BLACK
SNOW

ALSO BY JAMES M. SCOTT

Rampage:
MacArthur, Yamashita, and the Battle of Manila

Target Tokyo:
Jimmy Doolittle and the Raid That Avenged Pearl Harbor

The War Below:
The Story of Three Submarines That Battled Japan

The Attack on the Liberty:
The Untold Story of Israel's Deadly 1967 Assault on a U.S. Spy Ship

BLACK SNOW

Curtis LeMay, the Firebombing of Tokyo,

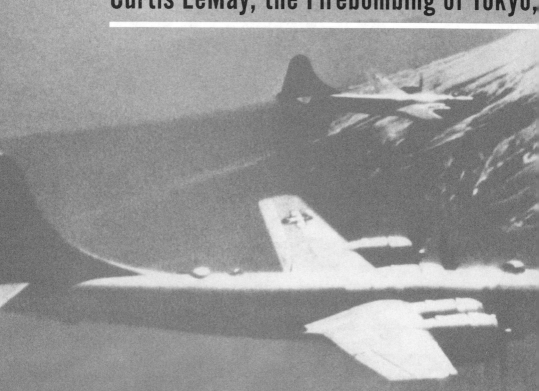

and the Road to the Atomic Bomb

JAMES M. SCOTT

W. W. NORTON & COMPANY
Independent Publishers Since 1923

For information about permission to reproduce selections from this book, write to
Permissions, W. W. Norton & Company, Inc., 500 Fifth Avenue, New York, NY 10110

For information about special discounts for bulk purchases, please contact
W. W. Norton Special Sales at specialsales@wwnorton.com or 800-233-4830

Manufacturing by LSC Harrisonburg
Maps by Michael Borop
Book design by Beth Steidle
Production manager: Louise Mattarelliano

ISBN 978-1-324-00299-4

W. W. Norton & Company, Inc., 500 Fifth Avenue, New York, N.Y. 10110
www.wwnorton.com

W. W. Norton & Company Ltd., 15 Carlisle Street, London W1D 3BS

1 2 3 4 5 6 7 8 9 0

For Isa and Grigs,
I pray you never experience such destruction.

"There will be no distinction any longer between soldiers and civilians."

—GEN. GIULIO DOUHET
THE COMMAND OF THE AIR, 1921

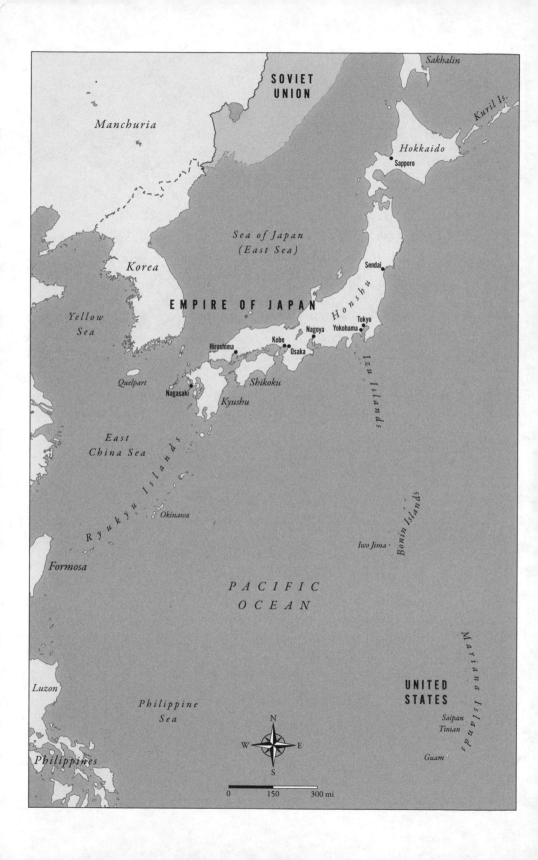

CONTENTS

The B-29, with a tail the height of a three-story building, was America's largest and most sophisticated bomber during World War II.

PART I

A Spark

"There has never been anything that has come which has changed war the way the advent of air power has."

—BRIG. GEN. WILLIAM "BILLY" MITCHELL
FEBRUARY 5, 1926

CHAPTER 1

"It is Thanksgiving Day in the United States and Americans all over
the world will rejoice in the fact that today Tokyo is being bombed."

—TIM LEIMERT, CBS CORRESPONDENT
NOVEMBER 24, 1944

Brig. Gen. Haywood Hansell, Jr., brooded in the predawn hours of
November 24, 1944. From the control tower of Isley Field on the
Pacific island of Saipan, the forty-one-year-old commander could see
the faint outlines of the 111 B-29 bombers lined up on the taxiway, ready at
daybreak to roar down the runway and lift off for the first strike on Tokyo.
The wiry southerner, whose pointy nose and narrow eyes had long ago
earned him the nickname Possum, had originally planned the mission for
November 17, but heavy rains and fluctuating winds had prompted him
to scrub the raid just as pilots prepared to take off. A typhoon that roared
ashore hours later validated his decision but also forced him to abort the
mission six more times in the days ahead, much to the frustration of anxious aircrews as well as Hansell's superiors in Washington, eager to open
a new front in the air war against the Japanese empire. "The delays," one
pilot griped, "were nightmarish." Others had quipped that the B-29, the
newest bomber in America's arsenal, was easily the best plane that never
left the ground.

But finally this morning the skies had cleared. Relief washed over him. Hansell had spent his life building up to this moment. He had relatives who had fought in the American Revolution, the War of 1812, and the Civil War. His own father had served as an army surgeon with tours in the Philippines and China; Hansell's first words as a baby, in fact, were in Mandarin. The general's youthful appearance, accentuated by red hair and fair skin, camouflaged a drive that had made him both a daring fighter pilot and a gifted thinker who helped design the air force's war plan against Germany. At his core, however, Hansell was a gentleman, whose love of writing verse had made him the air force's unofficial poet laureate. The genteel general, who recited Shakespeare and adored Gilbert and Sullivan operettas, approached combat in a similar manner. He despised the firebombing of cities that defined the British air war in Europe, advocating instead that America execute daylight precision raids designed to knock out an enemy's industry while minimizing civilian deaths. "The idea," he once wrote, "of killing thousands of men, women and children was basically repugnant to American mores."

The mission this Friday morning—codenamed San Antonio I— reflected Hansell's philosophy. Bombers would lift off at one-minute intervals, each carrying a five-thousand-pound payload. Aircrews would then fly in formation more than fifteen hundred miles north across open ocean to penetrate the Japanese capital, defended by 375 fighters and more than 150 antiaircraft guns. The target was Nakajima Aircraft Company's factory in the Tokyo suburb of Musashino, just ten miles west of the Imperial Palace. Japan's oldest aviation company, Nakajima was the largest producer of airframes and engines, punching out half the nation's combat planes and 30 percent of the engines. The sprawling factory, built in 1938 and expanded throughout the war, now stretched across 130 acres and occupied almost 3 million square feet of floor space. At its wartime peak in May 1944, the plant employed 45,000 workers, who could produce on average 1,200 airplane engines a month. "There is," one intelligence report stated, "no more important target in the Jap aircraft industry than the Nakajima engine plant at Musashino."

America had invested heavily to arrive at this pivotal moment. The

United States had spent $3.7 billion to develop the four-engine bombers that lined the crushed coral taxiway on Saipan, making the B-29 the single most expensive weapons system of the war. The exorbitant price tag of Boeing's aeronautical monster did not account for the casualty toll—25,000 dead and wounded—exacted by the capture of the Mariana Islands of Saipan, Tinian, and Guam. This prized Pacific real estate placed Tokyo for the first time within range of American bombers, a fact reflected in the enemy's ferocious fight, including the largest suicide charge of the war, which led to 4,300 Japanese deaths in the span of just fifteen hours on July 7, 1944. "It was," recalled Marine Frank Borta, "a continuous meat grinder." To the horror of American troops, thousands of Japanese civilians who lived on Saipan had blown themselves up, waded arm in arm into the sea, or jumped off cliffs to avoid capture. "It's just the damnedest feeling deep in your stomach when you see somebody die like that," remembered sailor Leonard Bock, "especially women and young kids, babies even."

Six days after the June 15, 1944, invasion, the first aviation engineers had waded ashore, tasked with turning the forty-eight-square-mile island into Hansell's airbase. The job was herculean. Not only had the battle reduced Saipan's towns and villages to rubble, but the island's few roads could handle little more than bullock carts. Crews labored twenty-four hours a day, breaking only to watch the bombardment of neighboring Tinian, just three miles across the water. "The artillery fire was terrific," Maj. Henry Williams wrote in his diary. "The percussions would go right through your head." Engineers armed with dynamite, jackhammers, and bulldozers leveled hills, blasted coral quarries, and cut roads through sugarcane fields, moving a staggering 4 million square yards of rock. Crews scavenged a boiler, pipes, and valves from an old Japanese sugar mill to set up an asphalt plant to pave roads and runways. "Day and night the equipment continued to turn," one report noted. "Sometimes it appeared that only faith and hope kept the wheels turning, but the earth and coral continued to move."

Rogue Japanese snipers heightened the challenge, targeting laborers, trucks, and planes in an effort to disrupt progress. Marines picked off an average of thirty-five to fifty a day. In one of the more dramatic encounters, Second Lt. Henry McCoy, armed only with a jammed carbine, jumped into a jeep and gave chase after one enemy fighter who had set fire to a plane, an act that would earn him the Silver Star. "He ran over the Japanese soldier," his citation coolly stated, "made a circle and hit the enemy soldier twice again." Climate was another hardship. "Tropical downpours drenched the men, the heat was intense, water was scarce," one journalist observed. "The flies pressed unmercifully against sweaty bodies and had to be pried from one's eyes, ears and nostrils." Workers battled not only dengue fever but shortages of wire, lumber, and tires, the latter a precious commodity since the rugged landscape shredded truck tires in as little as seventeen days. "A handful of ordinary ten-penny nails," one army report noted, "were at a greater premium on the island of Saipan than a handful of rubies."

On October 12, Hansell arrived aboard the first B-29, the *Joltin' Josie, the Pacific Pioneer*, bringing bulldozers and earthmovers to a sudden standstill. Workers shielded their eyes from the bright sun to watch the silver bomber circle and touch down. "A great cheer went up," one officer wrote. "The thrill that went through all was almost electric in effect." That excitement masked the voluminous work that still remained. Monsoon rains in July and August had washed out roads and slowed construction. Hansell had arrived expecting to find two airbases, each with twin 8,500-foot-long runways, the required distance needed to put a 140,000-pound bomber into the air. Of the two airfields under construction, only one was able to accommodate the heavy bombers—and it had only one 7,000-foot runway, with just 5,000 feet of it even paved. There were likewise no barracks, machine shops, or mess halls. Fueling consisted of a handful of tanker trucks. "Ground crews," Hansell wrote, "put up borrowed tents in what was certainly one of the most disorderly military encampments of the war."

Work on the Tinian airfields lagged far behind schedule while the bases on Guam that would serve as the future headquarters of Hansell's 21st Bomber Command had not even been laid out. But construction setbacks were only part of Hansell's challenge. The B-29 remained a troublesome new airplane. Engines erupted in flames, and gun-sighting blisters fogged or even blew out at high altitudes, all perilous threats on a mission that required pilots to fly several thousand miles over hostile ocean. Hansell likewise depended on callow crews. None had more than one hundred hours of flying experience in B-29s. Few had even a fraction of that in the high-altitude formation flying that the general envisioned for his crews over Tokyo. To help train them, he had requested that B-29s reporting to Saipan practice flying in formation. To his surprise, the air force refused, stating that the B-29s did not have the range to fly 2,400 miles from Sacramento to Hawaii in formation. Hansell was stunned. If his superiors didn't think his planes could cover that distance, how did they ever expect them to make it to Tokyo and back?

Another challenge Hansell discovered was a lack of target data for Japan, even though his mission was to take the air war home to the empire. Aircrews fortunately remedied that intelligence gap on the beautiful morning of November 1, when the first reconnaissance plane buzzed the enemy's capital at 32,000 feet, capturing 7,000 images. From those black and white photos, the first glimpse of Tokyo's factories, steel mills, and shipyards emerged. Like jigsaw puzzles, analysts assembled the images into mosaics, pinpointing the airfields that encircled the capital and could throw up fighters to intercept the B-29s. "We've learned more about Japan in the past ten days," an astonished Hansell acknowledged, "than we knew in the past ten years." Since bombers would have to fly without fighter coverage, Hansell's primary mission was to obliterate Japan's aircraft industry, a move designed to cripple the enemy's ability to put more planes in the air. "Every crew," Hansell wrote, "was required to trace its photo map, mark landmarks and target runs, and then redraw them from memory—over and over."

But Hansell's worries ran far deeper.

Army Air Forces commander Gen. Henry "Hap" Arnold, the father of the B-29, was anxious for Hansell to justify America's gamble on the pricey bombers. More important, if Hansell's bombers could crush Japan and prevent a bloody invasion, it would at last demonstrate the need for an independent air force, a cause Arnold had championed for decades. To accomplish this goal, Arnold had established the 20th Air Force, a brand-new command under his direct control and with only one objective: destroy Japan. This guarded setup was designed to insulate his fledgling B-29 force from other Pacific commanders, like Gen. Douglas MacArthur in Australia and Adm. Chester Nimitz in Hawaii, all of whom were hot to steal his bombers for other missions. Arnold's new air force included the 20th Bomber Command under Maj. Gen. Curtis LeMay, tasked with flying missions out of China against southern Japan. But the prize of Arnold's new air force was Hansell's 21st Bomber Command. Far closer to Japan, the Marianas guaranteed that not just Tokyo but all of the enemy's critical industrial cities would soon be viewed through a bombardier's eyepiece.

Beyond Arnold, Hansell felt pressure from other leaders as well as the war-weary public, ready for a speedy end to a conflict that devoured ninety-six cents of every federal dollar spent. Army Chief of Staff Gen. George Marshall made that clear in a meeting when he pressed Hansell for an answer as to how long it would take to begin strikes against Japan.

"I hope to launch the first operation by six weeks after we get there," Hansell replied.

"What's going to take so long?" Marshall bluntly demanded.

Other senior officers had questioned whether Hansell, viewed largely as an academic and a planner, had the right temperament for such a demanding combat job. That was true of Lt. Gen. Barney Giles, who served as deputy commander of the Army Air Forces and chief of the Air Staff.

"Possum, I hope everything works fine for you," Giles had told him. "You have an awfully tough job to do. General Arnold is going to be very impatient."

Each week, it seemed, had only brought more setbacks.

The navy had originally planned to launch carrier strikes on Tokyo in the days leading up to the raid, which Hansell had welcomed since the attacks would draw enemy fighters away from his bombers. But the navy, with its flattops tied up in the Philippines, had suggested Hansell abort or at least postpone the mission. Hansell knew that wasn't an option. By acquiescing, he would send a message that his bombers could not operate independently of the navy, which ran counter to Arnold's purpose in setting up the 20th Air Force.

More disturbing news had arrived while Hansell waited for the typhoon to pass. Arnold had circulated Hansell's mission plan for evaluation among senior air force officers. Lt. Gen. George Kenney, who served as MacArthur's air commander and had more experience than most battling the Japanese, wrote to Arnold, urging him to cancel the strike. Kenney believed not only that the B-29s lacked the range but that Japanese fighters would shred them. Arnold forwarded the letter to Hansell, alerting him that others on his staff whose opinions he respected shared Kenney's concerns. Though Arnold did not order Hansell to abort the mission or even modify it, the general's message was clear. If the mission failed, it would be his fault—and his alone. Hansell had been warned. "The effect," he later wrote, "was chilling."

But Kenney wasn't the only one to doubt the mission.

Brig. Gen. Emmett "Rosie" O'Donnell, who as commander of the 73rd Bombardment Wing would lead the mission, passed Hansell a handwritten letter, arguing that the general should abandon the daytime raid or at least switch it to evening to give bombers the protection of darkness. "Failure of the mission," O'Donnell wrote, "would produce a disaster which far exceeds any military advantage that would accrue from success."

Hansell was shocked at the insubordination, telling O'Donnell that if he refused to fly the mission, he would put a letter of reprimand in his file. "Are you," Hansell pressed his senior commander, "reluctant to lead your wing on the forthcoming mission?"

O'Donnell relented.

His superiors, his mission commander, and even the weather seemed against him. "Hansell," one veteran wrote, "felt about as alone as any commander in history."

But there was no turning back.

The orders had been issued, the planes fueled, the bombs loaded. Hansell had been sent to this battered island in the middle of the Pacific to execute this mission, to bring the power of the American air force home to the Japanese Empire. The mission was a go. In his final briefing with the aircrews, the general focused not on the historical significance of the mission or the myriad obstacles he had overcome, but on the practical aspects of the raid.

"Stick together," he instructed his men. "Don't let fighter attacks break up the formations. And put the bombs on the target. If the bombs don't hit the target all our efforts and risks and worries and work will be for nothing. That's what we're here for."

The aircrews listened.

"If we do our job," he concluded, "this is the beginning of the end for Japan. Put the bombs on the target. You can do it."

Anxious aircrews rolled out of canvas cots at three-thirty that morning and slipped on flight suits before heading to breakfast and a final five a.m. briefing. Airmen wagered whether the mission would again be canceled. Second Lt. Herbert Kelly of Wisconsin asked friend and fellow pilot Chester Marshall if he thought the mission would take off.

"Yep, we'll go," Lieutenant Marshall declared. "My sure-fire reasoning is this: today is Thanksgiving back in the States."

"I hope you're right," Kelly replied. "This wait is killing me."

Crews climbed into the backs of trucks for the trip to the airfield, where flight prechecks were made via flashlight. Each bomber weighed 137,000 pounds, more than a third of that attributed to the 8,000 gallons of fuel sloshing around inside each plane's eleven tanks. Three 500-pound incendiary and seven 500-pound demolition bombs added to the weight; so did the 6,000 rounds for the .50-caliber machine guns plus another 120 rounds for the 20-millimeter tail cannon. Orders mandated that planes fly in five combat groups of two squadrons each at 31,000 feet. Mount Fuji, the iconic snow-capped symbol of Japan, would serve as the initial point, where crews would begin the bomb run over the Nakajima factory. If they were unable to reach the target, the airmen were ordered to bomb the docks that lined Tokyo Bay.

Marines had made a final sweep of Isley Field for Japanese infiltrators, a so-called rabbit hunt that killed 240 and netted nearly 50 prisoners. Hansell, who had touched down only forty-one days earlier, watched from the tower like a conductor poised before a symphony of destruction. The mission he had worked so hard to prepare—and on which the fate of his career rested—was now in the hands of the 1,221 pilots, navigators, and bombardiers.

First Lt. John Cox, the airplane commander of the *Lil' Lassie*, gathered his crew under the left wing. "Men," he said, "we've finally made it, after all those months of training. Today's the day it pays off, so let's go out there and show them what we can do!"

Shortly before six a.m., dawn illuminated the eastern horizon, revealing a handful of cirrus clouds that captivated Marshall. "I don't think I've ever seen a day awaken so beautifully," he wrote in his diary. "A morning like this has got to be a good omen."

Flashbulbs popped as the two dozen reporters who had traveled to Saipan to document the raid photographed General O'Donnell climbing up into the *Dauntless Dotty*. Maj. Robert Morgan joined him in the cockpit, the pilot of the famed B-17 *Memphis Belle*, which had flown twenty-five missions over Europe before making celebrated rounds on the war bond circuit. A handful of news reporters would fly as observers. Moments later blue smoke filled the morning air as the first crews fired up the engines, making the ground tremble.

Ambulances and fire trucks lined the runway, where rescuers stood armed with fuselage-cutting tools. Bulldozers idled, ready to push any cracked-up plane off the runway so the mission could continue. Hundreds of engineers jockeyed with sailors and Marines to watch the historic flight, standing shoulder to shoulder and even atop vehicles. "Right now there are ten million guys who would give anything to change places with us," one pilot told reporter Denis Warner. "In about seven hours we will be only too glad to change with any one of them."

The first bombers taxied toward the runway, where Catholic, Protestant, and Jewish chaplains stood ready to bless each plane. At six-fifteen a.m. O'Donnell's bomber thundered down the strip and lifted off. Gene

Rider, a reporter with Columbia Broadcasting Company, described the scene for his audience. "It is," he narrated, "at once monstrous and graceful."

The second bomber followed one minute later.

Then the third, fourth, and fifth.

One after another the bombers swarmed into the skies.

There was no turning back now.

CHAPTER 2

"No part of the Japanese Empire is now out of our range,
no war factory too remote to feel our bombs.
The battle for Japan has been joined."

—GEN. HAP ARNOLD
NOVEMBER 24, 1944

Hansell wasn't the only one brooding.

General Arnold, half a world away in Washington, had more at stake on the mission's success than anyone, a fact that no doubt contributed to the three heart attacks he had suffered in just the last two years. The fifty-eight-year-old Arnold, whose boyish grin had long ago earned him the nickname Hap, short for "happy," had come of age alongside the development of aviation. A 1907 West Point graduate, he had learned to fly from none other than Orville and Wilbur Wright, taking to the skies above an Ohio cow pasture in a primitive biplane crafted from cypress and canvas. Only after a bug hit Arnold during landing, forcing a doctor to later peel its wing from his eyeball, did early aviators finally adopt the trademark goggles. Arnold completed his aviation course in just ten days in May 1911 to become one of only two qualified pilots in the army. But the lessons of the bookish brothers, with whom Arnold would eat his Sunday meals, went far beyond aviation. "More than anyone I have ever known or read about," he wrote, "the Wright brothers gave me the sense that nothing is impossible."

Arnold applied that philosophy to his career, establishing the army's first flight school in the Washington suburbs while pushing the bounds of early aviation. Not only did he earn the distinction of being the first military man to fly more than a mile high, but he was also the first pilot to deliver the mail. Arnold once even beat carrier pigeons in a race from Portland to San Francisco. But a near tragedy in the fall of 1912 threatened to sideline his promising career. On a flight to observe artillery fire in Kansas, his aircraft suddenly spun, stalled, and then dove. Only seconds before certain death, he wrested control of the plummeting plane and landed. "At the present time," he wrote his commanding officer, "my nervous system is in such a condition that I will not get in any machine." To friends, Arnold confessed that his flying days were over. "That's it," he told one fellow pilot. "A man doesn't face death twice." The pain of failure haunted him for four years until he finally summoned the courage to climb back into a cockpit. "When I'm going to die," he finally realized, "I'm going to die."

Like the Wright brothers, aviation visionary Brig. Gen. Billy Mitchell was another powerful force in shaping Arnold's early career. In the waning days of World War I, Mitchell planned and led 1,476 Allied planes in the largest raid behind German lines, a feat that earned him the Distinguished Service Cross. Mitchell went on to predict the attack on Pearl Harbor—eighteen years before Japanese planes swarmed the Hawaiian skies. He likewise saw a future in which infantrymen would parachute behind enemy lines and commercial airliners would whisk passengers between New York and Europe in a matter of hours. The flamboyant general, who hunted tigers in India and had once met the King of Siam, scored one of his greatest victories in 1921 when his airmen sank the captured German battleship *Ostfriesland*, a triumph that foreshadowed the end of the dreadnought. For aviation to achieve its true promise, Mitchell preached that America needed an independent air force separate from the army.

Though a hero to young officers like Arnold, Mitchell's airpower crusade drew the ire of reluctant War Department leaders, including Gen. John "Black Jack" Pershing, who had commanded American forces in World War I and later served as army chief of staff. Pershing became one of Mitchell's greatest antagonists, claiming he had been infected with the "Bolshevik Bug." "An Air Force acting independently," Pershing scoffed, "can of its own account neither win a war at the present time, nor, so far as we can tell, at any time in the future."

A savvy officer with powerful family connections—his late father had served as a Wisconsin senator—Mitchell took his battle public, courting the press and members of Congress. "Billy, take it easy," Arnold had cautioned his friend. "We need you."

His own mother even warned him: "Keep cool and use good judgement," she cabled.

But Mitchell refused. "When senior officers won't see facts," he replied, "something unorthodox, perhaps an explosion, is necessary."

That explosion came in the form of a six-thousand-word manifesto he delivered to the press on September 5, 1925, in the wake of two aviation tragedies. Mitchell accused senior War Department leaders of incompetence, criminal negligence, and near-treasonous handling of the nation's fledgling air services. He demanded that the air service be made an independent branch, separate from the army and navy. "The lives of the airmen are being used merely as pawns," he wrote. "Our pilots know they are going to be killed."

That reckless statement landed Mitchell before a court-martial in Washington on charges of insubordination. To defend him, the aviator hired Illinois congressman Frank Reid, who over the course of fifty-two days turned the trial into a public spectacle on the importance of aviation, grabbing headlines in newspapers around the country. Throughout the trial, Arnold hustled to help his friend, feeding the defense records and spending nights huddled in strategy sessions. Arnold even risked his own career, testifying on Mitchell's behalf. In the end, the panel of ten generals, who included Douglas MacArthur, found Mitchell guilty, ultimately sentencing the dashing airman to a five-year loss of rank, command, and duty as well as the forfeiture of all pay and allowances. "Billy was licked, of course, from the beginning," a wiser Arnold later wrote. "There was nothing left for him to do but resign from the Army."

With Mitchell gone, Arnold and other young aviators continued the crusade, visiting Capitol Hill and firing off letters to lawmakers pushing for an independent air service. Senior War Department leaders, wounded from the public drubbing, were finished with Mitchell and his disciples. Maj. Gen. Mason Patrick, head of the army's air service, summoned Arnold. "You can resign from the army," he said, "or you can take a court-martial."

A stunned Arnold found that he now faced the same fate as his mentor, even though his only crime had been to lobby lawmakers. "How long do I have to decide?"

"You have twenty-four hours," Patrick told him.

Arnold called his wife, Bee, asking her to meet him at the Ellipse, a park in front of the White House. On a bitter winter day, he asked her what he should do. Bee reminded him that two years earlier his superiors had asked him to lobby a California congressman for a bill the air service supported. Why was it right then and wrong now? She urged him to fight.

"I was hoping you'd say all that," he replied.

Arnold's decision proved problematic for the army. A public court-martial risked reigniting the Mitchell furor. Furthermore, such a trial would expose the army's hypocrisy of ordering an officer to lobby, only to punish him later for the same activity.

"In your opinion," Patrick asked, "what's the worst facility we have in the entire Air Service?"

"There's no doubt about that," Arnold replied. "It has to be Fort Riley, Kansas."

"Good," Patrick told him. "You are now the commanding officer of an observation squadron there."

Arnold dutifully accepted his exile to Kansas, though he had learned a valuable lesson. If he wanted to fight for an independent air force, he would need to work within the system, not try to tear it down from the outside, as Mitchell had done. Arnold later acknowledged that while

Mitchell's trial might have boosted the public's perception of airpower's importance, it ultimately set the cause back among senior officers inside the arthritic War Department. "They seemed to set their mouths tighter," he wrote, "draw more into their shell, and, if anything, take even a narrower point of view of aviation as an offensive power in warfare."

Over the years, Arnold managed to advance up the ranks, despite a notoriously stubborn and maverick spirit that erupted into periodic clashes with his commanders, as evidenced by the efficiency reports that swelled his personnel file. "Inclined to be disloyal to his superiors and prone to intrigue for his personal advantage," complained one.

"In an emergency," added another, "he is liable to lose his head."

Upon arrival at a duty station, his new commanding officer asked Arnold if he had read his most recent evaluation. "It's so bad," he told him, "it makes you stink."

Arnold even managed to infuriate President Franklin Roosevelt, who once banned him from the White House and threatened to exile him to Guam. "Oh boy," Treasury secretary Henry Morgenthau told his staff afterward, "did General Arnold get it."

Despite such rebukes, those who worked with Arnold could not help but admire his tenacity. "His idea of a good time," recalled his personal pilot, Brig. Gen. Eugene Beebe, "was to work all day at the office." Though he was not a visionary like Mitchell, Arnold possessed an uncanny ability to grasp the big picture plus a dogged drive. Impetuous and impatient, the general refused to read papers more than one page in length, shunning exploratory thinking for recommendations and solutions. "Arnold was not a thoughtful man," Hansell observed. "He was not a strategist. He was not a philosopher. He was a doer." The hard-charging general, who had repeatedly risked his life to advance aviation, demanded the same dedication from his subordinates. He yelled, banged on his desk, and held grudges. Few felt much warmth from the irascible general despite a head full of grandfatherly white hair. "Hap," O'Donnell later said of Arnold's nickname, "is a misnomer."

The general's subordinates often echoed O'Donnell. "He was utterly ruthless when he felt that someone let him down," one said.

"He's kind of like an elephant," added another, "he never forgot a fault."

"Awfully rough on nonproducers."

Arnold's hard work, however, had generated results, even if he battered egos and torched friendships along the way. The general, who took command in 1938 of an air service comprised of twenty thousand aviators and a few hundred planes, had in just six years grown it into a global strike force that counted nearly 2.4 million airmen and eighty thousand fighters, bombers, and transports. Throughout it all, Arnold never lost sight of his early mentor's goal of creating an independent air force, even as he now found himself the one accused by younger officers of being reluctant to change. "People," Arnold later wrote, "have become so used to saying that Billy Mitchell was years ahead of his time that they sometimes forget it is true."

The nineteen years following Mitchell's trial had served as a valuable learning curve, allowing Arnold time to cultivate relationships with important leaders like General Marshall, whose support he would depend upon to break away from the army. Those years likewise witnessed a technological boom, as the antiquated planes Arnold had once flown gave way to the muscular four-engine bombers that could deliver seismic payloads far behind the enemy's lines. The general had realized, too, the importance of nurturing a cadre of senior air officers who could one day lead the service, requiring most of them to serve overseas in combat. The outbreak of fighting had exposed a host of new challenges, from developing tactics to morbidly calculating loss estimates for airmen and planes. "No war is ever like the last," Arnold recalled, "and in the case of the air power of World War II, there was no precedent at all."

As the war moved into its climactic act, Mitchell's unfulfilled dream haunted Arnold. To make the case for an independent service—and to win over holdouts—Arnold needed his air force to own an equal share of the victory alongside the army and navy.

Time was fast running out.

The air war in Europe, which bomber advocates had sold as a fast and painless path to victory, had devolved into a slog, becoming the conflict's longest battle. More American airmen, in fact, would die in the skies over Europe than the Marine Corps would lose in the entire war. In the end, the infantry still had to storm the beaches and retake villages, towns, and cities.

But Japan offered Arnold another chance, a blank canvas on which he could paint the awesome power of his air force. Much was at stake. Not only would success validate Arnold's decision to invest in the B-29 but it could save hundreds of thousands of American lives, troops who might not otherwise have to battle inside cities like Tokyo, Nagoya, and Osaka. The job of breaking Japan now fell to Haywood Hansell, Arnold's trusted former chief of staff who had helped build the new 20th Air Force. But loyalty and even friendship mattered little to Arnold compared with results. "He'd have fired his own mother," one aide said, "if she didn't produce." Arnold made that clear to Hansell. "These first few major missions of yours," he wrote to him on the eve of the Tokyo strike, "are of particular significance."

———

THE B-29 WAS the perfect weapon to bring the horror of war home to the Japanese people. But the graceful silver bombers, which Hansell watched charge one after the other down the Saipan airstrip that Friday morning, masked the incredible struggle designers, engineers, and fabricators had faced lifting this airplane off the drawing board.

The tortuous path to arrive at this dawn takeoff had begun on January 29, 1940, when the army air force mailed design requests for a new long-range bomber to America's top four airplane manufacturers: Boeing, Douglas, Consolidated, and Lockheed. Underlying the new proposal was a fear that Germany, which had invaded Czechoslovakia and Poland, could overrun much of Europe, including Great Britain. In such a scenario, even the new B-17, with a range of two thousand miles, would have no bases in the region from which to operate. Germany might then move into South America, which would directly threaten the United States. That plain manila packet, stamped with the War Department's official seal, set in motion what would become the biggest gamble of Arnold's career and hopefully spell the downfall of Japan.

Three weeks later Boeing delivered.

Engineers at the aircraft company, which had designed and built the four-engine B-17 Flying Fortress that would soon dominate the skies over Europe, had already started exploring concepts for an even larger bomber capable of greater ranges, giving Boeing an advantage over its competitors. On June 14, 1940—the same day Nazi troops marched into Paris—the army wrote Boeing a check for $85,652 to design its model. Ten weeks later—and before Boeing had even completed the mockup—the army awarded the company a $3.6 million contract to build two flying prototypes. "It was so large and complicated," Arnold wrote, "that it required about ten thousand drawings before it was possible to put it into production."

In May 1941, as Germany's nine-month bombing campaign against British cities known as the Blitz reached its climax, the army placed its first order for 250 B-29s—a staggering commitment for a plane that so far existed only as a plywood model. In the wake of the attack on Pearl Harbor six months later, the War Department upped that order to 750 bombers, a fraction still of the nearly 4,000 the army would eventually purchase throughout the war. To tackle the design, Boeing employed a force of 3,500 engineers and 700 mechanics. "His life was that B-29," recalled Hap's chief of staff, Brig. Gen. Lauris Norstad. "Arnold was into every damn detail." Curtis LeMay, whose 20th Bomber Command would fly B-29s out of China, echoed Norstad. "Hap took the chances, cut the corners, and ordered this unique airplane into production before the prototype was even completed," LeMay said. "Arnold took a calculated risk of unprecedented proportions—everything could have exploded in his face."

And it nearly did.

While engineers hustled with pencils and slide rules to finish designs, laborers raced to build the factories, roads, and houses needed to accommodate the army of workers required to mass-produce the B-29. Over the course of the war, four primary factories would hammer out the new bombers, including Boeing's sprawling plant in Renton, just a few miles south of the company's headquarters in Seattle. In addition, the government selected Wichita, Kansas; Omaha, Nebraska; and Marietta, Georgia, areas battered by the Great Depression that would benefit from the infusion of capital. Labor costs in the South and the Great Plains were a fraction of city wages. Plus there were no unions that might disrupt work or a need to camouflage structures. Ethnicity was a factor as well, as the government intentionally selected regions with fewer immigrants who might be sympathetic to Communist or Nazi ideologies, a move officials believed lessened the threat of sabotage. Wichita, home to aircraft manufacturers Beech and Cessna, had experienced aviation workers. The farming communities of Marietta and Omaha likewise guaranteed the availability of able hands familiar with tractor and equipment repair. Thousands of subcontractors churned out everything from spark plugs to wing flaps, while materials poured in from all over the nation, ranging from Minnesota steel to Arkansas aluminum.

Construction of the B-29 was an aeronautical gold rush. The promise of steady jobs attracted tens of thousands of prospective laborers, sparking a massive influx that dramatically shaped local communities. Boeing's Wichita plant sprawled across 185 acres and featured 2.8 million square feet of floor space. Some 26,000 workers labored in ten-hour shifts, seven days a week. Time off consisted of every other weekend. Workers hammered out six thousand homes in Wichita for aircraft employees, including an entire new town called Planeview, complete with four large elementary schools, a high school, and eighteen acres of playgrounds. Along with homes and schools, workers built a bowling alley, a barber shop, and even a theater, where residents could unwind and catch John Wayne in the movie *In Old Oklahoma*. Others enjoyed Bible classes, volunteered for the Boy Scouts, or grew victory gardens. Home to residents from forty-two different states, Planeview mushroomed into the seventh-largest city in Kansas, prompting residents to christen it the "Miracle City." "Grandmothers," one reporter observed, "who never wrestled with anything more intricate than a wood stove up until two years ago are building Superfortresses at Wichita."

Similar stories played out in other communities. The $73 million Marietta factory, which enclosed an area equivalent to sixty-three football fields, was the largest industrial plant south of the Mason-Dixon Line, requiring its own steam power plant. At its peak, the factory employed twenty-eight thousand workers from all backgrounds, ranging from dwarfs able to wriggle into tight spaces to the blind who sorted dropped rivets that littered the plant floor. The most famous employee, however, was Helen Dortch Longstreet, the widow of Confederate general James Longstreet. On the West Coast, workers engineered one of the more creative solutions to camouflage the twenty-six-acre rooftop of Boeing's plant in Seattle, where technicians assembled the first B-29 prototype. Boeing recruited Hollywood art designer John Stewart Detlie, who had worked on the 1938 film *A Christmas Carol* and earned an Academy Award nomination three years later for *Bitter Sweet*. Under Detlie's direction, designers built a fake neighborhood atop the plant dubbed "Wonderland," which featured several major streets, fifty-three homes, and even a gas station. To maintain the illusion, workers on break would unwind on burlap lawns and in the shade of more than three hundred trees made from chicken wire and feathers.

The completed B-29 was an engineering marvel, constructed out of 55,000 parts along with 600,000 rivets. Dubbed the Superfortress because it dwarfed its predecessor—the B-17 Flying Fortress—a single bomber required no less than 27,000 pounds of aluminum plus another ten miles of electrical wiring. With a tail that rose as high as a three-story building, the B-29 flaunted the largest propellers ever fitted onto a plane, along with a gigantic 141-foot wingspan—twenty feet longer than the Wright brothers' first flight. An onboard electrical plant powered 152 motors, which controlled everything from the wing flaps and the landing gear to the doors of the double bomb bays. For defense, the Superfortress touted twelve .50-caliber machine guns and one 20-millimeter cannon, operated by a computer that calculated the lead, parallax, windage, and gravity. The hemispheric bomber could fly four thousand miles across the ocean, a task that required a railroad tanker car's worth of fuel and oil. Engineers had spared nothing, from pressurized cabins that allowed aircrews to operate free of oxygen masks at altitudes as high as seven miles to built-in ashtrays where the eleven-man crew could stub out cigarettes. Curtis LeMay described the B-29 as an "aerial battleship." The famed aviator Jimmy Doolittle gushed that it "staggers the imagination."

Despite the accolades, one critical question still dogged America's newest bomber, on which taxpayers so far had spent $1.5 billion to order 1,665 planes.

Would it fly?

Engineers put the aerial monster to the test on September 21, 1942. The job that afternoon fell to Boeing's legendary test pilot Eddie Allen, a slight man with a head of thinning hair and a pencil-thin mustache reminiscent of the one worn by Hollywood heartthrob Clark Gable. The B-29 prototype roared down the runway at 3:40 p.m., lifting off into the blue fall sky. Seventy-five minutes later Allen touched down, swarmed by anxious engineers.

"She flies!" he reported with a grin.

More tests followed, which revealed problems with the bomber's 2,200-horsepower Wright Cyclone engines. On a test flight in December, two of the bomber's four engines failed at 6,800 feet. Technicians replaced the engines, only for another one to die again on a follow-up flight, a pattern that soon plagued the new planes. At 12:11 p.m. on February 18, 1943, Allen again piloted one of the prototypes into the skies, climbing up to five thousand feet. Five minutes into the flight, Allen radioed that the number-one engine had erupted in flames. The crew used a CO_2 bottle and believed the fire was under control, but Allen opted to land.

"Tell us if at any time you think you need fire equipment," the tower instructed.

Allen radioed again at 12:21 p.m.—just ten minutes into the flight—informing the control tower that he had dropped to 2,400 feet and continued to descend. "Request immediate landing clearance," he said. "Order crash equipment to stand by."

"Cleared to land, wind south ten, runway thirteen," the tower replied.

Tensions soared as fire and rescue crews rolled into action.

"Allen!" one of the crew members shouted over the intercom in a transmission the tower heard. "Better get this thing down in a hurry—the wing spar's burning badly!"

The situation suddenly devolved into a catastrophic crisis, as the crippled bomber droned over streets, businesses, and homes, trailed like a comet by a tail of smoke. "Have fire equipment ready," Allen radioed. "Am coming in with a wing on fire."

The burning bomber buzzed just twelve hundred feet over downtown Seattle. On the streets below, pedestrians gazed skyward at the wounded plane. "Flames were shooting out from the bomber's engines," truck driver Russell Looker later told reporters.

Radioman Harry Ralston bailed out, only to land atop a high-tension electrical wire. "There was a blinding flash," Looker said. "Then he dropped to the ground." Engineer Ed Wersebe likewise jumped, but at the low altitude his parachute failed to save him.

On the ground, people could see the flames had reached the cockpit just as the bomber tore into the five-story building of the Frye Packing Company. The meat processing plant exploded in flames. The crash killed Allen and all ten crewmen plus twenty-one others, a figure that could have been much higher had the tragedy not occurred during the plant's lunch break. "It was," LeMay later said, "a test program disaster of unparalleled proportions."

Arnold, who had staked his career on the B-29, was horrified. He called Maj. Gen. Oliver Echols, the air force's chief material officer at Wright Field. "Look, we're in trouble about this thing," he confessed. "What're we going to do?"

"I'll send you some of our best people," Echols replied.

But problems continued to plague the B-29 as the months rolled by. Despite more than two thousand changes, the bomber's engines continued to overheat. "You could hardly get one in the air and bring it back without an engine fire," recalled Paul Tibbets. Other times the bomb bay doors randomly opened and closed. On a flight at twenty-five thousand feet, the cabin pressurization system failed, blowing a crew member out of a gun-sighting blister. He fortunately wore a parachute and was found two hours later. "I was just sitting there practicing my gun sight," he later told his superiors, "and all of a sudden I felt like somebody hit me in the fanny with a truck and out I went."

Politics only exacerbated Arnold's challenges. "Within the air force itself there were certain people who didn't think that we should spend our time and effort on a bomber that far advanced," recalled Brig. Gen. Kenneth Wolfe, the B-29 project director. Arnold faced greater pressures than just those in the War Department. The general had assured President Roosevelt that the B-29 would be ready for combat at the start of 1944. Roosevelt, in turn, desperate to keep Chinese Nationalist ruler Chiang Kai-shek in the war, had promised him the bombers would soon operate from his country, targeting southern Japan. Not only would Arnold's failure to deliver upset Chiang Kai-shek, but it likewise validated British prime minister Winston Churchill's fears that the $3 billion bomber was a wasteful diversion of capital that could have gone to fighting the Germans in Europe.

"Everything," Roosevelt complained, "seems to go wrong."

"The B-29 business," added presidential aide Harry Hopkins, "has been an awful headache."

The mounting frustrations, however, did little to fuel results. "It is my desire," a frustrated Arnold wrote in October 1943, "that this airplane be produced in quantity so that it can be used in this war and not in the next." Design changes continued to slow the process. Rather than reconfigure the main assembly factories, Boeing set up modification centers to remedy defects. Those centers, originally located in Marietta and Omaha, ultimately demoralized plant employees, prompting Boeing to move them to Denver and Birmingham, where 5,200 workers climbed over the bombers. By the end of 1943, each B-29 needed an additional 25,000 worker hours for modification, a figure that jumped to 61,000 hours. By January 1944, ninety-seven B-29s emerged from the factories. Of those, only sixteen were actually flyable. Arnold visited the Wichita plant that month, where he walked down the assembly line, pausing in front of one bomber. Armed with a black grease pencil, he signed his name on the fuselage. "This is the plane I want—right here," the general said. "I want it before the first of March."

Arnold returned to Kansas two months later, expecting to watch the first bombers depart for the war in Asia. Instead he learned that not a single plane was ready. "I was appalled at what I found," he later wrote. "There were shortages in all kinds and classes of equipment." The general, in what was later dubbed the "Battle of Kansas," ordered the B-29 to take precedence over all air force projects. He assigned Brig. Gen. Benny Myers and Col. Bill Irvine to run the project. The building of such a complex weapon, which depended on myriad subcontractors for everything from engines to radar, resembled a symphony without a conductor. Irvine immediately set up a system to track work on every single bomber. Boeing shipped in an additional six hundred laborers, many of whom toiled outside in subfreezing temperatures and snow in electrically heated flight suits. "We charted each airplane," Irvine said. "Everything that happened to that airplane around a 24-hour clock went on the chart."

At seven each morning, Arnold called with one question: "How are we doing?"

Three weeks later, on March 26, the first bomber rolled down the runway and lifted off, starting the journey halfway around the world to join the fight against Japan.

Scores more soon followed.

The Battle of Kansas had been won.

Aircrews assigned to the B-29 marveled at the revolutionary silver bombers that rolled week after week out of hangars around the country. "It was so big," recalled pilot William Cooper, "that I just couldn't imagine that it would fly." Cooper's reaction was common. "There may be bigger planes in the future," humor columnist Jack Tarver wrote in the *Atlanta Constitution*. "But right now the B-29's the only one I know of where it takes three cents for the tail-gunner to send a postcard to the pilot." The Superfortress impressed even veteran airmen like Hansell. "She was a thoroughbred," the general wrote. "She had heart and she could take an astonishing amount of punishment and still keep flying till she brought you home." But it was the simple comfort of the pressurized cabin that won over many. "The most pleasing thing about the B-29," recalled gunner John Alebis, "was that we could fly it in our tee-shirts."

The 157,000 hours that had been needed to build the first bombers fell, by the end of the year, to just 30,000 hours, resulting in the production on average of four planes a day, as American workers hustled to assemble a fleet capable of raining ruin on Japan. Few were as relieved as Arnold, who had nurtured the sophisticated bomber from an idea into a reality. "The B-29," Norstad recalled, "was a dream of the Old Man's." Arnold's tenacity and the risks he took earned accolades from many. "The most courageous decision he made in all was the acceptance of the B-29 before the damned thing had ever flown," Hansell said. "He built factories to build these airplanes, and gave them top priority at a time when the airplane was still in test stage. That was a tremendous gamble." But the biggest gamble was yet to come. The B-29 now had to deliver on its promise—and knock Japan out of the war. "Never before in the history of warfare," LeMay said, "has so much been expected of a single weapon."

CHAPTER 3

"The sight of all those bombs dropping on the
Tokyo war machine does my heart good."

—MAJ. ROBERT MORGAN
NOVEMBER 27, 1945, LETTER

Hansell paced the control tower.

Across Saipan, bulldozers grumbled and snorted, while every ten seconds trucks loaded down with coral rolled one after another out of quarry pits, seemingly oblivious to the mission under way that morning. Hansell had watched his first bomber lift off at 6:16 on that Friday morning of November 24, 1944. The last had followed two hours and thirty-eight minutes later. Of the 111 bombers that climbed into the skies for the first strike against Tokyo, 23 turned back over fuel and mechanical problems. The other 88 Superfortresses had pressed on across the immense ocean toward the Japanese capital, carrying a combined total of 277.5 tons of bombs in their bellies.

The stress of the mission weighed heavily upon Hansell. Would Japanese fighters pounce on his crews, as Gen. George Kenney had predicted? Or would the hundreds of antiaircraft guns that guarded the capital shred them and end his career?

Hansell would have an answer soon enough.

In the meantime, the general no doubt would have agreed with the quip made by one of his airmen in the cockpit of a Tokyo-bound B-29 that morning. "The Wright brothers should have stayed in the bicycle business," the flier said. "Then we wouldn't be here."

The first bombs-away report reached Saipan at twelve-fifteen p.m.

O'Donnell had made it.

Hansell's headquarters relayed the report to Washington, where twenty-four minutes later the War Department broadcast the first news flash of the mission to the world, buoying the morale of American families who sat down that Thanksgiving Day to dinner. "A large task force of B-29 aircraft today attacked strategic industrial targets in the city of Tokyo," Hap Arnold said in a statement. "The first group over the target accomplished visual bombing and observed that its bombs fell within the target area, causing an explosion and fires."

Hansell waited for his bombers to return. The afternoon sun drifted across the western sky. The searing midday light faded to a warm gold and then gray with the approach of dusk. Crews lit smudge pots, which cast a faint glow to mark the runway at Isley Field. The first bomber touched down at 7:26 p.m. Over the next three hours and thirty-three minutes, the others returned, many of them with just a few hundred gallons of gas left in the tanks.

"We caught them with their pants down and gave them a hell of an afternoon," O'Donnell told the gathered reporters that night. "The Japs just weren't on the ball. I was utterly amazed at the lack of organized fighter opposition or effective anti-aircraft. We didn't run into anything. I don't know whether they didn't have it or weren't ready."

The next day reporters in New York tracked down O'Donnell's seven-year-old son, Patrick. "Boy," the youth exclaimed. "Bombing Tokyo! I guess he can just about do anything."

News of the raid would soon dominate papers nationwide, part of a choreographed public relations campaign spearheaded by Lt. Col. St. Clair McKelway, a career journalist before the war who had ink in his veins. His great-uncle and namesake edited the *Brooklyn Eagle*, while his brother ran the *Washington Star*. McKelway, who donned glasses and sported a mustache and a receding blond hairline that accentuated his large forehead, had started his own career as a messenger for the *Washington Times-Herald* before working his way up to the prestigious *New Yorker*, landing a job at just twenty-eight writing profiles of police officers, gangsters, and arsonists. He understood people and the power of detail and narrative. "His communiques," one colleague wrote, "were masterpieces, vibrant, full of color and life."

McKelway applied those skills on Saipan. Nineteen reporters, all anxious to transmit stories of up to five thousand words, would have overwhelmed the communications system, prompting McKelway to devise a clever strategy. "Correspondents were advised to write advance stories as if the take-off had actually transpired and to include the background material they had already gathered," he wrote. "These stories were sent to Honolulu by airmail and by telecon, classified as Top Secret." Media relations staff had previously airmailed photos of the Superfortresses to Washington as well as gathered two thousand questionnaires from ground personnel that could be fed to hometown newspapers. Within three hours of the first bombs falling on Tokyo, Washington unleashed the flood of stories, totaling more than 100,000 words.

Headlines across America heralded the strike.

"Tokyo Airplant Smashed, Fires Rage in City," trumpeted the *New York Times*.

"B-29s Took Jap Capital by Surprise," echoed the *Washington Post*.

"Just the Beginning," predicted the *Christian Science Monitor*.

To complement the press—and in another brilliant public relations maneuver—the air force arranged to display a B-29 at Washington's National Airport that holiday weekend, offering a special showing Saturday afternoon for reporters and members of the cabinet and of Congress, as well as senior military officers. The first to preview the silver Superfortress, which had come directly from the Marietta plant, were none other than George Marshall and Hap Arnold, the latter no doubt relieved that his beleaguered bomber was finally in combat against the heart of Japan. More than 100,000 spectators followed them that Sunday, forcing the bus company to double its regular schedule to the airport. Even then fifteen thousand cars created a massive traffic jam. To enhance the experience, air force workers displayed forty 500-pound bombs along with 160 fifty-gallon gasoline drums, a move designed to illustrate the eighteen tons of aviation fuel required for a round trip to Japan. Four hundred spectators filed through the War Finance Committee's on-site trailer armed with $25—the equivalent today of $350—that allowed them to scribble their name on a bomb destined for Tokyo.

"I want the Japs to know about my little greeting," a woman from Brooklyn said as she signed her name on a bomb.

"No wonder we have to buy more bonds," exclaimed another woman as she marveled at the towering Superfortress.

Despite the public relations bonanza, the first Tokyo mission was largely a bust.

And Hansell knew it.

In contrast to the fears of some senior officers, Hansell fortunately had lost only two planes: one collided with a damaged Japanese fighter, while the other ran out of fuel and crash-landed in the ocean 140 miles north of Saipan. A destroyer fished the crew out of the water nineteen hours later. But the mission's results failed to justify the cost of the bombs, the 172,471 rounds of 20-millimeter and .50-caliber ammunition, or the 731,353 gallons of fuel required to power his B-29s. Just twenty-four of Hansell's bombers actually targeted the Nakajima Aircraft Company's plant during the two-hour-and-twenty-minute raid. Sixty-four others, most unable to see because of clouds, resorted to radar to unload on nearby dockyards. Six bombers failed to attack any target. Postwar records would later reveal that only forty-eight bombs exploded inside the target area, damaging just 1 percent of the buildings and 2.4 percent of the machinery. The attack, which killed fifty-seven workers and injured another seventy-five, did little to slow production. "The bombing," Hansell conceded, "left much to be desired."

The earlier pressure on Hansell worsened. Not only was Arnold anxious for him to produce results, but now the American public expected it, thanks to the media's lionization of Hansell as the public face of the air war against the empire. "This Possum," declared the *Saturday Evening*

Post, "is Jap Poison." Twenty-four-year-old Maj. Ralph Nutter, who had fought with Hansell in Europe and now served as his command navigator, accompanied the general to debrief the crews. Hansell's stress was obvious. "He was in no mood," Nutter noted, "to congratulate O'Donnell for his leadership of the mission."

The friction between Hansell and O'Donnell ran deep, predating the latter's complaint on the eve of the first mission. A thirty-eight-year-old Brooklyn native, O'Donnell had a ruddy Irish complexion and a tendency to blush that had long ago earned him the nickname Rosie. Lean, muscular, and with a hawklike nose, O'Donnell was a natural athlete in his youth, playing varsity lacrosse and swimming at West Point. His reputation as the fastest cadet in the 1928 class had landed him a coveted spot on the football team even though he didn't know how to play, much less run with the ball. "I thought," O'Donnell later joked, "you carried it like a watermelon." He quickly picked up the sport, playing substitute half-back to All-Americans Harry Wilson and Red Cagle and later serving as assistant coach from 1934 to 1938. O'Donnell had proved himself in combat, battling the Japanese in the disastrous early days of the war in the Philippines, earning the Distinguished Flying Cross. A charismatic leader, O'Donnell inspired loyalty in his men, a trait he could trace back to his youth when he was elected student body president at Manual High School. Maj. Jack Catton, pilot of the *Joltin' Josie,* which had brought Hansell to Saipan, lauded O'Donnell. "I would do anything for him," he said, "absolutely anything."

Arnold likewise trusted O'Donnell, tapping him in 1943 to serve on his advisory council, a handpicked group of talented young officers the general depended on every day. "Your job," Arnold once said, "is to do my thinking for me." O'Donnell had used his perch on the general's council to challenge the strategy of daylight precision strikes against Japanese industry, urging Arnold in February 1944 to strip the bombers of guns and abandon formation flying. Such moves would lighten the B-29s, extend flying range, and reduce engine stress. To limit the threat from Japanese fighters, O'Donnell advocated flying night missions and firebombing cities, a position he continued to push the following month, when Arnold chose him to command the 73rd Bombardment Wing. O'Donnell further outlined his views in a memo on June 7, 1944, listing the pros and cons of firebombing versus precision strikes. The extensive pros on his four-page memo made clear O'Donnell's preference for fire raids.

"Requires less fuel."

"Losses will be small."

"Japanese morale would suffer."

When Hansell took charge of the 21st Bomber Command in August, he was shocked to find O'Donnell prepping his crews to fly night missions. Given the rudimentary nature of radar, Hansell believed, such tactics would never allow his crews to pinpoint and destroy critical wartime factories. He ordered O'Donnell's aircrews to begin crash-training for daylight precision attacks, organizing practice flights from Kansas over the Gulf of Mexico. "Opposition to this change," Hansell wrote, "was severe."

But O'Donnell had refused to give up.

The tenacious airman fired off a seven-page letter to Arnold on August 8, warning that the small force of available B-29s could never knock out Japan's industry via pinpoint bombing. To maximize the punch, he again urged Arnold to firebomb the enemy's cities at night. "Civilian morale in Japan should certainly be considered an important target," O'Donnell wrote. "The Japanese people have never had to submit to a real attack and on the few occasions recorded where they have suffered natural disaster, such as in the Yokohama earthquake and succeeding fire, they did not stand up well as a people to their adversity."

Arnold shared the letter with Hansell and Curtis LeMay, whose 20th Bomber Command was charged with flying B-29 missions out of India and China against targets in southern Japan. LeMay shot down O'Donnell's suggestions. So did Hansell.

Hansell no doubt took O'Donnell's letter as a slap, considering he had gone over him to complain to Arnold. "I realize that we will face many difficult operational problems," Hansell assured Arnold, "but I decline to believe that we are licked before we start."

Arnold sided with Hansell and LeMay.

But O'Donnell continued to press Hansell, pitching him a plan on

November 4 to send one-third of his force each night to Tokyo with incendiaries. Such a move, he argued, would reduce the bombers parked on the hardstand that might be targets for a Japanese raid. Hansell again shot him down. During the long weather delay that preceded the first mission, O'Donnell vented in his diary. "I have 108 airplanes on hand," he wrote, "and not one has yet done a job." Hansell's insistence on precision strikes, he felt, had cost them plenty of chances to hit the enemy. "The lack of flexibility," O'Donnell continued, "has us stymied. I am more than ever convinced that the plan for our initial employment is not good." The delays had cost America the element of surprise. "We lost an excellent chance to catch them psychologically unprepared," O'Donnell concluded. "We could have been driving them nuts."

The buildup of frustration led O'Donnell to confront Hansell on the eve of the first mission to Tokyo, a move that prompted the general to consider firing him. Hansell's fear of rattling the already shaky nerves of his aircrews was all that saved O'Donnell. "I was torn," the general later wrote in a personal letter. "It is dangerous to entrust an important and hazardous mission to a man who says he doesn't think it can be done."

But festering tensions between the duo had already become obvious among senior officers on Saipan, who grew nervous of a potential showdown. "Rumors are in the air here concerning Hansell-O'Donnell discord," Col. Samuel Harris wrote in his diary. "I have a feeling the going out there is going to be rough and I don't mean combat missions. Remind me not to get caught in the middle. If I have to take sides it will be Rosie all the way."

O'Donnell, despite his tactical objections, had celebrated the Tokyo strike with some of his men, opening a bottle of 1914 bourbon to pass around. "I look at the mission as a damn good warm up flight," he wrote in his diary. "Invaluable to the crews because of the confidence they will derive from the experience. Nothing mysterious about it from now on."

Hansell wasn't so generous when he walked into the mission debriefing. The strike might not have done much damage, but his bombers had flown to Japan in formation, dropped bombs in broad daylight over the enemy's capital, and made it home safely.

"This first mission," he told O'Donnell, "has proven that high-altitude daylight missions are feasible. We can improve our bombing accuracy with more training and experience."

Hansell then focused his ire.

"The results of a night mission," he added, "would have been catastrophic."

Nutter, who noted that the tone of Hansell's comment made it clear it was a reprimand, shot a glance at O'Donnell. "I could see he was astonished," Nutter later wrote. "I wondered about the relevance of Hansell's comment. Catastrophic for whom?"

———

ANXIOUS TO REBOUND, Hansell ordered a second strike—code-named San Antonio II—three days later against the same plant. Eighty-one bombers lifted off that Monday, only to find Tokyo again shrouded in dense clouds, forcing them to divert to secondary targets.

The mission was a failure.

So was the third.

These early raids revealed an unexpected challenge: Japan's weather. Hansell was no stranger to the hardship that weather conditions posed. He had battled it in Germany, where fog often enveloped English airfields, making takeoffs and landings perilous, while fronts over the continent moved six times faster than in the United States. "The weather," Hansell once griped, "was actually a greater hazard and obstacle than the German Air Force."

But Japan's weather was even worse.

Impenetrable clouds often blanketed the island nation, limiting visual bombing to an average of just three days per month. Aircrews could fall back on radar bombing, but such tactics were far less accurate, raising the fear of missed targets and increased civilian deaths. Clouds were not the only obstacle. The collision of frigid winter air masses over eastern Asia with the warm Pacific currents produced violent jet streams that raged over Japan at speeds of up to 230 mph, rivaling the gales that battered Mt.

Everest. Flying downwind pushed groundspeeds over 500 mph, making it impossible for the bombardier to see the target, much less hit it. "The bombsight," recalled Lt. Col. David Burchinal, "couldn't handle it."

Flying upwind, however, slowed bombers to 125 miles per hour, essentially stalling planes over the target and making them vulnerable to Japanese antiaircraft fire. "You would be there," one pilot quipped, "until you ran out of fuel." The challenges frustrated Hansell. "Experience to date," he wrote after the first few missions, "indicates that the most vital factor influencing every operational decision and the performance of every operational mission is weather."

But Hansell faced an even greater struggle.

The air war against Japan—just like his battle with O'Donnell—was shaping up as a pivotal test not only of his leadership but also of his fundamental beliefs about bombardment, ideas he had developed during the interwar years and that had since come to define him.

Hansell was, in many ways, an accidental aviator. He had rejected an offer to attend West Point in what was no doubt a blow to his father, enrolling instead at Georgia Tech, where at 125 pounds he had made an unlikely football player and boxer. Upon graduation in 1924 with a degree in mechanical engineering, he worked as a boilermaker until an interest in aeronautical engineering enticed him to enlist in the Army Air Corps in 1928. Even then Hansell viewed learning to fly only as a prerequisite for what he believed would be his future life's work designing aircraft. "From the minute he got in the airplane," biographer Charles Griffith observed, "his whole life turned around; he had found the direction his life had needed."

Hansell began his aviation career as a fighter pilot, performing aerial tricks in the early 1930s as a member of the acerbic Louisianan Claire Chennault's "Three Men on a Flying Trapeze," a traveling acrobatic team designed to bolster enthusiasm for army aviation. The trio christened the group with that name after belting out the original nineteenth-century British folk song in a bar, celebrating their first performance at the opening of a new airport in the rural town of Macon, Mississippi. "We did every acrobatic maneuver in the books and some that weren't,"

Chennault remembered, "all in perfect formation." Once during practice, Hansell's wing jammed the tail of Chennault's elevator, locking his control stick, though the talented airman fortunately was able to wrestle his plane to the ground. "It is sheer chance that we lived through it," Hansell reflected. "If we had kept at it long enough, we certainly would have been killed."

Hansell traded his cockpit seat for a classroom in 1934, spending four years as a student and faculty member at the Air Corps Tactical School at Alabama's Maxwell Field. There the young fighter pilot landed amid a like-minded community of passionate aviators. "We considered ourselves a different breed of cat," recalled Carl Spaatz, who would later command American air forces in Europe and the Pacific. "We flew through the air and other people walked on the ground. It was as simple as that." In the wake of Billy Mitchell's trial, the school's white stucco classrooms had evolved into an incubator for the bomber's future. Not since the invention of gunpowder had a new technology so upended warfare, offering a promising solution to trenches filled knee-deep with mud, rats, and excrement that haunted the nightmares of infantrymen. Along with Mitchell, students pored over the writings of Italian general Giulio Douhet, another airpower pioneer who had seen the potential of aerial combat just a few years after the Wright brothers stunned the world at Kitty Hawk. "The skies," Douhet predicted in 1910, "are about to become a battlefield as important as the land and sea."

Much like Mitchell, Douhet's fervor led him to clash with his superiors, resulting in his court-martial and one-year imprisonment. But Douhet never wavered, publishing his seminal work *The Command of the Air* in 1921, the same year Mitchell sank the battleship *Ostfriesland*. "To have command of the air," he wrote, "means to be in a position to wield offensive power so great it defies human imagination." In his writings, Douhet painted an apocalyptic picture of cities ravaged by bombs and poisonous gas with no distinction between civilians and soldiers. Such destruction would in turn trigger widespread national terror. "Normal life would be impossible in this constant nightmare of imminent death and destruction," he theorized. "The time would soon come when, to put an end to the horror and suffering, the people themselves, driven by the instinct of self-preservation, would rise up and demand an end to the war."

Such ideas were like catnip to the fervid advocates of airpower, who soon became known as the "Bomber Mafia," a group that recruited Hansell into its ranks. "Nothing could stop us," recalled Laurence Kuter, a former fighter pilot turned bomber enthusiast. "This was a zealous crowd." That fanaticism, however, sparked fights, pitting bomber advocates against those who believed that future warfare would still demand fighters. "The Douhet book," a frustrated fighter instructor once griped, "became the secret strategic bible of the Air Corps."

The B-17's introduction in 1935 only emboldened the mafiosi, who felt that the muscular four-engine bomber signaled the end of the fighter. Not only could the Flying Fortress soar higher and faster than most pursuits, but it sported solid armor and an eventual arsenal of thirteen guns. Bomber devotees were so confident in this new weapon that some argued the school should abandon its curriculum on fighters. Hansell found himself in the awkward position of opposing his former mentor and fellow instructor, whose strong convictions he believed made him "egotistical and narrow-minded." "Chennault," Hansell said, "figured there were only two kinds of people—those who agreed with him and those who didn't."

Hansell's newfound passion often overflowed from the classroom into social settings, where parties devolved into heated arguments, occasionally keeping his children awake. "There were no other subjects of conversation," Hansell recalled, "and a few drinks did not serve to mellow the intensity of the contention." One time at a dance, a fellow officer went so far as to confront his wife. "Tell Possum," he said, "to get his head out of the clouds."

But Hansell refused.

He saw the bomber as a powerful tool to paralyze an enemy's industrial capacity, though without resorting to incinerating cities, as Douhet advocated. A modern nation, he theorized, resembled a house of cards, built atop a web of interdependent industries required to produce everything from bullets and bombers for the military to ovens and cars for civilians. Each of those networks had an Achilles' heel that, if destroyed, would crash the entire system. Blasting power plants, for example, would cripple not only munitions factories but also food production. Bombing key bridges and marshaling yards likewise could arrest the movement of raw materials, such as the coke needed to fuel steel mills. In a last-resort scenario, cities could be targets, but only electrical, water, and transportation systems, which if destroyed would force a mass exodus of civilians and overburden an enemy government. The best means to execute such attacks, Hansell believed, was daylight precision bombing, a move that guaranteed maximum accuracy and spared unnecessary deaths. "We may find the air force charged with breaking the will to resist of the enemy nation," Hansell wrote in a 1939 lecture. "Let us make it emphatically clear that that does not mean the indiscriminate bombing of women and children."

Hansell further refined those ideas when he landed in Washington later that year, tapped by Arnold to help set up an Air Force Intelligence Division. His mission: identify the industrial and economic chokepoints of Germany, Italy, and Japan. Faced with the rise of Hitler, the group zeroed in on Germany, focusing on the nation's petroleum industry as well as its electric power and distribution system, much of which had been built in recent decades. Intelligence out of wartime Germany was scarce, so the group turned to American banks in New York, which had financed the construction. This was a windfall; the banks handed over blueprints and schematics, allowing war planners to develop target folders. Hansell complemented that research with a visit to England as an observer, where the British loaded him up with boxes of valuable intelligence. The British social formalities, which reflected his own southern upbringing, left a lasting impression. He started carrying a swagger stick, adopted the expression "chap," and for the rest of his life would close his letters with "Cheerio."

Following Hitler's invasion of Russia in June 1941, Hansell jumped to the Air War Plans Division, joining what would become a four-person team with Lt. Col. Harold George, Lt. Col. Kenneth Walker, and Maj. Laurence Kuter. This tight-knit group, all former faculty at the Air Corps Tactical School, represented the dons of the Bomber Mafia. George had flown one of the bombers during Billy Mitchell's famous sinking of the

Ostfriesland. He later risked his own career to testify on the general's behalf at his court-martial. Walker had developed what had become the de facto credo of the mafia: "A well-organized, well-planned and well-flown air force attack will constitute an offensive that cannot be stopped."

The airmen's job was to formulate the first strategic air plan for a worldwide war. It was a tremendous assignment—and Arnold gave them only nine days to complete it. Adding to the challenge, the general departed for the Atlantic Conference in Placentia Bay, Newfoundland, leaving them alone without his guidance. The officers worked out of the unair-conditioned penthouse atop the Munitions Building on Constitution Avenue, cooled only by oscillating fans in an August heat wave that sent temperatures soaring into the upper nineties. "When you put your hand down on your desk," Hansell recalled, "your papers would stick to it."

But the mission was far larger than crafting a war plan.

For many millennia, armies and navies had fought in ships powered by sail and oarsmen and with infantries armed with bows and swords, which had given rise to defined doctrine, strategy, and tactics. That wasn't the case with airpower. The wood-and-fabric biplanes that had made their first-ever combat appearance during World War I—largely for reconnaissance and artillery spotting—had been replaced by four-engine aluminum bombers that for the first time could turn whole nations into battlefields. This technological explosion opened the door for an entirely new role for airpower. "The European War," as Billy Mitchell quipped in 1926, "was only the kindergarten of aviation." The plan Hansell and his team hammered out would define the mission of the air force and its future, a fact not lost on the men. "If the task was staggering," Hansell said, "so too was the opportunity." Should, for example, airmen try to defeat Germany alone by obliterating its industrial capability? Or should the air force take a more limited approach, weakening Germany enough to allow an invasion by ground troops? Another possibility was for the air force to play a totally subservient role to the infantry. "We wrestled as a group," Hansell said, "with this fundamental problem."

The 139-page plan the men completed at one-thirty p.m. on August

12, 1941—stamped with the wonky acronym AWPD-1, derived from the group's name—codified many of the theories the bomber advocates had debated in the muggy classrooms at Maxwell Field. The plan, which Hansell described as "the most important single event in the evolution of the Air Force," mapped out an aggressive role for the fledgling service in World War II, one focused on daylight precision bombing from altitudes as high as five and six miles above the earth. Rather than burn cities, the airmen's strategy called for selective strikes. This echoed President Roosevelt's plea for nations to avoid killing innocents, which he issued on September 1, 1939, as German forces marched into Poland and ignited the war in Europe. "The ruthless bombing from the air of civilians in unfortified centers of population during the course of the hostilities," Roosevelt said, "has sickened the hearts of every civilized man and woman, and has profoundly shocked the conscience of humanity." Selective attacks, the airmen reasoned, were not only morally superior but could bring about a faster and more economical victory, requiring fewer sorties and bombs, with less risk to American lives. Rather than beat a nation to death, you simply slit its jugular.

The airmen identified 154 targets, from airplane factories and dams to refineries, that if destroyed would in theory cripple Germany. To accomplish this goal, the team forecast the need for 2,165,000 airmen and an estimated 61,800 fighters, bombers, and transports, providing the blueprint Arnold would later use to grow the air force. The plan furthermore estimated how much ordnance would be required, and it factored in loss and replacement figures for planes and crews. "The scope of the air proposal," Hansell said, "was simply staggering."

Despite the hard work, a "slumbering dread" hung over Hansell. "A plan," as one historian wryly wrote, "that should have been assembled by dozens of experts in a period of months was written by four young men in nine days while their boss was out of the country." That plan, based solely on theory, called for taxpayers to spend billions of dollars and would send tens of thousands of men into the skies over Europe to fight and die.

What if they were wrong?

The war in Europe was the ultimate test—and it exposed the plan's critical flaw. The British, who had battled the Germans since 1939, had begun the war executing daylight precision strikes, just as the Americans planned. The ferocity of German fighter attacks, however, forced them to abandon such tactics in favor of firebombing cities at night, a term the British euphemistically referred to as "dehousing." But Hansell and his colleagues believed America could succeed where the British had failed. That confidence rested upon two factors. The first was the top-secret Norden bombsight, an analog computer made from more than two thousand parts that promised incredible accuracy. Developed and produced at a cost of $1.5 billion, the sophisticated instrument's price tag rivaled that of the atomic bomb. The second factor was the supposed strength of the B-17, whose bristling guns convinced many that it could soar solo far behind enemy lines. "We hung all our hopes," Hansell said, "on the capability to penetrate unescorted. We hung all our hopes on the effectiveness of defensive gunfire."

"God knows, I hope you can do it," British Bomber Command leader Sir Arthur Harris said, "but I don't think you can."

Harris was right.

Despite the ballyhooed view of the B-17's invincibility, German pursuits pounced, like aerial Rottweilers, highlighting the failure of bomber advocates to push for the development of long-range fighters that could accompany missions deep into Germany. "Many a B-17 crew," a vindicated Chennault later wrote, "had to go down in flames under the gun and rockets of Luftwaffe fighters before the bomber radicals learned that bloody lesson."

American airmen returned to base with horror stories. During one mission, the explosion of a plane hurled the body of a gunner back, where it hit the number-two propeller of the plane behind it, splattering blood and flesh all over the windscreen. "In order to see," a military psychiatrist later reported, "it was necessary for the pilot to borrow a knife from the engineer and scrape the windscreen." Exhausted aircrews suffered weight loss and insomnia. Others battled nightmares and tremors. "I'll give you a little clue how to fight this war," one commander instructed his men. "Make believe you're dead already; the rest comes easy." Many turned to alcohol. "I'd go back to the bar at night and a few familiar faces wouldn't be there," recalled Robert Morgan, pilot of the legendary *Memphis Belle*. "I would concentrate on the scotch in front of me. That scotch was my instrument panel through those nighttime navigations."

Hansell witnessed these struggles, trading his desk job in Washington for command of the First Bombardment Wing in England. After each strike, he met with his group commanders to review, sessions he characterized as a trial by fire. "I dreaded them," he said, "because the essential ingredient of our effort to learn by experience—and learn quickly—was absolute honesty. The mistakes had to be exposed and acknowledged. It was a soul-searing ordeal."

The air war had not only revealed flaws in Hansell's plan but laid bare his personal weaknesses as a combat commander, challenges that would haunt him in the fight against Japan. Though at ease with the air force's top leaders, he appeared nervous and uncomfortable among fighting crews who were his subordinates. The general shied away from tactical discussions, only to come alive when analyzing the enemy's economy and computing how much bomb tonnage would be required to flatten a target. "He was a proud military theorist," one aide observed, "but he had never been accepted as one of the boys in an operational unit." Such men saw Hansell as a planner, not as a predator, a background that had conditioned him to cordial dialogue and decisions made through compromise and consensus. The atmosphere in Europe was far different, with blunt and pointed debate among commanders who woke up each morning to find fewer faces around the breakfast table.

Ralph Nutter, who served as then Col. Curtis LeMay's navigator, remembered the first time he met Hansell, soon after the general took command of the wing on January 1, 1943. Though he would later work closely with Hansell on Saipan, Nutter knew little at that time of the general, other than that he was one of the architects of America's air plan and was considered a rising star in the air force. Nutter contrasted Hansell with LeMay, the gruff and normally reticent commander of the 305th Bombardment Group, one of the four units that made up the general's wing. The burly colonel with a head of jet-black hair propped up his reputation not with a swagger stick but with his dogged skills in the skies. "After working for LeMay for almost six months, I had the utmost confidence in his leadership. It seemed apparent to me that he was born to command a combat unit," Nutter said. "Hansell, on the other hand, knew the formalities of military command but gave no appearance of charisma or inner strength."

That first meeting was brutal, as LeMay grilled Hansell on everything from inexperienced gunners and poor bombing accuracy to the lack of escorts. "Without fighter support, we'll be unable to protect our crews," he declared at one point.

"Who," LeMay barked another time, "was the sad sack who put those thirty-caliber peashooters in the nose?"

"What's the use of flying over a target if we're not going to hit it?"

A pragmatic pilot and commander, LeMay used his complaints to segue into proposed solutions, including a pioneering new formation that would maximize defense as well as extended bomb runs to improve accuracy. The inquisition left Hansell visibly upset, but to the general's credit, he offered to fly with LeMay on his next mission, a strike on a locomotive plant in the northern French city of Lille on January 13. Though the wing commander and LeMay's boss, Hansell did not assert any control, riding in silence in the right-hand seat next to the colonel. Over the target, five German fighters attacked. Nutter opened fire with his thirty-caliber machine guns. "I could hear cannon shells and pieces of shrapnel hit our aircraft."

Nutter looked back and saw two bombers collide and fall from the sky, followed by a few white parachutes. As the plane returned to England, the flight engineer appeared next to Nutter, handing him a Spam sandwich. "Compliments of General Hansell," he said.

Back on the ground, Nutter thanked Hansell.

"Those head-on fighter attacks on the bomb run were not pleasant; you deserved it," the general said. "I must say, this mission was not a happy experience."

Happy or not, the mission served as a powerful lesson. The genteel Hansell might have recoiled at the combative tenor of his subordinates, but his success—and that of his plan—depended on the creativity and courage of men like Curtis LeMay.

German fighters and flak weren't the only threats to Hansell's plan. Bombers that were needed to pummel the enemy's homeland were diverted for the November 1942 North Africa invasion. Not only did fewer planes put more pressure on the remaining crews, but Hansell's plan would work only if America deployed enough bombers to break Germany's industrial back. "Our fears were realized," he later wrote. "Political necessity was more compelling than military strategy." Another crisis arose in January 1943, the same week Hansell took to the skies with LeMay. Prime Minister Churchill had grown increasingly hostile over America's insistence on daylight precision strikes, convinced that without fighter support, the bombers would never make it deep into Germany. During the Casablanca Conference to plan Allied strategy, Churchill persuaded Roosevelt to abandon such raids and join the Royal Air Force on night missions to firebomb cities, a decision that not only abrogated Hansell's plan but represented a significant moral shift for the United States. Maj. Gen. Ira Eaker, commander of the Eighth Air Force and a close friend of Hansell, flew to Morocco to salvage the plan. Eaker proposed to the prime minister that the best solution was to combine America's daylight precision strikes with the British nighttime fire raids. Not only would such a plan allow Americans to pinpoint hard-to-hit targets and reduce air congestion; more important, it would force Germany to suffer around-the-clock attacks and exhaust its citizens.

"Young man, you haven't convinced me that you are right," Churchill conceded, "but you have convinced me that you should have a further opportunity to prove the case."

Other challenges surfaced. The German economy, which Hansell and his fellow mafiosi had thought would collapse like a house of cards, proved to be far more resilient. Rather than surrender, workers rebuilt factories, dispersed machinery, and imported supplies from occupied countries, forcing bombers to return to targets again and again. "We couldn't envision," LeMay later wrote, "how resourceful or determined the Germans really were."

Hansell returned briefly to Washington to direct the modification of the air force's war plan in 1942, and the following year he led the creation of the Combined Bomber Offensive, an Allied offensive strategy to attack Germany. At no point, however, did he waver from his commitment to daylight precision bombing, even as German fighters brought down bomber after bomber, climaxing with the twin strikes against the ball-bearing plants at Schweinfurt that cost the United States a staggering 120 bombers and prompted a temporary suspension of raids deep inside Germany. "Combat experience dictated changes in tactics," Hansell acknowledged, "but the basic strategic concepts and doctrines stood up astonishingly well."

Hansell, however, did not.

In June 1943, as American losses piled up, General Eaker looked to replace the head of the Eighth Bomber Command, one of the top air force jobs in Europe. Eaker knew that few leaders had the experience and background of Hansell, but he saw in his friend the same weaknesses his subordinates witnessed. "Hansell has been carefully considered for eventual Bomber Commander," Eaker wrote to Arnold. "He is nervous and highly strung, and it is very doubtful whether he would physically stand the trial and responsibilities."

Hansell landed back in Washington, helping to plan the air war against Japan. Far removed from the front lines, he was again in his element. Hansell had learned invaluable lessons in Europe, which he now applied in the creation of the new 20th Air Force. Unlike the European theater, the Pacific theater had no overall commander; rather, control was split geographically between Gen. Douglas MacArthur and Adm. Chester Nimitz. For the B-29 to exert maximum pressure, it was imperative that the new force operate independently and not be pulled into either's orbit. To bypass the politics, Hansell proposed that the Twentieth be headquartered in Washington, with Arnold serving as the commanding general and executive agent for the Joint Chiefs of Staff. On April 12, 1944, the joint chiefs approved the unorthodox command structure, creating what was effectively an independent air force in the Pacific. "We were operating beyond the battle area controlled by either of them—far beyond," Arnold said. "Without a single over-all commander in the Pacific, MacArthur and Nimitz each visualized the operation of the Twentieth Air Force as being for the benefit of his particular campaign plans."

Arnold looked past the concerns of Eaker and others when he tapped Hansell in August to lead the 21st Bomber Command, the air force's top combat job in the Pacific. Hansell would go from planner to prosecutor in the war against Japan. Lt. Gen. Barney Giles, who served as deputy commander of the Army Air Forces, begged Arnold to reconsider. "He's a very fine staff officer," Giles warned, "but he is not a tactical commander."

"I think you have judged him too fast," Arnold countered.

Giles ran through the myriad obstacles Hansell would face, from opening new bases to training crews. "I'm awfully afraid," Giles said, "you will relieve him."

"No, I won't," Arnold assured him. "I won't."

Arnold no doubt felt a measure of loyalty. By then, the balance of power in the skies over Europe had finally flipped. The arrival of the P-51 Mustang, equipped with drop tanks, gave the ferocious fighter enough fuel to protect bombers on missions all the way to Berlin. The buildup of bombers allowed America to launch raids with more than a thousand planes, devastating Germany's aircraft plants, oil refineries, and ship and railyards. Hansell couldn't help but feel vindicated. "Americans," he wrote, "came out of the war in Europe with their faith in daylight, precision destruction of key industrial targets intact and fully justified."

Many of the same problems Hansell battled in Europe he now faced in the war against Japan, including too few bombers and skeptical combat commanders.

But in other ways, his challenges were greater.

In England, Hansell had benefited from established airfields maintained by the British, but in the battered Marianas he operated from primitive bases, dependent upon a supply line that ran across the Pacific. His crews fought powerful jet streams in the heavens and a troublesome new airplane forced to fly extraordinary distances over an unforgiving ocean. The expectations of Arnold and the attitudes of the American public had changed. After 1,088 days of war, people were exhausted. It had taken more than four years of combined British and American bombings to push Germany to its breaking point, yet the air war against the Japanese homeland was only now beginning. No one had the patience for a similar slog.

The conflict had to end—by any means possible.

Even Roosevelt, who only a few years earlier railed against killing civilians, had done an about-face in greenlighting Churchill's plan for America to join the firebombing campaign.

After the failed Tokyo strike on November 29, 1944, Nutter walked back to headquarters with Hansell. Much like Don Quixote, his favorite literary character, Hansell was powerless to break his fixation, confessing that despite three bad missions, he was not discouraged.

"It's my air plan that is defeating Hitler in Europe," he said.

His command navigator listened.

"It will defeat Japan, too," Hansell concluded.

But Nutter wasn't so sure, questioning whether Hansell's devotion to the doctrine he had helped develop years earlier in the classrooms at Maxwell Field had become an obsession. "I wondered," Nutter wrote, "if anyone could persuade Hansell to change his tactics? It had become a matter of will and ego. He was determined to prove that his critics were wrong."

CHAPTER 4

"Today the enemy came in rows of silvery wings."

—KIYOSHI KIYOSAWA
DECEMBER 27, 1944, DIARY ENTRY

Emperor Hirohito stewed.

The forty-three-year-old ruler of Japan could only watch from his palace in the heart of Tokyo as his empire crumbled. With his slight frame, stooped shoulders, and oddly high-pitched voice, the bespectacled Hirohito more closely resembled a librarian than a wartime leader, an image reinforced by his quiet and occasional clumsy mannerisms along with his pursuit of solitary hobbies. In his free time, he wrote poetry, studied natural history, and collected starfish as part of his passion for marine biology. When stressed, he often talked to himself, a peculiarity that had no doubt increased given Japan's reversal of fortune.

Gone were the heady days of victory that followed the destruction of much of America's powerful Pacific Fleet anchored in the cool waters of Pearl Harbor. Hirohito's forces had quickly captured Guam, Wake, and the Philippines from the United States, Hong Kong and Singapore from the British, and the oil-rich Dutch East Indies from the Netherlands. In a few short months, Japan had built an empire that stretched across 20 million square miles and seven time zones, putting one-quarter of the world under the emperor's control.

The Japanese public had soaked it up. A pile of fan mail nearly a foot high landed daily on the desk of Pearl Harbor attack architect Adm. Isoroku Yamamoto, while after the capture of Singapore thousands of adoring subjects serenaded the emperor with shouts of "banzai."

Residents couldn't thumb through a newspaper or tune in to the radio without reminders of Japan's victories. "Our men are now among the world's immortals," declared the *Japan Times & Advertiser*.

"We are the greatest people in the world," echoed a radio broadcaster.

The press went so far, in the spring of 1942, as to boast that it would be easy for Japanese soldiers to storm the beaches of California and sweep the nation. "The contention," argued the *Japan Times & Advertiser*, "that the United States cannot be invaded is a myth."

But Hirohito's dream of a Pacific empire was a mirage, vanishing as a string of defeats—from Midway and Guadalcanal to New Guinea and the Marianas—robbed the nation of almost 2 million soldiers, sailors, airmen, and marines. America's submarine blockade starved Japan of imported resources, ranging from the bauxite it needed to build fighters to the coal that powered its steel mills. The greatest loss, however, was oil, the lifeblood of a modern military that powered bombers, tanks, and aircraft carriers. The loss of fuel forced the Imperial Navy to park its battleships in port, relegating these once muscular symbols of the nation's sea power to antiaircraft duty, and sparked the creation of the kamikaze force, monsoons of metal and flesh that rained down on advancing American forces.

Japan's wartime failures reverberated on the home front. Just beyond the gates of the immaculate palace grounds, garbage littered the streets, now empty of cars and buses with the exception of the occasional abandoned automobile. The few emergency vehicles puttered around on charcoal. Sanitation crews diverted as much as 30 percent of the capital's sewage into Tokyo Bay. Desperate for metals and minerals, the government demanded that residents hand over everything from teapots and hibachis to watches, gold teeth, and even precious diamonds, which could be used to produce radios. Buddhist priests relinquished hanging bells and gongs from temples. Scrap drives robbed Tokyo of park benches and cemetery fences, lampposts, and even the handrails on bridges. Workers toppled columns for the metal grilles and pried up boilers and yanked radiators, heating pipes, and public telephones from walls, all of which scarred buildings and marred the streetscape. "Tokyo had never been a beautiful city, but it was now dirty as well as homely," recalled French journalist Robert Guillain. "Every morning the capital awoke a little more sordid, as though stained by the sinister night into which it had just been plunged."

The war had taxed Japan's labor force, which was already at full employment at the time of the attack on Pearl Harbor. "This was a politician's dream," noted historian Thomas Havens, "but a mobilizer's nightmare." The government eliminated the twelve-hour workday restriction, marched prisoners into factories, and shuttered nonessential businesses, ranging from book and toy stores to art, dressmaking, and typing schools. Eleven thousand small shops closed just in Tokyo. In a hustle to round up more laborers, Japan barred men from working as barbers, sales clerks, and railway conductors. In June 1944, Okayama added tombstone cutters, tree surgeons, and gardeners to the list. Bars, restaurants, and kabuki theaters closed and authorities bolted the wooden doors on Tokyo's more than three thousand teahouses, putting ten thousand geishas out of work. "A geisha out of her element is like a bird fallen from its nest," Guillain wrote. "Many even let themselves be drafted into the labor service where hands trained to pour sake and arrange flowers learned to sew white-silk parachutes and fashion aluminum parts."

One after the other, basic necessities had vanished, from sugar and soap, to thread, matches, and medicine, forcing the Japanese to scrounge for substitutes. Newspapers doubled as toilet paper while cowhide gave way to shark, salmon, and whale skin, creatively dubbed "sea leather." Residents sipped sake made from acorns and sweet potatoes and smoked eggplant and persimmon leaf cigarettes. Engineers tried unsuccessfully to make gasoline from shale and sardines and extracted oil from pine roots, going so far as to build nearly forty thousand distilleries, including some on the fairways of Tokyo's tony golf clubs. "Traveling through the country," observed Japanese journalist Masuo Kato, "one could see evidence of the failure of the program in the many piles of pine roots abandoned and rotting by the roadside." When charcoal became scarce, Tokyo bibliophiles burned home libraries for fuel. No one was exempt from sacrifice, including the deceased. "One borrows coffins for the dead but cannot buy them," journalist Kiyoshi Kiyosawa noted in his diary. "They are used any number of times."

As the war dragged on, wages plummeted and inflation soared. "Money," said Kimi Tatebayashi, "was practically worthless." Dwindling food allowances forced residents to haggle on the black market. "Everything was rationed," recalled Ayako Koshino, a kimono maker. "Even a tiny mackerel had to be divided among ten families." Others pilgrimaged to the countryside in search of vegetables, an experience Philippine diplomat León María Guerrero described in his diary. "The trains were packed full of grim housewives loaded down with knapsacks knobby with potatoes or redolent of radish," Guerrero observed. "Fish blood dripped from the baggage racks." Authorities tried to crack down, prompting women to bundle bags of rice to resemble babies. Seafood became a delicacy as the lack of fuel slashed in half the amount caught, robbing the population of an important source of protein. Residents foraged for greens in vacant lots and graveyards. Ishii Tominosuke, a librarian in Odwara, made soup from the dandelions he plucked from his stone wall. Others feasted on family pets. "Merely to subsist," Kato wrote, "had become the goal of each Japanese."

The government mobilized 3 million students aged ten and older to toil on farms and in factories, a figure that equaled almost one-tenth of the nation's workforce. One of those laborers was twelve-year-old Katsumoto Saotome, from a poor working-class family in downtown Tokyo's Mukojima ward, the son of an alcoholic father and a mother who worked as a seamstress. The slender youth, who was often ridiculed for his poor performances in his school sumo tournaments, worked seven days a week from eight a.m. until five p.m. at the Kubota Iron Works on the banks of the Sumida River, a factory that helped crank out tank engines. Every day, wearing his white kamikaze headband featuring a red rising sun, he piled scrap metal atop trolley carts. He and two other students then pushed the carts up to the furnace, his lunch tied to his waist to prevent someone from stealing it. Rain or snow, Katsumoto struggled amid the shower of sparks, his hands growing callused. "The hunger was the hardest for me," he recalled. "The amount of rations got smaller and smaller day by day."

In another blow to home life, authorities after the fall of Saipan broke up families, ordering the evacuation of more than 350,000 third- through sixth-graders from major cities and resettling them in more than two thousand rural resorts, inns, and temples spread across twelve prefectures. Yoneko Moriyama recounted the debate in her household. "Let's all die together in Tokyo," her grandmother insisted.

"Who says we're going to die?" her mother replied.

"Let's at least," countered her father, "try to save the children."

Moriyama remembered the last supper before she and her brother boarded the train. "Every good thing to eat that could be found in the house was put on the table," she said, "around which we all sat with faces that seemed to prophesy the end of the world."

Many children paid a heavy price for safety. Homesick youths ran away only to later be found wandering the train tracks that most seemed to think would deliver them home to Tokyo. Others wet their beds and grew despondent. Schoolteachers, who evacuated and cared for the students, monitored their letters home, afraid that mentioning hardships might worry parents. "Mother, as soon as this letter arrives, please come to see me that very day. Please, mother," one sixth-grader wrote. "Mitsuko might die if you don't come to see me."

The evacuees likewise battled food shortages. Students bullied one another, and desperate teachers swiped food from the youths. Children resorted to eating snakes and stream crabs as well as tooth-cleaning powder, paint, and crayons. Only the lice grew fat. "On sunny days we stripped the children naked and boiled their clothes to kill the lice," recalled Mitsuko Ôoka, a teacher. "The water would turn red from all the blood the lice had sucked."

Life in the cities was just as hard. Fights broke out on trains, and worker absenteeism in factories spiked. Ill health plagued many, from weight loss and fatigue to chronic diarrhea. The infant mortality rate climbed, while older children suffered from rickets, a disease sparked by a prolonged vitamin D deficiency that causes soft and deformed bones. Mothers were often too malnourished to nurse, forcing hospitals to bottle-feed newborns radish and turnip juice, both rich in vitamin C. Kyoto resident Tamura Tsunejiro captured the struggle of many in his diary: "We simply are waiting to starve to death." Desperate residents turned to thievery to survive. Food vanished through open windows and from community gardens. An Osaka University professor, arrested for stealing tomatoes, was sentenced to five years in prison. People swiped everything from overcoats and shoes from the entryways of homes to keys and doorknobs from inns. Passengers stripped trains of hanging straps and even the leather upholstery. "Japan," journalist Kiyosawa lamented in his diary, "has become a nation of thieves." French reporter Guillain agreed. "All that was pleasing in Japanese life had perished."

The government struggled to prop up the nation's morale by announcing bogus victories in the press, an industry militarists had dramatically reshaped to control public opinion. Under the guise of a newsprint shortage, the government had forced the mergers of many major newspapers, slashing them from 848 down to just 54, most only a few pages long. Reluctant owners faced suspension or even closure, often over trumped-up offenses. That was the case with the *Japan Advertiser*, accused of offending the imperial family with a blurred photo of the eight-year-old crown prince. "At that point," editor Wilfred Fleisher recalled, "I felt that the situation was almost hopeless." Such hostile moves succeeded. "By the time the war began the newspapers had become no more than official bulletins," Kato said. "Any newspaper that wished to remain in business had to be an enthusiastic supporter of Government policy."

But residents increasingly saw through the lies. How could Japan be victorious if American bombers were buzzing the capital's skies? "We are clearly being pushed back by the enemy. We are losing," novelist and poet Jun Takami complained in his diary. "Why can't they write it plainly and appeal to the people? It's the same old story." Others questioned whether the war was even worth it. "We should have the courage, come hell or high water, to give up the fight," Tokyo resident Aiko Takahashi wrote in her diary after the loss of Saipan.

Despite the private grumblings, few dared to speak out, much less revolt. In the years leading up to the war, authorities had built societal guardrails to control public opinion, including revising textbooks to indoctrinate the youth on the importance of citizenship, nationalism, and the divinity of the emperor. Universities purged professors, while police banned or confiscated controversial books. "During recess periods," recalled reporter Joseph Newman, "I frequently saw boys, who could not have been more than twelve years old, being taught by army officers how most effectively to bayonet straw dummies set upon the playground of a primary school."

As far back as 1925, Japan had passed the first of a series of sweeping laws designed to curb speech and later even public assembly. A force of so-called thought police monitored unions, political parties, and educational organizations and interviewed the friends, neighbors, and family members of potential suspects, arresting some seventy-six thousand people. But even those draconian efforts failed to silence the increasing bitterness of an exhausted and starved citizenry. "We used to talk about Tojo and his cohorts, wondering what kind of clothes they wore and what kind of food they ate," recalled the wife of a Nagoya farmer, referring to the former prime and defense minister, Hideki Tojo. "We were darn sure it wasn't the kind that we ate."

Stories abounded of frustrated residents running afoul of authorities over even trivial complaints. Police in Nagasaki scolded a baker for publicly doubting Japan could win the war. "Are you a Japanese or not?" officers implored the man.

Authorities went further in Tokyo, slapping a woman over a similar outburst. "It's not possible," she lamented afterward, "to say anything at all while on the trains."

This discontent was not lost on senior leaders. "The people are disgusted with the military and with the government," Reserve Gen. Kanji

Ishiwara wrote in his diary in September 1944. "They do not care any more about the outcome of the war."

In a radio address, the minister of agriculture urged people to carry on despite the suffering. "By covering up the fact that you are hungry, you are a samurai."

Such empty slogans did little.

The brutal winter of 1944–45 only compounded the misery, as temperatures plummeted, freezing the water inside homes where fuel-starved residents could do little more than shiver beneath tattered blankets. "Nothing's quite as hard on old bodies," the seventy-five-year-old Tamura wrote in his diary, "as the cold." The daily struggle to endure wore down civilians. "People in the bath silently stare at the ceiling in exhaustion," novelist Futaro Yamada wrote in his diary. "From the women's bath on the other side of the partition, one used to hear chattering and laughter, voices calling and children bawling, noisy as frogs on a June night in the countryside. But now there is only a silence like death."

The fear that American bombings would intensify only exacerbated the strain, a reminder hammered home each time the air raid alarms screeched and the antiaircraft guns opened fire, rattling the doors of nearby homes and raining shell fragments down atop tile roofs. "People in Tokyo," Guillain recalled, "thought nightly of the coming fire."

Everyone knew it could not go on forever.

"The days are coming," Kiyosawa wrote in his diary, "that will decide history."

———

HANSELL CONTINUED to struggle.

On December 3, he launched San Antonio III, once again targeting the Nakajima Aircraft Company's factory in the Tokyo suburb of Musashino. He hoped at last to deliver a knockout punch, to scratch the fighter and bomber engine plant from his target list.

Eighty-six bombers roared off Saipan's crushed coral runway early that Sunday morning. Of those, just fifty-six attacked the factory. The raid killed sixty workers and wounded twenty-one others, but destroyed only 5 percent of the buildings and 2 percent of the plant's machinery, furnaces, and automobiles. Strike photos revealed that only 1 percent of the bombs dropped over the target hit within one thousand feet of the aiming point. Much to Hansell's frustration, the attack delivered at best a glancing blow. "The results of the bombing," the after-action report concluded, "are considered to be unsatisfactory."

Hansell followed that strike with several missions against Nagoya, Japan's third-largest city. Perched along the coast 160 miles southwest of Tokyo, Nagoya had developed around a graceful 334-year-old wooden castle that dated back to the shoguns. In more modern times, the city had evolved into an industrial powerhouse, home to Mitsubishi's sprawling engine works factory and airframe plant, the latter of which offered a staggering 4.25 million square feet of floor space. "This is the largest aircraft assembly plant in the world," an intelligence report observed, "and unquestionably one of the most important targets in the Japanese Empire."

Ten days after the Tokyo strike, Hansell ordered operation Memphis I. Seventy-one bombers walloped Mitsubishi's engine works plant, killing 246 workers and wounding another 105. Hansell's most successful attack to date flattened 15 percent of the plant and left another 20 percent in shambles, ultimately slashing production from 1,600 airplane engines to 1,200 a month. Hansell's bombers returned to Nagoya on December 18, hitting Mitsubishi's airframe factory, then pounded the engine works plant a second time four days later. Neither of the latter Nagoya raids, however, did damage comparable to Memphis I.

In the last strike of the year, on December 27, Hansell ordered his bombers to once again return to Tokyo. The target: Nakajima Aircraft Company's Musashino factory.

But this fourth raid, just like the ones before it, was a bust.

Hansell's aircrews had flown eight missions against Japan in a little over one month, targeting three factories in Tokyo and Nagoya. His crews had burned through more than 4 million gallons of aviation fuel and dropped 1,655 tons of bombs.

None of the strikes, however, despite killing some workers and damaging a few buildings and machinery, had succeeded in destroying a single plant.

Japan's war machine still hummed.

Photos taken on the latest mission over Tokyo, in fact, revealed that workers had repaired the previous damage to the Nakajima plant. It was as if the earlier strikes had never happened. "The results of the bombing," the report once again concluded, "are unsatisfactory."

Each day, each mission, the pressure mounted on Hansell. "The weather was just too damn bad," he complained. "It whipped us." Heralded just one month earlier in the news back home, Hansell now found the press filled with stories of his struggles.

"High Winds Hamper Forts," read a headline in the *Boston Traveler*.

"Weather Proves Handicap," added another.

"Kinks in B-29 Attacks Wait for Solution."

Possum's problems only worsened.

Outraged by the strikes, the Japanese retaliated, launching air raids from Iwo Jima, some seven hundred miles northwest of Saipan. Home to two Japanese airfields, the eight-square-mile island reeked of rotten eggs, the product of volcanic vents that belched sulfur fumes from the earth's belly. At twelve-fifteen a.m. on November 27, just hours before crews lifted off for the second Tokyo strike, two enemy bombers swooped down on Isley Field, drawn like moths to the portable lights that maintenance crews had set up to make final adjustments to the B-29s. Ralph Nutter, who reviewed the bomb route with lead pilots and navigators, heard the engine roar along with the rattle of machine guns. He charged outside the operations hut alongside the flight line to see the planes just fifty feet overhead. One zeroed in on a parked B-29. "It was immediately engulfed in flames and exploded with tremendous force, knocking the three of us to the ground," he said. "I shook my head to clear it and saw an unexploded bomb a few feet away."

The phone inside the Quonset hut rang. Nutter climbed to his feet and darted back inside. "Nutter," Hansell exclaimed on the other end of the line, "aren't you the officer of the day? What are you doing to stop this attack on our mission?"

The command navigator fell silent, unsure of how to answer.

"Nutter," Hansell repeated, "are you there?"

The Japanese strafing had punctured the fuel tanks on a bomber as well as a nearby gas truck. The plane burned furiously. Before Nutter could answer, another blast knocked him again to the ground. From his back he yelled into the phone: "There's nothing I can do sir!"

The explosions shook Saipan. Gunner John Ciardi, who had earned a master's in creative writing from the University of Michigan before the war, stumbled outside his tent. "The smoke went up in a high smudge, thousands of feet into the moonlight, roiling black fumes highlighted on all the undersides of their contortions by the orange fire," he wrote in his diary. "Then it blew. I could feel the concussion all the way down the hill, a good two miles."

Hansell rolled up to the flight line in a jeep a few moments later, greeted by Nutter in his now muddy uniform. "Are you hurt?" he asked.

"No," Nutter replied. "There's debris and a fire from a burning B-29 blocking the runway access. No one can take off until the runway is cleared."

The general ordered Nutter to phone the Seabees to bring a bull-dozer. "I watched the scene with fascination and horror," Nutter later wrote. "This type of war was beyond my comprehension, and yet another unforeseen problem for Hansell." Others agreed. Col. Samuel Harris, commander of the 499th Bombardment Group, spent the rest of the night brooding. "Little could be done until daylight except keep the fires from spreading and taking care of injured personnel," Harris wrote in his diary. "This morning's examination revealed the true picture and bad it was. Six airplanes damaged beyond our ability to repair."

But the day had only begun.

Japanese fighters swarmed in at 12:05 p.m., just as many were sitting down in plywood mess halls to a lunch of roast beef and canned peaches. "The strafing came so suddenly that only those standing near a shelter were able to reach it," one report noted. "The remainder had to hit the dirt where they were or try to crawl under some tent or other fancied shelter." Hansell raced to the field with Col. John Montgomery, his deputy chief of staff for operations. "As we came up a rise onto the flying field, I found myself looking straight into a Japanese fighter that was strafing the area," he said. "I brought the jeep to a halt and sought shelter under it. Quick as my reaction had been, it still was not quick enough. Colonel Montgomery was already there."

Antiaircraft guns opened fire, targeting the Japanese Zeros that buzzed overhead. "The noise was terrific," pilot Chester Marshall wrote in his diary. "It sounded as if every gun on the island was going full blast." John Ciardi, who had watched the earlier raid, charged outside the mess hall just as gunners blasted one of the fighters. Parts from the wounded plane rained down atop the mess hall roof as the Zero plummeted to the ground nearby. Ciardi and others ran to the crash site to find two strips of plowed and smoldering earth, revealing where the Zero had hit and bounced before coming to rest, its engine buried underground. Little was left of the plane apart from crumpled fuselage metal that resembled tin foil and a twisted prop blade. "There were pieces of the pilot everywhere," Ciardi wrote in his diary. "His torso lay off to one side looking like a smoky roast. His head and both arms and legs were scattered around in the debris. The gunner that got him came racing down in a jeep and passed us before we reached the wreck. He had already cut off the parachute and was holding it as his private booty!"

The forty-five-minute raid destroyed three B-29s, seriously damaged three others, and banged up twelve more. It killed a medical clerk in the hospital and left others with burns as well as cuts and abrasions from diving for cover atop sharp coral. "It was an extremely daring attack and well executed," Harris wrote. "They caught the island defense with their pants down." The colonel, like many, was exhausted when he finally sat down to put pen to paper. "This day has really been something," he concluded, "so long it feels like two."

Hansell met with the island's army, navy, and marine commanders to improve defense. The Japanese attackers had flown so low that the pilots had avoided radar detection by the picket boats that patrolled the waters north of the island. By the time naval lookouts spotted the planes, they had only a few minutes to warn the airfield. Fighter patrols over Isley Field were ordered increased while technicians hustled to install radar atop Mount Tapochau, the highest point on Saipan. Hansell dedicated 160 of his command's .50-caliber machine guns to supplement the island's antiaircraft batteries and ordered his bombers to throttle Iwo Jima, executing raids on the enemy stronghold on December 8 and again on Christmas Eve.

After Japanese bombers returned again two nights later, crews began to adopt their own safety measures. A major and several lieutenants moved into a coral cave. Others started sleeping outside, tucked amid the rocks. "There was a tremendous increase in the eagerness with which air-raid shelters were being built," observed the 73rd Bombardment Wing's report. "The tent without one became a rarity." The strain of flying fifteen-hour missions, dodging flak and fighters, only to return home to battle sleepless nights because of enemy air raids, wore on the already exhausted crews. "There are Jap raids galore," one officer complained in a letter. "It's getting so everyone scrams at the slightest noise." One shell-shocked airman, dressed in full combat gear including a helmet, gas mask, leggings, and a knife, refused to leave his air raid shelter, which he had stocked with K-rations. "It's a pitiable case of pure panic—he hasn't been out of his clothes or his equipment since the first strafing raid, and he won't get more than 10 yards from a shelter," Ciardi wrote in his diary. "Someone that is in immediate charge of him has sense enough to leave him alone, but what he really needs is some competent psychiatry."

Chester Marshall recounted in his diary on December 4 how one tail gunner, after flying five combat missions, returned to his bunk and unholstered his .45 pistol.

"Well, boys," he reportedly said. "This is it."

The airman then shot himself.

The Japanese struck again at four a.m. on December 7, three years to the day since the attack on Pearl Harbor. Hansell watched from the airfield. "A couple of B-29s had been hit and were burning brightly," he recalled.

"They lit up the sky, and the oncoming Japanese aircraft was clearly visible." The enemy bomber charged down the runway, strafing the hardstands. Hansell dove to the pavement as antiaircraft batteries pounded the plane with tracers, likely killing the pilot. The bomber crashed one hundred yards from Hansell. Just as he climbed to his feet, the bombs and fuel exploded. Bulldozers and earthmovers joined the fight, rumbling through the flames to push burning planes aside and cover them with dirt to extinguish the fires. "It was the most amazing sight I have ever seen. No one knew for sure that there were not bombs in those flaming masses. Fifty-caliber ammunition was going off like firecrackers," Hansell wrote. "The scene was an animated illustration out of Dante's *Inferno*."

The all-clear came at daybreak. Marshall jumped into a jeep and rumbled down to the flight line to check on his crew's plane, *Lil' Lassie*. En route he encountered the wreckage of the twin-engine Japanese bomber, which had disgorged the bodies of five airmen. Corpsmen gathered the remains of the enemy dead. "It was a gruesome scene and very nauseating," Marshall wrote in his diary. "I excused myself and relieved my stomach of all its contents."

Marshall spotted *Lil' Lassie*. "In the hardstand, where our plane was parked, there was nothing left except a few scattered parts and a totally unrecognizable, tangled wreck of what was once an airplane—ours!" he wrote. "*Lassie* was down for good this time."

Aircraft commander John Cox arrived at the field moments later, surveying the damage alongside Marshall. American workers had invested more than 150,000 hours to build a bomber that had spent less than thirty in combat. "Flames and smoke billowed from our hardstand. Our B-29 was dying in the inferno! The firefighters were doing their best, but it was all over," he remembered. "Silently, we stared at the funeral pyre that had been our airplane."

"Well," a disgusted Cox finally said. "We're grounded again."

But the threat didn't come just from the air. Rogue Japanese soldiers lurked amid the ruins and in caves. During the November 29 mission to Tokyo, three Japanese soldiers hid near the end of the runway, trying to shoot down B-29s. "Occasionally, they would attempt to stab us in our tents or steal food or personal property," Nutter wrote. "Some of our tent mates became so nervous that whenever they heard a noise outside they would rush out, ready to shoot anything that moved. The continuous gunfire made sleep almost impossible."

Not all such encounters turned violent. On December 17, five airmen out hunting war souvenirs, ranging from pistols and swords to flags abandoned on the battlefield, spied two children. Upon closer inspection, the airmen discovered an entire Japanese family, including a visibly pregnant mother, father, and five children living in a cave. Other times starving enemy troops walked into camp and surrendered. Pilot George Savage remembered one such soldier, dressed only in a pair of shorts. "That was the most scared individual I ever saw in my life," Savage said, "because he thought he was going to be beaten to death."

Japanese raids and rogue soldiers were not the only unexpected challenge.

A storm hit Saipan the night of December 13 as Hansell struggled to bring his bombers home from a mission to drub Nagoya's Mitsubishi engine plant. The general, joined by O'Donnell and public affairs officer St. Clair McKelway, stood outside on the tower platform in the rain, eyes aimed skyward. No one spoke. "Overhead," McKelway observed, "the first airplanes coming in and circling were occasionally visible on top of the rain and fog which had settled down over the stretch of earth on which they wanted to land."

"Visibility zero," pilots radioed. "I am out of gasoline. Request instructions."

The tower operator remained calm, advising them to continue to circle. The only hope was for the storm to dissipate before the bombers burned through the last few gallons of gasoline. Thunder grumbled while the occasional flash of lightning illuminated the sky. Through breaks in the clouds, the officers could see a line of red and green flying lights, which reminded McKelway of a distant train rumbling across an American landscape.

The bright fingers of searchlights combed the clouds as ambulances and fire trucks gathered alongside the runway. The silence endured. "The rain fell and drained inside Possum's and Rosie's raincoats, streamed down their backs, down their chests, over their stomachs, down their thighs, their legs, their ankles, into their muddy soldier's shoes," McKel-way wrote. "There was nothing they could do and there was nothing they could say."

Fifteen minutes turned to twenty.

Then twenty-five.

"It's breaking over there," Hansell finally announced.

O'Donnell looked where he pointed.

Several minutes later the first stars popped through the ceiling of clouds. The generals could see the elegant shapes of the silver bombers. It was time to bring them home. "They began landing one by one," McKel-way recalled. "An hour or so later they were all down and safe in the arms of their ground crews, their grease-monkey mothers and fathers."

Someone on the platform finally broke the tension. "I don't want any more of that, with a hundred damn airplanes up there and no place for them to go."

Hansell said nothing, but smiled.

"A hundred airplanes," O'Donnell added, "and a thousand kids."

———

THE JAPANESE REBOUNDED from the surprise of America's initial raids. Enemy fighters roared up to blast Hansell's bombers while antiair-craft fire filled the sky with lead. On the December 3 mission over Tokyo, aircrews fended off 523 fighter attacks. Ten days later, following a strike on the Mitsubishi Aircraft Engine Works in Nagoya, thirty-one planes limped back damaged, including twenty-six perforated by flak. The dam-age report from that mission gave a glimpse of the violent aerial combat that crews faced in the skies over the enemy's homeland.

"Nose window broken by bullets."

"Bombardier's window cracked by flak."

"Exploding shells through left and right outboard wings."

In the first eight missions against Japan, Hansell had lost twenty-three bombers, though only seven were confirmed destroyed by the enemy, including Japanese pilots who rammed planes in suicide missions. "Last seen," one report sadly noted of a bomber, "with two engines out and losing altitude with fighters continuing attacks." The loss of fuel brought down other planes. So did mechanical failures. Eight others, however, simply failed to return. "Circumstances surrounding its fate," one report noted, "are unknown."

Morale of the airmen, which had soared a month earlier on the eve of the first attack, plummeted. Not only did crews battle the enemy in the skies over Japan, but engine problems continued to plague the B-29s, robbing the airmen of confidence in their weapon. "This airplane has more bugs in it than a Tennessee mountain bed," Col. Sam Harris complained in his diary. Others echoed Harris. "Sometimes," recalled pilot Charles Hawkes, "we wondered whether the battle was with the Japanese or the B-29."

Arnold meanwhile stepped up the pressure on Hansell, much to Possum's frustration, though it shouldn't have come as a surprise as his former chief of staff. Arnold had likewise micromanaged Ira Eaker when he commanded the Eighth Air Force in England. "I do not feel," Eaker once pushed back, "that I am a horse which needs to be ridden with spurs." No sooner had Hansell set up a communications link with Washington than Arnold started peppering him with demands. "The machine worked 24 hours a day all right, without stopping. Most of the messages seemed to consist of questions that I couldn't answer," Hansell later wrote. "I began to understand the meaning of the remark ascribed to Lord Palmerston to the effect that the disintegration of the British Empire had begun with the invention of the telegraph."

In the wake of the Japanese raids on Saipan, Arnold complained that photos he had seen showed the bombers parked too close together, making them easy prey. "I cannot understand Jap planes coming over in the daytime and apparently making several passes at the field during a period of 45 minutes with no mention whatsoever made of our own fighters even attempting to prevent such strafing," Arnold wrote. "Just what do our fighters do out there, or don't we have any fighters?" The air force commander highlighted the fact that on each mission three to four bombers ditched in the Pacific on the return to Saipan. While he understood some planes suffered battle damage, many appeared to ditch without any definite cause provided. Arnold demanded Hansell's staff analyze the problem immediately and give a full report, including recommendations to eliminate the problem. "In my opinion, the B-29 cannot be treated in the same way that we treat a fighter, a medium bomber, or even a Flying Fortress," Arnold wrote. "We must consider the B-29 more in terms of a naval vessel, and we do not lose naval vessels in 3's or 4's without a very thorough analysis of the causes and what preventive measures may be taken to avoid loss in the future. This same reasoning must apply to our B-29s."

In another letter, Arnold griped about the high percentage of bombers that aborted missions before ever reaching Japan. The general singled out the December 27 strike on Nakajima Aircraft Company's factory, where twenty-two out of seventy-two bombers turned back. "We must not and cannot let this continue," he wrote. "I want to hear from you about this with reasons." Hansell likewise felt threatened by his former subordinate Curtis LeMay, whose crews flew B-29 missions against targets in southern Japan. "Arnold's staff," Nutter said, "would send him memos describing the success of LeMay's operations in China, which angered Hansell, who didn't appreciate the comparison of his bombing accuracy with LeMay's."

Hansell's relations with O'Donnell continued to sour. Nutter felt Hansell, who appeared overwhelmed with combat as well as administrative struggles on Saipan, was letting his personal animosity cloud his judgment. "He appeared lonely and withdrawn, seemingly engaged in a duel of nerves and will with Rosie," Nutter recalled. "He had to know that he could not make his program succeed if his aircrews were hostile toward him. He also knew that O'Donnell was not alone in opposing high-altitude precision daily bombing over Japan."

But it wasn't just Hansell.

O'Donnell did a poor job of masking his frustration, convinced that the unsuccessful early missions had validated his belief that Hansell's strategy was wrong. In private letters, he vented that the Bomber Command staff was worthless. "From the very first day," he complained, "they were more of a hindrance than a help." The heavy takeoff weights, combined with the grueling climb to thirty thousand feet and the insistence that crews fly in formation, strained the already trouble-prone engines. Hansell was trying to apply tactics he had used over Europe against Japan, which O'Donnell felt were two different problems requiring different solutions.

"We don't mind dying for a cause," O'Donnell confided in an aide, "but dying when you are not accomplishing anything is a different matter."

For O'Donnell, this was no longer an academic argument over tactics, the kind Hansell had once relished during his days as an instructor at the Air Corps Tactical School. Unlike Hansell, who monitored the missions from the safety of Saipan, O'Donnell led his crews through black clouds of bursting flak while dodging enemy fighters. Problematic tactics killed men. O'Donnell was reminded of that every time he sat down to write letters to the mothers and fathers, wives and siblings of the men killed in the heavens over Japan. "It was with deep regret," O'Donnell wrote in one such letter, "that I learned of the death of your son, Raymond, as a result of wounds received while participating in a combat mission over Nagoya."

"I realize," he added in another letter, "there is little I can say to comfort you, but we are sharing with you the hope that he survived."

"Please accept my deepest sympathy during these trying times."

One loss had particularly anguished O'Donnell. On the December 3 mission to Tokyo, Col. Richard King had trailed O'Donnell's formation. The commander of the 500th Bombardment Group, King had been a star football player and team captain at the Citadel. Japanese fighters had jumped the bombers en route to the Nakajima factory, costing King two engines. "Dick's ship was last seen descending at a rate which made it seem improbable that it could make the sea," O'Donnell wrote his wife. "It was also under heavy attack of approximately twenty Jap fighters on the way down. No chutes were observed." Unbeknownst to O'Donnell, King had, in fact, made it out of the plane, though he would suffer cruelly for the rest of the war as a prisoner of the Japanese. "I don't have to tell you what I think of Dick," O'Donnell concluded. "His poorly concealed love and affection for you, his competence, his deep interest in the welfare of his men and officers, his devotion to duty, his fighting spirit and his loyalty to superiors combine to make him one of the most outstanding men I have ever known."

The friction between the generals frustrated the crews. "There is uncertainty everywhere, orders canceled, rewritten and canceled again," Col. Sam Harris griped in his diary, adding that he was losing respect for Hansell. "Ignorance, inefficiency and doubt. It must straighten out soon or this outfit will go to hell in a hurry." Two weeks later Harris returned to the struggle. This time he blamed O'Donnell for being too cautious. "Someone has to start running this show," he wrote. "We need a heap less Chiefs and hell of a lot more Indians."

Hansell called a meeting with O'Donnell and his crews.

O'Donnell began the session, praising his aircrews for their hard work despite the high wind and poor weather. The commander then turned the meeting over to Hansell. "I don't agree with General O'Donnell at all," Hansell began, his face a scowl. "I disagree with him strongly. I don't think you people are making a maximum effort."

The crews listened.

"You have not been earning your pay," Hansell barked at the crews. "You whine and complain about the wind, cloud cover, and the B-29's mechanical problems. The combat conditions and weather here are no worse than our Eighth Air Force crews faced over Germany. In fact, the flak, fighters and the losses we experienced were much worse."

The meeting lasted less than five minutes before Hansell stormed out. O'Donnell's diary left no doubt that the duo's already poor relationship reached a new low. "I was distinctly disappointed in Hansell as a leader," O'Donnell wrote. "He lost much of what little prestige he had." Nutter was equally shocked. "This was not the Hansell I had known and worked for in England. I had always admired him as a sincere, idealistic, and dedicated leader," he wrote. "This conflict with the 73rd Wing had to be resolved before it led to a disaster."

Nutter sat down for supper in the mess hall that night with weather officer Maj. Tom Bowman. Nutter told Bowman that in Europe, even when Hansell struggled with subordinates, he never allowed it to become so tense or personal. Nutter asked if he should intervene.

"You can't be serious," Bowman replied. "I've been studying the weather over Japan for two months. The cloud cover, jet stream winds, and visibility will be worse in the next few months. If our crews couldn't see their targets in the last two months, they sure as hell won't be able to see and hit them this winter. Who is going to be blamed for that?"

Nutter knew he was right, but he couldn't let it go. After dinner, the two men walked out of the mess hall. Nutter tried to steer them toward Hansell's tent, prompting another rebuke. "You can't do anything about the problems between Hansell and Rosie," Bowman warned. "There's a lot more involved than the jet stream or cloud cover over Japan."

But Nutter refused to give up.

"You're a fool," Bowman finally told him.

Nutter strolled alone over to Hansell's tent. Through the open flap, he could see the general armed with a book. "Sir," he asked, "are you busy?"

"Can't you see I'm reading?" Hansell shot back with a scowl.

Nutter glanced at the title, *Lee's Lieutenants*, an examination of the Civil War general Robert E. Lee and his senior officers. Was Hansell looking at Lee's struggles for solutions to his own? Nutter wondered. "Yes, sir," he said. "Have a pleasant evening."

Nutter returned to his own tent.

"You're back early," Bowman said.

"You were right," Nutter replied.

CHAPTER 5

"We want to emphasize that we are not bombing people. We are bombing the Japanese war machine."

—LT. GEN. MILLARD HARMON
NOVEMBER 25, 1944

The pressure on Hansell only intensified.

The general was one of the few leaders who still preached the idea of precision bombing of military targets. Much of the world had long since diverted down the moral off-ramp, embracing as a necessary means to victory the killing of civilians and the destruction of cities first articulated by airpower visionary Giulio Douhet. Each failed strike on Tokyo and Nagoya, however, brought into sharper focus the looming question that hung over Hansell.

How much longer could America refrain?

The path to this pivotal moment began three decades earlier during World War I, when Germany first deployed zeppelins to terrorize Londoners. The primitive attacks by dirigibles and biplanes, however, paled compared to the horror the world would witness as fleets of four-engine bombers darkened the skies. This time Japan was the first, launching a brutal two-year campaign against the Chinese city of Chungking, the world's first capital to suffer systematic bombing. From 1939 to 1941, the emperor's airmen hit Chungking 268 times, prompting comparisons to Pompeii and forcing the nearly half-million residents to crowd inside tunnels dug deep into a mountain. The single worst attack occurred on May 4, 1939, when bombers killed 4,400 people, injured another 3,100, and destroyed thousands of homes. Nearly four times as many people died in that one raid than died in all of Germany's attacks on England during World War I. "The city of Chungking boiled in a sudden upheaval of flying wreckage and black dust," wrote missionary and author Robert Ekvall. "By nightfall the entire horizon was red with fires that threatened to burn the rock of Chungking clean of human life and habitation."

Germany followed Japan's lead.

After failing to knock out England's airfields, radar installations, and shipping, Germany switched tactics, firebombing British cities in an effort to crush civilian morale. In what later became known as the Blitz—short for the German word *Blitzkrieg* or "lightning war"—Luftwaffe commander Hermann Göring set his sights on London, the sprawling British capital and home to 8 million men, women, and children. For the baptismal raid on September 7, 1940, Göring used the codename Loge, the demigod of fire in Wagner's opera *Das Rheingold*. That unseasonably warm Saturday afternoon, 348 bombers accompanied by 617 fighters lifted off from airfields in France, forming an aerial armada that stretched across eight hundred square miles. British fighter squadron leader Sandy Johnstone, on patrol that afternoon, broke through the haze at sixteen thousand feet. "I'd never seen so many aircraft," he recalled. "As far as you could see, there was nothing but German aircraft coming in, wave after wave."

That same sense of awe struck others on the ground, who aimed their gazes skyward at what proved to be the largest assault on England since the Spanish Armada arrived off British shores in 1588. "At first we couldn't see anything," remembered American journalist Virginia Cowles, "but soon the noise had grown into a deep, full roar, like the far-away thunder of a giant waterfall." The capital's air raid sirens sounded at 4:43 p.m. as the Germans zeroed in on the commercial docks and gasworks that lined the Thames River in the city's East End, an area comprising not only vast warehouses but also worker cottages and pubs. Pressure created by the high-explosive blasts literally tore the pants and ripped the shirt off eighteen-year-old Len Jones, who had stepped outside his home to watch. "You could actually feel your eyeballs being sucked out," he said. "I was holding my eyes to try and stop them going."

Fires erupted along the docks as warehouses packed with barrels of rum exploded. Burning rubber sent plumes of asphyxiating black smoke skyward. Flaming barges floated down the river. "Send all the bloody pumps you've got," fire station officer Gerry Knight radioed as he watched the inferno. "The whole bloody world's on fire!"

Fourteen-year-old Olive McNeil emerged from her family's shelter after the first wave of bombers. "The sky as far as I could see all around me was orange and pink," she said. "It glowed making everything look like fairyland." Fireman Jim Goldsmith, racing to help, observed the same. "You didn't need any lights or maps to find the way, you just headed for the glow in the sky."

German bombers returned for a second strike followed by a third, ultimately dropping 625 tons of high-explosive bombs and 800 incendiaries, each packed with 795 pounds of explosives. The attacks on what later became known as "Black Saturday" killed 436 people and left another 1,600 wounded. Firemen meanwhile battled more than a thousand blazes. "The monstrous inferno before us was like nothing I or anybody else in this century had ever seen," American journalist Vincent Sheean wrote. "It was like a vision of the end of the world."

German bombers returned the following evening.

And the next.

For fifty-seven consecutive nights, bombers pounded the British capital. By the end of September, the death count had climbed to 6,945, with another 10,615 injured. The casualties nearly doubled by the end of October. Mortuary teams had the awful job of assembling the remains of the dead, a jigsaw puzzle of arms, legs, and torsos. "The stench was the worst thing about it—that and having to realize that these frightful pieces of flesh had once been living, breathing people," recalled Frances Faviell, a civil defense volunteer. "If one was too lavish in making one body almost whole, then another would have sad gaps. There were always odd members which did not seem to fit, and there were always too many legs."

Terrified residents sought shelter nightly in backyard bunkers, department store basements, and even church crypts, where the less scrupulous went so far as to pry off lids, dump out the bones, and crawl inside. No fewer than 177,000 men, women, and children crowded nightly atop subway platforms, sparking a cottage industry of entrepreneurs who marked out spots in advance and then sold them at prices that rivaled the cost of a decent hotel room.

German bombs damaged or destroyed forty thousand homes a week. Others wrecked hospitals, schools, and graveyards, hurling the remains of the dead for hundreds of yards. After each raid, rescuers clawed through collapsed buildings, hoping to find survivors before they suffocated or drowned from ruptured water mains. "We were saturated with blood, dirt and stinking sweat," remembered Stanley Rothwell. "Our uniforms were now stiffened with clotted blood, we were impregnated with the acrid fumes of cordite and explosives and old brick dust."

The Germans saved the most devastating raid for four days after Christmas, hammering the heart of London with 120 tons of high-explosive bombs and 22,000 incendiaries. Luftwaffe pilots reported that the smoke rose more than 14,000 feet while residents forty miles outside the capital marveled at the fiery glow. The heat from 1,400 fires was so intense that asphalt ignited and railroad tracks buckled. Aluminum fittings and glass liquefied; fleeing residents found that the broiling pavement melted rubber soles. The conflagration incinerated nearly a third of the city, including seventeen churches, among them thirteen designed by legendary architect Christopher Wren in the wake of the Great Fire of 1666. Fortunately St. Paul's Cathedral—Wren's masterpiece as well as his final resting place—survived despite being hit by twenty-eight incendiaries. "You have all seen big fires, but I doubt if you have ever seen the whole horizon of a city lined with great fires," American journalist Ernie Pyle wrote. "There was something inspiring just in the awful savagery of it."

But London wasn't the only city to suffer.

The Germans realized that strikes against smaller cities might better undermine morale, guaranteeing that more residents personally experienced the terror. Bombers pounded Birmingham and Bristol, Liverpool and Manchester, Southampton and Belfast. The symbol of this frightful strategy, however, became Coventry. A medieval city of 238,000 residents barely a hundred miles northwest of London, Coventry had evolved into the home of one of England's largest armaments manufacturers. On the clear night of November 14, 1940, more than five hundred bombers pummeled the city, sparking an inferno visible as far away as the English Channel. "When we reached the target there was a huge sea of flames," recalled pilot Gunther Unger. "I have never seen such a concentration of fire during a raid, not even on London."

German bombers hammered the city for some ten hours; so long, in fact, that many of Coventry's antiaircraft batteries ran out of ammunition in the hours before dawn. Sunrise revealed that the raid had destroyed or damaged two-thirds of the city's homes, stores, and offices. Among them was Coventry Cathedral, a fourteenth-century Gothic sanctuary upon whose organ composer George Frideric Handel had once played. The city resorted to mass burials for the 568 people killed, since mutilation had left one of every two bodies unidentifiable. "I saw a dog," recalled survivor Jean Taylor, "running down the street with a child's arm in its mouth." The devastation prompted the Germans to invent the verb *coventrieren*, which meant "to raze a city." "Coventry," the British historian of the raid, Frederick Taylor, noted, "had quickly become the proverbial measure of airborne horror."

The bombing campaign, which ended only when Germany launched the invasion of Russia in June 1941, stretched on for 246 days, ultimately killing 43,500 men, women, and children and wounding another 257,636. The raids left 2.25 million people homeless. But the German effort to break civilian morale failed. If anything, the nightly terror attacks sparked a desire for vengeance. Bomber Command leader Sir Arthur Harris, who was enraged when he watched London burn on December 29, 1940, captured that sentiment. "They sowed the wind," he declared, "and now they are going to reap the whirlwind."

The British had begun the war so concerned with killing civilians that pilots were prohibited from bombing enemy ships in port. Germany's battering of Warsaw in September 1939, followed by Rotterdam in May 1940, led to an easing of restrictions, prompting strikes on military targets, like railyards, airfields, and arms factories. The Blitz, however, erased the last of those restraints. On December 12, 1940—in retaliation for the destruction of Coventry—the War Cabinet ordered a strike on Mannheim: not a raid on military targets but an attack on the largely residential city center. That mission, however, paled compared to the fury the British would unleash fifteen months later, once the air force had amassed enough planes and bombs to take the war home to Germany. By that time, too, British policy endorsed the firebombing of cities, putting the bull's-eye on the backs of civilians. "The primary objective of your operations," the Air Ministry ordered on February 14, 1942, "should now be focused on the morale of the enemy civil population and, in particular, of the industrial workers."

"Bomber" Harris, as he was later known to his men, jumped at the task, eager to scratch German cities off his hit list. A former farmer and gold miner in Rhodesia, Harris was a ruthless and tenacious commander; he chain-smoked Lucky Strikes while guzzling Dr. Collis Browne's mixture to quiet his ulcers. "He gave," one historian noted, "no sign of fearing God or man." Harris approached his job with a vulgar glee, which seemed more fitting in the rough-and-tumble colonies than in the parlors of English high society. "We can wreck Berlin," he once crowed, "from end to end." The mustachioed commander had taken the helm just as England abandoned daylight precision strikes, which Harris disdainfully referred to as "panacea" targets. "He believed that there were no short cuts to defeating Germany from the air," wrote historian Max Hastings. "It was necessary to concentrate all available forces for the progressive, systematic destruction of the urban areas of the Reich, city block by city block, factory by factory, until the enemy became a nation of troglodytes, scratching in the ruins."

Harris first targeted the Baltic seaports of Lübeck and Rostock, whose lack of significant industry guaranteed only minimal defense. These trial attacks burned 60 percent of both cities, including Lübeck's ancient cathedral, which dated back to 1187. The destruction horrified Joseph Goebbels, the Nazi propaganda minister: "Community life in Rostock is almost at an end." Harris then turned to the industrial heartland of Germany, blasting cities inside the Ruhr Valley, an area that produced much of the nation's steel, coke, and synthetic oil. Harris sent more than a thousand bombers to hit Cologne on May 30, 1942, an attack that killed 480 people, leveled or damaged almost 13,000 buildings, and left 45,000 residents homeless. "Our new methods," Winston Churchill bragged in a letter to President Roosevelt, "are most successful."

Other cities soon followed.

Bombers burned Dortmund, followed by Wuppertal and then Düsseldorf. The Germans were Harris's greatest teacher. "We learned as much from their few successes as from their failures," he wrote, "from what they did as from what they did not do."

Harris sent bombers back to blast cities multiple times, realizing that it took workers longer to recover from the second strike than the first. Rather than spread attacks out over an entire night, which logic originally predicted would exhaust civilians, Harris discovered it was more effective to concentrate strikes over a shorter period of time and a tighter area. Such attacks were far more likely to spark an inferno and overwhelm fire departments. Harris likewise experimented with ratios of high-explosive and incendiary bombs, the first used to blow out windows and roofs to allow the easier spread of fires sparked by the latter. "The Germans invented the Blitz," he wrote, "without appreciating its strategic possibilities."

But Harris did.

On the night of July 24, 1943, he launched Operation Gomorrah, named for the biblical city wiped out by God in a fury of fire and brimstone. His target: Hamburg, Germany's second-largest city, which cranked out warships and submarines. Over the course of eight days, bombers repeatedly blasted the industrial city. The worst of the raids came on July 27. That night more than 700 planes decimated Hamburg with 2,313 tons of bombs, using a destructive recipe of one-third high-explosive bombs and two-thirds incendiaries. The dry weather and low humidity coupled with the city's density triggered an inferno that sent smoke 20,000 feet in the sky and could be seen 200 miles away. "Tens of thousands of individual fires were joined in a very short time into major area fires, which caused firestorms of hurricane force," the Hamburg police later reported. "Trees, a meter in diameter, were broken off or uprooted, roofs of houses swept away and human beings hurled to the ground or sucked into the flames."

Winds reached speeds of 170 miles per hour, ripping children from the arms of their parents. Temperatures inside the conflagration soared to nearly 1,500 degrees, melting glass and tiles. "The heat," concluded the U.S. Strategic Bombing Survey, "turned whole city blocks into a flaming hell." Those who chose to escape often got stuck in the molten asphalt. "They fell and didn't get up again," recalled survivor Wolf Biermann. "Like flies in the hot wax of a candle." Thousands of others perished inside shelters, where some were reduced to piles of ash. Rescuers found mountains of bodies pressed against sealed doors, as though scrambling to escape. The fortunate ones passed out before death claimed them. "The very small children fell asleep first," recalled one survivor, "then the four-to-six-year olds, then the slightly older, then the adolescents and finally the old."

The hell storm, the remnants of which would smolder for a month, incinerated 8.5 square miles of Hamburg, killing 45,000 men, women, and children. More people died in one night than in the entire nine months of the Blitz. The raid destroyed 275,000 homes and damaged almost 110,000 others, leaving nearly 1 million people homeless. "Hamburg," recalled Minister of Armaments and War Production Albert Speer, "put the fear of God in me."

He was not alone.

Such horrific attacks had appalled Haywood Hansell, who reviewed the strike photos with Curtis LeMay. Unlike Hansell, who was morally opposed to such attacks, LeMay saw value in the burning of Hamburg. The British raid had killed tens of thousands of civilians, but littered among the ruins of the gutted city were wrecked armaments plants vital to the German war machine. Civilian casualties were a price the British were willing to pay to destroy the enemy's war capability. The divergent views of Hansell and LeMay personified the larger debate among American leaders over the future of bombing strategy as the war dragged on. Should commanders continue precision strikes or follow the British lead and burn the enemy's cities?

Despite America's long-standing commitment to precision bombing, war planners, in fact, had already started to prepare for a possible switch to firebombing cities, a process that had begun with the design and development of a new incendiary bomb. The Blitz had not only demonstrated the terrifying potential of incendiaries, whose destructive power proved five times greater than high-explosive bombs, but also revealed just how far behind America was in the development of flame weapons. In 1941, as German planes set English cities ablaze, America had only two designs for incendiaries, both pirated from the British. Hap Arnold furthermore had grown alarmed about potential shortages of magnesium, a critical incendiary component of those designs. The air force commander demanded a replacement.

Before the war, Louis Fieser, a defense researcher and organic chemistry professor at Harvard, had begun developing explosives made from gasoline thickened with rubber. The Japanese capture of Malaya—a dominant supplier of the world's rubber—forced Fieser to look for an alternative. In February 1942, he discovered he could turn gasoline into a gel by mixing it with aluminum naphthenate and aluminum palmitate, from whose combined names Fieser derived the much simpler "Napalm." On Independence Day 1942, Fieser tested his weapon on the Harvard soccer field, setting off an explosion whose temperatures soared more than 2,000 degrees and sent an oily cloud over the Cambridge campus.

Standard Oil Development Company meanwhile designed the delivery mechanism for Fieser's invention, settling on a six-pound hexagonal cylinder that used simple canvas streamers in place of fins. An impact fuse in the nose ejected the flaming jellied gasoline from the bomb's tail, hurling it up to three hundred feet. The bombs could be packaged in 100- or 500-pound clusters, designed to break apart in the air and fan out over dense residential areas.

This new weapon was dubbed the M69. To test the bomb, analysts sought to create as realistic a target as possible. In March 1943, workers built mock German and Japanese villages at Dugway Proving Ground in Utah. This remote stretch of desert seventy miles southwest of Salt Lake City guaranteed not only secrecy but also clear skies and low humidity, which would help dry lumber, better replicating the wood found in older homes. "The enormity of the effort that went into building those Dugway structures was amazing," recalled Hoyt Hottel, a Massachusetts Institute of Technology professor who worked on the project. War planners focused on roof design, since bombs would have to penetrate them to start fires inside homes in order to maximize destruction. Standard Oil recruited Jewish architect Eric Mendelsohn, who had fled Germany in 1933 amid the rising antisemitism of Hitler's Third Reich. Mendelsohn designed three, two-story apartments with brick exteriors, each with tile-on-batten roofs, mirroring construction typical of cities in northern Germany. Three other apartments featured slate-on-sheathing roofs, similar to homes found across the Rhineland. All the units had attics, a common feature in German homes. These designs represented eight out of ten homes in industrial areas across Germany that would soon fall under Allied bombs.

Analysts likewise studied roof designs in Tokyo, Yokohama, Nagoya, Kyoto, Osaka, and Kobe, determining that tile or sheet metal made up 80 percent of them. To spearhead the design of the Japanese village, Standard Oil hired architect Antonin Raymond, a protégé of Frank Lloyd Wright who had spent eighteen years in Japan before the war. Raymond had worked with Wright, in fact, on the landmark Imperial Hotel in Tokyo. "It certainly was not an easy task for me and my wife to be instrumental in devising means of defeating Japan," he later wrote. "In spite of my love for Japan, I came to the conclusion that the quickest way to terminate this war was to defeat Germany and Japan as quickly and as effectively as possible."

Raymond designed two apartment buildings, each with twelve homes, divided by a narrow eight-foot street that mirrored the alleys that crisscrossed Japanese cities. Mimicking Japanese construction required creativity, down to swapping out nails for wooden pegs. Workers used Russian spruce in place of Hinoki cypress, at one point diverting a ship of lumber headed for Oregon into port in San Francisco. Adobe gathered from the Southwest stood in as the plaster used to slather Japanese walls. Air Force officers in Hawaii hustled to collect woven tatami mats from Japanese homes and temples, shipping them to Utah. To guarantee enough of the iconic floor covering, workers even set up a local factory to produce them.

Construction of the two villages took just forty-four days, which included a concrete observation bunker 450 feet away designed to withstand the hit of a 500-pound incendiary dropped from 20,000 feet. To apply the finishing touches, Standard Oil recruited two German furniture makers along with the authenticity division of RKO Radio Pictures in Hollywood, the studio behind 1933's classic *King Kong* and Orson Welles's 1941 landmark film *Citizen Kane*. Throughout the homes, workers placed upholstered sofas, easy chairs, and dining tables along with throw rugs and even window drapes. Technicians applied the same detail to the Japanese village, including sliding screen doors, mattresses, and seating pillows commonly found in Tokyo homes. "In the bedroom," one government history noted, "the single beds were placed together in pairs, with a crib adjacent, reflective of a young family with an infant."

Over the course of that summer, the villages were attacked again and again. The end result of such destruction, analysts realized, was the perfect weapon for the incineration of Japanese cities. "The M69 bomb was the most effective of the bombs tested," touted one report, "and showed itself to be a potent weapon against Japanese construction."

But war planners did far more than just develop a new incendiary.

Though abhorrent to Hansell, the concept of burning the enemy's cities had percolated among American leaders long before Japanese planes battered Pearl Harbor. As early as 1932, airpower prophet Billy Mitchell advocated such a strategy in the event of war against Japan, highlighting that nation's vulnerability to fire based on its reliance on wooden construction. "These towns," he wrote, "form the greatest aerial targets the world has ever seen." Gen. George Marshall, in a secret press conference just three weeks before the war's outbreak, echoed Mitchell. "There won't be any hesitation," he said, "about bombing civilians."

Such ideas ran counter to the strategy of precision bombing that the air force ultimately adopted. In May 1943, however, as German cities smoldered, air intelligence analysts began to reassess whether a switch to fire attacks might be warranted in the fight against Japan. Armed with city plans, population statistics, and fire and weather data, war planners determined that Japan's wooden construction and extreme density made an ideal target for incendiaries. Researchers proceeded to carve cities up into three zones, with the first being the most vulnerable to fire, often consisting of congested residential areas filled with small factories.

An October 1943 report by air intelligence analysts concluded that 1,690 tons of M69 incendiaries would set uncontrollable blazes in twenty Japanese cities, an area that counted three of every four priority bombing targets. Those fires would destroy utilities, incinerate stockpiles of food and clothing, and leave 12 million people homeless. Such catastrophic attacks would slash production by 30 percent for up to six months. "The type of bomb concentration discussed," the report noted, "is calculated to start sweeping fires in heavily built-up urban areas, utilizing the combustible materials in Japanese construction as 'kindling' for conflagrations capable of destroying factories and other military objectives over wide areas."

The report went to the Committee of Operations Analysts on November 1, an organization of military leaders, lawyers, and economists. Created by Arnold eleven months earlier to examine the German economy and select industries to destroy, the group had since shifted its focus to the Pacific in preparation for the B-29 campaign, gathering around a conference room table in the Pentagon to brainstorm how best to destroy Japan. That November the committee rushed to finalize its report, prioritizing the nearly half-dozen Japanese industries America should target, including aircraft manufacturing, steel, merchant shipping, ball bearings, and electronics, like radio and radar. Attacks on urban industrial areas, which until that time had not been contemplated, sparked heated debate among committee members. "I felt that it was wrong for the air force to turn from precision bombing to area attack," Col. Guido Perera, a former Boston lawyer and the secretary of the group, later wrote. "The Committee finally agreed to include the system in its report provided that it did not take precedence over primary precision target systems." The incendiary study arrived so late—three days before the committee met to draft its report—that members could make no judgment on the accuracy of the figures. "The effect upon the Japanese war effort," the group conceded in its report of November 11, "would be very severe but probably cannot be expressed in percentage."

The following February, however, the committee was tasked to update its findings based on new intelligence, giving them a chance to explore incendiary attacks. On May 12, 1944, a special incendiary subcommittee was created under the direction of naval Commander John Mitchell. The air force intelligence analysts who prepared the October 1943 report were brought on board along with economists and fire experts. The group further split into three subdivisions, one to look at force requirements to execute such raids, another the vulnerability of the targets, and lastly a team to examine the economic effects that might arise from a successful incendiary attack. Analysts considered not only Japan's architecture and city design but also the nation's extensive history of fires, ranging from the 1923 earthquake and subsequent conflagration that burned up much of Tokyo and Yokohama to a more recent 1940 chimney fire that sparked an inferno that razed 6,500 buildings in Shizuoka. To better understand these blazes, analysts solicited help from Canadian and British insurance adjusters who had worked in Japan at the time. One even had helped with the redesign of Tokyo after the 1923 fire.

The group determined that Japan's flammable cities were a far more promising target for incendiaries than Germany. The six major urban areas of Tokyo, Kawasaki, Yokohama, Nagoya, Osaka, and Kobe—home to one out of every five Japanese—had a greater concentration of industrial workers than Germany's twenty-five leading cities combined. Furthermore, these six urban areas counted a third of Japan's industry and half of the priority industries America sought to destroy, ranging from aircraft and ordnance factories to chemical plants and radar manufacturers. Analysts determined that the best strategy would involve a series of massive back-to-back strikes, which would overwhelm firefighters and prevent leaders from dispersing industry and relocating residents, creating firebreaks, and improving air raid protection. "The best chance of creating social chaos and administrative failure," one report stated, "lies in a concentration of attacks against all targets in the shortest possible period."

To accomplish this, war planners estimated America needed thirty tons of incendiaries per square mile in Tokyo and twenty tons for the other cities. "Successful incendiary attacks," analysts predicted, "would destroy 70 per cent of the houses in the six major cities and would result in the estimated death of 560,000 persons." Targeting homes was the key to societal breakdown. Not only did Japan depend on residential workshops for wartime production, but such attacks killed laborers, burdened survivors, and overwhelmed authorities. That, in turn, slashed military production and impaired the enemy's will to fight. "The principal product of an incendiary attack is housing destruction," concluded a September 4 report to the Committee of Operations Analysts. "Housing destruction, casualties, and administrative breakdown cause absenteeism, and absenteeism reduces production."

The full Committee of Operations Analysts began evaluating such attacks in September 1944. The group's directive was to revise its original November 1943 study based on two assumptions for how America might defeat Japan. The first called for defeat via an aerial and naval blockade coupled with bombardment. The second mirrored the first, only it climaxed with an invasion of Japan's industrial heartland. Burning cities would destroy factories and erode Japan's war-making capabilities, but the committee concluded it would have no real effect on the existing frontline fighting strength, making an invasion all the more perilous. Firebombing Japan therefore depended upon whether America wanted to end the war through attrition or by troops storming the beaches. "These six cities do form a promising target," Lt. Charles Hitch said in the afternoon meeting on September 13. "It is therefore a matter of some importance to decide just what kind of war we are proposing to fight against the Japs."

The committee returned to the discussion the following morning. In the ten months since the completion of its original report—and after several years of war—national morale had changed. No longer did the public or the brass have the patience for a drawn-out war in Asia, particularly following the brutal fight in Europe. America had to defeat Japan quickly. That led members to suggest scratching industries like steel, which would only be a valuable target if war planners anticipated a long fight and wanted to wipe out Japan's ability to make more aircraft carriers and tanks. The elimination of such target systems elevated the importance of fire raids. "It is clear that incendiary attacks do not have much effect on front-line strength," affirmed Dr. Edward Mason, a Harvard economics professor. "What it does do is to reduce substantially overall industrial output, distributed over a whole range of items and tremendous property destruction, loss of life and disorganization of the economy and society."

The idea of societal disruption emerged again during the September 27 meeting. Air intelligence officer Col. William Burgess asked what effects fire raids might have on the civilian population, Japanese leadership, and the will of the people to follow them.

"Would bedlam be created?" he asked.

To answer that question, the committee summoned Commander William McGovern, with the Office of Strategic Services. A political scientist and explorer who once sneaked into the closed kingdom of Tibet disguised as a servant, McGovern had studied in Japan during his youth and later worked as an Asia correspondent for the *Chicago Times* in Tokyo. He enthusiastically advocated incendiary attacks. "The Japanese are extremely brave, as we know, but they are also given to panic," he told the committee. "The panic side of the Japanese is amazing."

Japanese children, raised in wooden cities, grew up terrified of fire, the one disaster, McGovern said, guaranteed to spark a mass panic. Tokyo made a particularly inviting target. Not only was it the center of the nation's politics, but also of Japan's cultural life and even national identity. The destruction of the capital would resonate with every Japanese.

"The closer you get to the center of Tokyo, the heart of Tokyo," McGovern said, "the greater the psychological effect."

The committee's revised report of October 10, 1944—completed two days before Hansell touched down on Saipan—drastically changed the target priority list for Japan. Though the report projected two scenarios for Japan's defeat, the first was largely immaterial since the army already planned to invade Japan the following year. The original six target systems had been slashed in half. No longer did the committee recommend that bombers blast steel mills, ball bearing plants, or electronics factories. Members instead urged the air force to first wreck Japan's airplane industry. As soon as America owned the skies, the committee advocated, bombers should incinerate Tokyo, Yokohama, Kawasaki, Osaka, Nagoya, and Kobe.

Such a recommendation, however, failed to consider the struggles of Bomber Harris, who wielded fire night after night in his crusade to reduce Hitler's cities to wastelands of rubble and rebar. "In the past eighteen months," Harris wrote on November 1, 1944, "Bomber Command has virtually destroyed forty-five out of the leading sixty German cities."

But Germany still fought.

And fought.

Even after Harris's staggering blow to Hamburg, factories rebounded to 80 percent capacity in just five months. Hamburg had shown that destroying a city, as Italian general Giulio Douhet once advocated, did not guarantee victory, particularly in a totalitarian state like Germany, where the Nazi party had infiltrated all aspects of daily life, from the church to trade unions, and where speaking out meant the firing squad. With a nation fighting for survival, there was no way to predict how many civilian deaths or how much destruction was needed to ensure surrender. That was the unknown variable in this equation of ruin, one that neither Douhet, Harris, nor members of the Committee of Operations Analysts ever solved.

Though Possum had long resisted fire raids, his superiors in Washington were increasingly persuaded, if not downright excited. Arnold, who publicly opposed such attacks as "abhorrent to our humanity, our sense of decency," preached a very different gospel to his aides in private. "This is a brutal war," he said. "The way to stop the killing of civilians is to cause so much damage and destruction and death that the civilians demand their government cease fighting." Even Roosevelt, who once vehemently objected to bombing civilians, had softened his views. He greenlit the development of the atomic bomb in October 1941 and personally ordered the first bombing raid on Tokyo on April 18, 1942, a mission led by Jimmy Doolittle. "Urban areas are profitable targets," Arnold assured the president, "not only because they are greatly congested, but because they contain numerous war industries."

The Committee of Operations Analysts urged the air force to execute a single test incendiary strike against Japan, one that would allow them to gauge the effectiveness of such attacks but not tip off the Japanese to a potential shift in tactics, giving the enemy the time to disperse industry. On December 18, Washington ordered Hansell to execute a full-scale incendiary attack against Nagoya. "The purpose of this attack is two-fold. First, to destroy as much of the city as possible to reduce its industrial capacity; second, to determine the effectiveness of our incendiary weapons particularly the M-69 in aimable clusters," orders stated. "The performance of this mission is an urgent requirement in order that future operations may be planned with far greater assurance as to our capabilities than we now possess."

The directive had come from Arnold, but Hansell saw that Norstad was the one who had actually signed it. Possum was furious. He had worked hard to retrain his aircrews to fly daylight precision missions, only for Norstad to now undermine him. More important, a mission designed to "destroy as much of the city as possible" was the antithesis of America's long-standing policy of precision bombing, guaranteeing mass civilian deaths, which he abhorred. Hansell challenged the operation; Norstad assured him the proposed mission did not represent a change in tactics, but was only a test operation. "Future planning?" a suspicious Hansell later questioned. "Was the switch to area urban bombing already under way?"

CHAPTER 6

"We just couldn't seem to get that target out of our system, mainly because we just couldn't seem to hit it."

—SECOND LT. CHESTER MARSHALL
DECEMBER 3, 1944, DIARY ENTRY

Brig. Gen. Lauris Norstad touched down on the island of Guam on January 7, 1945, one week after Hansell had moved his headquarters 135 miles south from Saipan. The thirty-seven-year-old Minnesotan, who grew up the son of a Norwegian immigrant and Lutheran minister, served as Arnold's chief of staff, a job Hansell had held until the general tapped him four months earlier to lead the 21st Bomber Command. Tall, elegant, with wavy blond hair that reflected his Scandinavian roots, Norstad had long counted Hansell as a close friend. Both were products of the Air Corps Tactical School as well as members of Arnold's cadre of handpicked young officers groomed to help lead the air force. A 1930 graduate of West Point, Norstad, much like Hansell, had fought in Europe, where he had worked closely with Gen. Dwight Eisenhower. "Norstad," the D-Day commander later wrote, "so impressed me by his alertness, grasp of problems, and personality that I never thereafter lost sight of him. He was and is one of those rare men whose capacity knows no limits."

Arnold's mounting frustration had reached a climax following the release of Hansell's first prepared press statement on December 27, 1944, in which he attempted to sum up his initial thirty days of operations. "These first accomplishments have been encouraging but they are far from the standards of perfection," Hansell wrote in remarks McKelway helped draft. "We have not put all our bombs exactly where we wanted to put them and therefore we are not by any means satisfied with what we have done so far. We are still in our early, experimental stages. We have much to learn and many operational and other technical problems to solve."

Far from the standards of perfection?

Not by any means satisfied?

Experimental stages?

Hansell's "sober report," as it was described in newspapers nationwide, horrified Arnold. The general had spent more than $3 billion to build an aerial armada of B-29s, a figure that failed to include the priceless human capital required to capture the Marianas. He likewise had staked the future of an independent air force on his ability to bomb Japan into submission. In just a few words, Hansell had sabotaged him. What would Roosevelt, the Joint Chiefs of Staff, Congress, and the American people think of such defeatist remarks?

Hansell had made the great political mistake of speaking the truth.

And it doomed him.

Norstad had grown increasingly irritated with his friend, who he felt had shown "utter absolute complete and irreversible lack of competence." More important, Hansell had resisted his push to firebomb Japan. In Possum's clumsy comments, Norstad saw an opportunity, urging Arnold to fire him. "I was more than a hatchet man," he later told an air force historian. "I had to decide to take the action before we lost the god-damned war." Arnold reluctantly agreed, but he resisted Norstad's suggestion that he fly to Guam and deliver the blow in person. "The Old Man," he later said, "really had come to a point where he was torn between his great fondness for Hansell—very warm personal feeling— and what had developed."

Hansell asked if Norstad wanted a tour, but he declined. Inside his quarters, Norstad leveled with him. Hansell was out. Curtis LeMay would replace him. The news shocked Hansell, who had worked his entire career to earn such a coveted job. The task had certainly been more difficult than Hansell expected. He had suffered thirteen Japanese raids, which had destroyed eleven of his B-29s and damaged another forty-nine. His airmen battled ferocious weather and airstreams along with a troublesome new airplane prone to engine fires.

And then, of course, there was Rosie O'Donnell.

Despite all those challenges, Hansell had persevered. He had been a good soldier. Now Norstad, one of his oldest and closest friends, stood before him, taking it all away. "I thought the earth had fallen in," Hansell confessed. "I was completely crushed."

Hansell knew Norstad was anxious to test firebombing cities, but he said he doubted LeMay would be so quick to abandon air force doctrine. Five weeks, he pointed out, was hardly enough time to test the feasibility of daylight precision bombing.

Norstad agreed, but added that Hansell failed to understand the incredible pressure on Arnold. Germany had proved far more resilient than expected, launching rocket attacks on English cities and introducing the war's first jet fighter. On the ground, American troops, after successfully storming the beaches of France, had bogged down in the Ardennes Forest. The Battle of the Bulge, which in just six weeks would ultimately cost America seventy-five thousand casualties, foreshadowed the horror that awaited infantrymen if forced to storm the beaches of Japan. The United States needed to end the war and by any means possible.

Hansell was too civilized a fighter for what America now needed.

Norstad offered Possum the job of LeMay's second-in-command, a toxic suggestion that would normally never have been considered, but one that pointed to the haste of Hansell's termination. Neither Arnold nor Norstad had bothered to ready a cushy landing pad for the general's once-trusted chief of staff. Hansell declined the job. He had fought alongside LeMay in Europe and even advocated for his promotion to brigadier general. He knew it would only poison morale for him to hang around. "I had every confidence in General LeMay," Hansell later said. "I knew him well enough to realize he needed no second string to his bow."

The next day, Hansell wrote a letter to Arnold, requesting reassignment to a training base. His sadness and exhaustion were obvious. "I am being relieved of the best job in the Air Forces; my energies are, at least temporarily, spent," he wrote. "It has been my lot to prepare for and pioneer both the air offensive against Germany and that against Japan. I should like a job now which will afford me the time and opportunity to rehabilitate myself."

LeMay landed on Guam at dawn on January 9. The general climbed down from the plane to find Hansell, ever the gentleman, waiting on the tarmac to escort him to his headquarters to meet Norstad. Back in England, LeMay, then a colonel, had been Hansell's subordinate. Now, despite being three years his junior, LeMay outranked him; the youngest major general in the air force. LeMay still had no idea why he had been summoned to Guam. "All we'd heard was that the new B-29's over there in the Marianas didn't seem to have been earning any Merit Badges," he later wrote. "At least their performance wasn't satisfying Hap Arnold."

At headquarters, Norstad informed LeMay that he would replace Hansell in the Marianas while operations in India and China would be phased out. "We'll select a new commander for the Twentieth Bomber Command; and he'll stay in India, but only temporarily," Norstad said. "The operations will be slowed. They can keep on with their system of on-the-job combat training against those lower targets; but they'll have to stop busting their ass to get supplies up to China."

LeMay, never one for words, listened, his expression unchanging.

"Just as fast as we have new fields open, the Twentieth Bomber Command will be redeployed up here, and everything will be under the Twenty First, and under you."

The meeting was awkward. Though Hansell and LeMay were not close friends, the two shared a mutual history and respect for each other. LeMay told Hansell he hoped he would advise him once he took command. He likewise feared Hansell might believe he had engineered his firing, but Possum put him at ease, telling him he knew such a move was not in LeMay's character. "If he was going to be replaced by anyone," Hansell assured him, "he was glad it was LeMay. He was the best heavy bomber commander in the air force."

Hansell pressed LeMay about whether he planned to firebomb Japanese cities or continue his policy of daylight precision strikes. LeMay was not opposed to incendiaries, if such weapons could destroy military targets, but he told Hansell he planned to adhere to the doctrine Possum had developed. Hansell hoped he would. More was at stake than just victory. "When the war was over," he reminded LeMay, "they would be judged by the way they had won it."

Outside the mission planning room, Hansell ran into McKelway. "Mac," he said to the public affairs officer, "I think there's something you ought to know."

The general escorted him into a corner of the planning room, where the two sat atop a table. Work swirled around them as officers strung worsted thread on maps, outlining in bright red an upcoming strike on a Kawasaki airframe and engine plant near Kobe. Technical sergeants, meanwhile, computed air speed, gasoline reserves, and bomb loads. Hansell briefed him. "LeMay is coming here to take over the command," Hansell informed him. "I'm out."

McKelway sat stunned.

"I'm leaving for the States as soon as LeMay has had time to fly back to China, wind up his business there, and fly back here. That's what Norstad came out to tell me."

"Holy God," McKelway finally sputtered. "What is this all about?"

"I'm not entirely sure," Hansell said, struggling. "I don't *think*—"

McKelway noted his consideration and emphasis of that last word.

"—that they are dissatisfied with the way I've been running things. There is nothing to indicate that."

McKelway hung on Hansell's every word.

"I think what's happened," the general continued, "is that the boss has decided LeMay is the best man to go on with this from here on out. I think that's really it. I think the boss considers LeMay as the big-time operator and me as the planner."

Norstad summoned McKelway later that day for a fifteen-minute conference, relaying to him that air force senior leaders were pleased with how news correspondents had so far covered the B-29 story. At the end of the meeting, McKelway asked him about Hansell's firing.

"We're personal friends. We've done a lot of tough jobs together. And I'm the one that has to come out and tell Possum we're not letting him keep the best job in the Air Forces today," Norstad told him. "The reason is that General Arnold—and all of us, including, I think, Possum—now know that this LeMay is the best man in the Air Forces right now for this particular job, the job of carrying out what Possum and the rest of us started. LeMay is an operator, the rest of us are planners. That's all there is to it."

Maj. Gen. Curtis LeMay would rise to become one of the war's great combat commanders.

PART II

The Fire

"We'll make them wish the airplane had never been invented."

—GEN. HAP ARNOLD

JANUARY 14, 1945

CHAPTER 7

"I had to select a man for the job who had experience, knowledge, judgment, but who was also cold as steel when it came to sending out his missions. I selected Curt LeMay."

—GEN. HAP ARNOLD
NOVEMBER 7, 1948, LETTER

Curtis LeMay was everything Haywood Hansell was not.

The thirty-eight-year-old general with jet-black hair and hazel eyes lacked the social grace and polish of his poetic predecessor, a factor derived from his less than privileged upbringing. LeMay stood just over five feet nine inches tall, yet weighed close to two hundred pounds, a girth that pressed against his uniform and showed in his pudgy jowls. His physical resemblance to a bulldog mirrored his stern reputation, which, coupled with his dislike of chitchat, had earned him the nickname "The Diplomat." That was the kinder of LeMay's many sobriquets. Those on the receiving end of the general's wrath preferred "Iron Ass."

Unlike Hansell, who was raised in comfort as the son of a southern aristocrat and army surgeon, LeMay had suffered a hardscrabble childhood in Ohio, one whose adversities had shaped the warrior he had grown up to become. LeMay's father had struggled to hold down a job as a painter and carpenter in Columbus, often uprooting the family on his nomadic quest for work. His mother cleaned houses to make sure LeMay and his five younger siblings had enough to eat. In 1914, after his father lost his construction job, the family climbed aboard a train west to Montana, lured by the promise of work on a ranch. That job, like so many others, soon vanished. His father rebounded, landing work south of Butte City as the wintertime caretaker of a fish hatchery used by a remote sportsmen's club. "Never shall I forget that ride in the open wagon," LeMay recalled. "A snowstorm lashed us most of the time."

LeMay found Montana to be a seven-year-old's paradise. Wooded mountain slopes ringed the valley where the family lived while bald eagles and hawks circled the skies. The experience taught him other invaluable lessons. "My father," LeMay said, "was perfectly willing to sit with his socked feet up against the shiny stove fender, while the frost snapped and crackled outside." To provide food for his family, the young LeMay would grab a piece of raw meat, trudge through the snow, and fish. One time he landed a trout so big that he struggled to drag it to the cabin. His father would lift his feet so the youth could pass. "I didn't stay for long; just got warm for a few minutes, and then hustled back to try to catch another fish."

The family moved to California in 1915, drawn by a guarantee of work offered by LeMay's uncle Oscar. The grueling trip to Emeryville via wagon and railroad was a bust. The family arrived to find that his uncle had enlisted in the army and shipped out to the Philippines. "Oscar was gone," LeMay said. "No house, no job, no anything else." LeMay's father eventually found work in a cannery while the youth scored his own job shooting sparrows for a nickel a piece that his neighbor then fed to her cat. That year, however, was transformational for LeMay. The Panama-Pacific International Exposition came to nearby San Francisco, featuring famed stunt pilot Lincoln Beachey, who had recently concluded a 126-city tour in which 17 million people had watched him perform aerial loops and rolls. Poet Carl Sandburg was so impressed with the daring airman that he wrote a tribute to Beachey. Orville Wright described him as "the most wonderful aviator the world has yet seen."

Eight-year-old LeMay wholeheartedly agreed. Each afternoon as

Beachey buzzed through the California skies, the mesmerized youth aimed his gaze toward the heavens. On March 14, 1915, Beachey took off for his second flight of the day, guiding his German Taube monoplane up over San Francisco Bay. When Beachey hit three thousand feet, he shut off the power and began his stunt dive. Fifty thousand spectators watched as he raced toward the water before pulling back on the controls. "At that moment," a *New York Times* reporter wrote, "the wings crumpled, and the aeroplane, turning over and over in its fall, plunged into the bay. Thousands of spectators rushed to the near-by waterfront, but with the exception of a few splintered fragments of the aeroplane floating on the surface of the water, no sign of the wrecked machine could be seen." Beachey's death shocked LeMay, who found that again and again he looked up expecting to see the airman overhead in the skies. "I wondered a little where he had gone," he later wrote, "but mostly I wondered how he felt when he was alive and flying."

The family migrated east to Columbus via Pennsylvania in 1919, where LeMay hawked newspapers to earn cash for school books and clothes, offering his extra earnings to his mother, who resumed cleaning houses. The industrious youth saved his money and bought a secondhand bike, which allowed him to extend his range selling papers. He also delivered Western Union telegrams and packages from department stores and candy companies. In high school, LeMay had no time to play football or baseball or chase girls. Summers were equally as hectic as he swapped school for a job as an ironworker. Few teachers took much interest in him. Nor did his parents. "There may have been nights when I looked up into the darkness and held to the opinion that I was carrying a load which not many other people were carrying," he recalled. "Usually however I was too tired to lie there and grieve about what I was missing out on."

In the fall of 1924, LeMay enrolled at Ohio State to study civil engineering. It cost $650 a year, a fee he paid himself while living at home. After his father took a job in Youngstown, prompting his parents and younger siblings to relocate yet again, LeMay moved into the Theta Tau house on Olmstead Avenue, the civil engineering fraternity. The organization not only gave LeMay his first real social interaction with his peers but also revealed how much he had missed as he hustled newspapers and telegrams through high school. On the eve of the first big social, he confided in his friends that he had never attended a school dance.

"LeMay," one of his fraternity brothers prodded him, "you will have to go down to a dance studio this afternoon, and take a dancing lesson."

It was a decision he never regretted.

LeMay likewise found a home in the ROTC program and landed a job at the Buckeye Steel Casting Company, which hammered out railroad car chassis. He worked six days a week from five p.m. until three a.m., which left his days free for class and put thirty-five dollars a week in his pocket. "It was hard work, but I liked it," he later said. "Only trouble was I needed more sleep than I was able to manage." After a long night setting molds, LeMay soon discovered, he was too exhausted to study. To make it work, he reasoned, he would have to sacrifice his grade in his nine a.m. class. "By sleeping in one class I managed to stay awake through the rest of the day and be fit for work at night," he wrote. "It was just that little margin of sleep which I needed."

Aviation continued to soar in popularity. Charles Lindbergh flew solo across the Atlantic in 1927, followed a year later by Amelia Earhart. LeMay had never forgotten his earlier fascination, an interest he rekindled his last year of school when six Army planes landed in a pasture west of Columbus. LeMay and several friends from his ROTC program ventured out to meet them. Starstruck, LeMay was paralyzed, unable to ask the fliers a single question. The next morning, he eagerly waited to watch them all take off. "One after another they went bumping away; one after another clouds of dry grass and dust and leaves and gum-papers and Lucky Strike wrappings blew in the wind," he recalled. "Then they were gone, lifting, circling, pressing farther and farther into the west." The experience mesmerized him. "Every time I closed my eyes for a long while afterward all I could see were those leather flying helmets and goggles," he said. "All I could hear were the sounds of those Liberty engines."

LeMay graduated with honors from his ROTC program in 1928 only to realize he was fifteen hours shy of earning his engineering degree. His morning slumbers had cost him. Anxious to learn to fly—and armed with a reserve commission in the army—LeMay opted to finish college later. His hopes of flying dimmed when he learned that several thousand applicants had flooded the air corps, all competing for the roughly one hundred spots. Furthermore, reserve officers were number seven on the list of priority for flying school. Active-duty army ranked at the top of the list, but there were no spots for ROTC graduates. He then noticed that the National Guard was second on the priority list, which gave him an idea. LeMay hustled down to see the commander of the 62nd Field Artillery Brigade of the Ohio National Guard.

"Sir," he announced, "I would like to enlist in one of your batteries."

"Why all the eagerness?"

LeMay decided to level with him, telling him about his desire to learn to fly and how he had determined that the National Guard offered him the best odds.

"I guess that there's some method in every madness. I've got a vacancy on my staff right now—I need an ammunition officer. Why don't you take that?"

The commander escorted LeMay across the street to the Ohio Statehouse, where he resigned from the reserves and was commissioned as a second lieutenant for field artillery in the National Guard. "My application as a National Guard officer applying for admission to the Army Air Corps flying school went in just as fast as it could be processed."

LeMay then waited.

And waited.

As summer gave way to fall he contemplated enrolling again in college to finish his engineering credits and graduate. Before he handed over the money for class, he decided to fire off a telegram to Washington. "Urgently request information concerning my appointment as flying cadet in the November class," LeMay cabled on September 25, 1928. "If I cannot be accommodated in this class I wish to complete my thesis at Ohio State University."

His answer arrived one day later.

"Your enlistment as a flying cadet for November class has been authorized."

LeMay was ecstatic. His creative end run around the army's bureaucracy had worked. But now he faced an even bigger test. "I used to wake at night and think about washing out," he said. "Just twenty-five percent of the would-be cadets were making it at that time; the standard washout rate was seventy-five percent." Those fears haunted him as his train rumbled west to California's March Field, where his new quarters consisted of a holed tent. The program required eight months of ground school and basic flying in California. Those candidates who passed then moved to Kelly Field in Texas for four more months of advanced flying.

LeMay struggled under the tutelage of Peewee Wheeler, who he realized was a gifted flier but a terrible teacher. The apprentice airman watched in horror as Wheeler's students washed out one after the other. LeMay contemplated asking for a new teacher, but such a move countered his personality. He was a fighter, always one to stick it out regardless of the obstacles. LeMay's challenge worsened on the day of his flight test when he drew instructor Red MacKinnon as his examiner, known among the airmen as the toughest appraiser.

LeMay soon learned why.

"God damn it!" MacKinnon shouted at one point. "That's all wrong!"

LeMay botched maneuvers after a simulated power failure, proved unable to perform a snap roll to the right, and in the end landed long. "Altogether it wasn't one of my better days," LeMay later wrote. "And I knew it."

"Well, son," MacKinnon said after he climbed out of the plane. "By Jesus Christ. I don't know whether to wash you out, or give you a chance and send you on."

LeMay couldn't breathe.

"I guess," MacKinnon replied slowly, "that I will send you on, after all. But I'll keep my eye on you, and see how you do."

LeMay's fortunes improved when he landed former World War I pilot Joe Dawson as his next instructor. LeMay learned more from Dawson in two weeks than he had in months under Wheeler. LeMay completed his eight months with 164 hours in the cockpit and then transferred to Kelley Field for advanced training in the summer of 1929. In Texas the students split up into different areas of aviation: pursuit, observation, and bombardment. LeMay chose fighters. "We had our normal training in fighters: formation, night flying, cross-country. Then we used to go down and fly the airplanes of the Bomber people, the Attack people and the Observation people," he remembered. "Everybody flew everything that was on the field."

On October 12, 1929, LeMay graduated from flight school. He resigned from the National Guard and was commissioned a second lieutenant in the air corps. His first assignment was with the First Pursuit Group in Selfridge, Michigan, an outfit, he soon learned, with too few planes for its pilots. Despite the stock market crash and the subsequent Great Depression, cities continued to open airports, often requesting army pilots to perform acrobatic shows at the ceremonies, a job that kept LeMay and others in his squadron flying. At the same time, LeMay began to feel haunted by his failure to finish his degree. His efforts to convince his superiors to allow him time to complete college failed. "Most of the people surrounding me were people with degrees," he said. "I became certain that there might be embarrassments and disappointments in the future if I didn't have a more solid scholastic background."

In the spring of 1931, a fellow flier, who was engaged to a girl at the University of Michigan, arranged a blind date for LeMay and another officer. On the night of the date, the two young women peered through the curtains of Mosher Hall dormitory at the two airmen who approached. "I think I'll take the fat one," Helen Maitland said to her friend.

The fat one, of course, was LeMay.

The daughter of a corporate lawyer in Cleveland, Helen had studied nursing at Western Reserve before enrolling at the University of Michigan to do postgraduate work as a dental hygienist. "I was attracted to her from the start," LeMay said. "She talked plenty, couldn't seem to stop. And it was all in a bubbling effusion which I found myself rather enjoying. She'd skip from one topic to another, like a dancer just hitting the high points."

Helen's academic success made LeMay ashamed of the fact he had not yet graduated. When he drove her home that night, he confided in her of his ambition to finish his degree as well as his struggles with the army to accomplish it. "It's up to you," she said. "You've got to use your best resources, whatever they are. Figure out a way. You might take your commanding officer into your confidence, if you haven't done so already. But there must be a way."

LeMay took her advice. He devised a plan to return to Norton Field in Columbus, where there was only one regular-duty officer and a few sergeants who would no doubt welcome a little extra help. He discovered that regulations allowed an officer to detach from service for five months and twenty-nine days. Anything longer required a permanent change of station. He could barely fit in the work he needed at school in that time. "It would be necessary to report to school just a few days late and leave just a few days early," he said. "But I thought this might be arranged with the college authorities." LeMay was right. His commanding officer and the university officials gave him the green light, while the officer at Norton Field generously allowed him to have mornings to attend classes if he agreed to work afternoons and weekends. Life was far easier than his earlier college days, when he worked all night in the steel mill. He no longer had to worry about food or money. "I had the world by the tail," he said. "For the first time in my life I seemed to know what it was like to be young and alive."

LeMay finished his exams early and returned to Michigan. Like his high school dances, he missed commencement and the chance to walk proudly across the stage. His diploma later reached him by mail, but that paper confirmed he was finally a college man.

The young airman continued to periodically date Helen, who worked in Akron as a hygienist. On a visit to see her in October 1933, LeMay learned she had agreed to marry another man. "I was thunderstruck at being presented with the news of Helen's engagement. An engagement not to me, but to someone else," he said. "She seemed very smug about it. She told me that night, chattering with her usual colorful detail; the fiancé was a doctor, busy at some clinic down in Brazil now, but planning to meet her in Bermuda for a marriage ceremony there."

The news horrified LeMay, who in his stoic manner refused to plead with her to change her mind. "Well, Curt," she asked at the end of the evening, "when are you coming back?"

"Not coming back," he replied.

"You're not?"

"Nope."

Despite LeMay's obstinance, the couple soon reconciled, marrying on June 9, 1934. LeMay had little time to settle in after his honeymoon in a Cleveland hotel before the air corps ordered him to Hawaii. The two years he spent on Oahu would mark a pivotal turning point in his career. LeMay had previously studied celestial navigation under famed Australian aviator Harold Gatty, who in 1931 helped the pilot Wiley Post set the world record for circling the globe, a 15,474-mile journey the duo accomplished in a single-engine plane in eight days, fifteen hours, and fifty-one minutes. On Oahu, LeMay decided to start his own navigational school to spread Gatty's gospel. At the same time, LeMay, much like Hansell, underwent a metamorphosis in his views on the strategic importance of bombers. Though a pursuit pilot by training, he had since realized fighters alone could never win a war. "The fighter aircraft was purely a tactical phase of warfare. If you desired a strategic role, you had to get into Bombardment," he said. "It would be *the* strong arm. Perhaps, in the end, the primary arm of the Air Force."

LeMay landed in Virginia with the Second Bombardment Group in 1937 under the tutelage of Lt. Col. Robert Olds. A bomber advocate ten years his superior, Olds, like Arnold, had been close with Billy Mitchell, even risking his own career to testify on his behalf at his trial. In an interview upon his retirement decades later, LeMay would credit Olds as the single most important figure in his thirty-five-year career. Olds did what neither LeMay's teachers nor his parents seemed capable of doing. He took an interest in him, harnessing the young airman's drive and resourcefulness as he worked to shape him as an officer. "I can't imagine any experience more demanding and more valuable to a young officer than a tour of duty serving under Bob Olds," LeMay recalled. "He was the first man I'd ever come in contact with who really penetrated my thick skull with a sense of urgency in getting things done."

LeMay's tenure with Olds came at a critical juncture for the air service. Olds commanded the first operational units of the B-17, a four-engine bomber that would prove vital in World War II. Olds demonstrated his faith in LeMay when he tapped him in August of that year to serve as his personal navigator during a two-day joint exercise with the navy. The goal: find and bomb the battleship *Utah* in the waters off the West Coast. The aviators faced stiff headwinds, as the same anti-airpower tensions that Billy Mitchell battled twelve years earlier still permeated the War Department. The admirals, in particular, took a dim view of the air force, believing that bombers usurped the navy's territory. "The Navy," LeMay later said, "had loaded the dice for this crap game, but still we were going to play with them."

Under the rules, navy reconnaissance planes would first find the *Utah*—in an exercise area that consisted of over 100,000 square miles of ocean—and radio the coordinates to the army. The B-17s would then take off and attempt to belt the battlewagon with dummy bombs. The exercise would run from noon on August 12 until the same time the following day. Bombers were not allowed to attack after dark, which gave them limited light each day to find and hit the *Utah*. The massive distances likewise meant that if the *Utah* steamed at the outer edge of the exercise area, then there was no way that the B-17s could take off from shore and even reach it before dark. The odds seemed stacked against them. Olds made the decision that his airmen would take off and head out to sea and await the coordinates.

As nightfall fast approached, the navy finally reported the *Utah*'s coordinates. LeMay plotted the course. The bombers broke through the fog to find nothing but empty seas. A search of the area as night descended revealed nothing. Olds doubted his navigator, emphasizing to LeMay that the future not only of the B-17 but of the entire air force was at stake. "You were selected to fly lead navigator because I thought you were the best in the Group."

LeMay assured him his navigation was correct. To prove it, he took a new reading, plotted the bomber's location, and predicted the estimated arrival in San Francisco.

"This is it," he said, handing the details to Olds in the cockpit.

"I hope you're right, Curt."

LeMay returned to the cockpit about ten minutes before arrival, watching moments later as the city lights began to show through the fog in the distance.

"By God. You were right," Olds said. "Then why didn't we find the *Utah*?"

"Maybe they gave us the wrong position," LeMay said.

Olds woke him up early the next morning to tell him the navy admitted the coordinates were one degree off. That one degree translated into sixty miles.

That morning the coordinates were off again, but this time the bombers had flown low and fanned out, covering more ocean. Shortly before noon, the *Utah* came in sight.

"That's it," LeMay announced, binoculars trained on the battleship.

At five minutes to noon, the B-17s closed in on the target. Sailors scrambled out of the way as the bombs fell. "I remember watching the first bomb which smashed into the deck. It sent splintered pieces of wood flying in every direction," LeMay said. "We clobbered her." The airmen scored three direct hits in an exercise, like Mitchell's attack on the *Ostfriesland*, that revealed yet again the obsolescence of the battleship and infuriated the brass. "The Navy," Hap Arnold later said, "raised hell like a country gentleman finding poachers on his property."

LeMay continued to build on his success. In February 1938, Olds tapped him as lead navigator on a mass flight of B-17s south to Argentina, a feat that would require buzzing the Andes Mountains. Ira Eaker, who was then on the air staff, pulled Olds aside. "Bob," he said, "this is a very significant flight, upon its success may depend whether we get any more B-17s from Congress. How could you select a lieutenant as your navigator?"

"Because Lieutenant LeMay is the best damned navigator in the Army Air Corps."

The flight was a stunning success, earning the group the prestigious MacKay Trophy and foreshadowing the not-too-distant future when

American bombers would lift off from England and pulverize German cities. "We proved," LeMay later said, "that we could go anywhere in the world with these airplanes." On a personal level, the young lieutenant received a letter of commendation from Secretary of War Harry Woodring. "You have brought great credit," Woodring wrote, "to yourself and to the Army of the United States."

LeMay helped pioneer air routes across the North Atlantic and conducted a survey of fourteen airports from South America to Iraq, a twenty-six-thousand-mile journey that laid the groundwork for wartime supply routes to Russia and the Middle East. "This outstanding flight," read LeMay's citation for the Distinguished Flying Cross, "reflects the highest credit on the military forces of the United States." Over the years, LeMay's personnel file swelled with similar accolades from his superiors, many of whom highlighted his navigation skills, dogged work ethic, and determination in solving problems. "Forceful and aggressive in obtaining his objectives," one evaluation read. "Is at his best when given an outline of the general result and allowed to work out his own plan, which he will do with marked efficiency."

"A level headed, serious worker, who is not satisfied with a job done unless it is well done," added another.

"Has a brilliant career ahead."

Though forceful and aggressive on the job, LeMay remained reserved in person. He distrusted intellectuals, whom he viewed as dreamers much like his derelict father. A pragmatist, LeMay valued hard work over intellect. "If a man is really motivated and he really wants to get something done, he'll get it done," he once said. "He may have to work ten times harder than someone who is a little more knowledgeable or smarter or better prepared but if he's got the motivation he'll get it done and this counts a lot with me." A life spent struggling to fend for himself had robbed LeMay of opportunities for social growth, rendering him awkward in gatherings. As such, he disliked public speaking. "Humor," one subordinate wrote, "isn't one of the general's strongest points." LeMay instead saved his affection for his wife and daughter Janie, born in February 1939, whom he adored. "He was much softer individually than one would give him credit for," recalled Paul Carlton, an aide. "Very few people knew how human he really was." LeMay, who in his downtime liked to fish, hunt, and tinker with cars and a ham radio, likewise was loyal to his friends. That said, he was not ignorant of his rigid reputation, even poking fun of himself in a letter to Helen. "I understand," he wrote, "that in some circles it is thought that I definitely don't have an affectionate side to my character."

In May 1942, following the attack on Pearl Harbor, LeMay was chosen as commander of the 305th Bombardment Group, a brand-new outfit made up of four squadrons at Salt Lake City. That July, the outfit relocated to Muroc Army Air Field in the Mojave Desert northeast of Los Angeles. LeMay's job was to turn new recruits into combat airmen ready to take the war home to the Germans and the Japanese. "Most had never seen a B-17," he said. "Some had never seen any combat airplane before." The challenges kept him awake at night. "How," he wondered, "could anybody ever have the gall to bring a rabble like this into battle?"

Ralph Nutter was one of LeMay's early recruits. A student at Harvard Law School, Nutter had enlisted in the Army Air Forces the morning after the attack on Pearl Harbor. The first flight he ever took was from Maxwell Field in Alabama to Sacramento's Mather Field, where he trained as a navigator before heading to Muroc. The husky LeMay looked far different than the dashing airmen Nutter had seen in Hollywood movies. "He didn't look like a glamorous pilot," Nutter recalled. "There was no vanity in his appearance." LeMay's tough approach and gruff demeanor had already earned the colonel several other nicknames among the troops, including "Smiley" and "Old Poker Face." Nutter's squadron commander Maj. Joe Preston gave him some advice on dealing with LeMay.

"When he gives you an assignment," he said, "get it right the first time. When he asks a question, get to the point. He doesn't want to hear any bullshit."

Nutter listened.

"He believes talk is cheap," Preston continued, "and that you learn more by listening than talking, so he doesn't judge people by words or promises. He judges them by what they do. Performance is the beginning and the end for him. He's fair, but tough as nails."

"I can forgive a mistake—once anyway," LeMay often told his men. "But God help you if you ever lie to me."

LeMay drove his men, but he also believed in giving them time off.

"Enjoy it," he warned them. "Don't think this is my combat policy. If you want to raise hell, get it out of your system now. Once we get overseas you'll be confined to base until I decide you can hold your own in combat. It may take a long time."

In October, as LeMay prepared to move his group to Europe to join the fight against Germany, he came down with what he believed was a bad cold. The colonel powered through the pain at his desk that morning with coffee. Around lunch time he took a swig of his drink only to spew it all over his shirt. LeMay stepped into the latrine to clean up, catching a glance in the mirror. "Something," he said, "was radically wrong with my face and mouth."

LeMay hustled to see the flight surgeon, who diagnosed his sagging right cheek and jowls on sight. "You've got Bell's palsy," the doctor told him.

Terror washed over LeMay, who sat frozen for a few moments. "It sounds perfectly horrible," he finally stammered. "What in the *hell* is Bell's palsy?"

The doctor explained that it was a condition, often sparked by a viral infection, that caused inflammation and damage to facial nerves, prompting paralysis. In extreme cases patients could not close their eyelids, while drooping lips prompted others to drool.

"Are you going to do anything about it, or *can* you do anything about it?" LeMay pressed. "What's the treatment?"

In most cases, the flight surgeon said, it cleared up over time. In cases where it didn't, some people had undergone shock therapy. Others had turned to massages. Those who sought treatment, the doctor added, fared about as well as those who opted to do nothing. LeMay might not have liked the way he looked, but he did not have time to be sidelined for remedies that might not even work. "You've named my treatment," he announced. "Goodbye."

"One thing," the doctor hollered after him as he left. "Be sure to keep the right side of your face warm, and stay out of drafts."

That would be all but impossible.

Before flying out for England, the colonel summoned his airmen, instructing them to be mindful of military courtesy, demonstrate good behavior, and avoid pub brawls.

"But if you do get into a fight," he concluded, "don't get licked."

LeMay's mentor Robert Olds, who had guided the young officer over years and on missions around the world, cabled him on the eve of departure. "It is a source of gratification to me to know that you have overcome all obstacles and have developed an outstanding group under adverse conditions in an exceedingly limited time period," Olds wrote. "Our interest will remain with you while you are in the combat zone, and I have every reason to expect that your conduct under combat conditions will reflect credit on the Army Air Forces."

LeMay touched down in England in late October 1942 to join a fight unlike any other he had ever experienced. Miles above the earth where temperatures plummeted as low as sixty below zero, crews battled not only German fighters and antiaircraft guns but also frostbite and oxygen deprivation that could knock an airman unconscious in minutes. The cold on this heavenly battlefield was powerful enough to cauterize wounds and weld skin to metal. To fend off the elements in unpressurized cabins—and at altitudes that rivaled the summit of Mount Everest—airmen wore heated suits and donned heavy gloves, sheepskin boots, and oxygen masks. "Every position in the plane was vulnerable," wrote historian Donald L. Miller. "There were no foxholes in the skies." At night LeMay would lie in his bunk and question whether he was up to the job. "What do you know about how it feels to be in combat?" he asked himself. "Will you stand up? Will you have the nerve to ask them to stand up to it?"

Life on the ground was little better as the Americans bedded down in frigid Quonset huts at Grafton Underwood Airfield before eventually settling in at Chelveston Airfield near Cambridge. "The mud was atmosphere," LeMay recalled. "You breathed it in even if you didn't want to, it was under your nails, it was in grooves of your hands. We took off in it, flew in it, often had to abort because of it." But the mud was only part of the colonel's challenge. Despite his earlier efforts, LeMay's crews remained woefully ill-prepared. "We had practically no air-to-air gunnery; very little high-altitude bombing; no high-altitude formation; no group formation until we got in the concentration area, not having enough airplanes to make a formation," he said. "The navigators had no long-range navigation. Each first pilot had about 100 hours in a B-17. The average total flying time among pilots was 400 hours. The bulk of the pilots were right out of flying schools; they learned to fly B-17's, and came over seas."

Soon after he arrived, LeMay ran into Col. Frank Armstrong, who had led the first daylight raid over France, earning the Silver Star, the nation's third-highest medal for heroism. LeMay arranged for Armstrong to brief his pilots; the men were eager to soak up his words. Armstrong warned them that the German flak was horrific.

"If you fly straight and level for as much as ten seconds," he concluded, "the enemy are bound to shoot you down."

The odds seemed stacked against LeMay.

The colonel pushed aside his concerns and started preparing. Short-range fighters could not accompany the B-17s on long missions, leaving the bombers to defend themselves in the skies over enemy targets. Sloppy formations often doomed aircrews, making them easy prey for German fighters, who picked off the stragglers. To maximize the defense, LeMay experimented with new formations. His first test flight with his crews was a "complete debacle." As the pilot of the lead bomber, LeMay struggled to see his planes, much less organize them in the skies. That night the frustrated colonel lay awake, replaying the flight in his head, when an idea suddenly hit him with such force he sat up in bed.

"Top turret," he said aloud. "That's where I belong."

LeMay climbed out of his bunk, grabbed a chart, and started sketching. The formation he worked out involved eighteen bombers—three squadrons of six—flying in what was later called a wedge-shaped combat box. The formation resembled the tip of a spear, with a lead group of six bombers followed by a squadron below to port and another above to starboard. This three-tiered structure not only guaranteed that each bomber's .30- and .50-caliber machine guns had an unobstructed field of fire but also allowed the planes to bomb without breaking formation. As soon as the weather permitted, LeMay returned to the skies with his airmen, climbing up into the top turret, where he had a view of his bombers. He plugged in the radio extension and began directing each bomber into position. "We've got to circle our wagons," he radioed. "Our only chance of survival is to maintain a tight formation. A tight, close formation will concentrate two hundred guns anytime the Nazis attempt to fly through our formation."

A better formation helped solve the challenge of German fighters, but it did nothing for the antiaircraft fire. Furthermore, LeMay's review of strike photos and postraid reconnaissance images revealed that airmen weren't hitting their targets. Those misses, he surmised, resulted from the pilots taking evasive maneuvers to avoid flak, which only scattered the bombs. Every missed target meant that aircrews would have to return again and again—battling more fighters and more flak—until the shipyard, refinery, or airplane factory was destroyed. How could LeMay defend his bombers and increase accuracy? "As soon as you cross the enemy coast you have paid the price of admission," he said, "whether you hit the target or not."

Despite Armstrong's insistence, LeMay harbored doubts about the accuracy of German flak. Ten seconds seemed an awfully short time for an antiaircraft battery to zero in on bombers five miles overhead and flying at speeds of 150 miles per hour. If his hunch was correct, then bombers would be able to fly a long, straight run over a target, a move that would improve accuracy. But how could LeMay prove it? Inspiration roused him again on a sleepless night, prompting the colonel to climb out of bed, pull tight the blackout curtains, and rummage through his footlocker. There in the bottom he found his old artillery manual from Ohio State. "Why the hell I ever put that in the locker," he later wrote, "I'll never know."

But it was fortunate he had.

Armed with a pencil and notepad—and with a sweater wrapped around his shoulders to fend off the November cold—he attacked the problem. Based on intelligence estimates, he figured out how many guns the Germans operated, the type, and the rate of fire.

"You've got to imagine what the actual situation will be," he repeatedly told himself. "You've got to figure out their precision fire."

The pencil charged down the paper as he hustled to solve the equation. The answer he computed by lamplight in the middle of the night stunned him. For a German artillery battery to bring down a bomber in the upper stratosphere would take 372 rounds. There was no way, LeMay realized, the enemy could hurl up that much flak in just ten seconds. Armstrong was wrong. But who was LeMay—armed only with his nearly two-decade-old artillery manual and no combat experience—to challenge the expertise of a veteran pilot?

LeMay knew there was only one way to test his theory. The group's first combat mission was scheduled for November 23, 1942, a raid on the German submarine base at Saint-Nazaire along the west coast of France near the city of Nantes. LeMay briefed his men.

"If we're going to St. Nazaire we're going to get some bombs on that target, by God," he told them. "And this is the only way I can see to do it."

Zooming in on the French coast, LeMay spotted the target and began his bomb run. German antiaircraft fire thundered, peppering the skies with black clouds, all of them far below. Ten seconds passed—and nothing happened. LeMay kept his focus as the seconds rolled into minutes. Before he knew it, his bombs were gone and the target vanished behind him. "We flew straight and level for four hundred and twenty seconds, after we first saw that target and came in on the bomb run," he wrote. "Not one of us was knocked down by ground batteries."

LeMay had shattered the myth of Germany's flak, leading to the adoption of his revolutionary new tactics by the entire Eighth Air Force. "I felt if ever there was a man in the right place, at the right time, it was Colonel LeMay," Nutter later said. "I finally understood what he had been trying to do with our group ever since July back at Muroc. His tough discipline and what originally seemed like iron-ass demands began to make sense to me." Others in his outfit agreed. "If LeMay said two and two are five, I'd believe it," added Theodore Beckemeir, "because I know he would have the facts to prove it or he wouldn't have said it."

Saint-Nazaire was the first of many missions as LeMay and his men pummeled cities like Lorient, Rouen, and Antwerp. Targets ranged from submarine bases and railyards to steel mills and ordnance depots. The weeks soon turned to months. The German air force adapted. Fighters learned to attack head-on to try to break up a formation, while others dropped parachute explosives from above. The Germans even repaired a crashed B-17 and used it to infiltrate one formation. "As long as LeMay was our leader, most of us believed we could hold our own against the Germans," Nutter said. "Failure was not in his vocabulary."

"We'll shoot our way in and back from a target," LeMay often told his men.

That ferocity along with his quiet demeanor kept his men disciplined.

"We were more afraid of him," one officer recalled, "than Hitler."

While Hansell and Eaker stressed over proving the concept of daylight precision bombing, the job of propping up that strategy fell to LeMay, who week after week climbed into the skies to battle German fighters and flak. "The only thing I was thinking about was living for the next twenty-four hours," he said, "trying to keep my outfit alive and the airplanes flying." LeMay believed that a commander should have no friends, a view that guaranteed that no combat decision would ever be affected by personal loyalties. The good of the group always outweighed the good of the individual. "I'm not supposed to be liked," he often told senior aides. "I don't have the luxury of liking or disliking people." Nutter, who became LeMay's personal navigator, came to appreciate the loneliness of command. "He taught me that some loss of life had to be expected in every battle," Nutter wrote. "Loss and death went with the territory; if victory were to be achieved, some lives had to be sacrificed for the greater good."

LeMay hammered that point home after a bomber dropped out of formation to help a parachuting crew under strafing attack by German fighters. The enemy pilots then peeled off and attacked and destroyed the second bomber. The unnecessary loss infuriated LeMay.

"We aren't fighting a Hollywood war here," he barked at his men. "Leave the glory, the false heroics, and the sentimentality to the actors and the sob sisters."

LeMay's tough but fair and consistent approach earned the respect of his airmen, who came to champion their fearsome leader. That was evident the time he climbed down from his B-17 to refuel, a cigar clenched between his teeth. A member of the ground crew pulled LeMay's crew chief aside. "Doesn't the general know that the plane might explode?"

"It wouldn't dare," his crew chief responded.

LeMay's fellow group commanders—many of whom were more experienced—were surprised at the rookie's success. His airmen had fewer losses and less aborts and put more bombs on target. "His group," recalled Leon Johnson, who commanded the 44th Bombardment Group, "was leading everyone else." Eighth Bomber Commander Ira Eaker paid LeMay a visit after he heard grumblings that the colonel had sent his gunners to the range for practice immediately after an arduous mission. "German fighters flew by my plane so close I could have hit them with my Colt .45," LeMay said. "If we don't shoot better than that tomorrow, we won't come back. These crews are great kids and I want to bring them back alive."

Eaker agreed.

Johnson and Eaker were not the only ones to notice LeMay. The colonel's tenaciousness earned him a commendation letter from the general he would one day replace on Guam. "The superior leadership demonstrated by you," Hansell wrote, "has been greatly responsible for the improvement of combat bombing, gunnery and formation techniques." The efficiency reports that filled LeMay's personnel file echoed Hansell. "This officer," observed Doolittle, "is unusually gifted as an airman and as a combat leader." Maj. Gen. Frederick Anderson, who succeeded Eaker as head of the Eighth Bomber Command, agreed. "Devoted to his command, but if necessary for the carrying out of directives, he will push his command to the breaking point. Loved by his men even though he works them harder than any commander of my knowledge," Anderson wrote. "In my opinion, one of the greatest combat leaders developed in this war."

LeMay was promoted to brigadier general and commander of the Third Bombardment Division in September 1943. As in his college days when he juggled his studies and his work in the steel foundry, he found he was lucky to stretch out at two or three in the morning. Even then he struggled to fall asleep. In his letters to Helen he often lamented his exhaustion. "Most nights, I get my sleep in four hour stretches or less," he wrote in one letter. "I wonder," he added in another, "if there will ever come a time when I'll get all the sleep I can use."

The long hours and the distance likewise strained his marriage; he failed to write as often as Helen preferred, a fact that prompted her to repeatedly scold him. "It certainly would be fun to get a nice, cheery letter from home for a change," he complained in one note. When LeMay did put pen to paper, his letters were short, a few lines, a paragraph or two at most. "I'm sorry you haven't received as many letters as you would have liked," he griped to her in one. "I'm doing the best I can; however, my primary job is putting bombs on Germany and yours is being as understanding and helpful as possible under the circumstances. I suppose it is impossible to expect anyone 3,000 miles away from the fighting to understand war."

LeMay did make it home briefly after a year, during which time he visited his family in Cleveland for a few days. He was stunned at how much his daughter, Janie, had grown.

"Daddy, I want you to go out on the porch with me," she said to him on a frigid November night. "I want to sit in the porch swing."

"Let's stay inside," he pleaded. "It's real nice in here."

LeMay's efforts to persuade his four-year-old failed, so together father and daughter sat on the swing for an hour. Afterward Helen shared their daughter's motivation with him. "Janie wanted the neighbors to *see* me," LeMay later wrote. "Some of the kids had told her they didn't believe that she had a father, and she wanted to prove that they were wrong. Must have been the warmth of her affection which kept me from catching cold."

Despite the ebb and flow of the war, and the sagging morale, LeMay drew inspiration from his men, who day after day lifted off to battle the enemy. Many, he knew, would never come home. The final letter from one fallen airman to his family greatly affected the normally reserved LeMay. "I sometimes wonder what I have ever done to deserve the command of an outfit like this," he wrote to his wife. "You have always complained about my not being sentimental enough. I think sometimes I'm too soft to properly fight a war. After raising these kids from pups and leading them against the best pursuit and anti-aircraft defenses in the world, and having them come through the way they have, it hurts like hell to lose them."

LeMay's tenure in England came to an end in late June 1944, soon after the Allies stormed the beaches in France and just shy of the two-year anniversary of when he had first touched down in England. Hap Arnold had bigger plans for LeMay.

"You're going to India and China," one of the general's aides told him. "B-29s."

Arnold tapped LeMay to lead the 20th Bomber Command, replacing Brig. Gen. Kenneth Wolfe, who had been fired for failure to perform after only three missions. Wolfe had helped shepherd the Superfortress through its difficult development before landing in a remote corner of Asia, where he faced an equally daunting challenge spearheading Operation Matterhorn, the war's first B-29 offensive. In an ironic twist, Hansell, who at the time served as Arnold's chief of staff, had played a role in Wolfe's downfall, harping on him over his poor bombing accuracy and failure to take instructions from Washington, complaints that would dog Possum a few months later in the Marianas. "With all due respect to Wolfe, he did his best," Arnold wrote, "but LeMay's operations make Wolfe's very amateurish."

LeMay knew little about the recently organized 20th Air Force and even less about Boeing's new Superfortress, but he welcomed the challenge. "There would be much to learn, all over again," he wrote. "New theater, new equipment, new personnel, an entirely new set of problems." LeMay first insisted that before shipping out to India, he spend a month at Grand Island Army Airfield in the prairies of Nebraska to learn to fly the B-29. His experience only confirmed the struggles Arnold had with getting the revolutionary plane airborne. "B-29s had as many bugs as the entomological department of the Smithsonian Institution," LeMay said. "Fast as they got the bugs licked, new ones crawled out from under the cowling."

On August 29, LeMay touched down in Kharagpur, about seventy miles west of Calcutta. The general had gone from the fog and mud of England to the heat and humidity of India, which was so oppressive that he had to change out of his sweat-soaked uniforms several times a day. But weather was only one challenge. "As we piled out of the airplane, anxious to see our new base, my heart sank," one pilot remembered. "This was not the civilized war we had expected to fight, for there were no barracks, no paved streets, nothing but insects, heat and dirt." The headquarters of LeMay's 20th Bomber Command was, in fact, located in an old political prison. The general bunked in the home of the former warden just outside the walls, a luxury considering many of his staff lived in native *bashas*, bamboo huts with dirt floors and thatched-straw roofs. "From what I have seen of India," LeMay wrote in a letter to his wife, "it is another one of those places that I am *not* going to visit again after the war."

LeMay's job was to take the war home to the Japanese. To do so, bombers would base in India, yet fly missions from forward airfields across the Himalayas in China. In preparation, 6,000 American troops and 27,000 Indian workers had built five airfields around Kharagpur, complete with prefabricated administration buildings and hangars made of steel frames and canvas. An even greater project played out around the Chinese city of Chengtu, the capital of the province of Szechwan. More than 300,000 conscripts plus 75,000 hired workers, paid just a quarter a day, constructed four 8,500-foot-long runways and fifty-two hardstands for each. "The strips had been built by coolie labor: thousands of families, from tots to creaking old grandsires, lugging those water-worn stones from along the dry beds of the rivers, pounding them up, rolling them into place," LeMay said. "It was like depending on a gang of ants."

Aircrews had flown the first mission on June 5, 1944, targeting railyards in Bangkok. That was followed ten days later by a raid out of China against Imperial Iron and Steel Works at Yawata on the southern Japanese island of Kyushu, marking the first time the mainland had been bombed since Jimmy Doolittle throttled Tokyo on April 18, 1942. In the nearly three months since that first mission until LeMay took command, aircrews had flown a paltry seven raids. An experienced veteran against the Nazis, LeMay's first priority was to test the Japanese in combat. On September 8, 1944, just ten days after arriving in India, the general lifted off at 5:40 a.m. as an observer on a 108-bomber raid against Showa Steel Works in Anshan, Manchuria.

As the bombers zoomed in on the target, fighters rose to challenge them.

"Now we'll see what they can do," LeMay thought.

To the general's surprise, the enemy fighters misjudged the speed and missed the planes. None of the bombers were shot down, and only a few were hit by flak. "I finally got a personal crack at the Japs," LeMay wrote afterward to Helen. "If all the Jap opposition is like what we ran up against, this war is going to be a lot easier than the one I just left."

The 20th Bomber Command's lackluster start, LeMay realized, stemmed not from ferocious enemy fighters or antiaircraft fire but the logistical nightmare of shuttling planes from India to China in order to then strike Japan. "The scheme of operations had been dreamed up like something out of *The Wizard of Oz*," he complained. "It didn't work. No one could have made it work." The absence of usable railroads, ports, or highways meant that all supplies, including fuel needed for a mission, had to first be flown in from India, an aerial pipeline that taxed planes and aircrews. To fuel a single bomber for a raid on Japan required seven trips across the eastern end of the Himalayas—diminutively dubbed "the Hump" by the aircrews—just to import enough gasoline. To bring enough fuel for a raid of 100 bombers, similar to the size of LeMay's strike on Anshan, planes had to make a staggering 700 trips. But the sheer number of flights was only part of the problem. "It was a grueling hell, climbing the big bombers over the rugged Himalayas—the roof of the world. It was 1200 miles of the worst flying imaginable," LeMay later wrote. "The mountains were a veritable smorgasbord of meteorological treachery—violent downdrafts, high winds, and sudden snowstorms—all served up in temperatures 20 degrees below zero. As if they needed any reminding, the crews could frequently glimpse the 29,028-foot peak of Mt. Everest thrusting up through the clouds just 150 miles from their flight path."

The plan, which was put in action before the capture of the Mariana Islands, was sparked by the clamor of President Roosevelt and Chinese Nationalist ruler Chiang Kai-shek to hurry up and bomb Japan. At the time, China was the only option. Even with the B-29's formidable range, however, much of Japan remained beyond the reach of the Superfortress, limiting raids to Kyushu. Tokyo was just too far. Not only did he face logistical challenges, but his crews lacked experience. LeMay unloaded in a letter to Norstad two days after his Manchuria raid. "They are finding out how to fight the same as our first outfits did at the beginning of the war, by the trial and error method," he wrote. "We need experience from the combat outfits. We shouldn't be breaking people into combat in B-29s, it's too expensive." The myriad challenges kept LeMay up most nights. "Airplanes were going down over the Hump all the time, or they were busting up on the strips in India and China alike," he wrote. "I'd lie there on my cot, after finally getting to bed late in the muggy night, and try to battle the thing out."

LeMay implemented many of the same strategies that had worked in Germany. He organized schools to develop the best pilots, bombardiers, and navigators, who could then lead the formations. He likewise swapped out the four-ship formation that crews had been using for his combat box that had worked so well in Europe. He also alternated missions against the Japanese mainland with raids on closer targets, flying out of India, where fuel was more plentiful. That also allowed aircrews to fly more often, giving them valuable combat experience. Bombers hit the naval base in Singapore, oil refineries on Sumatra, and aircraft factories on Formosa. LeMay opened up back channels with Communist ruler Mao Tse-tung, even though the United States was allied with his enemy, Chiang Kai-shek. Mao controlled vast regions in northern China, and

LeMay wanted to secure his help when American bombers crashed there. To sweeten the deal, LeMay sent Mao a C-47 filled with medical supplies, with the hope that Communist doctors might use them to treat banged-up American airmen.

LeMay likewise networked with native tribes outside the control of either Chiang or Mao, offering to pay them for rescuing any downed crews. Amid such negotiations, one of LeMay's officers barged into the office. The tribes didn't want cash, he said, but opium.

"What am I going to do?" the officer asked. "I haven't got any opium."

"We have to get the crews," LeMay replied. "Get the opium. Go buy it."

"I can't put that down on the accounting."

"I don't give a damn what you put down," LeMay barked. "Get our men out."

The rescue of American airmen, for accounting purposes, was officially logged as purchase of "fertilizer."

Arnold, who in his letters criticized Hansell, applauded LeMay. "You have the full confidence of me and the staff here," he wrote in one letter.

"The fine work your people have been doing here is providing a standard for the other B-29 units," Arnold added in another.

"Keep up the good work."

Despite LeMay's aggressive efforts, the best he could hope for still was four missions a month, a rate that was too little to do much real damage to the enemy. The entire setup in China was fatally flawed, a fact known not only to LeMay but also to his superiors in Washington. Norstad informed him in October of a potential move to the Philippines, where MacArthur had landed on the island of Leyte. LeMay worried that even there a base would be too far from Japan to consistently hit it, and his forces would end up having to bomb shipping. "I believe," LeMay replied, "that the B-29 should drop bombs on Japan proper and nothing else." Still, he conceded that "almost any base would be better than the one we have." Arnold agreed. "One of our major interests," he wrote LeMay, "continues to be to get you out of China."

That opportunity arrived in January with his summons to Guam. Despite the challenges Hansell faced, LeMay felt confident he could overcome them. After China, how much harder could it be? He likewise relished the chance to take the fight to the heart of the enemy empire. "The Marianas," he wrote, "would be the beginning of the end of the road to Tokyo."

CHAPTER 8

"I don't mind being called tough, since I find in this
racket it's the tough guys who lead the survivors."

—MAJ. GEN. CURTIS LeMAY

On January 19, 1945, LeMay touched down on Guam, concluding a
4,100-mile direct flight from India. That night the general settled
into a tent, while work crews hustled to build him a home on the
island that would be ready in several weeks. Even in a tent, however, conditions were a step up, a fact that his aide Maj. Theodore Beckemeir noted
in the command diary. "The climate is delightful," he wrote. "After India,
this place seems like paradise."

Some of Hansell's supporters viewed LeMay with suspicion. The general's reserved demeanor, noted St. Clair McKelway, did not help ingra-
tiate him with the officers. In fact, the public affairs officer felt that by
civilian standards, LeMay, who hid the residual effects of his Bell's palsy
behind a cigar or a pipe, appeared rude. Others, however, understood a
change was needed, including Col. Sam Harris, who was thrilled to learn
of Hansell's firing. "Praise be to Allah," Harris wrote in his diary. "LeMay
is known to be a very good if slightly rough operator—we can take the
roughness if there is a sense behind it."

Outside the Marianas, senior air officers and War Department leaders agreed with Arnold's decision. Many had privately questioned Hansell's appointment months earlier to such a demanding combat job. One of them was Dr. Edward Bowles, a Massachusetts Institute of Technology professor and War Department consultant who worked with Arnold. "Possum was a weak sister," Bowles later said. "Likeable but weak." Col. Bill Irvine, the deputy chief of staff of the 21st Bomber Command, agreed with Bowles. "He should never have had the job," Irvine later said. "Hansell is a weasel compared to a lion."

The following day LeMay officially took the helm of the 21st Bomber Command in a ceremony where Hansell received the Distinguished Service Medal. McKelway asked LeMay if he might photograph the general shaking hands with Possum. The publicity-averse LeMay, who had tried to keep a low profile standing in the back puffing on his pipe, seemed surprised at the gesture and fumbled with his pipe.

"General," McKelway finally said, "please let me hold your pipe."

LeMay stepped forward, handing it to him.

"Where do you want me to stand?" he asked.

McKelway, who had spent his prewar career writing profiles for the *New Yorker*, had learned over the years to read people. At that moment, despite his exhaustion from being up all night gathering facts on the Kawasaki mission, McKelway caught either a look or a gesture from LeMay. He wasn't sure which, but regardless, the writer felt a sudden and unexplainable sense that this stocky new general was about to shake up his life, like a storm fast approaching on the horizon. "My God," he thought to himself, "if this LeMay turns out to be another great young Air Forces general, I will desert. I will run up into the hills and hide, like the Navy radio operator who stayed up there all those months the Japs were here on Guam. Couldn't I have a lousy, easygoing, mediocre general just for a few weeks, a few days? I want to relax! I've got to relax! Dear God, don't tell me this LeMay is as good as he looked just now!"

"Better get some sleep," LeMay warned him, interrupting his thoughts with a nudge.

McKelway just stared at the general.

"Thanks for holding my pipe."

Ralph Nutter returned from Saipan to catch the conclusion of the ceremony. LeMay, his old commander in England, greeted him warmly. So did Joe Preston, who had been his squadron commander back at Muroc soon after he joined the air force. Preston was the one who had first advised Nutter on how to handle the irascible LeMay. "Well Ralph, here we are, together again," Preston said. "We finally did get to the Pacific."

Nutter spotted Hansell, surrounded by several aides. The twenty-four-year-old found he was at a loss for words as he shook his former commander's hand. "I was learning," Nutter later wrote, "that war could ruin careers as well as lives." Hansell put him at ease, wishing him the best. "I'm sure you'll enjoy working with LeMay and Joe Preston again," he said. "Look me up when you get back to the States and let's talk about something besides the war."

Hansell had recovered from the shock of his firing but not from the disappointment. A few days before the ceremony, he sent a ten-page letter to Hap Arnold, analyzing his failures and addressing concerns the general previously had noted. Hansell described struggles to win over crews to daylight raids along with efforts to improve accuracy and reduce abortives. "I feel, on reflection, that I have erred in not passing on to you my problems in more detail," he wrote. "I have felt that my first consideration should be to solve my problems as best I possibly could, rather than to send complaints to you. Perhaps I have overdone this conception."

Arnold, who suffered his fourth heart attack of the war on January 17, responded a couple of weeks later as he convalesced. The general chose not to engage Hansell point by point, likely recognizing it would accomplish little. "I am cognizant of the great problems involved in pioneering a project of this type. You have my appreciation as well as my admiration for your excellent work," he wrote. "The job from now on is no longer planning and pioneering. It has become one of operating." LeMay, he added, was the air force's top operator. "I know," Arnold concluded, "that you join me in wishing him well in this great undertaking."

With LeMay in charge, Hansell did not linger, though he would at least leave on a high note. His final mission to hit the Kawasaki plant in Akashi the day before had been a great success. "Every important building in the engine and airframe plants was hit," he wrote. "Production of both plants was cut 90 percent. Production never recovered." Word had spread of Hansell's firing, and the glances and mutterings of subordinates had only exacerbated the stress he felt in his final days, prompting the normally light drinker to entertain a second glass of sherry at his farewell dinner, as he autographed a few photographs for his officers and men.

Afterward he gathered on the porch of his tent with members of his staff. McKelway asked what he planned to do next. Hansell told him he had requested a training wing, a job that would afford him a chance to rest, enjoy time with his wife and three young children, and see his parents.

"Then I'll be ready for whatever comes up," Hansell added. "I haven't had a day off in eight years and I think I'll take several when I get home."

Hansell ended the night in verse. As Col. John Montgomery strummed a guitar, the general belted out what proved a fitting tune, even if marred by his lack of vocal talent. "Old pilots never die, never die, never die," he sang. "They just fly away."

Before his departure from the Marianas, Hansell planned a short stop in Saipan, where he had arranged a visit with Maj. Jack Catton, the commander of the *Joltin' Josie, the Pacific Pioneer*, the bomber that had delivered him to Saipan less than a hundred days earlier, at a time when his career seemed so full of promise. The bomber was originally named just the *Joltin' Josie* in honor of Catton's wife. Hansell was the one who added *the Pacific Pioneer*. Possum had remained close with Catton, asking him to gather his crew and meet him at the hardstand. Master Sgt. Quentin Hancock, the bomber's crew chief, had long admired Hansell's swagger stick with a stiletto inside, the British symbol of command that he had carried for years. But those days were over. Hansell had gone from engineering America's air war against Germany and Japan—a vaunted job in which he had enjoyed the confidence of leaders such as Hap Arnold, Dwight Eisenhower, and Winston Churchill—to a backwater post far removed from the halls of influence where he would oversee crews practice bombing in the desert Southwest. "He had one consolation," Nutter observed. "He had been true to his beliefs and stood firm against area bombing, even if it had cost him his career."

On Saipan, however, he thought not of himself but of others, thanking each member of the *Joltin' Josie*, many of whom stood before him with tears in their eyes. Then he presented his swagger stick to Sergeant Hancock. "That just gives you an idea," Catton said, "of what kind of a man Hansell was."

———

LeMay spent his first few days visiting crews on Saipan and Tinian. The lagging morale and the poor shape of the command staff he had inherited stunned him, prompting him to vent in a letter to Norstad. "The road ahead always looks worse than the road behind," he wrote, "but after ten days here this job looks much tougher than the one I just left." Many of LeMay's concerns echoed the gripes O'Donnell had raised in private letters and that had contributed to his clashes with Hansell, highlighting Possum's struggles as an administrator. The staff, LeMay wrote Norstad, was "worthless." At the half-built headquarters on Guam, officers sat around waiting for a completed office to begin work. The combat units reported that headquarters was not only blundering and feckless but often made work harder. "My first job is to get this staff functioning," LeMay advised Norstad. "I'm afraid that this is going to require considerable weeding out and I probably will have to ask for replacement personnel."

LeMay knew of Hansell's struggles with O'Donnell. Though he might have agreed with some of Rosie's observations, LeMay would not tolerate insubordination; nor was he afraid of confronting his commanders. He made that clear to O'Donnell.

"I'll tell you," the gruff LeMay warned him, "I don't like what I see."

To Norstad, LeMay was blunt. "Rosie's outfit is in bad shape. I get the impression that from Rosie on down they think the obstacles too many and the opposition too heavy to crash through and get the bombs on the target," he wrote. "You had better start warming up a sub for Rosie in case we have to put him in." LeMay echoed his frustrations in a letter to his wife. "I have my legs worn down to my knees from running around and the more I saw the more work I found to do," he wrote. "I have a brand-new staff, new base, new units, and I'm new. Nothing is shaken down yet. There is so much work to be done that it looks as though it will never be accomplished."

One of LeMay's concerns centered on the poor shape of his base, whose construction fell to the navy. His ire skyrocketed when he secured a list of priority projects. LeMay scanned the first page, then the second, third, and fourth. Not until the fifth page did he find any army projects. "The Navy had been hard at work otherwise," he wrote. "They had built tennis courts for the Island Commander; they had built fleet recreation centers, Marine rehabilitation centers, dockage facilities for inter-island surface craft, and every other damn thing in the world except subscribing to the original purpose in the occupation of those islands. The islands were attacked and taken and held because we needed them for air bases to strike against Japan."

LeMay still stewed when he received a dinner invite from the theater commander, Fleet Adm. Chester Nimitz. He fished a clean albeit wrinkled uniform out of his bag. LeMay showed up to find chandeliers and white tablecloths adorned with sparkling silverware. "Everyone was standing around in starched white uniforms having a drink," he recalled. "I felt like a skunk at a family reunion." That multicourse dinner, which featured soup, fish, and a roast, was soon followed by one hosted by the island commander, Adm. John Hoover, which was equally as nice though with a few less Filipino mess boys. Next he received one from Vice Adm. Charles Lockwood, the submarine force commander, aboard his flagship, *Holland*. "Cocktails, hors d'oeuvres, roast beef," he remembered. "You name it, we had it."

Each invitation only underscored how woefully ill-prepared LeMay was as he returned home each night to his tent. "The Navy," he later said, "always treated us rather like stepchildren in the Marianas." To prove his point, LeMay reciprocated, inviting everyone to dinner at his place, including Fleet Admiral Nimitz. The evening started with drinks at his tent from a bottle of liquor he scored off a sailor. That was followed by dinner in a Quonset hut. "We took especial pains to serve up the best flight-rations available. That's what we were living on: canned stuff," he said. "I'll give the web-footed guests credit, and report that they stood up like real men throughout it all. Didn't complain, told stories, were right good company."

LeMay followed Hansell's tactics, though he ordered his crews to drop down to around twenty-five thousand feet to dodge the jet streams, a move that sparked alarm among the airmen who wielded altitude like a shield against fighters that struggled to operate in the thin air five miles above the earth. "The extra 5,000 feet was our margin for life," John Ciardi wrote in his diary. "In it we saw home again, and warmth, and wife-flesh, and neon, and country furrows, and the lost language." In another entry, the gunner wrote that LeMay's decision underlined the "complete expendability" of the crews. "I'd frankly bow out if I knew how to," he confided in his diary. "If I do get killed, it will be because I lack the courage to quit and accept the humiliation."

The day after he took command, LeMay sent his bombers on a training mission to hit the Japanese-held island of Truk in the Caroline Islands. Three days later he ordered a strike on the Mitsubishi Aircraft Engine Works in Nagoya. Only twenty-eight of the seventy-three planes that lifted off made it to the factory. "From landfall to and over the target," the mission report noted, "an almost total undercast at 14,000 feet offered only fleeting glimpses of the ground." Thirteen other bombers aborted the mission, including one that ditched a few miles from Saipan after two engines failed. The rest, battling heavy clouds, unloaded on the city of Nagoya. Crews endured 626 fighter attacks, resulting in the loss of another bomber and damage to thirty-one others. Postwar records showed the attack set the Mitsubishi factory back only thirty engines. "Bombing results," the report concluded, "were considered unsatisfactory."

LeMay followed that strike with an attack on the Nakajima plant in the Tokyo suburb of Musashino on January 27, a mission stymied once again by clouds. Japanese fighters intercepted the bombers before crews even reached the mainland, forcing gunners to fend off 984 attacks, including suicide pilots who rammed the B-29s. LeMay lost a staggering nine out of seventy-six bombers. Thirty-two others were damaged.

"Crews reported enemy fighter opposition," the mission report observed, "of unparalleled intensity for this theater."

These early missions underscored LeMay's challenges. Before leaving India, he had used his goodwill with Mao Tse-tung to set up a weather station. Even that, along with the daily weather strike missions out of the Marianas, failed to provide him with reliably accurate predictions. The weather and the clouds were just too volatile, leaving LeMay some months with as little as three clear days to bomb. "The worst part is that you have to forecast those days accurately," he said, "and then make sure you're over those targets on those specific days."

Beyond the weather and the jet streams, LeMay had inherited inexperienced crews and maintenance challenges made all the more difficult by the extreme distances and altitudes his airmen had to fly. In India, he had centralized the maintenance program in order to repair planes faster and keep them in the skies longer. "You can't drop bombs," he often said, "from a grounded plane." LeMay envisioned the same system in the Marianas, a twenty-four-hour assembly line where, for example, mechanics specializing in radios worked exclusively on radios, while new technicians trained under them. Before LeMay had time to even propose this new approach, Col. Bill Irvine pitched the identical idea.

"Go ahead and do it," LeMay instructed.

The results were immediate. Airborne planes failing to bomb the primary target because of mechanical problems fell from 18.5 percent in January to 12.6 percent in February and then again in March to 6.8 percent. Streamlining maintenance would ultimately slash the time needed to replace an engine from three days to just four hours. The move likewise would quadruple the average monthly flying time of each bomber to 120 hours.

LeMay analyzed several months of previous missions, discovering that weather had allowed crews to bomb visually that month just 38 percent of the time. That was down from 45 percent in December and would plummet to just 19 percent the next month. Meteorologists warned LeMay that the estimated seven clear days he could expect in February would fall to five in March, to three in April and May, and then to only one in June. Visual bombing would soon no longer be an option. Radar bombing, which Hansell had despised because of its inaccuracy, would be LeMay's future, whether he liked it or not. Most of LeMay's radar operators were gunners, whose lack of training showed in their poor bombing results. LeMay fired off a message to Arnold and Norstad, requesting a minimum of forty radar operators to train his crews. "It is," LeMay wrote, "imperative that I have capable radar operators in my tactical aircraft if I am to operate efficiently against the Japanese mainland in the coming months."

As he had done in England and India, LeMay fell back on training. Any obstacle, he reasoned, could be overcome with proper study and preparation. Japan was no different. "Within one day of his arrival," recalled aircraft commander John Cox, "the directives started down the chain of command." Col. Sam Harris, who had been caught in the struggle between Hansell and O'Donnell, welcomed the change. "He seems to know exactly what he wants," Harris wrote in his diary, "and I suspect will likely get it."

LeMay instituted poststrike reviews with his wing commanders to examine tactical doctrine and troubleshoot any problems. Hansell had organized a lead school in late December, but LeMay revamped it, starting the first class on January 24 under Col. Joe Preston. He likewise launched a radar school. "All kinds of training courses were initiated overnight, and special techniques in bombing, pilotage, gunnery, navigation, and so on were introduced," McKelway recalled. "Crew members attended special classes day and night."

Outside the classroom, crews climbed in the skies to train. Just as he had done in England, LeMay joined his men in the air, taking to the radio to organize them.

"If you can't lead the formation," he barked, "turn it over to the deputy."

His approach impressed many of the airmen. "It was the damndest thing you ever saw in your life," Jack Catton recalled, "LeMay following those squadrons over our practice targets watching the sighting activity and the handling of the formation, the turns. It was fantastic!" The sudden focus on practice frustrated at least a few of the airmen, who knew each mission flown brought them closer to home. "We were ordered out for another training mission this morning," Marshall griped in his diary. "All the time I thought we were here to fight a war."

Despite his reserved demeanor, LeMay couldn't help but worry. Norstad had made it clear on the day he took command what was expected of him. "What General Arnold wants is the greatest possible number of bombs dropped on our priority targets in any given period of time," he wrote to LeMay. "I am sure that you fully appreciate this."

LeMay did, and he voiced those same concerns to his staff. "General Arnold has crawled out on a dozen limbs a thousand times to get the physical resources and funds to build these airplanes and get them into combat. Now he finds they're not doing well. He's determined to get results out of this weapons system. The turkey is around my neck. I've got to deliver."

Norstad made it clear to LeMay what would happen if he failed. "If you don't get results, you'll be fired," he warned him. "If you don't get results it will mean eventually a mass amphibious invasion of Japan, to cost probably half a million more American lives."

LeMay wasn't the only one worried.

The increased ferocity of the enemy's fighter attacks exhausted his crews even as the air force hustled to provide means to distract them. Across the Marianas, laborers erected thirty-two theaters, where airmen could catch actor Robert Alda as composer George Gershwin in the film *Rhapsody in Blue* or escape into the onscreen romance between Humphrey Bogart and Lauren Bacall in *To Have and Have Not*, a wartime adventure based on Ernest Hemingway's novel. Others relaxed in chairs fashioned from oil drums to watch *The Buckaroos*, a traveling variety show brought in from Oahu. Studious airmen perused more than thirty-five thousand titles that lined the shelves of base libraries or leafed through newspapers, including the *Coral Times* and *Poop from Group*. Pious airmen attended weekly Protestant, Catholic, or Jewish worship services. Workers hammered out a baseball diamond—named in honor of Col. Byron Brugge, who was lost over Tokyo in December—and fashioned a Quonset hut into an enlisted men's club, with a porch running the length of one side overlooking the ocean. "The club," the command historian bragged, "has an ideal location both for beauty and for convenience."

Troops drifted down to the beach to swim or peer through glass-bottom boxes at aquatic life in the crystal blue waters. "I'm getting started on a sun tan already," navigator Louis Kestner, Jr., wrote his parents from Tinian. "We felt like angels when we got here because everyone is so dark." Others hunted souvenirs amid the battle-wrecked towns and jungles, scavenging everything from guns and grenades to gold teeth. "Nudism had its heyday beneath the pines and rusty shower barrels until island command regulations and rumors of the arrival of scores of nurses demanded return to modesty and GI towels," noted the Sixth Bombardment Group's log on Tinian. Gin rummy and solitaire helped many pass the downtime. "Galleries of pin-up girls appeared on the walls and ceilings of shacks, tents, airplanes," a reporter observed. "Family snapshots were near every bed." One airplane commander built a picket fence around his hut where he grew marigolds, morning glories, dahlias, and sunflowers. Others planted vegetable gardens, watching crops of radishes, beets, and corn erupt in the warmth of the tropical sun. "We found you can grow almost everything that you can grow in the States," said Lt. Russell McManus, "and about twice as fast." The gardens provided a nice change from the otherwise bland food dished out in the mess halls. "Everything we eat," Lt. John Barcynski griped in a letter, "has beans in it except our oatmeal and coffee."

There were only so many ways, however, to fight boredom and anxiety before the caliber of activities devolved. A rodent infestation on Saipan, for example, sparked a grim tournament. "For every rat shot dead, a rat was painted above the front door," a reporter wrote. "For a wounded rat that got away, half a rat was painted up, and listed as 'a probable.'" Officers on Tinian got a small pig drunk on beer, while others taught interned Japanese children at Camp Churo to say derogatory comments in exchange for K-ration candy bars.

"Tojo's a bastard" was one such popular refrain.

More crews joined the fight each week. By the end of February, LeMay would count 34,003 officers and enlisted men under his command, a little more than half of the 63,000 he eventually expected. Saipan's rolling landscape had forced engineers to scale back plans from four 8,500-foot bomber runways down to just two at Isley Field. Across the narrow waters, workers toiled under the tropical sun on Tinian's North Field, where the inaugural B-29 had touched down on December 22, marking the completion of the first of six runways that would eventually give the island the distinction of being the largest airport in the world. "Sometimes I awake during the night, and when I look out of the tent, I think it snowed," Kestner, the navigator, wrote in another letter to his parents. "That's how white the coral is."

One hundred miles south, construction of Guam's four bomber fields required moving more than 500,000 cubic yards of coral, a feat that required as much as two tons of dynamite daily. The hum of activity amazed even Ernie Pyle, the grizzled war reporter who marveled at the sea of tents, Quonset huts, and warehouses that had mushroomed across the islands. "The roar of planes, the clank of bulldozers and the clatter of hammers is constant," he wrote. "It is a strange contrast to the stillness that dwelt amidst this greenery for so many centuries."

The herculean efforts to transform the Marianas into a small slice of America in the Pacific could not eradicate the fear that weighed upon the airmen. In Europe, a round-trip mission from England to Berlin clocked in at fifteen hundred miles. In the Pacific, crews covered that distance one way just to Tokyo. Battered airmen in Europe could likewise bail out over land and hope to evade the enemy or receive help from friendly locals in occupied countries.

There was none of that in the Pacific.

Crews gazed for hours on nothing more than dark waves, trying not to think about how a loose bolt or split rivet could force a mighty bomber down into the unforgiving ocean, where ditching was usually a death sentence. "Metal was our enemy. Its tiniest flaw, its first imperfection waited to drop us from the air," gunner John Ciardi wrote in his diary. "In every engine there is fire and death in more places than an eye can find, and it waits forever." Aircraft commander Lt. Wilfred Lind agreed. "Old Man Ocean is a mean devil, big, deep and rough," he wrote. "The myriad number of things that can put you down in that ocean makes my knees weak and I begin to wonder what I ever did to make God so mad at me." The continued plague of engine fires only exacerbated those worries, sending Louis Kestner's bomber into the swells only twenty-five days after he first touched down on Tinian and long before he had a chance to perfect the tan he had admired on his friends. "Most of the bombers we lost in the Pacific," LeMay lamented, "came down due to mechanical malfunctions."

Wounded by flak or enemy cannon fire, airmen had to endure an agonizing trip home of up to eight hours, aided only by tourniquets, pressure dressings, and intravenous plasma designed to treat shock. Medical records showed nearly one out of every five wounds was classified as severe, from compound fractures and amputations to frostbite. An exploding shell on one mission ripped the right foot off an airman; medics later counted more than one hundred flak fragments in the arms, legs, and torso of a tail gunner. For those who bailed out, life as a prisoner of war was brutal. That was the case for Robert Goldsworthy, who was shot down over Tokyo. Interrogators not only beat him with rifle butts but also tied his fingers together and rammed pencils between them, twisting them until his skin wore down to the bone. "As bad as were the beatings and mistreatment, far worse was the cold and the hunger. You can get used to a club," he said. "But no words can ever describe the torture suffered from cold and hunger."

Commanders meanwhile hammered out letters to the families of the missing and killed. Rosie O'Donnell would ultimately write nearly twelve hundred pages of such letters; so many, in fact, that he would fill three binders with carbon copies organized by the airmen's home states, letters he would keep for the rest of his life. Empty bunks spread like cancer, eroding the morale of other crews who knew that survival came down to chance. "We all often lived or died because of the difference made by a fraction of an inch, a fraction of a degree, or a fraction of a second," recalled Hoyt Clark. Ciardi echoed him, remembering the names of his missing tentmates in his diary. "It might have been anyone of us," he wrote, "or all of us, or me."

Survivors returned to base, testifying to superiors and friends of the horrors witnessed miles above Japan. "Left wing burned off as it spiraled down," one eyewitness report stated. "Plane was seen falling in two pieces with four enemy fighters circling."

"I saw the wing come off of one and the tail off the other," observed another.

"How we ever got back we'll never know," Second Lt. Robert Sollock said after landing with 147 holes and an unexploded shell lodged above a fuel tank. "It must have been because every one of us was praying. I can assure you there were no atheists aboard."

But the threat wasn't only in the skies.

Patrols hunted stray Japanese soldiers, who ambushed and killed troops. The brazen enemy at times approached close enough to enjoy outdoor movies. On Saipan, an African American regiment broadcast folk songs to lure out the enemy, while eleven-member kill teams combed the caves and jungles on Guam. To assist, Marines recruited a Japanese prisoner known as Taki to make broadcasts from a sound truck. "I know you like it in the jungle," he announced in Japanese. "I know it is fun to be hungry and hunted and to live like wild animals. I know you would not like American food and cigarettes and the care of American doctors."

The combination of threats exhausted the airmen. "Each month here," one officer wrote, "seems like a year." Many worried about their families at home. "Honey, I don't want to sound morbid," Col. James Connally wrote to his wife, "but if anything should happen to me remember I want you to be happy and raise our two as I know you will."

Ciardi channeled his fears into poems penned in elegant handwriting on the pages of his diary. "Our bombs," he wrote on his twenty-ninth birthday, "descend to save or kill us all." In one poem, Ciardi described the explosion of a B-29 during a crash landing, the roasted ammunition rattling beneath a monstrous cloud of black smoke. In another, he crafted a preemptive elegy, questioning whether he had met his end via bullets, the wind, or "a rip cord fouled with doom." Airman Kurt Porjescz's failure to return prompted him to again put pen to paper. "Clouds had them once," he wrote, "and wreckage mars them now."

The war, the machinery, the frailty of youth and life all haunted his work:

> We waken, and the cities of our day
> Move down a cross-haired bomb site in the mind.
> The thoughtless led, those only in the way,
> The powerful by intent, wake there and find
> Their jungles closing, each man tangled tight
> Into this day that may not last till night.

Poor bombing results that forced crews to return again and again to the same targets exacerbated the emotional toll on the airmen, whose flagging morale sparked concern among senior commanders. "Our crews," one command report noted, "began to fear their own aircraft and our field orders more than the devices of the enemy."

The solace Ciardi searched for in prose, others found in the occasional hoppy brew the service rationed. "The first beer I ever drank in my life was hot," remembered Second Lt. David Braden. The more crafty airmen learned to bootleg booze from dried fruit and sugarcane, a sweet and heady concoction dubbed Raisin Jack. "In spite of the high quality control exercised during the fermenting and distillation processes," recalled flight engineer Fiske Hanley, "many hangovers resulted from the partaking of this potent beverage."

The battle in the skies over Japan had only intensified as the enemy reallocated fighters and antiaircraft guns to protect Tokyo and Nagoya, an area the men dubbed "flak alley." Sgt. James Krantz experienced that on the January 3 mission. Moments after the *American Maid* completed its bomb run over Nagoya, gunfire from a Japanese fighter shattered the right blister. The rapid depressurization catapulted Krantz out of the plane at twenty-nine thousand feet. "One minute I was at my station," he recalled, "and the next I was flying through space."

The twenty-two-year-old gunner, who had two young daughters back home in Tennessee, fortunately had tethered himself to the bomber via a homemade harness he fabricated out of an old parachute rig. Krantz felt a jerk as his strap arrested his fall. His left foot hooked on the edge of the blister as his six-foot-tall, 170-pound body smashed against the side of the bomber, dislocating his left shoulder. The more than 350 miles per hour winds robbed him of his pistol and ripped off his oxygen mask and his gloves, exposing his skin to the minus-forty-degree temperatures. Krantz tried to pull himself back into the plane, clutching the cables from the torn-out gun sight, but he soon slipped unconscious, his body flapping against the fuselage.

Two fellow gunners tried unsuccessfully to haul him into the plane. The radarman joined the effort, but the airmen still struggled, foiled by the compartment's cramped conditions. The aircraft commander dispatched pilot Franklin Crowe, who leaned out into the slipstream and seized Krantz's shoulder holster. The lieutenant and the gunners then wrestled Krantz back into the bomber. He had been without oxygen for ten minutes. No one expected him to survive. The airmen hauled him to the radar room and laid him atop a makeshift bed of clothes. The men administered two units of plasma and oxygen and rubbed his frozen body continuously. Twenty minutes later Krantz miraculously opened his eyes. "I was the first man to fly over Japan head down at the end of a strap," he later said. "I just hope I'm the last."

Krantz was one of the lucky ones.

On the January 23 mission over Nagoya, where bombers battled more than six hundred fighter attacks, John Cox spotted smoke trailing from the number-one engine of a nearby Superfortress piloted by his friend Lt. Ken Smith. No sooner did Smith feather the propeller to reduce drag than his number-three engine began to belch smoke, forcing the bomber to slow as the formation turned back toward the coast to begin the long flight home. Cox and two other planes dropped out of formation, encircling the wounded bomber as enemy fighters pounced. "With each pass," Cox later wrote, "the intercom buzzed with fighter reports. The attacks must have lasted only about twenty minutes, but it seemed a lifetime."

The Japanese coastline soon fell behind them and the enemy fighters faded. Two of the bombers returned to cruise speed and pulled ahead, but Cox opted to remain. "Don't worry," he radioed Smith. "We're going to stay with you all the way back."

The battered bomber was only one of Smith's challenges. Over Nagoya a shell had exploded under the right side of the cockpit. Medical records later showed the blast hit Lt. John Miller in his perineum, fracturing the pilot's pelvic bones and severing the iliac vessels. Each beat of Miller's heart spilled more of his blood over his cockpit seat. Crew members, operating with oxygen masks in the depressurized plane, struggled to find a vein to inject Miller with plasma. The crippled number-three engine, which operated at only half power, leaked oil, prompting Smith to order the other airmen to lighten the bomber. "Everything not bolted down was dropped from every access port in his Superfortress," Cox wrote. "Weight was altitude and he was doing everything he knew to keep his aircraft flying."

Cox flew over and under the crippled bomber, noting the extensive flak and cannon holes before settling off the right wing. The slow speed was hard on both crews, who were already exhausted after the long flight up to Japan followed by the surge of adrenaline in the battle over Nagoya. The sun began to drop in the western sky as the minutes crawled past.

"Miller just died," Smith radioed.

The bombers droned on in silence. "What could we say?" Cox recalled. "The tone of his voice indicated an imminent morale breakdown. I didn't need much imagination to visualize what their flight deck crew had been through in trying to save Miller's life."

Cox knew he needed to distract his fellow airmen, who still had to get the wounded Superfortress back to Saipan. He began to pepper Smith with questions about his flight performance. The bombers dropped through the clouds, allowing Cox to glimpse Iwo Jima ten miles to east. Night descended upon them, a welcome protection against fighters.

As the bombers closed in on Saipan, Cox grew increasingly worried. "His fatigue was apparent," he wrote of Smith. "His responses were lengthier and it took more coaxing to keep him on course. His control was erratic. We slowly sank toward the sea."

Smith's number-three engine died, leaving him with only two engines. He feathered the prop to reduce drag. "Are you going to ditch?" Cox radioed.

"Not if I can help it," Smith replied.

Smith reduced his speed to 160 miles per hour and an altitude of four thousand feet as Cox radioed the tower and informed them of the trouble. Ambulances and rescue equipment stood ready. Cox anxiously awaited to see if Smith could even get his landing gear down.

"They're down and locked, I think!" Smith radioed.

The tower waved them off while crews cleared another bomber. Cox escorted Smith as he came around for final approach. To his relief, Smith brought the plane safely down onto the runway, an anticlimactic conclusion to a brutal day. Cox followed him down, discovering after sixteen hours that his legs struggled to support him as he climbed down from the bomber. "Looking at the rest of the crew, I could see they were in the same condition," Cox said. "No one shouted praises or celebrated. We were totally wasted and somewhat depressed."

The next morning Smith appeared at the Quonset hut with a bottle of whiskey in each hand. "John," he said, handing Cox the liquor, "this is for you and your crew."

CHAPTER 9

"It takes a little time for me to get used to going to sleep at night
knowing that I may be killed the next day."

—JOHN CIARDI
DECEMBER 16, 1944, DIARY ENTRY

As January gave way to February, life in Japan worsened. Air raids only added to the anguish of food shortages, gnawing hunger, and the raw winter cold. The raids initially sparked a feeling of suspense and even excitement as the sirens howled shortly before noon. The silver bombers would then buzz through the skies for several hours, prompting residents to marvel at what one described as the "fantastic glass dragonflies." Others with empty stomachs wondered what the aircrews had brought for lunch. The predictable pattern followed by the targeting of industrial areas on the outskirts of the capital created a false sense of security; residents even joked of the "regularly scheduled service" of the bombers. "Housewives stood in line to do their marketing before or after the danger period," recalled Masuo Kato, a journalist with *Domei*. "Most business transactions were arranged with the air-raid timetable in mind."

The Japanese sang a song to bolster morale against such strikes:

Why should we be afraid of air raids?
The big sky is protected with iron defenses.
For young and old it is time to stand up;
We are loaded with the honor of defending the homeland
Come on, enemy planes. Come on many times.

Since the start of the raids, the Japanese government had worked to assuage the public's fears, filling radio waves and editorial pages with propaganda designed both to prepare citizens for life under bombing while trying to maintain order. "We must face the situation calmly and collectedly," one such missive instructed. "Everyone in the country ought to be prepared," advised another. "There should be, however, no sense of uneasiness."

Newspaper headlines meanwhile published exaggerated accounts of Japanese air victories: "22 of Enemy Planes Raiding Tokyo Are Downed," trumpeted one.

"More than 90 Per Cent of Foe Planes Brought Down or Damaged," claimed another.

The *Mainichi* newspaper went so far in January as to state that American production could never keep up with such terrific losses. Another article described the enemy's surprise that Japan's cities seemed immune to fire. Other times the press published photographs of the wreckage of downed B-29s. In a macabre move, authorities drove trucks piled high with crashed bomber debris through neighborhoods, allowing residents to glimpse the twisted aluminum fuselage and even finger a pair of fur-lined boots. Philippine diplomat León María Guerrero, who recounted such a scene in his diary, observed how even the wreckage of such a once-mighty plane sparked awe among the resource-starved populace. That was hammered home for Guerrero as he watched an elderly man run his hands in wonder over a silk parachute.

"Well," the man finally announced, turning to a neighbor, "we'll build a bigger plane than that. But I'll tell you something. We shan't waste any silk on parachutes. Parachutes! Our soldiers don't need parachutes. They don't get shot down."

He was right. Japan had little use for parachutes, but not because its pilots were never shot down. Absent gasoline, the nation resorted to kamikaze attacks, sending pilots up to ram B-29s. The media celebrated these airmen, including twenty-one-year-old Cpl. Matsumi Nakano, who survived a strike on a Superfortress in the skies over the capital on December 3. "We want to lay the foundation for victory by the sacrifice of our lives," the press quoted Nakano in an address to students. "We don't want to die in vain."

This bravado camouflaged the reality that the war had entered a deadly new phase. Even though residents might have been slow to grasp it, Japan's leaders certainly did. That was evidenced by the four words Fleet Adm. Osami Nagano had uttered to Emperor Hirohito following the fall of the Mariana Islands: "Hell is on us."

Maybe not yet, but officials knew it would be soon.

To prepare, Hirohito approved the outline for Ketsu-Go on January 20, 1945, an ambitious army-and-navy operation to counter the anticipated American invasion. The strategy called for fortifying perimeter strong points, like Iwo Jima and Okinawa, while ground forces prepared to battle the enemy on Kyushu and the main island of Honshu. In anticipation, Japan planned to conserve its air strength for the invasion and would depend on kamikazes to crash into warships. Rather than battle on the beaches, military strategists envisioned a defense in the cities, towns, and villages. The backbone of this plan therefore would fall to civilians, who were being trained in schools and businesses to fight with bamboo spears. "The final decisive battle of the war," the plan's opening sentence declared, "will be waged in Japan proper."

At the same time, Hirohito took the unorthodox step of seeking advice on the war from former senior statesmen known as the *jûshin*, a move that had to be done in secret so as not to draw unwarranted attention from military leaders who might object. Despite interruptions from air raids, Hirohito met individually between February 7 and 26 with six former prime ministers, including Kiichiro Hiranumu, Koki Hirota, Fumimaro Konoe, Reijiro Wakatsuki, Keisuke Okada, and Hideki Tojo, and the former keeper of the privy seal, Nobuaki Makino. All pushed for the war's continuance except Prince Konoe. "When I think of the madmen leading the present situation," he once said, "I can't help but feel weary of life." In his February 14 meeting, Konoe urged Hirohito to make peace. Loss of the war would threaten the *kokutai*, the traditional imperial political system. "Regrettably," Konoe said, "I think that defeat is inevitable."

Hirohito pushed back, arguing that Japan needed one more victory first to guarantee a better position at the bargaining table.

"Is that possible?" Konoe pressed.

That, of course, was the critical question. Despite the worsening odds, Hirohito stood firm. "If we hold out long enough in this war, we may be able to win," the emperor said that day, "but what worries me is whether the nation will be able to endure it until then."

In the meantime, authorities hustled to adapt to American attacks. Interception devices picked up radio checks among bomber pilots prior to takeoff, which gave analysts up to seven hours of advance notice of a strike. Radar stations in the Bonin Islands provided details on the direction, altitude, and number of bombers, an effort complemented by a fleet of picket boats, which operated anywhere from eighty to a thousand miles offshore. Reports from radar operators in the Bonin Islands triggered confidential calls to the Tokyo Metropolitan Police Board as well as to all prefectural governments, military installations, wartime industries, and vital utilities. Not until coastal radar picked up the bombers did authorities issue the first public alert, giving residents in the invading path at least a half hour's warning.

Tokyo had seventy-seven air raid sirens to alert citizens in the heart of the old city. Fifty-six of those were twenty horsepower, meaning the sirens could be heard under ordinary conditions at a range of just 1.4 miles. The remaining twenty-one sirens were three horsepower, covering an area of just under half a mile. The rise in raids had prompted authorities to augment sirens with radio broadcasts, a faster and wider-reaching system.

After the first raid in November, authorities upped the pressure on residents to abandon the capital, particularly the elderly, expectant mothers, and families with children, bribing them with rations of precious commodities like butter and soap. To sweeten the deal, the government offered to rent out the homes of holdouts to generate revenue and even promised to house family members left behind in special quarters with added rations. "Strangely enough," observed Guerrero, "in a land supposed to combine the brutalities of feudalism and totalitarianism, nobody has yet thought of chasing excess population out at the point of a bayonet."

Japanese leaders realized that Tokyo's wooden construction and density remained a danger. To mitigate the threat, workers in late January 1944 launched the first of six operations to hack firebreaks up to 120 feet wide through the capital's congested neighborhoods, a job that in the end resulted in the flattening of 214,203 homes, shops, and factories.

But Tokyo was only the start.

Workers leveled houses and buildings in Osaka, Kobe, Kyoto, Nagasaki, and numerous other cities, ultimately destroying a total of 614,698. The government paid homeowners the equivalent of thirty-three dollars per thirty-six square feet. Renters received three to six months of free lodging. Household items, ranging from dishes and kitchen utensils to clothes and cupboards, could be sold to the city or stored in schools, temples, and theaters. "Grids were traced in straight lines running through flat, densely overpopulated neighborhoods where thousands of houses were marked for demolition," recalled journalist Robert Guillain. "The people living in them were given a week at most—sometimes only two or three days—to get out with their meager possessions, their bedding, their rags. Then the troops arrived and, often aided by schoolboys and older students, embarked on a kind of brutal, rapid sack of the city. Lined up for miles, khaki-clad soldiers smashed buildings, chopped at them with axes, pounded them with battering rams, pulled them down with ropes; in less than three hours, the old wooden houses crumbled into dust."

The poor shape of the nation's fire departments was another threat to public safety. The job of defending the capital, which sprawled across 213 square miles and on the eve of the war counted nearly 7 million residents, fell to just 8,100 firefighters, a figure far short of the estimated 12,500 needed. The war's drain on labor, gasoline, and resources had prompted the department to slash age and education requirements of new recruits as well as to shave training from three months down to just thirty days, the minimum needed for physical training and to teach classroom skills and pump and hose handling. The organization had only 980 operable trucks and pumpers, many of them hand-powered and commandeered from volunteer fire departments in rural communities. Of the three aerial ladders, only one worked, a German Magirus capable of reaching up to eighty-five feet and pumping five hundred gallons per minute. "The Tokyo fire department," one American report later noted, "was hopelessly inadequate."

But Tokyo fared better than most departments, which wrestled with constant manpower shortages. To guard the ancient city of Kyoto—home to some two thousand temples and shrines—Japan counted only 1,029 firemen. Departments likewise suffered from a scarcity of tools and gear, including carbon dioxide and foam extinguishers, both common in America. What little agencies did have was often broken or dated.

The lack of organized vehicle maintenance departments was another failing, one that evolved into an acute handicap as the war progressed and the military conscripted most mechanics. That led to a breakdown rate of one out of every five pieces of equipment. Many of the pumpers that departments did have were aged or inadequate. Japan's second-largest city of Osaka, home before the war to almost 3.5 million residents, still depended on the first American-made fire truck, a LaFrance that had been imported in 1918. "Firefighting equipment in common use," noted one report, "would, in a large part, have been shunned by small-town volunteer departments in the United States."

Japan, in contrast, banked on residents shoring up the nation's firefighting deficiencies. Across major cities, every ten to twenty households formed a neighborhood group called a *tonarigumi*, an organization whose roots reached back to feudal times. These groups, which normally collected taxes and distributed rations, served as the front line of civilian defense against raids. Neighborhood air raid wardens, often the only ones with any training, enforced the city's strict blackout regulations. "I can see light!" Akiko Oya recalled her warden's frequent nighttime shouts. "That'll be a target for enemy planes! Put it out!"

Armed with shovels, brooms, and bamboo water guns, these groups battled blazes, hoping to contain a fire until the professionals arrived. Many of the men wore steel helmets; mothers made air raid hoods for children, often fashioned from old kimonos. Kisako Motoki's mother sewed hers out of peach fabric, so she could easily spot her in a crowd. To guarantee compliance, Japan passed a national air defense law in 1937, which was revised in later years and required residents to remain at home and battle fires under threat of fines and even imprisonment. "To fight ultramodern incendiary bombs, the populace's basic weapons were straw mats soaked in water, little paper sacks of sand and, in quantity, water buckets that had to be filled from the cisterns at each house; bucket brigades were made up of women and girls and retired elders," Guillain noted. "It was officially drilled into them that with speed and order their equipment was adequate to put out even the most violent fires."

The government had proved equally ill-prepared in building bomb shelters. Not until July 1942 did the Ministry of Home Affairs issue its first order for shelters, which were little more than open trenches reminiscent of foxholes. The government mandated these dugouts be covered in September 1943. A month later residents for the first time were instructed to shovel home shelters, often just a hole in the garden. Masako Sato's family had no choice, given the surrounding pavement, but to pull up a tatami mat and dig one underneath their Tokyo home. The government, which offered plans for bunkers, provided no materials or cash. Construction fell entirely on the backs of the local governments, businesses, and homeowners. "Last year we were told to hide in closets, this year we must dig holes," an exasperated author, Kafu Nagai, wrote in his diary. "What will it be next year?"

In June 1944, the same month B-29s flew the first raid against the Japanese homeland, the government finally ordered tunnels bored into the sides of hills and mountains. These shelters, the only ones able to withstand the blast of a five-hundred-pound bomb, could accommodate only 2 percent of the urban population. "The government's interest," the U.S. Strategic Bombing Survey remarked, "was mediocre and basically insincere."

Japan's strategy for handling mass casualties was better but still far from adequate. Compared to American standards, the nation's hospitals left much to be desired, a by-product of years of war that had robbed Japan of vital imports. Most hospitals had only dated and poorly maintained equipment. Shortages of drugs, anesthesia, X-ray film, and developing chemicals were another challenge. Doctors and nurses performed surgery in filthy scrubs while operating rooms lacked soap and detergent and featured bloodstained tarpaulins. Cotton scarcity forced clinics to reuse surgical dressings. The same conditions plagued Japan's network of aid stations housed in medical offices, clinics, and factories. "Under these circumstances," one postwar report noted, "the standards of medical and nursing practice could be nothing but deplorable."

Japan had done little outside Tokyo to prepare for the possibility of mass deaths beyond instructing residents to sew identification tags inside clothes, listing an individual's name, address, neighborhood group, and in the case of children, school. No one appeared to consider what might happen to such tags in the event of a fire raid. Tokyo experienced an average of two to three hundred deaths a day in peacetime. The military had instructed mortuary service officials to prepare for up to thirty thousand more annually, a figure that would soon prove tragically low. Much of the government's focus instead was on how to cover up such fatalities. "Directives sent out from Tokyo to the prefectures stressed the importance of utmost secrecy in connection with deaths from air raids," one report noted. "Bodies were to be disposed of in secluded places and funerals were to be carefully screened from the public gaze."

The steady drumbeat of American raids brought Japan's failure to prepare into much sharper focus. That frustration reflected the change in the government's rhetoric. Gone was the early strategy to downplay the threat of attacks, replaced instead by efforts to vilify the United States. "We must once and for all," the *Mainichi* newspaper declared, "realize fully the foe's bestial character and thereby further enhance our determination to wipe him out." In his opening address to the Diet in late January, Prime Minister Kuniaki Koiso implored the public to defend the homeland. "The war situation is developing with ever-increasing tempo," he warned. "Today our country is faced with the gravest situation since the outbreak of the Greater East Asia War and has truly come to stand at the critical point of its rise or fall."

The early novelty of the raids faded as the daytime strikes on aircraft plants, combined with the nightly weather strike missions, meant residents never went more than a few hours without the shriek of air raid sirens, which interrupted sleep and further exhausted the hungry populace. "Some people became so weary of the frequent air-raid alarms," recalled Osaka resident Kikuko Ueda, "that they began burning their furniture as fuel, thinking that if it was going to be burned anyway, they might as well get some use from it."

The government's steady diet of propaganda, coupled with the censorship of Germany's incineration, left many confused and ignorant of the peril facing Japan, reflected in the stack of a dozen untouched water pails Guerrero spied in the basement of his apartment building. "The sidewalk ditch-shelters in our vicinity are still uncovered," he noted in his diary, "although some neighborhood associations are starting to shovel out the garbage that has accumulated in them." Artificial limbs dangled from stalls of prophetic shop merchants, while one elegant brothel used the promise of bomb safety to lure customers inside. The evening air raids led twenty-six-year-old Hisako Yoshizawa to sleep clothed. "How will the war turn out?" the Tokyo resident asked in her diary. "Most people no longer believe in victory."

That realization crystallized for many on January 27.

On that frigid Saturday afternoon, LeMay's Superfortresses, unable to reach the Nakajima plant, instead unloaded five-hundred-pound bombs mixed with incendiaries on the capital, pounding the tony shopping district surrounding the Ginza, dubbed the Fifth Avenue of Tokyo. Bombs blew out the windows of the five-story *Asahi* newspaper building, wrecked the Taimei National School, and caved in Yurakucho Station. Private homes erupted in flames; so did the Kirin Beer Hall, a Mikimoto pearl shop, and a branch of the Yasuda Bank. Across the city, people climbed to rooftops to view the acrid smoke, visible above the skyline for miles. Down below, in streets littered with rubble and roof tiles, firefighters rushed to the scene, as residents formed bucket brigades. Hoses snaked like tentacles through the streets as rescuers pulled the dead from the debris. "Until the very day the bombs were dropped over our heads," observed author Shuichi Kato, "we never believed it could really happen."

Koyo Ishikawa, the Metropolitan Police Department's photographer charged with documenting air raid damage, hustled to ground zero, where he was horrified by the carnage that greeted him at Yurakucho Station. As many as sixty bodies lay piled atop one another, some missing arms and legs. Intestines poked through the bellies of a few; others had gouged-out eyes. The blast had ripped the clothes and even underwear off most of the dead, leaving a wrecked tangle of flesh that made it hard for him to determine if the victims were male or female. Among the human wreckage he spotted several dead children. "An infant, who miraculously survived, clung to the already cold body of its mother, crying bitterly," Ishikawa wrote, "making us fully appreciate the cold ruthlessness of war."

Authorities roped off the area, but curious residents pilgrimaged to see where more than five hundred people died, the debris still smoldering days later. Guillain was one of them, joining the throngs of others who stood in awe at the wreckage of one of Tokyo's most vibrant areas. Amid the broken buildings, rubble, and ash, Guillain realized, was a vital message, one that finally managed to break through the years of government propaganda and lies. "It was from that raid," he later observed, "that the people of Tokyo knew the war was lost."

FACED WITH HELLACIOUS FLAK and fighter attacks over Tokyo and Nagoya, LeMay contemplated swapping targets. He set his sights on the Mitsubishi Aircraft Works in Tamashima, a port city on the Inland Sea near Okayama. LeMay ran his proposal by Norstad, who countered with his own idea. Rather than strike a low-priority target, Norstad recommended LeMay execute a test fire raid on Kobe, Japan's dominant seaport and sixth-largest city, home to more than 1 million residents. Kobe contained the nation's largest concentration of ship and marine engine construction; it also served as a vital rail hub and touted steel, rubber, and ordnance factories. But as the mission report made clear, those industries were not the only target. "The area selected for attack," the report stated, "was the highly congested core of the city, having a population average of over 100,000 per square mile."

Unlike Hansell, who had resisted firebombing raids for moral reasons, LeMay had no qualms. He had executed just such an attack against the Chinese city of Hankow in late December. LeMay ordered his crews to hit Kobe on February 4 in the first mission to involve two wings, Rosie O'Donnell's 73rd and the newly arrived 313th under the command of Brig. Gen. James Davies on Tinian. Out of the 129 planes that took off, only 69 made it to the target, fending off some 200 fighter attacks to drop 172.8 tons of bombs.

Despite the small size of the attacking force, the raid was surprisingly effective, killing thirty-eight people, injuring another 150, and leaving 4,350 homeless. Poststrike photos revealed that bombers had damaged or destroyed 1,039 buildings totaling 2,651,000 square feet, including vital wartime factories such as Mitsubishi Heavy Industries and Kanega-fuchi Soda Industry. "Of the dozen most important factories in Kobe, which accounted for over 90 percent of the city's essential war activity, one was almost completely destroyed, two were severely damaged and three others were lightly damaged," concluded the U.S. Strategic Bombing Survey. "February operations were reduced 40 to 60 percent at one of the city's two major shipyards and at two large producers of electrical equipment and rolling stock, and local output of fabric and synthetic rubber for Kobe's important rubber products industry was permanently wiped out. In addition, several food processing and woodworking plants were destroyed."

As Norstad analyzed the results in Washington, LeMay returned to precision attacks. His crews flew a strike on February 10 against the Naka-jima factory in Ota, about fifty miles northwest of the Imperial Palace. This 200-acre complex, which included 3.1 million square feet of floor space and employed a wartime peak of 52,778 people, built seven types of fighters, bombers, and suicide planes. Five days after that strike, LeMay sent his crews to hit the Mitsubishi engine plant in Nagoya, followed by another attack on the Nakajima plant in Musashino on February 19. LeMay intermixed these missions with attacks against Truk and Iwo Jima, the latter to help with the capture of the island. One week soon rolled into two, three, and then a month. Headlines in America, meanwhile, trumpeted the news:

"Kawasaki Plant Gutted by B-29s," heralded the *New York Times.*

"Huge Air Plant North of Tokyo Razed by B-29s," declared the *Chicago Tribune.*

"B-29s Again Hit Tokyo with Record Force," added the *Washington Post.*

But the poststrike photos LeMay pored over revealed a less jingoistic story. Unlike Japan, where authorities were eager to downplay the attacks, air force officials were afraid of overselling the results to the American public, who might then expect the war to end more quickly than possible. McKelway rushed to rein in the press, requesting the wire services and rewrite desks avoid headlines and leads with adjectives like "relentless," "smashing," "giant," and "huge." He also encouraged correspondents not to report on routine weather strike missions, which comprised just two or three planes, and to hold off on writing right after the raid. "Instead," one report noted, "the correspondents were persuaded to file their first detailed stories after strike photos had been taken and interpretation of the photos was available."

The stress of the war wore on LeMay, who had developed headaches in the wake of his battle with Bell's palsy. The pain eventually drove him to consult a doctor in India, who had failed to diagnose a cause. "I'm still having headaches," LeMay complained in a letter to Helen. "I guess I'm getting old and wearing out because they usually happen when I'm worried about something or tired." Unable to write about operations, LeMay often focused on his daughter, Janie, whom he had rarely seen since he deployed to England in 1942, forcing him to track her growth through photographs. He mailed her silver bracelets for Christmas and peppered

Helen with questions about her life. "Tell Janie," LeMay wrote in one letter, "the toads over here are as a big as dinner plates, so she probably would have trouble playing with them."

"How is Janie getting on in school now?" he asked in another.

"Did Janie have a birthday party this year and how did it go?"

More bombers and crews arrived each week in the Marianas, but LeMay's efforts to destroy Japan's factories failed to improve. None of his precision raids had knocked out a plant. America, in fact, had now hit the Nakajima factory in Musashino seven times, yet workers still cranked out engines and air frames. LeMay gathered with his wing commanders to review each strike, blunt sessions that resembled the ones with Hansell in England. His review of the strike on the Nakajima factory in Ota was brutal. The minutes of the two p.m. session show he repeatedly stressed to O'Donnell and Davies the importance of hitting the targets.

"What happened to your bombing?" LeMay pressed Davies.

"Sir," he replied, "I consider it good bombing."

"It was poor," LeMay countered. "Some of the bombs dropped a mile short of the target. I do not see how any bombardier using a bomb sight can miss the target by a mile."

"The dense smoke encountered above the target was a contributing factor," Davies said, "as it was difficult for the bombardier to orient himself on the target."

"The bombardier had two targets which he could bomb and had about a week in which he should have devoted to target study," LeMay replied. "We can never accomplish our job by going over and dropping a few bombs here and a few there."

Col. John Montgomery, LeMay's deputy chief of staff for operations, offered his opinion. Montgomery had flown the February 19 mission against Musashino. Bad weather had forced him to bomb his secondary target at Hamamatsu via radar. Montgomery reminded LeMay that he had been there from the start with Hansell. Japan's weather foreclosed any hope for success—and it was only going to worsen. "Our whole campaign will fail unless something is done to get a better delivery of bombs on the target," Montgomery warned. "We can bomb secondaries forever by radar and it would have little significant impact on Japan."

Montgomery shared more bad news.

"The word," he added, "is spreading around more and more in the Navy."

Despite his good relationship with Nimitz, LeMay knew the navy's rank and file resented the airmen, who required tremendous logistical support in the form of ships loaded with food and fuel. LeMay also couldn't escape the fact that carrier airmen had just launched the first raids against Japan, including a February 17 strike on the Nakajima plant at Musashino, which did more damage than any of the air force's previous attacks.

The navy was now a competitor in the race to knock out Japan.

General Arnold, who was still recovering in Florida, added to LeMay's pressure. Days before his January heart attack, the general had outlined his frustration over his force's failure to deliver a solid punch to the Japanese, a fact that threatened the entire B-29 program on which he had staked his career and billions of dollars of taxpayer money. The Superfortress had been sold not just as another bomber but as a war-winning weapon, a promise it had so far failed to deliver on. "Unless something drastic is done to change this condition soon," Arnold wrote, "it will not be long before the B-29 is just another tactical airplane."

The navy's strike on Musashino only heightened Hap's concerns. In a single mission, the navy had bested seven earlier raids by the vaunted Superfortress even as American newspapers boasted that Boeing's Wichita plant had produced its one-thousandth bomber. Why then, Arnold demanded, could his forces not muster more than sixty or eighty bombers for a strike? In a missive to his chief of the air staff, Lt. Gen. Barney Giles, Arnold questioned whether he needed a leadership change. "I know that there are one thousand other reasons for not getting two, three, or four hundred B-29s over Japan every other day. But all of these reasons must be pushed to one side with a grim determination to get the maximum number of B-29s over Japan on every possible occasion. This cannot be done if we accept excuses and don't face the issue," the exasperated general wrote. "From my viewpoint down here, I would not be surprised any day to see the control of the 20th Air Force pass to either Nimitz or MacArthur."

Giles rushed to assuage the impetuous general, assuring Arnold that operations would increase but reminding him that LeMay had inherited a monstrous job and needed time to implement changes. "When he took over the XXI a month ago, he was told by General Norstad that he would be given a free hand for a period of one month in which to institute a training and maintenance program that would insure the rapid attainment of the highest operating standards. Very radical measures have been taken by LeMay to accomplish this," Giles wrote. "Please accept my assurance that no one views this problem with any complacency. We will all continue to do our utmost to put effective tons of bombs on the critical targets in Japan."

LeMay found himself in the same precarious position Hansell had been in only weeks earlier when Arnold fired him. If anything, the pressure was even greater now. LeMay's results were dismal, the tactics questionable, and now the navy's agile fighters and bombers threatened to muscle him aside. Unlike Hansell, who had at least initially benefited from his long personal connections with Arnold, LeMay enjoyed no such relationship. He had met Arnold only once in person, when he passed through Washington en route from England to India. LeMay, who had landed his job through hard work, knew he could not depend on personal loyalty for protection. It was all up to him. "The system wasn't working," LeMay realized. "It was a different war with different weather and a different airplane. It called for a different solution."

And he had a radical idea.

One so unorthodox, it was best shared face-to-face. LeMay fired off a cable to Norstad, who was scheduled to visit in the middle of March. "I have been here long enough to become oriented and have a grasp on the status of the command," LeMay wrote. "I have made plans for the next two or three months that I can give you better by personal conference than by telecon. A visit by you now will pay greater dividends than one on March fifteenth."

LeMay closed with a cryptic lure.

"I suggest," he wrote, "you come out now."

LeMay let Montgomery in on his idea. "What do you think about going in at night at 5,000 to 7,000 feet and bombing with incendiaries?" he asked.

"I don't know what capability the Japanese antiaircraft have at that altitude."

"The only way we will know is to try."

The Kobe strike, though far from inflicting the destruction LeMay had seen in Hamburg, had still served as one of the command's most successful missions. Sixty-nine planes had sparked myriad fires, some of which recon photos showed still smoldered three days later. Norstad, who had long advocated incendiary strikes, messaged LeMay after the raid, urging him to fly another test mission. As the general mulled over possible plans, his new target list rattled off the teletype on February 19, revealing another shift toward firebombing. The orders still ranked aircraft factories as LeMay's top objective but made clear that any secondary or diversionary attacks should consist of incendiary strikes against urban areas. The directive likewise mandated that he aim any radar attacks against urban areas in Nagoya, Osaka, Kawasaki, and Tokyo.

LeMay got the message.

He had planned a joint operation with the navy to pound the Musashino plant on February 25, but weather forecasts called for clouds to blanket the island of Honshu, forcing him to fall back on radar. LeMay seized the opportunity for another firebombing test. This time he set his sights on Tokyo, choosing an aiming point 3.5 miles up the Sumida River, where the primitive radar would easily reveal the water–land contrast. Though he debated a nighttime strike with a drastic reduction of altitude, for now he chose to send his planes during the day and at twenty-five thousand feet. He would, however, send all three of his bombardment wings, including the newly arrived 314th under the command of Brig. Gen. Thomas Power.

Shortly past daybreak on the twenty-fifth, 229 bombers roared into the skies from runways on Saipan, Tinian, and Guam. Of those, 172 made it to the target, unloading 453.7 tons of bombs. On the ground, residents trudged through newly fallen snow into shelters as plumes of black smoke drifted skyward. "It was only early afternoon but quickly the skies darkened so that it seemed to be sundown," Guerrero wrote in his diary. "It gave us all who were watching a queer eerie feeling, a vague uneasy sensation of catastrophe."

And a catastrophe it soon was.

Fourteen-year-old Shizuyo Takeuchi, a mobilized high school student, lived with her parents in Tokyo's Joto ward in a complex of about two hundred wooden houses. Shizuyo had just walked home from her job at Fujikawa Electric Cable Company and settled in to study. Her father, who pedaled his bicycle each day to Tsukiji Market where he sold fruits and vegetables, had scrounged to buy her an expensive English dictionary, which she treasured.

The air raid siren interrupted her studies, sending Shizuyo and her mother outside to the dark narrow trench that served as the family's shelter. The teenager held her breath.

"The house is burning," her mother suddenly screamed.

Shizuyo looked up and saw smoke and flames pour from the two-story home. She leaped out of the shelter with her mother, grabbed a bucket, and filled it with water from the basin. "My heart was pounding," she recalled, "and my legs were shaking."

The teen hustled to battle the blaze, repeatedly racing in and out to retrieve buckets of water, glimpsing her mother through the dense smoke, like a ghost. The two collided in the kitchen, where her mother judged the situation to be hopeless. The duo had no choice but to flee. Neighboring homes on either side of the road burned, forcing Shizuyo and her mother to charge through a tunnel of fire toward a nearby snowy field. Only when she came to a rest did the stench of her singed hair flood her nostrils. She looked down at her throbbing right arm to find it scorched by flames, ultimately leaving a keloid scar she would carry for life.

The family spent that night with friends before returning the next day. Fires had gutted the majority of the houses in her neighborhood. Amid the ashes of her own home, she discovered her treasured dictionary. She picked up the book gently with both hands. The typeface appeared in gray on a crispy white page. Shizuyo let her eyes wander down the page. "The wind blew," she recalled, "and it turned into ashes right in front of me."

That Sunday raid sparked two dozen such fires, destroying 27,970 homes, shops, and businesses. The attack incinerated nearly one square mile of Tokyo, an area ten times larger than the destruction visited upon Kobe three weeks earlier. "Whole districts were set ablaze and, with the wind carrying smoke, sparks and ash from the fires, the day ended with a new wonder: black snow," wrote reporter Robert Guillain. "The city was paralyzed for the next two days by the fires, the bomb damage and the thick coat of snow that refused to melt." Hisako Yoshizawa was stunned at the expanse of burned-out buildings and at the survivors, many with blackened faces and hands, piling burned mattresses onto carts. "Living each day amid this destruction has become unbearable," she wrote in her diary. "Is this natural selection?"

Back on Guam, LeMay and his staff reviewed the poststrike photos. "This raid," one command report noted, "proved conclusively the vulnerability of Tokyo to mass incendiary raids." Lt. Col. David Burchinal, who flew the lead bomber on the raid, was more blunt in his assessment. "Japan," he said, "would burn if we could get fire on it."

Any doubts LeMay might have harbored, Arnold put to rest. "Extend my sincere appreciation to all ranks for their united efforts which resulted in the greatest number of Superfortresses to date bombing objectives in Japan," he cabled. "Also notify all concerned that we must continue our best efforts to insure that our B-29s reach their objectives in Japan in ever increasing numbers until Japan's will to wage war is cracked. Good luck."

HALF A WORLD AWAY, the air war against Germany reached its crescendo when the first of nearly eight hundred British bombers lifted off at dusk on February 13. The target that Tuesday night would come to symbolize the horror of the air war for generations to come.

Dresden.

Germany's seventh-largest city, Dresden had roots that stretched deep into history. The ancient city's elegant architecture, wealth of museums, and Baroque palaces had earned it the nickname "Florence on the Elbe." "Since the eighteenth century," observed historian Max Hastings, "the old town had stood for all that was finest, most beautiful and cultured in Germany."

War had brought a change in Dresden's fortunes. The population of 640,000 had swelled to as many as a million with the influx of refugees from the eastern front, where Russian forces closed in on Germany. Many of the peacetime factories hammered out armaments, from machine guns and searchlights to torpedo tails and military saddles. Dresden was no longer a cultural treasure but a vital rail and communications hub for the Third Reich.

Air raid sirens howled at 9:51 p.m. as the first wave of 244 bombers zeroed in on the city, sending residents down into basements and coal cellars. "We were told to lay on the floor and open our mouths, otherwise the concussion of the bombs would burst our eardrums," recalled Ursula Elsner, who was fourteen at the time. Others huddled shoulder to shoulder on benches, illuminated by candlelight. Some sobbed and prayed. "Nobody dared speak, even the children were quiet," one survivor recalled. "All one could see were eyes, wide with terror."

The first attackers unloaded 881 tons of bombs in fifteen minutes, a mix of incendiaries and high explosives. War planners depended on the latter to wreck stone buildings, cave in water mains, and make roads impassable for rescuers. More important, such bombs unleashed waves of air pressure, which smashed windows and doors and allowed winds to race through buildings, feeding hungry flames sparked by the incendiaries. Residents felt the tremble of explosions as dust filtered into shelters and the minutes dragged. A few brave souls emerged from bunkers after the initial wave of bombers passed. "Everywhere we turned, the buildings were on fire," recalled the painter Otto Griebel. "The more we moved into the network of streets, the stronger the storm became, hurling burning scraps and objects through the air."

A second wave of more than 550 bombers closed in on the target.

Bombardier Miles Tripp could see the glow from forty miles out, while over Dresden the flames were so bright that they illuminated the silhouettes of the planes in the skies. "The streets of the city were a fantastic latticework of fire," Tripp recalled. "It was as though one was looking down at the fiery outlines of a crossword puzzle; blazing streets stretched from east to west, from north to south, in a gigantic saturation of flame. I was completely awed by the spectacle."

A firestorm like the one that burned Hamburg feasted on Dresden, devouring the city building by building, block by block, mile by mile. Carbon monoxide snuffed out the lives of thousands inside underground bunkers, while temperatures outside soared, bubbling the tar on roads and igniting the resin inside trees. Residents plunged into reservoirs, only to be boiled alive. "Sudden gusts of wind made us grab at each other for fear of being blown away," wrote Anne Wahle, the American wife of an Austrian diplomat. "It was almost impossible to see through the sparks that kept whirling around us like a red blizzard."

More than 300 American bombers joined the battle the following day, dropping 771 tons of explosives and incendiaries in a precision strike aimed at the city's marshaling yards, though by then the damage had been done. Dresden, the ancient cultural heart of Saxony, was gone. The attack incinerated thirteen square miles of the city's historic center, killing an estimated 25,000 men, women, and children. Bombers flattened 75,000 homes and seriously damaged another 18,500. Much as in Hamburg, the massive destruction was a stroke of luck, a confluence of timing, weather, and wind. "Dresden," recalled civilian physicist Freeman Dyson, who worked with Bomber Command, "was like a hole in one in a game of golf."

German authorities forced prisoners of war to dig out the dead, a job the American soldier and future novelist Kurt Vonnegut later called "corpse mining." The bodies were so numerous that authorities resorted to burning them in the city's market square. Where vendors once sold fresh flowers, workers created massive pyres of five hundred corpses, soaked them in gasoline, and set them ablaze. Over the course of twelve days, workers burned 6,865 bodies. Rudolf Sparing, the German Overseas News correspondent, stated that Dresden could be spoken of now only in the past tense. "A great city," he said, "has been wiped from the map of Europe."

But the fury over Dresden was only beginning.

Not since Hamburg had British bombers so thoroughly devastated such a large German city, one that resonated in the imaginations of educated Europeans as a cultural treasure, like Rome or Paris. Week after week, month after month, Bomber Harris had waged his merciless air war against Germany, reducing scores of cities to ash. Yet it was the burning of Dresden that finally pulled back the curtain to reveal the ugly toll of such strikes, sparking an outcry that swept England. That anger was fueled in part by a dispatch from Associated Press reporter Howard Cowan that slipped through the censors. "The Allied air commanders," he wrote, "have made the long-awaited decision to adopt deliberate terror bombing of the great German population centers as a ruthless expedient to hasten Hitler's doom."

Nothing Cowan wrote was inaccurate. His only offense, as Hastings observed, was he was three years late in breaking the story. Twenty-four Christian leaders protested attacks on German cities while Richard Stokes rose to the floor of the House of Commons and read aloud Cowan's article. Is terror bombing, he implored, England's policy? "We shall live to rue the day we have done this," he howled. "It will stand for all time as a blot upon our escutcheon."

Prime Minister Churchill, who had once bragged to Roosevelt about the firebombing, increasingly shied away from the horror. In the summer of 1943, while at home reviewing film footage of bomb-wrecked cities in the Ruhr Valley, Churchill sat upright in his chair. "Are we beasts?" he declared. "Are we taking this too far?" Ever a political animal, the prime minister no doubt sensed that with Germany's defeat now imminent, history would judge England harshly. He fired off a memo to the British chiefs of staff and Chief of the Air Staff Sir Charles Portal. "It seems to me that the moment has come when the question of bombing German cities simply for the sake of increasing the terror, though under other pretexts, should be reviewed. Otherwise we shall come into control of an utterly ruined land," he wrote. "The destruction of Dresden remains a serious query against the conduct of Allied bombing."

Cowan's story likewise ricocheted around the United States.

"Terror Bombing Gets Allied Approval as Step to Speedy Victory," blared the *Washington Star*.

"Ruthless Terror Bombing of Reich Decided to Speed German Collapse," echoed the *Boston Herald*.

"Allies to Bomb Cities of Reich Unmercifully," declared the *Arkansas Gazette*.

Hap Arnold, recovering from his heart attack in Florida, demanded a report from Lt. Gen. Carl Spaatz, the senior American air leader in Europe. "This story," as one air force memo stated, "will certainly bring an avalanche of queries because it contradicts all of our announced policies and purposes of precision bombing." The irony, of course, was that American officials fretted over potential public backlash of fire raids in Europe while others in Washington urged LeMay simultaneously to incinerate Japan's cities.

Spaatz assured Arnold that American policy against Germany had not changed. The majority of Dresden's damage resulted from the preceding British attacks. On February 22, just three days before LeMay unleashed his fires on Tokyo, War Secretary Henry Stimson assured the press the same. "Our policy has never been to inflict terror bombing on civilian populations," he said. "Our efforts are still confined to the attack of enemy military objectives."

For now.

CHAPTER 10

"No other industrial nation is dependent on so small an area for so substantial a portion of its manufactured products as Japan."

—REPORT TO THE COMMITTEE OF OPERATIONS ANALYSTS
SEPTEMBER 4, 1944

LeMay continued to mull over his idea of a low-altitude incendiary strike. At night he studied intelligence reports along with scores of black and white photographs of targets, searching for signs of anti-aircraft guns that might bring down his mighty bombers. "I could never be certain just how good my intelligence really was," he said. "We had pictures; we couldn't find any low-altitude defense; but that didn't mean that it wasn't there."

Though his firebombing raids on Kobe and Tokyo had proved successful, neither had sparked the massive fires that had devastated Hamburg and Dresden. He was still missing the critical ingredient in the recipe for total destruction. LeMay began quietly polling a handful of airmen about going in low. A few, like Montgomery, thought it might succeed.

"God," others countered, "that would be slaughter."

LeMay needed a way to bring his airmen around to his idea of a low-altitude attack. He summoned Montgomery, instructing his operations officer to plan a mission against the Nakajima factory in Musashino. "Altitude," LeMay said, "fifty feet."

"Give me that again, General," Montgomery replied. "I have been up kind of late."

"Fifty feet," LeMay repeated.

"What do you mean?" a baffled Montgomery replied. "It won't work."

"Why won't it work?" LeMay pressed.

Montgomery rattled off a list of reasons. At such a low altitude, crews could not see well enough to navigate much less find the target. "When you drop the bombs, they are going to ricochet," he stammered. "You are going to have airplanes blowing up."

"If you can't plan that mission, I will."

Montgomery relented, gathering with other equally mystified staffers to plan the mission. LeMay approved the operation and instructed Montgomery to fly a practice mission with twelve bombers in columns of three over Kito Iwo, a small island off Saipan. Montgomery sent a cable to Rosie O'Donnell and awaited his response, which soon rattled off the teletype.

"Mistake in altitude. Two ciphers missing."

"Altitude correct," Montgomery messaged. "Fifty—repeat—fifty."

"General O'Donnell would like to talk to Colonel Montgomery," came the reply.

"Here."

"What is going on?" O'Donnell wrote.

"LeMay's orders."

"I will be right down there."

Montgomery informed LeMay, who instructed him to prepare the conference room while O'Donnell flew down from Saipan. LeMay gathered his senior aides at the round table, including his chief of staff, Brig. Gen. August Kissner, and colonels Bill Irvine, William Blanchard, and Montgomery. O'Donnell barged in and collapsed into the empty seat.

"Well, Rosie?" LeMay asked. "What is it?"

"I can't run that mission."

The room fell silent. O'Donnell had pulled this same stunt on Hansell on the eve of the first Tokyo strike back in November. This time, however, he faced a very different commander. Montgomery watched as LeMay pulled his cigar from his mouth and set it down.

"By God," LeMay said, "you will run it."

The general locked his hazel eyes on O'Donnell. No one spoke. O'Donnell finally dropped his gaze.

"Anything else?" LeMay asked.

"No," O'Donnell said, rising to leave.

As ordered, O'Donnell's crews flew the March 1 practice mission, which sparked rumors that spread like a wildfire throughout the command, just as LeMay wanted. The general knew that when orders came for his crews to fly at five thousand feet, his men would feel not fear but rather relief. "That," Montgomery later said, "is a great commander in action."

Radar remained a nagging challenge for LeMay, who knew it was vital for his plans. Norstad had gone so far as to fire off a letter to America's top airman in Europe, Lt. Gen. Carl Spaatz, begging him to spare any radar-trained crews. "We are convinced that every bomb we drop during the next six months will be worth several bombs dropped after that period," Norstad wrote. "Anything, from one crew up, will be of great help to us."

LeMay grabbed Dr. King Gould, a civilian radar expert from the Massachusetts Institute of Technology who was assigned temporarily to his command. "Look," LeMay told Gould, spreading out a chart of the island of Saipan. "You go up there and pick out a couple of the stupidest radar operators they have, and Lord knows that's pretty stupid. You go up and fly with them and see if they can fly over this spit of land sticking out on the northern side of the island. That's a real good land-water contrast. Go see if they can do that."

Gould did as instructed, reporting back a few days later. The news was bad. "I guess maybe they can do it," the scientist hedged. "But they sure need a lot of training."

Day in and day out, crews took to the skies. "We participated in another of General LeMay's practice missions," Chester Marshall wrote in his diary. "I believe now he really means it when he says we are going to practice until we learn to hit those targets." LeMay knew his men grumbled. "Hell," he replied, "I'm not here to win friends. I'm here to win a war. And the only way to do that is for my men to drop the max weight of bombs on the target."

The arrival of March brought heavy rains, turning the ground on Guam bloodred with mud. LeMay had ordered a precision strike on the Musashino plant for the first day of the month, but clouds over Japan forced him to delay the mission three times. "We have been having a hell of a time with the weather lately," he wrote in a letter to Norstad on March 3. "It looks like this situation will exist from now on." LeMay closed his missive with a nod to his earlier cryptic cable. "I am working on several very radical methods of employment of the force," he wrote. "Let me urge again the necessity for a visit from you as soon as possible."

LeMay launched his Musashino strike the following day, the eighth attack on the Nakajima plant. Much to the airmen's relief, the general ordered the attack at twenty-five thousand feet, though he planned an early-morning takeoff, putting his crews over Tokyo soon after daybreak. Of the 192 planes that took off, however, not a single one bombed the target. Heavy clouds forced crews to unload on the urban area of Tokyo, killing 650 people. Like the seven others before it, the mission was a bust. The enemy's war machine still hummed.

Victory was no closer.

THE TIME TO DECIDE had arrived.

LeMay hunkered down alone in the war room of his command headquarters, staring up at the maps of the enemy's homeland as the hours ticked past. At the outset, the 21st Bomber Command had been assigned nine priority targets that if destroyed would cripple Japan's aviation industry and give America control of the skies. In 2,037 sorties flown since November, bombers had failed to obliterate a single one. The Musashino plant, where workers each day continued to crank out engines and airframes, now stood like an emblematic monument to the air force's failure. Despite sending 835 bombers armed with 2,327 tons of bombs, the factory in the Tokyo suburbs had suffered only 4 percent damage.

The latest mission served to confirm yet again that high-altitude precision bombing did not work. Hansell had tried it and failed; so now had LeMay. Possum had clung to his principles, like a bucking bull, and watched in the end as his career was trampled.

LeMay didn't have that luxury.

As a boy in the frigid winters of Montana, he had learned that if he didn't fish, he didn't eat. The same had applied in college, where he paid handsomely for his education with years of sleepless nights in a sweltering steel mill. Those lessons had made LeMay a pragmatist. If he wanted to win the war—and save hundreds of thousands of American lives as well as his own job—he had to do what was necessary, even if it was morally grotesque.

But for LeMay, it was about more than just principles.

Similar to Bomber Harris, who came to rue precision bombing as a "panacea" before he embraced the burning of German cities, LeMay had lost his faith in the strategy that defined American bombing policy. Unlike Hansell, who relished arguments over bombing theory and the enemy's economics from the safety of his headquarters, LeMay had climbed into the cockpit and joined his men in battle. He had pressed on through black clouds of bursting flak and battled ferocious fighters on missions deep into the heart of Germany. Such operations, with their staggering losses over time, had eroded his confidence in daylight precision bombing. He came to view pinpoint attacks on key industry, which planners long promised would collapse the enemy's economy like a house of cards, as an illusion. "That's just about like searching for the Fountain of Youth," he once wrote. "There is no such thing; never was."

In LeMay's mind, there was no shortcut to victory. "You've got to kill people," he said, "and when you kill enough of them, they stop fighting."

Japan needed to learn that lesson.

Over LeMay hung the fact that if he could not bring Japan to its knees through bombing, American troops would have no choice but to slosh ashore on the enemy's beaches in what promised to be a brutal fight. The Pacific already was littered with blood-soaked islands where American troops had battled the enemy's fanaticism, from Guadalcanal and New Guinea to Peleliu and Tarawa, the latter so gruesome that *Time* magazine had called it "One Square Mile of Hell." Just seven hundred miles north of Saipan, Marines were currently slugging it out for the sulfuric island of Iwo Jima, a thirty-six-day brawl that would cost America nearly 27,000 casualties, including 6,800 killed. Japan would count more than 20,000 dead. The battle was so grisly that *Time* and *Life* reporter Robert Sherrod stumbled across a string of intestines fifteen feet long. "Along the beach," he wrote, "lay many dead. About them, whether American or Jap, there was one thing in common. They died with the greatest possible violence. Nowhere in the Pacific war have I seen such badly mangled bodies. Many were cut squarely in half."

The Battle of Manila, which had finally ended that week on March 3, gave American war planners the best approximation of what an urban fight inside Japan's cities might involve. Some seventeen thousand enemy troops had fortified the Philippine capital, using land mines, overturned trucks, and railroad axles sunk upright into the pavement to block more than fifty intersections. The Japanese converted modern concrete-and-steel-reinforced buildings into fortresses, barricading passageways and forcing American soldiers to fight room by room through university halls, hotels, and even Rizal Memorial Stadium. The twenty-nine-day battle not only flattened 613 blocks of the former Pearl of the Orient but led to an estimated 100,000 dead, many of them massacred by the Japanese. "If anything should happen to Tokyo," one American general wrote to his wife after surveying the city, "the Japanese have asked for it."

The plan LeMay formulated was extreme—a 5,000-to-8,000-foot incendiary attack on the enemy's capital. Such a move would bring his aircrews in under the raging jet streams and clouds that had wrecked so many previous missions. The lower altitude would put less strain on the engines, improve radar and target accuracy, and allow the B-29s to carry more bombs. The flip side, however, was that it would expose his crews to flak and fighters, turning the strike into a potential turkey shoot. To counter this, LeMay opted to abandon formation flying and push his attacks from day to night, providing his airmen the cover of darkness. Previous missions typically counted around a hundred bombers. For this one, LeMay planned to send every plane in his arsenal. More than three hundred would lift off from Saipan, Tinian, and Guam and rendezvous in the skies over Tokyo in a mission appropriately dubbed Operation Meetinghouse.

LeMay decided to swap out not just his tactics but also his target lists. Gone was the pinpoint focus on the enemy's aircraft industry. Instead he planned to unleash his bombers on downtown Tokyo's crowded civilian neighborhoods, putting the bull's-eye on the kitchens, living rooms, and bedrooms of Japan's workers. Many such homes doubled as small factories, a vital cottage industry that fed parts to Japan's ravenous war machine. The general hoped the combination of low altitude, heavy incendiaries, and Tokyo's dense wooden construction would at last release the genie of destruction from its bottle, conjuring a firestorm like what had ravaged Hamburg. This was no ordinary mission—and LeMay knew it.

This was murder.

Men and women. Boys and girls. Toddlers and infants. Incendiaries did not discriminate. The fires would consume everything and everyone in their frightful path, from factory and armaments workers to artists, teachers, and housewives.

"If we lose," LeMay confided to an aide, "we'll be tried as war criminals."

Beyond the ethical considerations, the proposed mission ran contrary to America's long-standing bombing policy, the gospel Hansell and other instructors had preached at the Air Corps Tactical School in the years leading up to the war. America had clung to those tactics throughout the fight in Europe, resisting British peer pressure to firebomb cities. "We should never allow," Gen. Ira Eaker warned in a January 1945 letter, "the history of this war to convict us of throwing the strategic bomber at the man in the street."

Even though LeMay justified the mission for its destruction of Tokyo's home factories, there was no doubt that this strike represented a tremendous moral shift for the United States, which until this moment had opposed the intentional killing of civilians. In the previous month, at the urging of Norstad and the Committee of Operations Analysts, LeMay had already crossed that line, executing test incendiary missions against Kobe and Tokyo along with pummeling the Ginza. But those missions paled compared to the strike he now envisioned. If successful, incinerating Tokyo could prove one of the most consequential and potentially controversial decisions of the war—and it would be made not by the president, the Joint Chiefs of Staff, or even Hap Arnold but by a thirty-eight-year-old field commander.

Unlike Europe, where a deep bench of senior airmen existed to debate and push back against questionable ideas, here on the battered island of Guam there was only LeMay, hunched over a table, a cigar hiding his drooping jowls. Arnold had fired the one leader who had opposed such tactics. Neither Chester Nimitz nor Douglas MacArthur exerted any real influence over LeMay's operations. LeMay reported only to Arnold, who had been sidelined by a heart attack. In his place stood Larry Norstad, a brigadier general whom LeMay outranked and saw, not as an authority figure, but as merely a conduit to Arnold. Norstad was a yes-man, a pencil pusher, a cog in the military machine incapable of making the hard choice LeMay now faced. LeMay furthermore did not trust him. He had witnessed the way Norstad orchestrated the firing of Hansell, one of his closest friends. He harbored no illusions that Norstad, whom he barely knew, would be any more loyal to him. If anything, LeMay suspected Arnold's chief of staff wanted him to fail so that he could slide in and take his job. "Norstad would never go out on a limb for anybody in his life," LeMay said. "I got no direction from him."

Though he discounted Norstad, LeMay wanted, without actually briefing Arnold, to make sure his unorthodox plan would not run afoul of the air force commander. "You know General Arnold," LeMay cryptically asked Norstad. "Does he ever go for a gamble?"

Norstad, who knew nothing of LeMay's proposed mission, assured him that Arnold would support anything that would hurry up and win the war.

LeMay saw that as a green light.

He would go it alone. If the mission failed, Arnold could deny involvement or even knowledge. Failure would fall directly on LeMay. He would be the one savaged by the press. Arnold could then fire him and hopefully resuscitate his B-29 program. "It was my decision," LeMay said, "my responsibility, my neck that was on the block."

Beyond Arnold, LeMay had to consider the fate of his airmen, the pilots, bombardiers, navigators, and radarmen. He would send them barely a mile above the earth into the heart of Tokyo, a city guarded by some 300 fighters and more than 600 guns. LeMay's antiaircraft experts warned him he could lose as many as 70 percent of his bombers. That would mean more than 200 airplanes and 2,000 souls. LeMay had studied the target photos and was persuaded that Japan lacked low-level guns. He also knew the enemy had only two units of night fighters. Months of consistent high-altitude daytime attacks meant that a low-level midnight strike would catch the Japanese off guard, like an aerial sucker punch. "You don't gamble the lives of your people," he reasoned. "You take calculated risks."

Despite that confidence, LeMay couldn't shake the fear that he might be wrong. He had harbored similar doubts back in Europe, when he worked to defeat German flak.

But the risk here was even greater.

What if he was sending thousands of American kids on a suicide mission? He imagined the flood of parental hate mail that would swamp his inbox and haunt him for life. "Dear General," he envisioned one mother writing. "This is the anniversary of my son Nicky being killed over Tokyo. You killed him, General. I just want to remind you of it. I'm going to send you a letter each year on the same date, the anniversary of his death, to remind you."

Lt. Col. Pinkham "Pinky" Smith entered the war room, interrupting LeMay's thoughts. The tactical officer apologized, having failed to spot LeMay.

"No, Pinky, don't go away. I want to talk to you," LeMay said, putting Smith at ease. "There is something I've been thinking about—a new way of hitting them up there in the Empire. And I want you to draw me up a field order and a plan."

Smith listened, his skin crawling. "General," he finally stammered when LeMay finished briefing him, "when we get down to details, I will need some more information."

"Call me when you need me," LeMay said. "One more thing, Pinky. I don't want anyone—anyone at all, mind you, who is not absolutely vital—in on this. I want it kept quiet as possible."

TOKYO, LIKE MOST of Japan's cities, owed its very existence to the nation's rugged landscape, as the mountains that dominate 85 percent of the volcanic archipelago long ago forced development to crowd coastal river valleys. From its humble beginnings as a fishing village half a millennium earlier on the vast Kanto Plain in the shadow of majestic Mount Fuji— an active volcano that soars twelve thousand feet high—Tokyo evolved into the third-largest city in the world, bested only by London and New York. With a peak wartime population of nearly 7 million, Tokyo counted more residents than Japan's next five largest cities combined. Divided into thirty-five wards, the city stretched across 213 square miles—an area ten times the size of Manhattan—and in some districts counted a density of more than 135,000 people per square mile. Tokyo served not only as the national seat of government and power but as Japan's great commercial, industrial, transportation, and communications center, home to its top hospitals, universities, department stores, museums, and theaters.

The Imperial Palace, tucked away behind stone walls and wide moats, stood at the heart of the congested city. The 531-acre compound dotted with towering pines served not only as the capital's largest open space but also as the home of Emperor Hirohito, his wife, Empress Nagako, and the couple's six children, who ranged in age from six to nineteen years old. The Imperial Diet, Japan's bicameral legislature, sat just a few blocks southwest of the palace. Hailed as the largest public structure in Japan, on which workers had toiled for nineteen years, the Western-style parliament building featured numbered lifts and long carpeted corridors that connected the 390 rooms. The Diet's defining feature, however, was its central granite tower, capped with a pyramid that climbed more than two hundred feet above the Tokyo skyline, making it the capital's tallest structure and prompting comparisons to the Metropolitan Life Insurance Building on Madison Avenue. To the east of the Diet ran the Ginza—Tokyo's shopping area that was bombed on February 25—where before the war wealthy patrons had perused department stores that featured escalators and high-speed elevators.

Beyond its central business district, much of Tokyo's industry centered on small feeder factories, often run out of homes. On the eve of the war, the city counted more than forty-five thousand such workshops, the majority employing fewer than five laborers who churned out textiles, ceramics, and tools. The war's outbreak had prompted many to close, freeing up workers for absorption into larger wartime factories that produced airplane engines and fuselages. Most of these crowded the western shores of the bay, running south for twenty-five miles into the neighboring cities of Kawasaki and Yokohama. These three cities formed an expansive industrial complex—complete with refineries and chemical plants, serviced by a network of railroads and highways—that was the beating heart of Japan's war machine. Not only was Yokohama the nation's second-largest port, but the waterfront city housed shipyards and dry docks for repair. "Kawasaki," added the U.S. Strategic Bombing Survey, "contained the greatest single concentration of industrial plants in the country, nearly all of them producing the materials of war."

Despite Japan's rise as an industrial and military powerhouse, the nation had failed to shed much of its feudal and agrarian roots. Westerners accustomed to the magnificent capitals of Paris, London, and Rome often found themselves shocked by the region's coarse and austere appearance, devoid of much of the grand architecture, spacious parks, and marble monuments that defined American and European cities. Most Westerners disembarked from steamers in Yokohama, their heads filled with postcard images of snow-capped mountains and lacquered temples, only to be welcomed by grimy warehouses and belching smokestacks. The twenty-mile drive from the port to central Tokyo was equally jarring, as the industrial eyesore gave way to ramshackle wooden shacks with corrugated metal roofs that hugged either side of the highway. Poverty ran rampant. Farmers dressed in rags and wooden clogs drove oxcarts; locals shuffled along barefoot even in the winter cold. "Everything was gray, monotonous, squalid," wrote American author Helen Mears, describing her first impression. "This was squalor."

Tokyo's four-square-mile business district, as most soon discovered, resembled a Hollywood backdrop of Westernization. Behind the modern high-rises stretched a sea of traditional two-story wooden buildings. These were intercut by suffocating alleys—some paved, others not—crowded with vendors hawking dried seaweed, bean-jelly candy, and tubs of live fish. Odorous canals, many offshoots of the Sumida River that bisected Tokyo, snaked through the capital, often clogged with coal barges and pole boats. The city's wealthier families lived west of the palace, while the poor packed districts in the south and the east surrounding factories. Entire families bedded down at night on straw mats in tiny wooden houses heated by charcoal braziers, which reflected Tokyo's primitive past. "These homes," wrote Canadian-born journalist Willard Price, "were so small as to make the Manhattan apartment seem spacious." Mears lived in one of the city's more modern residences, which had electric lights, a two-burner gas stove, and cold running water. "These conveniences," she wrote, "familiar to the slums of American cities, were in Tokyo practically Park Avenue luxuries."

American war planners realized that it was precisely this dense wooden construction that made Tokyo such an inviting target for incendiaries. History had demonstrated the city's unique vulnerability when a 7.9-magnitude earthquake struck two minutes before noon on September 1, 1923, a force so powerful that seismographs as far away as America and Europe captured it. "How long it lasted, I don't know," remembered American businessman Otis Poole. "We just hung on for dear life and waited for doom." The quake that warm Saturday morning, followed by more than two hundred major aftershocks, buckled roads, twisted train tracks, and snapped telegraph lines. Riverbanks crumbled, and bluffs slid into the sea as a forty-foot tsunami crashed ashore, wiping out seaside villages. Survivors recalled a deep roar, like the grumble of distant thunder, that swept across Tokyo and Yokohama, a chorus of collapsing hotels, offices, and homes. The pulverized concrete hurled a choking cloud of yellow dust into the sky, obscuring the sun. "It was as if life had been blotted out," Poole added, "the end of the world."

But the horror had only begun.

Chemical plants, laboratories, and apothecary shops that were filled with combustibles soon ignited as the earthquake ruptured gas lines and toppled lunchtime stoves in homes and businesses. Just sixteen seconds after the quake, the first fires were reported. The early blazes, fueled by the winds of an approaching typhoon, ballooned to 134. Ruptured water mains left firefighters impotent to battle the blazes as this unstoppable army of fire marched across the capital, nourished by the city's wood-and-paper construction. As the afternoon faded, terrified residents fled, often blocked by collapsed bridges. "In the obscurity of night we could clearly discern how quickly the flames were spreading, assuming the most phantastic shapes, like mythological monsters with beak and talons grasping for prey," wrote survivor Joseph Dahlman, a German literature professor at Tokyo Imperial University. "It was a scene of ghastly beauty." Sparks ignited the hair of some; others plunged into canals, only to boil in the superheated waters. "Hell," one official Japanese report noted, "was indeed let loose on earth."

That was true for the more than forty thousand men, women, and children trapped in the roughly twenty-acre open area of the Army Clothing Depot as the flames suddenly morphed into deadly fire tornadoes. "Frantic cries for help and prayers in frenzy now came, from tens of thousands of throats, making a tremendous din that rose even above the cracks of combustion and roar of fiery tempest," wrote journalist Kazutomo Takahashi. "All in vain!" When the conflagration finally burned itself out after forty-six hours, Tokyo was gone. The catastrophe had killed up to 140,000 people, many of them hastily cremated in the days afterward, when the rancid smell of death was so pervasive as to make aviators retch in open-air cockpits three thousand feet above the ruins. In addition to destroying tens of thousands of offices, factories, schools, and hospitals, the tragedy left another 2.5 million homeless. "The Yokohama and Tokyo disaster," wrote an editor with the *Japan Weekly Chronicle*, "did as much damage in twenty-four hours as the warring armies on the Western Front did in four years."

In the years after the earthquake, as Japan hustled to rebuild, engineers added six major avenues, each 120 feet wide, and cut more than one hundred new streets through the capital to serve as firebreaks. Only 1.7 percent of Tokyo before the quake had been parkland, a figure dwarfed by the 20 percent in Paris, 14 percent in Washington, and 9 percent in London. To remedy that, city officials built three large new parks—Sumida, Hamacho, and Kinshi, totaling more than seventy acres—along with nearly one hundred smaller ones, many of them doubling as school playgrounds. Even with the additional parks, only 3.7 percent of the rebuilt capital served as open space. The earthquake's deadly lessons, however, soon collided with economic reality. A 1927 depression dragged on until 1931, prompting officials to relax building regulations. That was followed by a 1938 ban on steel for private construction. The rebuilt Japanese capital, much to the delight of American war planners, consisted of 98 percent wood and paper. The city was just as vulnerable to fire now as it had been twenty-one years earlier. "Tokyo," LeMay declared, "would be our target—the primary target, the secondary target, and the *only* target."

CHAPTER 11

"Behind every combat mission flown by the Superforts
lay an incredible amount of training, planning, sweat,
sacrifice and just plain guts."

—MAJ. GEN. CURTIS LeMAY
NOVEMBER 19, 1945

At four-thirty p.m. on March 6, LeMay summoned his wing commanders and key staff to his Quonset hut headquarters to brief them
on his plans to strike Tokyo. Rosie O'Donnell was the veteran of the
group, having been in the Marianas since before the first mission to Tokyo
back in November. John Davies had joined in December as commander
of the 313th Bombardment Wing, based on Tinian. Answering to the
nicknames Skippy and Big Jim, the California native stood six foot four,
with close-cropped wavy hair. Like O'Donnell, the affable forty-year-old
had flown in the Pacific in the early days of the war. The newest arrival
was Thomas Power, commander of the 314th Bombardment Wing, on
Guam. A thirty-nine-year-old son of Irish immigrants, Power had grown
up on Long Island. Like LeMay, he harbored a love of flying, inspired by
Charles Lindbergh. He also matched LeMay's tireless work ethic. Though
colleagues considered him bright and dynamic, Power had a fiery temper

and a tough reputation as a leader who exercised control through fear. "He was," one aide recalled, "a very intense guy."

LeMay opened the meeting with a rundown of the command's history from November through February, noting that daylight precision strikes had failed to work, a fact that needed little explanation among the assembled airmen. He then transitioned into his plan for a low-level incendiary attack on the enemy's capital. If successful, LeMay planned to follow it with rapid strikes against Nagoya, Osaka, and Kobe, hoping in just a few days to incinerate the urban areas of those critical cities before the enemy had time to develop countermeasures. "I want to get in and out of the empire before the Japs make things too costly for us."

Unlike Germany, which had superior radar-controlled antiaircraft guns, Japan relied largely on searchlights to pinpoint invaders. LeMay likewise noted that Japan had only two units of night fighters capable of targeting his bombers. "I'm going to send you in," he announced, "at five thousand feet. And without guns, gunners, or ammunition."

O'Donnell whistled.

"I'm removing the ammunition because I'm afraid crews will be shooting at each other more than they will Japs," he continued. "Then, too, we'll save about 3,000 pounds by eliminating ammunition which will give us another ton and a half of bombs."

LeMay singled out Montgomery, whom he had talked to in advance. "Do you have any comments or suggestions?" he asked.

"I concur," he said. "If we don't start hitting targets, soon we'll be the targets."

"You've convinced me," one of the wing commanders said. "But I don't know if we can convince our crews that this isn't a suicide mission."

"It's your job," LeMay replied, "to convince your crews."

The staff departed to begin laying the groundwork for the mission. Nutter could not help but notice the sober demeanor of his colleagues. He had been with LeMay in Europe when he had made tactical changes that appeared radical. Every time, the navigator had learned, LeMay's instincts had proved correct. "He never," Nutter recalled, "failed the crews."

Norstad had taken off from Washington and would not arrive on Guam until the morning of March 9, the same day LeMay planned to hit Tokyo. No one in the chain of command above LeMay yet knew of the general's proposed change of tactics.

LeMay left the meeting and tracked down Colonel McKelway. A mission of this magnitude would generate significant press. LeMay needed to alert McKelway in advance. Montgomery had already dropped a hint to the former newsman. "We got some hot stuff coming up," he had warned McKelway. "LeMay is a pistol, a real pistol."

The colonel was ready when LeMay found him. "This outfit has been getting a lot of publicity without having accomplished a hell of a lot in bombing results."

McKelway listened.

"Tell Monty to fill you in on everything that's coming up," the general continued. "A lot of it can't be told until we know the Japs know what we're up to, but that's your baby. You see that what we don't want to get out doesn't get out."

"Yes, sir."

"This B-29 is a wonderful airplane," LeMay added, almost as an afterthought. "Let me know if you have any troubles I need to know about."

McKelway hustled to find Montgomery, flashing the duo's agreed-upon hand signal that it was urgent. "If I don't call you this afternoon," Montgomery said, "come over to the tent about eleven tonight and I'll give you a beer along with whatever it is you want."

"It's top-secret stuff," the newsman replied. "The Cigar said for you to fill me in on what's coming up."

McKelway swung by Montgomery's tent that night, listening in awe to LeMay's plan for Tokyo. He returned to his own quarters afterward, reading all night from the second volume of *Lee's Lieutenants*, which Hansell had given him before he left. "I could no more sleep than a rabbit," he said, "when I left him and went to my tent."

ON MARCH 7, Field Order no. 43 rattled off the teletype in the head-quarters of the three bombardment wings on Saipan, Tinian, and Guam, committing to paper LeMay's vision for the destruction of Tokyo. The bold mission, described in just four single-spaced pages, called for more than three hundred bombers to lift off at sunset two days later, a date chosen for its clear weather in the Marianas as well as for the flight to Japan. Crews with the 314th Bombardment Wing on Guam, located one hundred miles south of Tinian and Saipan, would roar down the crushed coral runway at 5:35 p.m. Airmen with the 73rd and 313th wings would launch forty minutes later. To prevent midair collisions with so many bombers in the skies, LeMay staggered the altitudes of each wing. The 73rd would fly out between 3,000 and 3,500 feet, then climb to 7,000 feet to attack. The 313th would cruise one thousand feet above and bomb just below, between 6,000 and 6,800 feet. The 314th would both fly and bomb in the range between 5,000 to 5,800 feet. "Radio silence," orders mandated, "will prevail en route to target except in case of an aircraft in extreme emergency."

To help with navigation, four special homing aircraft—two from the 73rd and two from the 313th—would take off twenty-five minutes before the main strike force. These planes would orbit between 24,000 and 27,000 feet, broadcasting a signal on four frequencies for an hour and a half to help guide the bombers. "The most capable radio opera-tors available will be assigned to the special radio planes," orders stated. "Jamming tactics may be employed by the enemy but 1 frequency of the 4 should remain open." The lower altitude and lack of formation meant planes would not need as much fuel, prompting the removal of bomb bay tanks. The Superfortresses would carry just 6,800 gallons in the wing tanks, with the exception of the 314th on Guam, which was allowed one bomb bay tank to boost its load to 7,300 gallons, enough to cover the extra two hundred miles.

Crews with the 73rd and 313th would carry an average of 14,000 pounds of incendiaries per plane, almost three times the weight crews hauled on the first Tokyo mission back in November. Crews with the 314th, given the need for extra fuel to fly from Guam, would carry just 10,000 pounds. LeMay designated the first squadron from each wing as pathfinders, ordered to mark the target area with M47 incendiaries designed to drop at hundred-foot intervals and explode on impact. Later crews would carry five-hundred-pound clusters of M69 incendiaries, the same bombs that had incinerated the mock Japanese village at Dugway Proving Ground in the Utah desert. These would drop every fifty feet and open between 2,000 and 2,500 feet above the ground, scattering thirty-eight bomblets to allow a saturation of twenty-five tons per square mile. "The M47 was chosen," the mission report stated, "to assure good penetration and initial fire spread of sufficient size to tie up the enemy's fire-fighting equipment and increase the potential effectiveness of smaller bombs to be dropped by later planes."

LeMay set his sights on what war planners described as Incendiary Zone 1, a highly flammable area in Tokyo's river delta known as Shitamachi or "low city." This roughly three-by-four-mile rectangle, when viewed from the air, resembled an irregular piece from a jigsaw puzzle. The Imperial Palace with its sprawling gardens marked the southwestern corner of the target area. From there the boundary ran north to Ueno Park, one of the capital's most prominent open spaces. The Joban railroad served as the northern boundary, ending at the Sumida River, which cut a diagonal line southwest back across the target area. The eastern border ran south midway between the Sumida and Arakawa rivers before making a ninety-degree turn west, crossing back over the Sumida and ending at the palace. This 11.08-square-mile area—spread across much of seven wards—included the Ginza and the financial district Marunouchi, home to government offices and newspapers, banks, and insurance companies. The area counted only six important targets, the most valuable being Hattori Co. The peacetime manufacturer of Seikosha watches cranked out fuses for artillery shells. The other vital targets included railyards, stations, and market areas. Much of Japan's heavy industry, including thirty-five vital targets, lay just beyond the eastern boundary, while steel mills and ship-yards were to the south.

But those weren't the mission's objective.

LeMay's focus was on Tokyo's home industries, the small workshops filled with lathes and drill presses tucked away in the capital's congested neighborhoods, which were not otherwise profitable targets for precision bombing. Ninety-five percent of the structures in this area were made of wood. Most consisted of two-story frame homes, each built on stilts 1.5 feet off the ground. Japanese carpenters shunned nails, preferring mortise and tenon joints. Large timbers served as foundation sills with four-by-four-inch stud walls and even larger roof rafters. Workers crafted floors from three-quarter-inch lumber; exteriors were fashioned from clapboard or bamboo lath and mud plaster. Clay tiles or corrugated sheet metal comprised the roofs. Tests had revealed such homes to be little more than kindling, burning to the ground in just twelve minutes.

Beyond destroying home industries, as the mission's target sheet made clear, LeMay's aim was to kill and displace thousands of workers, many of whom toiled in the larger neighboring factories. "Employment at scores of war plants throughout Tokyo and environs," it read, "would be directly affected by casualties, movement of workers out of the area, use of manpower in reconstruction, and probably lowered worker morale."

The targeted area all but guaranteed mass casualties.

A staggering 87.4 percent of the incendiary zone was classified as residential. The population in the area totaled 1.1 million men, women, and children or about 15 percent of the capital's population. The target included Asakusa, one of the city's most congested wards, home to more than 135,000 people per square mile. The population density in the other six districts—Fukagawa, Nihonbashi, Kanda, Honjo, Shitaya, and Arakawa—ran between 80,000 to 135,000, with an overall average of 103,000 per square mile. This residential area was one of the most crowded in the world, five times the average density found in American cities. The result was a seemingly endless horizon of tile and metal rooftops, which incendiaries could easily punch through and then spew

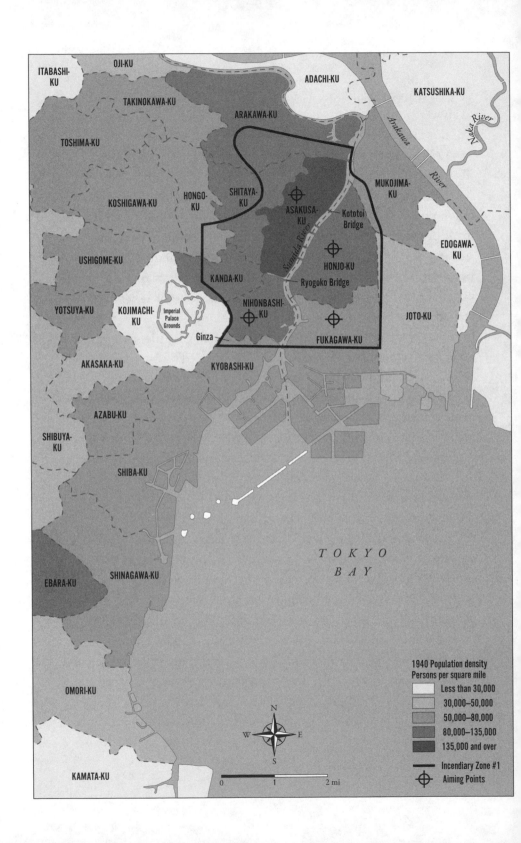

ITABASHI-KU

OJI-KU

ADACHI-KU

KATSUSHIKA-KU

TAKINOKAWA-KU

ARAKAWA-KU

TOSHIMA-KU

KOSHIGAWA-KU

HONGO-KU

SHITAYA-KU

ASAKUSA-KU

Kototoi Bridge

MUKOJIMA-KU

Arakawa River

Naka River

USHIGOME-KU

KANDA-KU

Sumida River

HONJO-KU

Ryogoko Bridge

EDOGAWA-KU

YOTSUYA-KU

KOJIMACHI-KU

Imperial Palace Grounds

NIHONBASHI-KU

FUKAGAWA-KU

JOTO-KU

Ginza

AKASAKA-KU

KYOBASHI-KU

AZABU-KU

SHIBUYA-KU

SHIBA-KU

T O K Y O B A Y

EBARA-KU

SHINAGAWA-KU

OMORI-KU

N
W   E
S

KAMATA-KU

0   1   2 mi

1940 Population density
Persons per square mile

☐ Less than 30,000

30,000–50,000

50,000–80,000

80,000–135,000

135,000 and over

Incendiary Zone #1

⊕ Aiming Points

flaming napalm upon wood-and-plaster walls and on floors covered with woven mats. The narrow alleys that serviced many of these homes—few more than twelve feet wide—were too small to accommodate most of the city's fire equipment. Efforts to hack firebreaks through such crowded districts likewise would be woefully inadequate. "It was calculated," one postwar report noted, "that, at one point in Tokyo, one could travel 800 yards in any direction before coming to a 100-foot-wide firebreak."

Those failings left the winding Sumida River as the largest firebreak in the target area, aided only by a few smaller rivers, canals, and thoroughfares. LeMay countered this by spreading his four primary aiming spots equally across both sides of the Sumida. Residents on the ground would be trapped with nowhere to flee. "No mission in history," Nutter marveled, "had ever been planned to create such mass devastation."

The following day—and with Norstad on a plane en route to Guam—LeMay sent his first message to Washington, alerting the air staff of his mission. With Arnold still recovering in Florida and Norstad somewhere over the Pacific, there was no one to stop LeMay. "Weather over Japan constitutes our greatest problem," he messaged, "rendering visual bombing impossible. For the next major strike, it is planned to alter drastically the pattern established by past operations. It is felt that inflexible pattern established in past has created opportunity to effect tactical surprise with a low altitude night incendiary attack on Tokyo by individual aircraft. Thorough study of all pertinent factors has been made. Indications are reasonable conclusive that this attack can be accomplished with maximum effectiveness and minimum losses."

———

NORSTAD TOUCHED DOWN at seven a.m. on March 9, hours before LeMay planned to incinerate Tokyo. The general and his chief of staff, August Kissner, greeted Norstad as he climbed down, accompanied by brigadier generals Patrick Timberlake, Edward Powers, Edgar Glenn, and Dr. Robert Stearns. The group then met, allowing LeMay to brief Norstad on the mission. Norstad, who had long pushed LeMay to firebomb Japan, liked what he heard, so much so that he fired off a cable to the 20th Air Force's public relations officer in Washington to prepare for a potential media blitz. "Operations tonight will be the largest yet if plan can be carried out," Norstad wrote Lt. Col. Hartzell Spence. "Its effect may be significant."

Across Saipan, Tinian, and Guam, thousands of airmen filed into briefing rooms, sitting atop benches and chairs. Others sticky with sweat leaned shoulder to shoulder against plywood walls. The heat soared and the air stagnated as nervous chatter flooded the rooms. All eyes aimed forward toward wooden stages and walls plastered with maps, where the briefing officers would address the crews about that night's mission. The airmen had developed finely tuned senses. After the Musashino raid on March 4, a notice tacked up on the bulletin boards had announced that there would be no more missions until March 9. That five-day lull on top of LeMay's altitude experimentations and alternating takeoff times had set the rumor mill spinning. "We felt a major change was in the offing," recalled pilot John Cox. "It was not long coming."

"It's a big one tonight," someone murmured as the crews waited.

"Yeah, every guy and his brother is going out."

Lt. Col. John Dougherty, commander of the 500th Bombardment Group, took the stage on Saipan. "Gentlemen," he began, "for tonight we have a new plan."

The room fell quiet as all eyes focused on him. "When you hear it," Dougherty continued, "you won't like it. But after you think about it a while—it makes sense. It should work." The Minneapolis native with sandy hair and blue eyes leaned against the lectern. "The best brains and the best information have been put into it. And if it does work, tonight can do more than any one raid ever did to bring the end of the war closer."

Dougherty and his operations officers outlined LeMay's plan. Briefers began with an explanation of Tokyo's vital role as the communications and railroad center of Japan. Workers in the city produced 95 percent of the nation's radio equipment, 75 percent of its telephone gear, and 40 percent of all its cars and motors. Capital laborers likewise hammered out 90 percent of its aircraft cannons and 30 percent of its engines and ball bearings. In addition, more than one-third of the nation's oil was refined in the capital. Not only would the attack disrupt industry, but planners noted that Tokyo's population density and wooden construction made the capital highly susceptible to fire. March marked the end of incendiary season.

Briefers laid out aerial routes into the heart of the city, where the main railroad bridge over the four-hundred-foot-wide Sumida River would serve as the radar aiming point. Radarmen would observe three bridges below this point and seven above it. Officers warned that there were several prisoner of war camps in Tokyo, but none were known to be in the target area.

Crews should fly with the lights out, wear red goggles, and expect antiaircraft fire, barrage balloons, and numerous searchlights. In addition, eighty airfields surrounded the capital that could throw up three hundred single-engine fighters and another sixty twin-engine planes. Lastly, planners cautioned the airmen not to carry any Japanese money, souvenirs, or diaries, and remember, if captured, give only their name, rank, and serial number.

Dougherty returned to the lectern. "Tonight there is no other target except Tokyo," he concluded. "Tokyo is our primary target, our secondary target, our target of opportunity, our target of last resort. Every single bomb will be dropped inside Tokyo."

In briefing rooms throughout the Marianas, crews processed the news. "The attack altitudes are what make the men's eyes pop," observed the 498th Bombardment Group's diary. "It is probably the most tense group that ever listened to a briefing."

"Most of us sat stunned in disbelief," Chester Marshall penned in his diary.

"We were dumbfounded and wondered if Bomber Command had gone crazy," added pilot Ben Robertson. "The tactics to be used on this mission were a complete departure from the design objectives of the airplane and, to us, tantamount to a suicide strike."

The new tactics promised to further undermine the already-low aircrew morale. "We were appalled at the briefing information. It violated everything we knew about flying and was a complete gamble with marginal data," Cox wrote. "As we left the briefing room it was apparent that even the briefers thought they would not see most of us again."

General Power, whom LeMay tapped to lead the mission, faced a tough crowd during his briefing with pilots, navigators, and bombardiers on Guam.

"Five thousand feet," someone hollered. "You have to be kidding!"

"This is stupid. It's suicide," another shouted. "Surprise may help us with the fighters. It won't help us with the flak."

Nutter shot a glance at LeMay, who puffed on his pipe. The outbursts brought no change in his stoic expression. Power resumed the briefing. "I would not lead this mission and we would not be sending you," he concluded, "if we thought it was an unreasonable risk."

An army of thirteen thousand men hustled to load bombs and attach fins and fuses while others fueled the fleet of Superfortresses. LeMay predicted his back-to-back strikes against Tokyo, Nagoya, Osaka, and Kobe would exhaust his stock of incendiaries, prompting a call to the navy. He alerted them that he planned to fly each bomber 120 hours that month, a statement that drew laughs from skeptical officers. "Nobody ever did this before. You can't do it."

"Well," a frustrated LeMay replied, "we're going to do it. And if you don't give us the supplies we need, we'll just sit here and go fishing."

That afternoon McKelway summoned reporters for a press briefing with Norstad and LeMay. The public affairs officer, who had been a loyal friend of Hansell, had eyed LeMay with suspicion when the reticent general first touched down on Guam back in January. As the days turned to weeks, however, McKelway's skepticism gave way to admiration. LeMay had sacrificed his personal life to fight in Europe and now in the Pacific, even though he had a wife and young daughter half a world away whom he rarely saw. The general worked tirelessly, stretching out only in the early morning hours, hoping to steal a few hours of sleep. LeMay alone,

McKelway realized, shouldered the awesome responsibility of this mission. "He was risking his own future, not only, I think as an Army officer, but as a human being," he wrote. "LeMay, I had begun to learn, was a very tough man, a very tough man indeed."

About fifty journalists who normally covered land and sea operations out of the navy's headquarters joined the assigned air force reporters for the pre-mission briefing. The officers laid down the ground rules for covering the mission. Reporters would watch the takeoff and then type up their stories, but McKelway would not release them over the wires until the first bombs-away report arrived, which would confirm the mission was a go. "The war correspondents," McKelway said, "would not be allowed to reveal that we were, by design, going in at low level, because the Japs might conceivably think that weather or miscalculation had caused this unexpected innovation and we wanted them to keep on thinking so until we had hit a couple more of their cities. Then we could reveal that we were deliberately going in low."

Unlike the first strike on Tokyo back in November, when eight reporters accompanied aircrews, only one journalist would fly this mission, the *Boston Globe*'s Martin Sheridan. The bespectacled reporter's tragic personal story made him appear an unlikely candidate to volunteer to fly a fire raid. On November 28, 1942, Sheridan, then a twenty-eight-year-old freelance writer and publicist, was hired to escort western movie star Buck Jones on a war bond drive, a busy day that included a visit to the children's hospital and a speech at Boston Garden, followed by the Boston College–Holy Cross football game. The duo, joined by Sheridan's wife, Constance Misslin, ended the evening at a dinner with two dozen movie executives at the Cocoanut Grove nightclub, one of the city's most popular spots, as evidenced by the thousand revelers who packed the club, whose official capacity topped out at just six hundred people.

Sheridan polished off the first course of oyster cocktail when he heard a commotion across the room. He ignored it, suspecting the ruckus was a fight among exuberant football fans. Seconds later a cloud of black smoke flooded the hall as fires attacked the cheap tropical decorations. As Sheridan and his party rose to leave, the lights went out, sparking terror among fleeing patrons. "I shall never forget," he recalled, "the screams and cries of the trapped, the crash and clatter of overturning tables and chairs, the smashing of dishes and glasses."

Toxic fumes toppled the reporter. On the ground in the dark, he flirted with consciousness, listening to the moans of other victims along with the hammer blows of fire axes. Cold water soaked him. A rescuer pulled Sheridan from the building, propping him up in a chair as he summoned a taxi to rush him to the hospital. "I sat there shaking," he said, "unable to see because both eyes had puffed shut from burns. My seared hands felt like the flesh was hanging from them." The blaze, which ranks as the worst nightclub fire in American history, claimed the lives of 492 people, including cowboy Buck Jones and Sheridan's wife. The reporter spent sixty days in the hospital, enduring seven blood transfusions and two skin grafts.

His burns left him ineligible for the Coast Guard, prompting Sheridan to join the *Boston Globe* as a war correspondent. Death no longer frightened him. "I went out there as a fatalist," he said of his time in the Pacific. "If you were going to get hit, you were going to get hit."

Two years later, aboard the attack-transport *Freemont*, a young sailor approached him. "You're Martin Sheridan, aren't you?" Howard Sotherden asked.

"That's right," he replied.

"Well," the sailor replied, "I'm the guy who pulled you out of the Cocoanut Grove fire."

On leave in Boston that fateful night, Sotherden heard the scream of sirens and chased the fire trucks to the club. The sailor rescued three others from the fire after Sheridan. "I was stunned beyond description," the reporter wrote in a front-page story on October 13, 1944. "Here in the Pacific I have suddenly found the man who saved my life."

In just a few hours, Sheridan planned to risk it once again.

Across the Marianas, pilots and navigators, bombardiers and flight engineers hammered out letters home, played cards, or stretched out on bunks in a futile effort to catch up on sleep. The weight of the mission hung over them. "We moped around most of the day after the briefing and listened as the guys cursed General LeMay," Marshall wrote in his diary. "As takeoff time approaches, apprehension increases to a degree higher than it was on our first mission. We *know* what can happen now."

The airmen ate an early supper before canvas-covered trucks rumbled up outside mess halls to retrieve them for the trip down to the airfield. Before anyone climbed up the bomber's ladder, aircraft commanders and co-pilots executed visual inspections of the Superfortresses, ranging from the tires and engines to the hydraulic lines, windows, and gun-sighting blisters. Crews then lined up to the left of the nose, with the co-pilot in the lead, followed by the bombardier, navigator, flight engineer, radar-man, and radio operator. The aircraft commander moved down the line, checking oxygen masks and parachutes, flight clothing, and identification tags. On Saipan, the chaplain of the 499th Bombardment Group seized this opportunity to walk from bomber to bomber. "Good luck, men," he told them. "Your chaplain will be praying for you."

With the ignition switches in the off position, ground crews pulled through the props, two men per each sixteen-foot propeller, spinning them to remove any oil from the cylinder. On board the Superfortresses, crew members ticked through extensive checklists. The flight engineer flipped on the cabin pressure, checked the oxygen and lights, and set the throttles to start. The radioman inspected the antennas and flare gun while the bombardier adjusted the altimeter, synchronized his clock, and investigated the camera equipment. Flight Officer Joseph Krogman, bombardier on the *Lady Annabelle*, swore as he worked down his checklist. "Sonofabitch," he muttered in the interphone. "Sonofabitch. Sonofabitch."

"Who's he talking about?" pilot First Lt. John Kearney asked.

"LeMay," replied aircraft commander Capt. Percy Tucker.

Up in the cockpit of each bomber, the aircraft commander and co-pilot ran through the list of more than two dozen items. Parking brake and chocks set?

Check.

Emergency landing gear release in place?

Check.

Emergency bomb bay door release?

Check.

With the lists completed, the aircraft commander signaled the ground crew to step clear. "Stand by to start engines," the co-pilot announced over the interphone.

The number-one engine sputtered to life, belching blue smoke as ground crews hovered nearby armed with fire extinguishers. "Engine operating normal," the flight engineer reported to the cockpit via the interphone. "Ready to start number two engine."

The second, third, and fourth engines grumbled into action, filling the air with coral dust. Ground crews scurried to yank out the wooden wheel chocks.

"Bomb bay doors closing," the co-pilot announced.

"Parking brakes off," the aircraft commander added. "Ready to taxi."

One by one the lumbering bombers rolled out of the hardstands, falling in line for the march to the runway, a parade of mechanical monsters. LeMay, accompanied by Norstad and other aides, climbed up into the control tower on Guam to watch as the sun dropped along the western horizon. One hundred miles north on Saipan, the deafening roar of hundreds of 2,200-horsepower Wright Cyclone engines was so loud that airmen on the neighboring island of Tinian could hear the thunder. The 73rd Bombardment Wing would send 161 Superfortresses to Tokyo that night. The 313th would add another 110 bombers, plus 54 more from the 314th wing for a total strike force of 325. Those bombers represented 84 percent of LeMay's entire arsenal, so many that even at fifty-second intervals it would still take two hours and thirty-four minutes to put all the bombers in the skies. "For almost a week," recalled Nutter, "most of us wondered if we were planning the greatest disaster in aviation history."

Picket and crash boats bobbed just off the islands in case any bombers ditched during takeoff. Between the Marianas and Japan, the navy stationed four submarines and three surface vessels to perform lifeguard duty. In the skies above, six bombers—colorfully known as Dumbos—

orbited to relay distress signals, direct submarines, and drop emergency equipment. Any damaged or distressed plane likewise could put down on Iwo Jima.

All eyes focused on the first bomber. A green rocket arced skyward, and the pilot released the brakes, starting down the runway. Five hundred feet turned to a thousand.

Then two thousand.

The 135,000-pound Superfortress, its massive propellers clawing at the air, increased speed and charged down the strip, its nose slowly rising in the muggy March air. At 5:36 p.m. the bomber left the earth, passed over the beach, and headed out to sea.

LeMay's great gamble had begun.

A Japanese mother and her children navigate the wasteland of Tokyo, which was flattened in American raids on the capital.

PART III

Inferno

"In a single night, the history
and fate of Tokyo were altered forever."

—KATSUMOTO SAOTOME
MARCH 9, 1945, SURVIVOR

CHAPTER 12

"We must not get soft—war must be destructive
and to a certain extent inhuman and ruthless."

—GEN. HAP ARNOLD
MARCH 7, 1945

Friday marked the end of a long week in Tokyo. The winter had been brutal, with more than forty-five consecutive days where the temperature failed to climb above freezing. The cold, along with the scarcity of food and heating fuel, had reduced life in the capital to a grind, interrupted only by the frenzy of air raids. A late February snowfall had camouflaged the scars of war, blanketing burned businesses and softening streetscapes that were robbed of benches and lampposts and pockmarked by craters and bomb shelters. "Filthy houses, blackened streets all awakened that morning transformed by its enchantment into a world of purest white," marveled reporter Robert Guillain, "where what remained of beauty in this afflicted city stood out like jewels against a setting of Oriental magic: pagodas with horned roofs, zigzagging pines, temple roofs with upswept eaves, a whole antique Japan reappeared, lined and mantled with ermine."

But the war was still very much a reality.

The headlines in the *Mainichi* newspaper that morning, which because of newsprint shortages had shrunk to just two pages, captured the struggle of Japanese forces fighting to hold on to Iwo Jima. Only a few days earlier reporters photographed the wife and eldest daughter of Iwo's ill-fated campaign commander, Lt. Gen. Tadamichi Kuribayashi, praying at the Sugahara Shrine. Another story heralded the so-called body crashers, the suicide pilots ordered to ram LeMay's bombers. An editorial that week attempted to prepare the public for what a few years earlier had seemed impossible. "All indications point to the certainty that the enemy, in an impetuous effort to terminate the war rapidly, contemplates landing operations on our mainland sooner or later," the paper wrote. "We, on our part, must crush the untoward enemy design and convince him of the futility of such an attempt by all means."

Tokyo authorities ordered dogs—already scarce in the capital—rounded up and killed, ostensibly because of a lack of rabies vaccinations. This followed the slaughtering of all the elephants, lions, tigers, and snakes at the Ueno zoo over fears that bombing might spark a breakout. The threat of defeat that hung over Japan prompted authorities to view all foreigners with suspicion and even contempt, including Germans, whose embassy warned its nationals to avoid visiting bomb-destroyed areas. That stood in marked contrast to the views of ordinary citizens, who were more concerned over soaring black market prices. "The impression one gathers," Guerrero wrote that day in his diary, "is that the Japanese, fantastic as it sounds, are indifferent to the war, divided by petty quarrels, bewildered by the disaster that is overwhelming them; they have lost touch with the government and lost faith; they are content to stand apart from a tragic adventure which they cannot understand and in which they have had no hand, absorbed in the intimate problem of the next meal, the next incomprehensible air-raid, while the vast wave of ruin looms darkly over their bent unseeing heads."

Signs of defeat surfaced daily, from the shriek of sirens that sent residents scurrying underground to the work crews tearing down homes to create firebreaks. Tokyo emptied out as wealthy families fled to the countryside and the government evacuated precious children. The only predictions of victory could be found in radio and newspaper propaganda.

Military police reported a deluge of defeatist rumors. "If enemy planes can attack the country," residents whispered, "then there is no way that Japan can win the war."

"Not even one out of a thousand firings from the antiaircraft guns is hitting the planes," others complained.

"It's going to be just like what happened in 1923."

The inevitability of defeat trickled down even to children, including eight-year-old Haruyo Wada, who was stunned to hear her father, Saburo, confide in a neighbor that he believed Japan was doomed, a comment that drew a rebuke. "Don't you ever say this," the neighbor warned him. "You don't know who is listening. It could be the police."

That Friday in the capital had been cold but clear. Those at home could tune in at nine-fifteen a.m. to hear a broadcast of the children's story "Brother's Savings Box," followed by an update on the fighting and a lecture on the literature of the Russo-Japanese War. The wind picked up throughout the day, whipping through the city's narrow streets and alleys. But the bitter breeze could not chill young Haruyo's excitement. The second-grader, who lived in the congested Joto ward with her parents and two siblings, had watched as many of her friends had evacuated Tokyo, leaving the neighborhood empty of most of her playmates. Her own school had finally closed its doors in the middle of February, shutting her off from the few others like herself who remained. "The town," she recalled, "was very empty and lonely."

But that week it all changed. The graduation of evacuated sixth-graders prompted a return of many students and families who had left for the countryside. Her Kameido neighborhood of modest wood-frame houses once again teemed with youthful energy. Of all the children, her favorite was Masao, whose family lived next door. The mischievous Masao would often get in trouble at school, prompting the teacher to force him to stand holding buckets of water as punishment. In the afternoons, the youth would wait at the school gate. "Don't you dare say anything about what happened at school to my family," he would say.

"I promise," Haruyo always replied.

His admonishment served as an excuse to wait so the duo could walk home together. Masao repaid the kindness when Haruyo got in trouble. As punishment, her mother would lock her outside, where Masao would invariably find her and oblige her wishes to play house, even providing broken plates he salvaged from his family's pottery business.

Haruyo and her friends played outside all day on Friday, immune to the cold. "Boys would be courageous soldiers," she recalled, while the girls all wanted to play nurse. "You got to take care of the wounded soldiers." In a neighborhood devoid of parks and gardens, the children played atop the family air raid shelter, which served as their military headquarters.

The afternoon sun faded and darkness approached. Haruyo heard her mother call her inside for dinner. The children promised to resume the game the next morning.

"I will see you tomorrow," Haruyo said, and hurried home.

She wasn't the only excited one.

In neighboring Fukagawa ward, Shizuko Nishio stood only hours away from celebrating her sixth birthday on Saturday. Shizuko's father, Juntaro, served as a local doctor, tending to the poorer residents in the working-class community. The family's relative wealth was reflected in their home's few amenities, including a refrigerator, washing machine, and telephone. To celebrate her birthday, Shizuko's mother planned a special dinner complete with her favorite dish of adzuki bean rice, a traditional recipe combining mochi rice with red adzuki beans, all topped with black sesame seeds and a touch of salt. Given the food shortages, such a meal was not easy to prepare, but her mother had visited many shops. "I have all the ingredients for your birthday feast," Soyo assured her daughter on Friday. "Tomorrow I will cook this for you."

Shizuko had another reason to be excited. Her nineteen-year-old cousin, Sumiko, was in town visiting from Gifu Prefecture. "I was so happy," she recalled, "because it was my birthday and my beloved and beautiful cousin was there to celebrate with me."

Metropolitan police photographer Koyo Ishikawa, the city's point person for cataloging raids, had taken advantage of the recent lull in bombings to catch up on work in the darkroom. The forty-year-old Ishikawa had informally begun his macabre job in the aftermath of the Doolittle Raid in April 1942. Armed with his trusted Leica, the bespectacled cameraman captured thirty-two images of the first attack on the homeland, including a couple of factories and a house hit by an errant bomb. Outside he saw the bodies of six people, including children, reduced to charcoal atop galvanized iron sheets, making it impossible to determine even the gender of the victims. "I prayed," he wrote, "for the souls of the deceased."

He then raised his camera and went to work.

The raids stopped for the next 961 days, until the first attack on the Nakajima factory in late November. Ishikawa had raced to the plant in the Tokyo suburbs that afternoon, spotting a formation of silver Superfortresses high in the skies. The photographer arrived to find bodies still being brought out along with the injured. "It was," he realized, "a battlefield."

Ishikawa was developing photos of the Nakajima strike when he was summoned to meet with Nobuyoshi Saka, the police superintendent-general. "I appreciate your hard work today. From now on, in my opinion, the air raids are going to be increasingly fierce, and the bomb damages greater," Saka began. "Would you continue taking photos?"

Ishikawa spotted a thick report on the superintendent's desk about the Great Kanto Earthquake. Saka picked up the file and flipped through it. The articles were strong, he said, but the photographs taken days later failed to convey the urgency of that tragic disaster twenty-one years earlier. Photographs were vital to telling the story. Unlike the Doolittle Raid, which had occurred at the height of Japan's power and at that time was unlikely to be replicated, everyone understood that the attack on Musashino was only the beginning.

"I'd like you to rush to the scene of the raid," the superintendent-general continued, "and get compelling images. Of course, I know it's very dangerous. You have to be ready to die. If you die, it is an honorable death in the line of duty."

Saka rose from his chair and approached Ishikawa, placing his hand on his shoulder. "I wish you good luck," he said. "But you should not die. You live to the end."

Ishikawa had jumped at the assignment, which had proved exhausting as the tempo of American bombings increased. He would photograph raids during the day and then work until three or four a.m. in the darkroom, developing images and making enlargements. There fortunately hadn't been a raid in five days, allowing him a needed reprieve.

But throughout the day, as he mixed chemicals and developed images in the darkroom, Ishikawa couldn't escape the sense that something wasn't right.

Where were the Americans?

———

THE ADRENALINE RUSH of takeoff faded as pilots, navigators, and bombardiers settled in for the seven-hour-and-fifteen-minute flight to the target. This was the agonizing part of the mission, the calm before the storm. Airmen listened to the drone of the engines, checked and rechecked instruments, and stared down at the desolate ocean. "We had hours to think of the many things you do when under high stress," recalled John Cox. "What was going to happen? Would we be able to do the job? Would we ever see home again? How did we get into this predicament? Many philosophies and religions were developed and polished during those long hours."

Fear consumed many, particularly on this unorthodox operation. Gone was the protective high altitude that the airmen had learned to trust on previous missions. Gone was the safety of defensive formations. Gone, too, was each bomber's firepower. Other questions loomed. Would Japanese fighters be waiting for them? Attacking Tokyo was like kicking a hornet's nest. Would the flak shred them? "At such low altitudes," First Lt. Charles Morgan said, "all effective ground weapons could be brought to bear on our aircraft."

The fate of the entire mission—and all their lives—hinged on one advantage. "We were relying very much," noted Staff Sgt. Robert Webb, "on the element of surprise."

But that provided little comfort.

On board the *Lady Annabelle*, Cpl. John Dodd fingered his rosary. "I can't do this," he said repeatedly while shaking. "I can't do this. I can't do this."

Flight Officer Joseph Krogman, the bombardier, kept up his colorful earlier refrain, blasting LeMay. "Sonofabitch," he muttered. "Sonofabitch." He wasn't the only one to curse the general.

Aircraft commander Cox and his co-pilot Chester Marshall flew in silence on the *Mary Ann*, listening to the gentle tunes broadcast by Radio Saipan, including the Cole Porter hit "Don't Fence Me In." The late-day sun slid down the western sky before vanishing into the cold Pacific Ocean, leaving only an empty gray horizon that soon faded with the onset of night. "We flew in absolute darkness and with no lights showing," recalled Capt. Charles Philips. "Hundreds of B-29s were all in the same general area, all headed in the same direction at approximately the same speed. None of us knew where the others were."

The aerial armada stretched across hundreds of miles of sky, a loose procession of Superfortresses hammered out by workers in Wichita and Renton, Marietta and Omaha. The bellies of these bombers carried thousands of airmen, some of whom came from big cities, like Los Angeles, Chicago, and Boston. Many others called small towns home, places like North Freedom, Wisconsin, and Seminole, Oklahoma. The airmen who grasped the controls, checked fuel levels, and monitored the radar were the sons of ranchers and railroad men, chicken farmers and truckers, welders and missionaries. Some of the older ones had wives at home and even children. The colorful names painted across the noses of the bombers often reflected those roots, including the *Mary Ann*, named in honor of crew chief Fred Reed's firstborn.

One hour turned to two.

Then three.

The aircrews passed to the east of Iwo Jima, where American marines had now battled for nineteen days against a fanatical enemy who had retreated underground into the honeycomb network of caves and tunnels. "Victory here," Marine Maj. Gen. Harry Schmidt told the press only the day before, "will be obtained only by slow, pulverizing pressure."

Another 150 miles to the north, aircrews buzzed the Japanese-controlled islands of Haha Jima and Chichi Jima, part of the volcanic Bonin Islands chain. Searchlights tried to snare them and antiaircraft guns thundered. "This fire was meager," observed the 505th Bombardment Group's report, "but was level, leading and accurate."

The brief excitement, however, soon passed, and darkness once again enveloped the bombers. Occasionally the airmen spotted the glow of phosphorescence on the dark waves below, as though constellations were reflected from the sky above. The weather north of the Bonin Islands at times deteriorated; crews battled thunderstorms and lightning as well as hail, sleet, and even snow. The worst was the St. Elmo's Fire, atmospheric electricity that resembled blue lightning and radiated from a bomber's nose or wingtips, a powerful and eerie enough phenomenon to unnerve pilots and cause temporary blindness.

Four hours rolled into five.

In the cockpit of the *Mary Ann*, Radio Saipan faded, replaced by Japanese broadcasts that neither Cox nor Marshall could understand but that served as a reminder that each minute, each mile brought them closer to Tokyo. A few of the airmen would later report hearing Tokyo radio play a few ironic American hits, including "Smoke Gets in Your Eyes," "My Old Flame," and "When Strangers Meet." *Boston Globe* reporter Martin Sheridan, the only man on his plane without a task, alternated watching the crew work with glancing out the window. "During the night, the plane passed through several sharp squalls with heavy rain," he wrote. "Then the weather would clear quickly and the sky would be full of riding lights. Occasionally, a lightning flash startled us. Then pale blue flames would pour from our exhaust."

IN HIS OPERATIONS CENTER on Guam, LeMay brooded. He had instructed his senior aides to get some rest, leaving only the all-night operations control staff and clerks. LeMay refused to follow his own advice, even though it would be hours before the first strike reports arrived.

Those, too, would be only bare-bones accounts—one per squadron—of the time over the target, method of bombing, results observed, and flak and fighter opposition. LeMay would not develop a clear picture of the attack until the first planes touched down the following morning. Norstad, exhausted after flying for several days, took him up on the offer, crashing in the general's quarters with the promise of a call if anything came up. LeMay settled in to a night of pacing. "I would have rather gone," he said. "It was no fun, walking that floor."

The gravity of the mission hung over the general, who had staked the lives of more than three thousand airmen, the reputation and morals of the United States, and the fate of an entire city. This night, one way or another, would define LeMay for the rest of his life.

FRIDAY TURNED INTO Saturday as the bombers closed in on Japan.

Airmen chowed down on a late-night supper of peanut butter sandwiches and oranges, chasing them with grapefruit juice. Others popped Benzedrine sulfate tablets to keep them alert. Crews grabbed steel helmets and slipped on thirteen-pound flak jackets, made with one-millimeter manganese steel plates sewn inside to guard against shrapnel.

Enemy picket boats bobbing offshore spotted the bombers. Flares arced skyward followed by antiaircraft fire, but the airmen pressed on toward the Boso Peninsula, the fat finger of shoreline that guarded the entrance to Tokyo Bay and provided radarmen with an easily identifiable land–water contrast. From there, crews split up, approaching the city from two directions. Airmen with the 314th Bombardment Wing would fly north across the peninsula, paralleling the bay's eastern coastline. A prominent jut out into the water—one that radarmen would have no difficulty discerning on the primitive scope—was designated the initial point, where crews would turn and begin the long run across the bay and into the heart of the city.

Pilots with the 73rd and 313th Bombardment Wings would fly a northwesterly course, following the rugged Pacific coastline until hitting a recognizable spit of land that served as the initial point for those crews to hook west and start their bomb run.

War planners had selected four aiming points inside the rectangular target area. The first was the center of Asakusa, Tokyo's most densely populated residential district, one that, the 21st Bomber Command's report later noted, had "virtually no firebreaks." The second and third points fell east of the Sumida River in the populous Honjo and Fukagawa wards, areas designed to guarantee an even spread of fire across the right half of the target zone. The final aiming point was the center of the Nihonbashi ward—the commercial heart of the capital—bounded by the Ginza, Tokyo Station, the Imperial Palace, and the Sumida River.

Night, coupled with the city's blackout regulations, helped hide the sprawling capital of Japan as the bombers roared across the Boso Peninsula. Despite the rudimentary radar, operators could clearly make out the dark waters of the bay alongside the bright light of land. The Arakawa River, which snaked south along the eastern edge of the target area, stood out so clearly that operators could even see several bridges. To the west, the scope showed the mouth of the Sumida as well as the moat that encircled the Imperial Palace.

Ships in Tokyo Bay as well as shore guns sprang to life, hurling flak into the heavens as the first pathfinder armed with 122 M47 incendiaries closed in on the city. The twin bomb bay doors yawned open. A mile above the earth—and traveling at more than 330 feet per second—the Guam-based bomber charged across the black waters of Tokyo Bay, ready to deliver the first punch in a catastrophic new phase of the war, one that threatened to devastate block after block, city after city, until Japan surrendered. LeMay's gamble came down to this moment.

To this minute.

At 1:07 a.m. the first bombs plummeted down toward the crowded capital.

The battle had begun.

THE TEMPERATURES TUMBLED in Tokyo. The bitter wind out of the northwest that had plagued the city throughout the day picked up, chilling those few souls brave enough to venture outside. Aiko Matani's father had shut down the family's bathhouse early while a freshly clean Tsuta Kawai hustled home. "A strong wind contributed to an uncanny fear," he recalled, "unlike anything I had known before." Inside the palace, Emperor Hirohito hunkered down, surrounded by his family and servants. Throughout the capital, families huddled around the *kotatsu*, a lattice box containing a charcoal hibachi and covered with a blanket that served as a common heat source. Light was a precious commodity given the city's strict blackout regulations. A bulb wrapped in black cloth cast just enough of a dim glow for families to eat supper. Others curled up in blankets atop futons, including soon-to-be-six-years-old Shizuko Nishio, excited to celebrate her birthday. "It was necessary to go to bed as early as possible in order to get some sleep before the raiders came," recalled journalist Masuo Kato. "Satisfactory sleep was almost out of the question in most cities from the beginning of 1945 to the end of the war."

Haruyo Wada prepared for bed after a dinner of curry rice eaten off her favorite floral dish. Despite the difficult times, her father, who sold spices to local noodle shops, could always rustle up flavorings, from mustard and curry to red and black pepper. The family of five slept in a row atop the tatami mats on the first floor. Like many children, Haruyo had learned a trick to disrobe. She took off her clothes and folded them in a pile in the order she needed to put them back on, a move that would allow her to dress in the dark in case of an air raid. To the right of her outfit, she placed her emergency pack, which contained extra underwear, her favorite green sweater with pink frills, and pieces of rock candy. More important, it held her collection of treasures, beautiful labels she lifted off bottles and cans by soaking them in water and then hanging them in a window for the sun to dry. To the left, she placed her air raid hood, which her mother had made from an old light green kimono. Last, Haruyo set her leather shoes atop her clothes, which would hold up better in the event of a raid. At eight o'clock, she climbed beneath the blankets, excited to wake up and find Masao and her friends.

The embattled Japanese government planned to celebrate Army Memorial Day the next morning. In preparation, Hidetoshi Matsumura, spokesman for the Imperial General Headquarters, took to the airwaves to broadcast a reminder to the capital's residents.

"The darkest hour," he announced, "is just before the dawn."

At ten-thirty p.m., radios again crackled to life, alerting citizens that picket boats had spotted enemy bombers approaching the mainland from the south. The alarm prodded twelve-year-old Katsumoto Saotome, who had spent a long day hauling scrap at Kubota Iron Works, to reluctantly climb out of his warm bed in Mukojima ward. One of his chores required him to break the ice that formed atop his family's water tank, which was used to fight fires. Katsumoto stepped outside, where the raw winter wind lifted the wooden trash can lid while the telegraph lines that ran overhead buzzed. Katsumoto grabbed a pick and broke up the top layer of ice, fishing out the larger slabs and dropping them in the street. Then he hustled inside, blowing on the tips of his freezing fingers. His family was gathered in the dark, illuminated by the glow of the radio, listening to news reports. The Eastern Army District announced that American bombers, spotted over the Boso Peninsula, had in fact turned back to sea.

"I'll repeat," the broadcaster announced.

Katsumoto felt relieved. His father appeared in the front door, dressed in his dark firefighting uniform and with a three-foot-long bamboo water gun strapped to his back.

"It's over," he murmured.

"Dad, tomorrow is Army Memorial Day, isn't it?" the boy asked.

"Yes. But apparently that was a sneak peak," his father replied, a reference to the popular rumor that the United States would use the annual holiday as a premise to attack.

Police photographer Ishikawa climbed up to the headquarters roof for a look. Though American bombers usually attacked during the day, the most recent strike on March 4 had come in the middle of the night. That odd change of habit nagged at Ishikawa, prompting him to remain at work even after he had finished for the day at five p.m. From the rooftop, where in recent months he had watched other fires erupt around the city during strikes, he looked out through his spectacles over the dark capital, feeling the bitter cold gusts of wind. Searchlights combed the sky; he spotted the single headlight of a car below.

The darkness shielded the Superfortresses, but lookouts heard the aerial monsters skimming the landscape at just five thousand feet, a deep rumble that made the hair rise on the back of one's neck. The American bombers had not, as the military reported, turned back to sea.

The enemy was here.

Survivors would later report that before the wail of sirens, the thunder of explosions, and the crackle of fires, the first real sound of the attacks was the rushed footsteps of air wardens racing through the streets and alleys. The grumble of the bombers soaring over the capital drowned out the footfalls, followed by the first detonations at 12:08 a.m.[*]

The 100-pound M47 incendiaries, dropped at one-hundred-foot intervals, rained down across Fukagawa ward in the southeastern corner of the target area. Two minutes later blazes erupted to the east in the neighboring Joto ward, just outside the designated incendiary zone, followed by Honjo ward to the north. Winds at that moment gusted between seventeen and twenty-five miles per hour, feeding the fledgling fires that benefited from days of bitter dry air that had robbed wooden homes and shops of precious moisture.

Tokyo was a tinderbox.

Across the sprawling capital, even as the first American bombers streaked through the skies and fires erupted, many residents still slumbered, curled up under heavy blankets in blacked-out homes. Japan's early warning system had failed.

Seconds turned to minutes.

And the bombers still came.

Soaring across the Boso Peninsula, pilots pulled back on the controls

---

[*] Tokyo time was one hour behind Marianas time.

and climbed to attack altitude. Bomb bay doors sprang open, and bombardiers sited the target.

On the ground, the air raid alarm finally sounded at twelve-fifteen a.m., seven minutes after the first bombs exploded, a delay that cost many residents precious time to evacuate. Incoming B-29s sowed a heavy north-south line of incendiaries across Honjo ward, creating a river of fire. Other bombs exploded in Ushigome, Shitaya, Nihonbashi, Hongo, Kojimachi, and Shiba wards. Blazes in Asakusa ward sent sparks skyward, which caught the wind and blew across the Sumida River into neighboring Mukojima ward, where Katsumoto Saotome lived. The boy, after breaking up the ice, had climbed back in bed and fallen asleep.

"Katsumoto," his father hollered, "get up!"

He popped out of bed, stunned at the dazzling light shining through the window. The family's two-story rented home straddled the northeastern border of the target area. He grabbed his air raid hood and emergency bag along with his prized treasure, a cloth bag of old pennies. He raced downstairs, where chaos greeted him outside the front door. Bombers roared overhead while the ground shook from explosions, and fire truck sirens shrieked. "In every direction I looked," Katsumoto recalled, "it was a sea of flaming red fire."

"Katsumoto, what are you waiting for?" his mother hollered from the entrance of the family's air raid shelter. "Quickly!"

Neighbors poured out of surrounding homes.

"We should've eaten those extra rations," she added. "It would be better to die on a full stomach."

"Stupid," his father said of her remark. "This is different from usual," he continued. "Katsumoto, get our luggage ready!"

"Yes," the boy replied.

"Hurry up."

"Yes."

"Shizuko?" his father asked.

"She's still sleeping," Katsumoto said. "I'll go get her."

He darted back inside and up the stairs beside the kitchen. The glow from the fires outside illuminated the wall calendar, allowing him to read the letters without light. Back outside, black smoke climbed into the crimson sky as sparks rained down. A B-29 roared overhead, dropping incendiaries. The family hustled to load mattresses and kitchenware onto a handcart in preparation for escape, leaving behind their pet cat, Tomi.

"My, how beautiful," Katsumoto's sister said of the fires.

———

SEVEN MINUTES AFTER the first Guam-based Superfortresses hit Tokyo, crews from Rosie O'Donnell's Saipan wing joined the battle. Then at 1:26 a.m., nineteen minutes after the attack started, the first bombers from Tinian unloaded. Inbound pilots could see the dreaded searchlights that now illuminated the horizon, eerie bright fingers anxious to grab hold of any aerial intruders. Japanese fighters climbed into the skies to greet them as enemy gunners fired antiaircraft shells, though most of the flak exploded miles overhead. "The Jap defenses," observed the 313th's mission report, "were caught by surprise."

An aerial freight train of terror rumbled through the capital's skies. Nearly ten tons of bombs fell on average each minute of the attack. The clusters blew open a couple of thousand feet above the ground, scattering six-pound canisters of napalm. Those hexagonal cylinders guided by canvas streamers tore through the tile roofs of homes and shops, factories and businesses, spraying flaming jellied gasoline on walls, tatami mats, and mattresses.

Fires spread, melding into other blazes, and the illumination grew, a beacon for the incoming planes. "We headed," recalled Staff Sergeant Webb, a radio operator, "straight for that glow on the skyline that had been visible for some time by now."

General Power, one of the first to arrive over Tokyo, circled the skies, armed with a red grease pencil to mark each new fire on a map. "I watched," the general said, "block after block go up in flames until the holocaust had spread into a seething, swirling ocean of fire, engulfing the city below for miles in every direction."

CHAPTER 13

"I know what it is like to fly through the fires of hell."

—ARTHUR TOMES
OCTOBER 26, 2002

U p on the rooftop of the metropolitan police department, which was located near the Imperial Palace just west of the target area, photographer Koyo Ishikawa watched a searchlight grab one of the bombers, followed seconds later by antiaircraft fire. To the east the sky began to glow red, signaling a major fire. He ran to the basement air defense headquarters to find the phones ringing nonstop. A large map on the wall glimmered with red and blue lights indicating reports of fires in Fukagawa, Asakusa, and Honjo wards. This was big.

Ishikawa popped in to see his section chief, informing him he planned to rush to the scene. "Are you sure you want to go?" his boss asked. "The air raid tonight is different."

The photographer was certain.

"Be careful," his boss concluded. "Don't die."

Ishikawa grabbed his Leica loaded with Kodak film and jumped into his police-issued Chevrolet, which he had depended on over the last three and a half months to photograph the previous raids in Musashino, Ginza, and the city center. Along Showa Road, a major north-south thoroughfare, fire trucks and police security vehicles overtook him, their sirens blaring.

The photographer reached the intersection of Asakusabashi, the southern edge of densely populated Asakusa ward. To the north, Ishikawa could see the swirling flames as the fires seared homes, shops, and businesses. To the east, residents fleeing Honjo and Fukagawa wards poured across the expansive Ryogoku Bridge, which straddled the Sumida River. The strained voice of a police officer directing escapees competed with the screams and cries of women and children. "The congestion," Ishikawa later wrote in his diary, "was indescribable."

The photographer realized it was impossible to drive farther, so he parked his Chevy next to the police box at the base of the bridge. Ishikawa grabbed his camera and battled his way across. On the far side he finally reached the Ryogoku Police Station, which was surrounded by a wall of fire and heat that made it difficult to open his eyes.

Inside the chief's office, a messenger delivered a report, his uniform in tatters and his cheeks covered with soot and eyes bloodshot. The raid had killed power to the station, but the dance of flames outside the window illuminated the office and made the pale skin of the chief's face glow. The situation, the chief told Ishikawa, was hopeless.

"You should evacuate," he advised him, "as fast as you can."

Ishikawa stepped back outside, where the wind and smoke hit him. Instead of making photographs, he focused on survival. "Everywhere I looked," he wrote, "there was only fire." He dropped to his knees and crawled, desperately searching for a place to shield himself from the wind. Around him people collapsed and died. He pulled one knee in front of the other, as the flames roared. Mattresses and bags ignited into fireballs, rolling down the street. Ahead Ishikawa saw a stream of fire rush, like a torrent, shooting up side streets and alleys, picking up bodies. Flames overtook a nearby house, then jumped to the next, hollowing out homes. "The heat mixed with sparks covered me. I wondered how long I'd be able to endure," he recalled. "I was prepared for this to be the end of my life."

He closed his eyes.

"Don't die," he heard a voice say in his head.

Ishikawa thought of his colleagues, the police officers on the front lines of this blaze, bravely struggling against the roaring flames to save lives. He climbed from his knees to his feet. The photographer felt the fury rise up inside him. The heat burned his cheeks, and he choked on the smoke as he stumbled forward, collapsing behind a crumbling stone wall that shielded him from the wind. Ishikawa looked skyward. Between the clouds of billowing black smoke, he spotted bombers crisscrossing the heavens, unloading more and more incendiaries, the low altitude a mockery. "The flames," he said, "reflected on them, making the huge bodies, four engines, and tails look deep red, literally the wings of the devil."

RESIDENTS ACROSS TOKYO slipped on air raid hoods and grabbed brooms and buckets and headed out into the frigid cold to prepare to battle the blazes. Others collected prized possessions, from ration books and photos to family heirlooms, depositing them in shallow garden shelters. Amid this scramble, Shizuko Nishio's father roused her from sleep.

"Wake up! Wake up!" he hollered. "Go into the shelter!"

She jumped out of bed in the early morning hours of her sixth birthday. The Nishio family lived in the heart of Fukagawa ward, just one block from the air force's southeastern aiming point. Like most families, Shizuko's father had constructed an air raid shelter on the property, but he had done more than many in building it, adding steel rebar to reinforce its strength. He likewise stocked it with water, dried biscuits, canned food, and medical supplies, enough to last the family for a week. Shizuko climbed inside with her mother, her cousin Sumiko, four nurses, and the housekeeper. Her father then hustled to his assigned aid station, only to return soon after with dire news. "Tokyo," he told his family, "will be finished tonight."

The family would never survive in the primitive shelter, he warned, instructing them instead to seek refuge across the street inside the Takahashi National School.

"Go," he said, "to that public shelter."

The seven of them climbed out, leaving behind the food and medical supplies. Sumiko and one of the nurses ran ahead and entered the school, but a man at the gate blocked the other five, telling them the shelter had reached its capacity of four hundred people.

"You all have to go somewhere else," he said.

But where?

Bombers roared overhead as flames tore through the city.

The family hustled toward Sumida Technical High School, approximately ten blocks to the southeast, entering the basement shelter. Others soon followed, swelling the total to about seventy, a mix of elderly neighbors as well as women and children, those who were too young to evacuate. Most of the men were either fighting in the war or outside battling blazes, as mandated by the law. The shelter, protected by an iron door, left much to be desired. The attack had killed power throughout the district, and there was no heat to fend off the freezing night air. Puddles of water covered the cold concrete floor, preventing anyone from sitting down. Many of the children, plucked out of warm beds only moments earlier, were tired. Shizuko's mother lifted her up and placed her atop her shoulders. Despite the misery, she was safe.

At least for now.

———

HARUYO WADA'S FATHER likewise rustled her out of bed.

"It's different tonight," he warned. "Get up!"

In the dark, Haruyo slipped on her clothes in the order she had taken them off. She grabbed her emergency backpack stuffed with her favorite sweater, candy, and bottle labels before pulling on her air raid hood and rushing outside. The wind chilled her. Several neighbors hustled past, hunched over like shrimp with bags on their backs, all headed toward the nearby Kameido Train Station, which served as the community's evacuation center since the new national school remained under construction. The distant horizon glowed red.

Haruyo spotted her friend Masao armed with a pole, breaking up the ice in his family's firefighting tank. The Wadas shared an air raid shelter along the sidewalk, which had acted as the children's command post hours earlier, with the neighboring Furuhashi family, the majority of whom were already seated down below. Haruyo's fourteen-year-old brother Sôichiro rushed to defend the factory where he worked, leaving her father Saburo alone to battle any blazes. The eight-year-old followed her mother and younger sister into the earthen shelter, which measured about six feet long and three feet deep. Her father and brother had helped dig it the previous year, shoveling the earth into sandbags that formed the curved roof and gave the bunker the appearance of a burial mound. The floor consisted of a slatted board with wooden seats along the wall. The air smelled of musty soil.

No one talked as the minutes passed.

Voices trickled inside followed by hurried footsteps passing overhead. The excitement increased with the sound of explosions and the crackling of fires. The calls of frantic parents searching for children blended with Haruyo's own cries. "The sounds came in layers, one noise over another," she recalled. "I was horrified. I put my hands over my ears."

Her father peered into the shelter.

"Get out," he demanded. "You will be steamed to death. Get out now."

The shelter had only one entrance, so if fire or smoke blocked it, everyone would be trapped. Haruyo's mother and sister climbed out. Haruyo rose to follow them when the next-door neighbor grabbed the back of her clothes.

"Stay here," Mrs. Furuhashi instructed her. "You will die if you leave."

Haruyo froze.

Her father had ordered her to leave; her mother and sister had obeyed. But now her neighbor demanded she remain. Haruyo reached down and snatched her clothes from her neighbor's hand and hurried up the exit. The entire landscape outside had changed. Fires engulfed nearby stores and homes while a flood of people rushed past.

Across the street rose a berm, on top of which ran the train tracks that led to Kameido Station. The family climbed the hill, which afforded them an aerial view of the neighborhood. Firefighters had arrived, spraying the flames with water, but the blazes accelerated, jumping from business to business and home to home. Haruyo's entire world was aglow. Her eyes moved down the block. Fires destroyed the neighborhood store where the children bought candies for a penny and the home of the local pediatrician, the kind gentleman who made house calls late at night to treat sick children. Gone, too, was Masao's house.

And her own.

———

WITH THE CART LOADED with kitchenware and bedding, Katsumoto Saotome and his family prepared to escape. He slipped on his cloth air raid hood, beneath which he had tied his kamikaze headband featuring the rising red sun. He wore his national defense uniform, which included a tag sewn on the chest that listed his school along with his name, home address, and blood type. To guard against the cold, he pulled on his brother's stiff white judo robe and a pair of gaiters to protect his legs. Underneath this outfit, he carried his emergency bag along with a rubber trumpet attached to his belt, which he needed to return to a friend. Last, he grabbed his pouch of treasured pennies, which rattled with each step.

The family's Mukojima home straddled the northern edge of the target area. They needed to make it only a few blocks north to reach safety. The winds from neighboring Asakusa ward, however, blew sparks south across the Sumida River, making it appear as though fires blocked any such path. Skies to the south, east, and west glowed red. A dark sliver of sky to the southeast appeared to offer the only promise of safety. Katsumoto took up a position to the rear of the family's two-wheeled cart, the type that would normally be towed behind a bicycle. "I pushed the back of the cart," he said, "while my father pulled it."

Sparks rained down, and the fierce wind out of the northwest blew against his back. Bombers continued to buzz overhead, searching out spots where fires had not yet started. Katsumoto failed to grasp the danger of the situation. Though he might lose his home, the twelve-year-old did not yet understand the threat to his life. "Once we reached the main road, we could see an avalanche of people running away from the blaze, some with mattresses or blankets around their bodies, some holding their children's hands, yet others clutching onto their valuables," he recalled. "They were all running frantically."

The family joined the southbound herd, all headed into the heart of the conflagration. "The air might catch on fire, don't you think?" his mother, Rin, asked. Katsumoto's sisters Shizuko and Sayoko flanked either side of the cart while his mother joined him in pushing, chattering nervously. At one point, he could see the fires reflected in her glasses. "Everywhere is burning," she continued. "What should we do?"

The family reached the Hikifune River. Once over the bridge, his mother suddenly announced she had to return home. She had forgotten to grab the photograph of Katsumoto's older brother, Kikuo, who had been conscripted into the army. A trip back to the house, the youth realized, would rival a journey through hell.

"Idiot," Katsumoto's father said without stopping. "Now is not the time to think of someone who isn't here."

His mother fell silent from the scolding. Katsumoto would later appreciate the pain she must have felt, imagining his brother's photograph melting in the flames.

The family ran into Mrs. Tori from the neighborhood and her only son, Iwao, who was in the same grade at school as Katsumoto. The family owned a local watchmaking business, though Iwao's father had been drafted into the military the previous spring.

"Oh, you," Katsumoto's mother exclaimed.

Her startled reaction reflected the frazzled mentality that affected so many at that moment, as evidenced by the crowds that included people carrying tatami mats on their heads and stones used to make pickled radish in bicycle baskets. Katsumoto spotted others with blankets around their shoulders, reminding him of the comic book hero Golden Bat. Mrs. Tori had done similarly, wrapping a mattress around her waist and tying it with a belt over which she hung a pair of clogs. Iwao did the same. He wore an adult's steel helmet with a floor pillow tied around his belly and back. He had several pairs of clogs dangling from his belt.

"Did you bring the watches, too?" Katsumoto jokingly asked.

"No," he said, "but I have clogs."

Katsumoto was impressed, remembering the radio mentioning that rubber-soled shoes might melt during incendiary attacks. The two families continued together. The cart had to squeeze through the crowds of people while sparks continued to rain down. "The fire was like a living thing," Katsumoto recalled. "It ran, just like a creature, chasing us."

The family hurried over the Tobu-Kameido train tracks. One of the cart tires bounced, sending the lid of a pot rolling down a nearby alley. "I immediately ran after it because I knew we couldn't replace that lid even if we had the money," Katsumoto said. "Everything was scarce, especially steel objects that were confiscated by the military to produce weapons and ammunition. If we didn't have that lid, we couldn't even cook rice."

A few steps ahead a father in an oversize coat escaped with his daughter, whom Katsumoto guessed was no older than four. A B-29 emerged from the purple flames, zooming so low that he thought it might hit a utility pole. The wings appeared bloodred.

"They're falling down on us," the man yelled. "They're coming down."

Katsumoto looked up and saw incendiary bomblets, which looked like flaming arrows streaking toward him. An explosion thundered. The boy dropped to the ground, clutching his rescued pot lid, and curled up like a dog. He squeezed his eyes shut, but he could still see the blinding flash of light. He blinked a second later to find a scene of horror. Flaming debris had struck the neck of the man steps in front of him. Another grazed the shoulder of a nearby woman and lodged in a utility pole, igniting it like a torch. Amid the carnage stood the young girl, miraculously alive but petrified and splattered with the blood of others.

His father emerged from the flames, only his face and mouth visible.

"Katsumoto," he cried, "what happened?"

MINUTE BY MINUTE, the inferno grew.

Inbound pilots could see the haunting red glow of Tokyo on the horizon from fifty miles away, a distance that soon doubled to one hundred miles.

And then two hundred.

One after the other, the bombers came, drawn like moths to a flame. Closer to Tokyo cockpit windshields framed a towering black cloud of smoke illuminated by the fires below, an ominous thunderhead rising thousands of feet.

Japanese gunners, who recovered from the initial shock of the attack, zeroed in on the invaders as powerful searchlights swept the skies. No sooner did a light seize a B-29 than others locked on and illuminated the silver bombers, allowing multiple gunners to focus their fury. The lucky ones unloaded their bombs and vanished back into the dark night on the far side of the target. But others were not so fortunate. Flak shrapnel tore through the thin aluminum skin with each deafening punch, severing hydraulic lines and shredding wires and even flesh. Communications systems failed, and gauge needles spun. Blinded pilots wrestled dead controls as engines erupted in flames. Two bombers exploded at 1:35 a.m. Another fell at 1:56 a.m., followed three minutes later by a fourth. "I saw several," recalled Lt. Bob Van Gieson, "go down in majestic slow-moving, burning spirals."

Searchlights soon zeroed in on Van Gieson's bomber, *Doc's Deadly Dose*. "Brilliant blue light filled the cockpit; light so intense it pained the eyes and blotted out the instrument panel," the aircraft commander later wrote. "Hammering explosions slammed the plane from every side! Shrapnel pierced the nose damaging the instrument lighting system."

But such attacks could not stop the raid.

Not tonight.

Bomber after bomber roared over the capital, a parade of aeronautical might that represented the culmination of Hap Arnold's crusade. "It is difficult to describe a conflagration ignited so swiftly and spreading so far," an amazed General Power scribbled in his notes. "At least a score of separate areas from fifty to a thousand city blocks were burning at the same time." The fear that had gripped many of the airmen on the long flight north gave way to awe and even wonderment. "It was mind boggling," remembered pilot Bob Vaucher, "to see so much on fire." The ground below appeared to move, like lava, prompting many of the airmen to compare the image to Dante's *Inferno*. "It felt like you were staring into the mouth of hell," recalled Second Lt. David Braden. "You cannot imagine a fire that big."

Others echoed him.

Staff Sgt. LeRoy "Trip" Triplett, a radarman on *Gamecock*, recorded what he saw in his diary. "As far as the eye could see, to the east and the north, there was a sea of flame, a mass of roaring fire that seemed to cover the city like a boiling cauldron," he wrote. "How could this fire ever be put out? How could anyone possibly live through the sea of hell?"

But the experience was far more visceral for some, as best described by *Boston Globe* reporter Martin Sheridan, who flew in the B-29 nicknamed *Patches*. "I not only saw Tokyo burning furiously in many sections," he wrote afterward, "but I smelled it."

He wasn't alone.

Smoke from the fires wafted up through the bomb bay doors and circulated through the Superfortresses. Pilots and navigators, gunners and flight engineers—long shielded from such carnage by miles of clouds and sky—inhaled the acrid aroma of the dying city, the scent of roasted bank ledgers and machine lathes, rooftops and floorboards, bedding and wardrobes. Mixed among the incinerated wood and paper, however, was the sickening stench of burnt flesh, from dogs and horses to mothers and fathers. The greasy scent sickened many of the airmen. "It was," as Capt. Charles Phillips would later write, "the smell of death."

A mile above Tokyo, the fires blazed so bright that airmen could read the dials on their wristwatches. Those at higher altitudes looked down upon the sleek silhouettes of other bombers. "The whole area," Chester Marshall wrote in his diary, "was lighted as if it were broad daylight." The ominous cloud over Tokyo grew, climbing more than twenty thousand feet. Crews had no choice but to fly through the storm of smoke and broiling heat where bits of paper and debris swirled, propelled into the heavens by the thermal updraft of a city aflame. Those same forces battered the bombers. "Crewmen," one reporter wrote, "rattled around inside the ships like bones in a dice cup." Phillips entered the cloud, hoping to hide from the flak, but immediately regretted it. "It was tumultuous. All my skill was required as an instrument pilot to bring us back to a wings-level condition, over and over again," he wrote. "Those of us in the forward crew compartment could actually see pieces of window and door frames flying by the airplane."

Those forces hurled airplanes higher into the sky. One bomber jumped from 7,000 feet to 12,000 feet in seconds. The heat flipped another bomber upside down.

"How the hell do you roll a B-29?" the pilot hollered.

"Pull back the throttles on one and two," the flight engineer replied.

Phillips popped out of the storm, his bomb bay empty, and banked his bomber to begin the long return flight to the Marianas. Until this moment, he had been focused on reaching the target and accomplishing his mission. "During this turn we began to grasp the enormity of the conflagration going on a mile or so below us," he recalled. "The explosions and fire resulting from the Pearl Harbor attack produced all kinds of horror, but this fire in Tokyo must have ranked as one of the most horrendous fires in the history of mankind." The gravity of the mission hit home for others as well. "This blaze will haunt me forever," another pilot said, crossing himself. "It's the most terrifying sight in the world, and, God forgive me, it's the best."

CHAPTER 14

"You could smell the flesh burning."

—FISKE HANLEY

OCTOBER 13, 1999

McKelway returned to the operations center around two a.m. The news reporters had watched the bombers take off and then sat down to type up their stories. McKelway would not release those articles until the first bombs-away reports confirmed the raid was under way.

The public affairs officer found LeMay seated alone on a bench, a cigar in his mouth, surrounded by walls plastered with maps, charts, and graphs. LeMay asked why McKelway wasn't in bed. The public affairs officer started to explain that he wanted to confirm the mission's success, but he sensed the general's attention was elsewhere.

"I'm sweating this one out myself," LeMay said. "A lot could go wrong."

McKelway listened.

"I can't sleep," LeMay continued. "I usually can, but not tonight."

McKelway collapsed on the bench beside him and fired up a cigarette.

"If this raid works the way I think it will, we can shorten this war," LeMay said. "In a war, you've got to try to keep at least one punch ahead of the other guy all the time. A war is a very tough kind of proposition. If you don't get the enemy, he gets you."

McKelway smoked and listened.

"I think we've figured out a punch he's not expecting this time," LeMay said. "I don't think he's got the right flak to combat this kind of raid and I don't think he can keep his cities from being burned down— wiped right off the map. He hasn't moved his industries to Manchuria yet, although he's starting to move them, and if we can destroy them before he can move them, we've got him. I never think anything is going to work until I've seen the pictures after the raid, but if this one works we will shorten this damned war out here."

LeMay looked at his watch.

"We won't get a bombs-away for another half hour," the general announced. "Would you like a Coca-Cola? I can sneak in my quarters without waking up the other guys and get two Coca-Colas and we can drink them in my car. That'll kill most of the half hour."

The duo climbed into his staff car and drove the hundred yards to his quarters. LeMay hopped out and retrieved the soft drinks. The officers drank them in the dark, staring at the wall of jungle. Fifteen hundred miles to the north, as LeMay sipped his sugary soda, a city burned. The normally reserved general chatted away, not about the mission but about India, no doubt anxious for a mental diversion from the stress that weighed upon him at that moment. "The way all those people are in India gets you down," he said. "It makes you feel rotten."

The men drifted back to the operations center. Tensions soared as LeMay awaited word from Tokyo. Had Japanese fighters shredded his crews? What about flak?

He had no idea.

The first bombs-away message arrived, which was forwarded to Washington at 2:55 a.m. "First aircraft bombed primary target by radar," it stated. "Several large fires reported."

Good news.

More reports, each relayed to Washington, amplified the information.

"Many fires, large fires and general conflagration," read another. "Enemy air opposition none to slight. Flak moderate to heavy."

"Observed reports of many fires. No enemy air opposition. Flak none," stated a follow-up message. "Visually reported general conflagration."

The previously empty operations center now hummed, as LeMay's senior aides arrived, poring over reports. "It looks pretty good," LeMay said to Montgomery. "But we can't really tell a damn thing about results until we get the pictures tomorrow night. Anyway, there doesn't seem to have been much flak. We don't seem to have lost more than a few airplanes."

News reporters likewise materialized, anxious for word of the attack. LeMay told them what he knew at two-thirty a.m. "From reports from planes at this hour I can say with conservatism that this looks good from our point of view and grim from the point of view of the enemy," he said. "There is a conflagration in Tokyo tonight. How big and how devastating it will turn out to be must be judged when all crews have returned and have reported their observations in detail. And the final proof will be in the photos that come in after that."

ON THE GROUND in Tokyo, bookstores burned.

So did noodle shops and fish markets, warehouses and apartments.

As the fires intensified, the resulting hot air rushed skyward, creating the thermal updrafts that battered the bombers. Carbonized resins from the wood, piggybacking on the escaping heat, oxidized in the air, turning into red or white hot embers that blew like seeds, helping to pollinate new blazes. The depletion of air at the center of the fire created a vacuum, pulling fresh oxygen in from the perimeter to fuel the growing inferno. That rush of air, which approached hurricane-force speeds, spawned a firestorm, as happened at Hamburg and Dresden. The windspeed at the blaze's perimeter climbed to twenty-eight miles per hour, which fanned the flames and bent the thermal updraft closer to the ground. That heat, unable to escape, turned the city into an oven. Soaring temperatures preheated homes and businesses, making them even more vulnerable to the encroaching fires. Winds swept embers through open doors and windows or deposited them on sills, eaves, and cornices.

The fires grew by the minute, feeding on the timber shops in Honjo and Fukagawa wards. In nearby Joto ward, the munitions factories and gasoline tanks of the Rising Sun Petroleum Company ignited along with the piles of coal at Kubota Iron Works in Asakusa. Five fires in Joto soon merged to create a single blaze that spanned the entire district. The same occurred in Asakusa, where four fires morphed into one. The flames from Fukagawa collided with the blazes in neighboring Honjo and Joto, creating a massive inferno that covered three wards. The Fukagawa Fire Department was the first to respond, dispatching fifteen trucks to battle the blazes. Incendiaries hit two of those, killing all the firefighters. Flames shortly swallowed the rest. Within half an hour, the Tokyo Fire Department was overwhelmed.

The winds at the blaze's perimeter reached fifty-five miles per hour while gusts inside the inferno topped out at more than seventy. Unlike a typical firestorm, which is stationary, Tokyo devolved into a conflagration, which one postwar study determined was at least four times more destructive. The winds drove the blaze leeward, creating a wall of fire three miles long that spread across the capital, feeding on block after block of homes, shops, and businesses. Residents could look skyward to see this terrifying phenomenon bearing down on them. "It seemed," recalled twenty-eight-year-old Seiichi Tonozuka, "like a wave crest approaching from beyond the ocean." The gale-force winds, sparked by the tidal wave of fire, tore trees from the ground and toppled cars and trucks. "Galvanized iron plates and mattresses soared into the air like pieces of paper," said fourteen-year-old Suzue Kobayashi. The winds proved strong enough to rip the clothes off people rushing through the streets.

The firebreaks that workers had hacked through the densely populated neighborhoods were hopelessly inadequate to arrest the advancing flames, but they did at least provide added paths for escape. Residents abandoned their futile efforts to fight fires with water guns, brooms, and bucket relays, crowding inside homemade shelters, with some going so far as to urinate on mattresses to keep them from burning. Others hustled toward the open grounds of temples, parks, and riverbanks or sought safety inside schools, government offices, and train stations, hoping the modern concrete and rebar construction would prove impermeable to fire. So many residents flooded the streets pushing carts piled high with bedding, kimonos, and kitchenware that police struggled to direct foot traffic, warning people not to stop and gawk. "Walk with your hand on the shoulder of the person in front of you," officers ordered. "If you fall, you're done."

People soaked air raid hoods with water from firefighting cisterns and used helmets to splash themselves, only to discover that the intense heat dried clothes in seconds. As temperatures soared, residents abandoned bikes, wagons, and bags, clogging already narrow alleys and bridges, which only slowed escape. Katsumoto Saotome passed an upright piano along the side of the road that someone had tried to rescue. Downed power lines and poles only added to the obstacles. Throngs of dazed escapees boxed in twenty-year-old veterinary student Kosuke Shindo, who found that he could turn neither left nor right. Refugees pushed from behind, cutting off his retreat just as new fires erupted ahead, blocking any escape forward.

Along wider streets, trams ignited as well as fire trucks and police vehicles. "The tops of utility poles," Tonozuka remembered, "bloomed like flaming flowers." Men, women, and children choked on acrid black smoke, the by-product of burning pine, bamboo, tar, and solvents. The smoke and the heat burned throats while eyes watered. Sparks rained down, singeing eyebrows and lashes. Others fluttered down shirt collars and up sleeves. "I couldn't breathe," recalled ten-year-old Kakinuma Michi. "I couldn't open my eyes." Many contemplated death. "What will happen to me?" Yoshiko Hashimoto wondered. "How painful will it be to burn to death?"

The glow of the conflagration turned night into day, illuminating the capital as if it were noontime. Asphalt roads softened into a sticky goo that clung, like quicksand, to bicycle tires and shoe soles. The fires produced a deafening roar like a freight train, drowning out the cries of husbands separated from wives, children from parents. "The pain caused by the heat and smoke," said twenty-six-year-old Aoki Hiroshi, "was beyond imagination." The winds sent bags tumbling down streets and ripped children from the grip of parents. "The town was a blazing hell," recalled Sumi Ogawa, "lit by the swirling and roiling flames."

Residents fled down narrow roads, which resembled tunnels through the flames. The superheated air caused people's clothes and even hair to spontaneously ignite. Evacuees gasped, struggling to breathe. Sixteen-year-old Minoru Tsukiyama, a mobilized student in Fukagawa, watched a first-grader struggle to remove his air raid hood, which had caught fire. "As if suddenly soaked in gasoline, his whole body burst into flames."

Fires cut off any escape route for nineteen-year-old Fumiko Naka-gawa, who had fled her Joto ward home with her father. Surrounded by flames, the duo had no choice but to huddle with others in a row in the middle of the street as buildings on both sides of them burned. A mother sat near Fumiko, her infant clutched in her arms. The baby began to cry, prompting the woman to suddenly stand. In a flash her hair ignited.

"Help!" she screamed, running around. "Help!"

With each step, the flames grew larger, turning the woman into a human torch. Fumiko watched in horror as the mother and her infant burned to death. But she wasn't the only one in the group. A young husband and wife shielded two children between them when the father suddenly caught fire. He refused to move, hoping to protect the infants.

"Please forgive me," he cried to his wife. "Please forgive me."

Eight-year-old Haruyo Wada witnessed similar horrors from her perch atop the berm where she fled with her parents. She saw a man try to save his horse, which caught on fire. "He held onto the rope of the horse really tight with both of his hands. He stayed right beside the horse," she recalled, "so he was burned to death together with his horse."

The fires spread to the bottom of the berm.

"We must run away," her father hollered.

The family held hands against the wind and fled down the tracks toward the Kameido Train Station. En route, sparks ignited Haruyo's green air raid hood.

"Take it off!" her father screamed.

She released her father's hand to untie the chin straps. A blast of wind seized the hood, carrying it up into the air. Another gust toppled Haruyo. When she climbed on her feet, she found she was separated from her parents. Steps in front of her, Haruyo spotted a person on fire, engulfed in blue and green flames, like a specter. The person raised a hand to warn her away. "It was so scary," she recalled, "but it looked so beautiful at the same time."

Haruyo backtracked only to tumble again, this time over a downed utility pole. She felt the burning heat on her back. Seconds later a hand grabbed her and pulled her away.

"Dad?" she hollered. "Is it you, Dad?"

The roar of the wind and the crackle of the fires drowned out any response.

"Are you my Dad?" she continued to shout.

But only chaos answered.

"Are you my Dad?"

The person who grabbed her pulled her down to the ground amid the sea of flames, wrapping himself around her like a protective cape. Smoke and sparks swirled. Other people piled on top. "We are Japanese," she heard someone shout. "We shall survive."

Haruyo slipped in and out of consciousness.

"Don't die," she heard someone plead.

She faded again.

THE FLAMES SPARED nothing.

Bathhouses burned. So did dentist offices and barber shops, grocery stores and florists. Tokyo's sea of congested residential areas fueled the inferno. Just as American tests in the Utah desert had demonstrated, fires attacked the wood and mud-plaster walls, while excessive heat cracked and splintered clay roof tiles. Fires raced through rooms adorned with tatami mats and sliding shoji doors. *Kotatsu* burned, along with chests of drawers and tables. Inside kitchens, the heat melted rice bowls and teakettles, fusing porcelain dishes together. Residents in the fire's path who sought shelter in the shallow bunkers the government had mandated perished. "Most of them," one report later noted, "were burned beyond recognition."

The solid concrete walls of schools, which served as designated evacuation centers, trapped heat like ovens. Men, women, and children crammed inside cavernous auditoriums, where in peaceful times students sang songs and celebrated graduations along with the emperor's birthday. Others overflowed into nearby classrooms and offices, stairwells and bathrooms, where desperate evacuees doused themselves with water from toilet tanks. Inside the community restroom of Takahashi National School in Fukagawa, where thirty or so people huddled shoulder to shoulder, a mother with a young child grabbed Tomoji Ishikura, a forty-seven-year-old office worker and fire defense leader. "Die with me," she begged. "Die with me on behalf of my husband."

Windows framed the horror outside. At Meiji National School in Fukagawa, nine-year-old Koiri Ino watched fires incinerate a block of houses across the street in minutes. The center of the blaze, he noted, burned bright white, indicating temperatures in excess of 2,400 degrees, hot enough to melt the water pipes. Sixteen-year-old Itaru Yamaguchi looked out the auditorium window at Kawaminami National School. "I suddenly saw a gruesome spectacle," the youth recalled. "It was a woman whose entire body was on fire, her hair burning bright red. She was screaming and desperately banging on the door of the auditorium. In the extreme situation I had to abandon the urge to save her, because of the increased difficulty people already had breathing and the danger letting her in would have posed to everyone inside."

The blizzard of embers ignited school gates, woodpiles, and playgrounds where children once enjoyed recess, warping metal sliding boards. Refugees battled to keep out the blazes, barricading windows with desks and organizing bucket brigades from school swimming pools. The lack of oxygen, however, threatened many who struggled to breathe and grew tired. The wired-glass windows began to crack. Evacuees fled up stairwells, hiding under second- and third-floor desks. Others escaped onto rooftops or plunged into frigid swimming pools. That was the case for Sumiko Morikawa, a twenty-four-year-old housewife in Honjo whose husband had been conscripted for army service. Sumiko climbed into the half-empty pool next to Yokogawa National Elementary School with her four-year-old son, Kiichi, and twin eight-month-old girls, Ryoko and Atsuko, one of whom she carried in her arms and the other on her back. Others soon crowded in the pool. Flames consumed the neighboring school, making it painful for Sumiko to even open her eyes as she swatted sparks away from her children. She could sense the agony of the twins, who cried and kicked at her with their tiny feet. "Mommy," Kiichi cried, "it's so hot!"

"Soon the flames will burn out," she assured him. "Please endure until then."

Twenty-five-year-old Mitsuko Terashima, who sought refuge inside the Neutralization National School in Honjo, watched as smoke seeped inside the building. "The windows in the hallway began to melt because of the fire around the school," she recalled. "It melts into a hole. It is unstoppable because the force of the fire is like a flamethrower."

Sparks invaded through liquefied windows and doors, setting fire to wooden shoe racks at school entrances and the curtains that hung in classrooms. Fires hopscotched through crowds. "Throw away your luggage," people screamed. "If you don't throw away your luggage you will burn to death."

But it was too late.

Corridors and stairwells functioned like chimneys, funneling superheated air and toxic gases throughout the buildings. Ishikura, trapped inside the bathroom at Takahashi National School, lost consciousness. Evacuees collapsed in hallways and school entrances. Hundreds passed out in pools, only to drown. The smoke and heat made it impossible for Sumiko Morikawa to open her eyes any longer. She could hear the voices of neighbors in the pool around her, crying out for loved ones. Her infant twins fell silent and succumbed while she desperately struggled to keep her son awake.

"Kiichi, steady! Don't fall asleep," she pleaded. "Don't leave me alone."

The fire roared, forcing her to shout.

"I want to see Dad," the boy finally muttered.

"Kiichi, let's try hard! We're going to see them all," she begged, shaking her son to keep him alert. "We're going to see Dad. Hold on, Kiichi!"

She then fainted.

Throughout Asakusa and Honjo, Fukagawa and Nihonbashi, these former places of learning and communal safety devolved into death traps for thousands. "I never thought," one survivor said, "that the whole auditorium would become a big crematorium."

Desperate evacuees at Sumida High School banged on the door of the basement shelter where Shizuko Nishio sat atop her mother's shoulders. Carbon monoxide poisoning led the youth, who only hours earlier had gone to sleep excited to celebrate her sixth birthday, to flutter in and out of consciousness.

"Shizuko," her mother called. "Shizuko."

The sudden pounding on the iron door perked her up. Shizuko expected that the adults would open up and allow the others inside. But no one moved. The threat of fire, smoke, and poisonous gas kept those inside rooted in place "Open the door," someone demanded.

"Let us in!" others cried. "Let us in!"

The voices grew more frantic.

More desperate.

But no one moved.

"They were shouting so hard," Shizuko recalled. "I naturally expected the adults inside the shelter would be sure to open the door, but the door was never opened."

Similar tragedies unfolded across the capital, as residents perished inside police boxes and post offices. Fires ravaged the two-story Tokyo Metropolitan Fukagawa Maternity Hospital, killing nearly 130 people. Scores more died inside the Sumida Branch of the Central Telephone Office and the Kameido Train Station. Beyond homes, schools, and government buildings, the conflagration claimed cherished cultural landmarks, including the Asakusa Kannon Temple with its five-story pagoda. "It burned," one survivor recalled, "completely in the blink of an eye."

To the south in neighboring Nihonbashi, residents swarmed the Meijiza Theater, a four-story concrete structure perched atop an expansive basement. The fifteen-hundred-seat theater, which was destroyed during the Great Kanto Earthquake in 1923, had opened again a decade later, this time designed to withstand both earthquakes and fires. A fire broke out in the basement dressing rooms, prompting some to suffocate. Others smashed windows and jumped out onto the street below. Fires ultimately killed some 350 people. "Life and death," one survivor said, "were decided in a short time."

While many sought shelter in concrete structures, others fled toward parks and the river. In crowded Asakusa, thousands rushed to Sumida Park, a sprawling forty-seven-acre oasis that ran along both the eastern and western banks of the river. The city had designed the park, which featured a promenade planted with cherry blossom trees, in the wake of the 1923 earthquake, as part of the effort to provide increased open space in the event of future fires. The military had installed an antiaircraft gun and erected barracks there for troops. Efforts by troops to block desperate residents from congregating soon failed as men, women, and children flooded the lawn, pushing carts and carrying bags. Evacuees overflowed onto the riverbanks, where some slathered their skin in mud to protect themselves. Others joined hands in prayer.

"Save me, Amida Buddha," evacuees chanted.

The Kototoi Bridge, trumpeted on postcards as one of the sixteen great bridges of Tokyo, spanned the river, linking the Asakusa and Mukojima sides of the parks. The low-strung steel bridge, supported in the middle of the river by two stone piers, stretched nearly eight hundred feet long and was almost seventy-five feet wide. Author Yasunari Kawabata described the park's elegant span as the middle rail of the letter *H*. Thousands of residents crowded atop the bridge along with bicycles, chests of drawers, and tea dais, giving the expansive bridge the feel of a flea market. "You had to step on people," one survivor recalled, "to cross the bridge."

Thirty-eight-year-old housewife Toshie Takagi, who had left her husband at home to battle the blazes, struggled with her three children to cross, the youngest an infant strapped to her back. The family's baggage made her job all the more burdensome. "You can leave your mother," she told her nine-year-old son, Tadashi. "Go on and cross over."

The superheated air, combined with the blizzard of sparks, set luggage in the adjacent park on fire. Refugees raced to the banks of the river, hurling mattresses and bags into the dark waters. The army barracks exploded in flames, and then suddenly the dead winter lawn erupted. "In an instant," one survivor recalled, "it turned into a sea of fire."

But it wasn't only the lawn.

"The bridge is on fire," someone screamed.

Like a bolt of lightning, flames shot across the span from Asakusa to Mukojima. "The heat," recalled Toshie, "ignited the bridge all at once. It was a white hot fire."

"Mommy, it hurts," Toshie heard her daughter Tamae cry.

People all around her toppled like dominoes. Others plummeted over the railing into the frigid river. Toshie jumped, but she was still close enough to the riverbank that she landed atop the concrete road below, injuring her back and breaking her left hand. The infant daughter on her back survived, but her other daughter Tamae and son Tadashi both perished in the fire. Their deaths would forever haunt her. "I wondered," she later said, "how to apologize to my husband for burning my children to death."

Similar tragedies unfolded atop other bridges that crisscrossed the target area. Twenty-four-year-old Honjo housewife Yoshiko Hashimoto, whose husband had reported to his duty station to fight the fires, fled with her infant son Hiroshi and parents atop the Sanno Bridge over the Tate River. Residents escaping Honjo collided with people fleeing neighboring Fukagawa, creating gridlock as both sides pushed against each other.

"Lie down," her father instructed her.

Yoshiko's infant suddenly cried. She pulled the baby off her back to discover that his cheeks glowed red from an ember trapped in his mouth. She jammed her finger into his mouth and fished it out as the family crouched in a huddle together. Her eyelashes melted, and her hair sizzled from the heat. Yoshiko's mother lay on top of her, and her father covered them all. Yoshiko closed her eyes and prayed. Even with her lids squeezed tight, she could still see the bright light of the flames. "I don't want to die," she thought. "I want to live."

Her father suddenly jumped up, grabbed her, and shook her shoulders. "Yoshiko," he shouted. "Jump into the river!"

She stood up. The fires framed her mother's face as she removed her air raid hood and placed it on Yoshiko. With her baby clutched in her arms, Yoshiko climbed atop the railing and leaped into the river. The frigid water jolted her as she kicked to the surface. A wooden raft floated past. She placed her son atop it and held on as the current pulled her under the bridge. On the riverbank, refugees huddled under sheets of metal roofing, chanting prayers. Yoshiko looked up to see flames flying across the bridge.

Near shore she spotted two men in a small boat. Yoshiko called out to them, begging them at least to help her son. The men reached down and pulled Hiroshi out of the water, followed by Yoshiko. Up ahead a wooden bridge burned. She could see the silhouettes of desperate people jumping into the water. Terror seized her. What if the bridge collapsed? "I hugged my child tight, squeezed myself into the bottom of the boat, and prayed to God," Yoshiko said. "The next thing I noticed, the fire was behind me."

As bridges burned, so did boats. People dove into canals, only for others to land on top of them. Carbon monoxide poisoned many, while others suffocated and drowned in the frigid waters. Oil spilled from a refinery in Fukagawa, setting the surface of the Onagi River ablaze. Elsewhere flames whipped across the surface. "As soon as I raised my face," one survivor recalled, "my hair and my face burned."

Nowhere seemed safe.

Twelve-year-old Katsumoto Saotomo and his family, having seen the glow of fires in the northwest near Asakusa, had fled south and unknowingly into the heart of the conflagration. New fires cut off the family's advance. "Direct hits fell one after the other to the front, back, left and right of us," Katsumoto recalled. "It was like an obstacle course. We just ran blindly." Utility poles, homes, and warehouses burned and collapsed all around them. "There was no choice," the youth said, "but to pray."

His sister spotted a tunnel of darkness, which was the Tobu rail line connecting Hikifune with Kameido. The houses along the tracks remained standing.

"Okay," his father said, "let's try."

Before departing, Katsuma scooped water from a cistern with his helmet and dumped it on the head of his son. The others did the same, soaking themselves to guard against the embers. Katsumoto's mother Rin suddenly announced that she had to urinate.

"It's not easy to run," she said, "when you have to go."

Her confession added a moment of levity, offering a reprieve from the exhaustion and terror that had seized them. Each member then took a deep breath and charged down the train tracks, battling the heavy wind that pushed them back toward the inferno. Katsumoto heard the roar of the flames and felt the warmth on his cheeks. His lungs burned from the smoke.

An ember ignited his mother's pack.

"Mom," Katsumoto shouted, "your backpack!"

She shed the bag without breaking stride.

The family charged ahead, passing several signal lights before crossing a small iron rail bridge. The smoke cleared. Other refugees emerged. The sudden sense of safety sapped Katsumoto's adrenaline. He felt exhausted, but his father urged them to press on to the river. "Before I knew it," he said, "dawn arrived."

CHAPTER 15

"The raid of 10 March was clearly one of the
greatest catastrophes in all history."

—U.S. STRATEGIC BOMBING SURVEY
MARCH 1947

Dr. Shigenori Kubota had endured a long night of waiting. A professor at the Imperial Japanese Army Medical School, Dr. Kubota doubled, during times of crisis, as the commander of Rescue Unit Number One, a twenty-four-person team comprised of nine doctors, eleven nurses, and four ambulance drivers. His mission: provide emergency medical relief to Tokyo. A second team half the size of his covered just the Imperial Palace. The twelve-fifteen a.m. air raid alarm had sent him running to the roof of the medical school, located west of the palace and outside the American target zone. On that cold March morning, Dr. Kubota looked east in the direction of Joto, where the atmosphere glowed crimson. This was no ordinary raid. The roar of airplane engines and the thunder of cannons reminded him not of battle sounds but of a funeral procession. "I had a fear," he said, "that this was the last day for Tokyo."

Orders finally arrived at 3:40 a.m. Dr. Kubota and his team climbed aboard the ambulances—equipped with four days of food—and rolled out of the gate ten minutes later. The night was silent and still, as the rescuers moved east through the capital without sirens. As the team closed in on the disaster area, smoke began to waft through the darkened streets. Dr. Kubota spotted the occasional burned structure. With each block, the damage worsened, from toppled utility poles and downed wires to the scorched remains of streetcars. The ambulances struggled to navigate roads littered with burnt wood and sheets of galvanized metal roofing along with abandoned carts and mattresses. Water bubbled out of ruptured mains; fires still smoldered in places. The eastern horizon soon lightened, signaling the approach of dawn.

Near the Ryogoku Bridge, the dead started to appear, but it wasn't until Dr. Kubota reached the top of the span that the magnitude of the tragedy struck him. "In the black Sumida River," he wrote, "countless bodies were floating, clothed bodies and naked bodies, all as black as charcoal. It was unreal. These were dead people, but you couldn't tell whether they were men or women. You couldn't even tell if the objects floating by were arms and legs or pieces of burnt wood." Corpses lined both banks of the river, piled one on top of another. Dr. Kubota could see the Earthquake Memorial Hall, which had been built after the 1923 disaster and had miraculously survived, but fires had reduced all the homes around it to ashes. "What caught my eye were the rows of burnt machine tools that could be seen endlessly in the vast burned area," he wrote. "There are numerous rows of machines everywhere, like elephants lying down."

Crowds gathered outside the Honjo government office, as authorities issued blankets and hardtack to survivors. Dr. Kubota disembarked, receiving orders to set up his relief station at Honjo National School. At six a.m. the ambulances moved out again. The roads were lined with charred corpses. Bodies stripped of clothes appeared pink, like steamed crabs. Up ahead in the morning light, he saw what resembled mountains of scorched lumber. The light brightened, and he realized the mountains were not lumber but piles of remains. Why, he wondered, were the dead congregated in piles? Then it hit him. People had sought shelter inside buildings, only to suffocate or die of carbon monoxide poisoning. The buildings had then burned, leaving only mountains of dead men, women, and children.

The ambulance could go no farther. Dr. Kubota climbed down and proceeded on foot. As he closed in on the school, he was stunned at the absence not only of smoldering homes but even of the household goods and utility lines he had previously seen. "Everything that could burn was burned out," he said, "and then blown away by the strong winds of the fire storm."

Dr. Kubota and his team reached the Honjo National School, a three-story concrete structure swarming with refugees. The doctor immediately went to work, clearing a corner in the auditorium before lining up desks and chairs. Within minutes, a maze of survivors wound around the cavernous room, all in need of help. Many of the patients, he discovered, suffered from conjunctivitis, an inflammation of the outer membrane of the eyeball that stemmed from the smoke and dust in the air. The medics washed eyes with saline solution and removed foreign objects. Other victims suffered burns and carbon monoxide poisoning. He removed shrapnel from one survivor's head, a fragment from an antiaircraft shell. Each patient had a story, including a family of nine who had survived by lashing themselves together with rope.

Dr. Kubota finally took a break for some fresh air, stepping outside the auditorium. The scene horrified him. Corpses filled the school playground, many huddled against the building's concrete walls. Others congregated around the doorway where he now stood, including women and children, still holding hands even in death. All had fled from the marching flames, only to die desperately banging on the door, fighting to get inside. The people in the auditorium, one of the survivors explained to Dr. Kubota, had held the door tight, refusing to allow them inside. The doctor listened in silence. "It was impossible to blame them," he wrote. "The situation had exceeded the limits of morality and given way to the instinct of self-preservation."

THE SUN ROSE OVER Tokyo that Saturday morning to reveal an apocalyptic wasteland. Gone were the glorious reds, purples, and blues that on any other morning would have heralded the start of a new day. Instead the sun, filtered through clouds of smoke, appeared gray, washed of all color, more reminiscent, one survivor later recalled, of the moon.

Ashes fluttered in the breeze like snowflakes. The heat that only hours earlier had caused clothes and hair to spontaneously ignite had vanished, replaced by the bitter cold of winter in a city where snow had fallen only days before. The only warmth survivors found this morning radiated from the smoldering ground. Gone, too, was the soundtrack of roaring winds, crackling fires, and screams, replaced by an eerie quiet interrupted only by the breeze.

The few survivors from the frigid rivers and canals dragged themselves up onto the banks, exhausted and shivering, anxious to soak in the warmth of the scorched earth. A few placed sheets of corrugated metal atop burning debris, creating a makeshift stovetop to dry shirts and pants. Others stumbled through this flattened landscape like zombies, with swollen and bloodshot eyes that stared blankly from faces smeared black with soot. Violent winds had robbed many of shoes and clothes, while the flames left others with singed hair and burns. Dazed and exhausted, many set off toward home, hoping to find missing husbands and wives, parents and children. "It was," one survivor said, "a procession of ghosts."

The conflagration had burned with such ferocity that by morning the fires had largely dwindled. There was no more fuel, nothing left to burn. Across the capital, the inferno had reduced house after house, block after block, mile after mile to rubble and ash, an empty landscape interrupted only by the occasional concrete building or chimney, marking a former bathhouse or factory. "I doubted my eyes," one survivor said, "as to whether it was Tokyo."

The dead not only littered the ground but also clogged rivers and canals. Corpses crowded the few surviving bridges. "There was still a light wind blowing," one journalist observed, "and some of the bodies, reduced to ashes, were simply scattering like sand."

The positions at times revealed a victim's desperate final moments. Parents died shielding children between them. Others perished hugging one another. A rescuer would later encounter a burned woman facedown with her fingernails covered in mud and blood. He rolled her over to discover a deceased infant she had placed in a hole beneath her. Seventeen-year-old Masako Kaneda, while searching for her missing sister, stumbled upon a scorched newborn at the feet of its deceased mother, still attached via the umbilical cord. Masako's own mother picked up the infant with both hands and placed it atop its mother's breast.

"Come," she said, "be born in a peaceful period next time."

Many of the dead were found in piles. A rescue team in Kameido attempted to pry apart what appeared to be a large block of charcoal in a bathtub in the ruins of a home, only to discover that it was a family of five who had burned to death while embracing one another. Haruyo Wada woke in the dark when someone grabbed her leg and yanked, pulling her out from under a pile of a dozen charcoaled corpses. Haruyo's father Saburo had found her hours earlier, crouching over her to protect her as the fires closed in on them. Amid the inferno that devoured Joto, other desperate residents had huddled around and on top them. The air, robbed of oxygen, had knocked Haruyo unconscious before the tidal wave of fire washed over them. The eight-year-old, wrapped in her father's embrace, had survived shielded in a cocoon of strangers.

Many of those who climbed inside the government-mandated home bunkers perished, as one survivor later described, "like roasted sweet potatoes." The blackened legs of others rose like chopsticks from now-dry firefighting cisterns. Not all were burned. Those overcome by carbon monoxide poisoning or who suffocated often appeared asleep.

A few, however, did survive, including Tomoji Ishikura, who woke up that Saturday inside the community restroom of Takahashi National School. Moments before he slipped unconscious, a young mother next to him had grabbed hold of his arm and pleaded with him to die with her on behalf of her absent husband. He now looked down and saw that she was gone, her deceased infant still cradled tightly in her arms.

On the morning of her sixth birthday, Shizuko Nishio remained with her mother in the damp basement of Sumida High School. The voices at the door, which had reached a crescendo of desperation, had long since fallen silent. The adults tried to pry open the door at daybreak, only to find it would not budge. When survivors finally wrested it open, those inside stared at a scene of horror. "There was a massive wall," Shizuko recalled, "of dead bodies."

The dead likewise swamped swimming pools. Eight hundred people died in the pool at Fuji National School in Asakusa. A similar tragedy unfolded at Futaba National School in Honjo, where hundreds of bodies floated facedown in the water, their backs all burned.

"If you are still alive," rescuers hollered at one pool, "raise your hand."

Sumiko Morikawa, who had escaped with her twin girls and four-year-old son Kiichi into a pool next to Yokogawa National Elementary School, came to her senses around dawn. Bodies packed the pool around her, while a handful of survivors had either gone mad or stood silent in shock. In her arms she held her son, whose lips had turned dark. Sumiko made her way to the side and climbed out of the pool. She reached up to remove the deceased twins from her back, only to find their tiny hands still clung to her shoulder, making it hard to separate from them. She laid the girls on the edge of the pool, both still dressed in the chrysanthemum-patterned kimonos she had put on them the night before. Side by side, Ryoko and Atsuko appeared asleep.

"Forgive me!" she cried. "Forgive me!"

Sumiko then focused on Kiichi, who was fading. A policeman alerted her of a nearby rescue station. Sumiko carried him there but could not find a doctor. She pressed on toward a friend's home, hoping to find dry clothes. Someone offered her a cup of hot tea, which she shared with her son. "Kiichi can drink," she thought. "He isn't dying. He will live!"

"Mommy," the boy muttered in what would be his last word before he died.

Dawn found Katsumoto Saotome, his parents, and two sisters gathered on the banks of the Sumida River in Mukojima. Unlike countless others caught amid the chaos, his entire family had miraculously remained together and survived the long night. As the sun inched skyward, the youth struggled to see, his vision blurred from the smoke. He stared down at his hands. The fires had burned the fingertips off his cotton gloves. Katsumoto looked back over the direction he had come from to find the capital gone. The eight-story Matsuya Department Store in Asakusa was the only structure still standing, a tombstone over the ashen cemetery of a city.

Police photographer Koyo Ishikawa came to his senses. Trapped in the fires of Honjo, he had collapsed behind a stone wall. He pulled himself into a nearby tub, where he survived with water from a spigot. Ishikawa had lost his Chevy and nearly his life, but through it all, he managed to keep his Leica. The slender cameraman climbed to his feet.

It was time to go to work.

Aid workers, like Dr. Kubota, opened rescue centers in those schools still standing that morning, passing out hardtack and blankets. Survivors scrawled messages on blackboards—first and last names and their destination—with the hopes that missing family might find them. Others used charcoal to scribble on pieces of unburned wood, leaving the primitive notes in the ruins of homes. Letters soon papered over the scorched remnants of utility poles. Masayoshi Nakagawa, who lost his two-year-old son in the inferno, found his home in ruins. With his six-year-old daughter in tow, he set out on an arduous journey to a relative's house. Warped steel safes dotted the flattened landscape, while black hexagons tattooed roadways, marking the fiery discharge of incendiaries. "We had to force ourselves to struggle on through mounds of debris and corpses; among the foul, pungent odors; and amid the groans of the injured and dying," Nakagawa said. "A man holding a frying pan gazed blankly at ashes that had been a house. Another squatted, dazed and helpless, in the middle of the street. Mothers frantically called for their children; small children screamed for their parents. I neither could nor wanted to do anything for the suffering people around me. My own suffering was too great."

Nakagawa's struggle was all too common—survivors barely able to help themselves, much less others. Haruyo Wada faced a similar dilemma as she stumbled home with her parents and sister. Amid a pile of blackened bodies, she spotted the pink flesh of a wriggling infant. She stopped, listening to its soft cries until her father pulled her away.

"Not now," he said.

Haruyo could only look back as the family continued, a scene that would forever haunt her. "I will never forget that little baby," she recalled. "My life was saved because a pile of people helped me to survive, but I could not save one life in return."

The magnitude of the destruction and loss was almost impossible to comprehend. Residents had gone to bed the night before, climbing under warm blankets, only to awaken to a world on fire. Morning brought confirmation that the horror had not been a nightmare but was real. Some went mad with pain and sorrow. "I can't tell you, it hurts so much I'm about to go crazy," a smoke inhalation victim told Dr. Kubota. "It hurts so much I'd like to cut open my chest and let some clean air in." Eighteen-year-old Toshiko Oikawa, while searching for her own family, encountered a distraught young mother, howling as she tried to nurse the dead infant she had carried on her back.

"Please kill me," she pleaded.

Similar scenes unfolded across Tokyo, as the adrenaline that propelled people through the night gave way to exhaustion and despair. Aiko Matani saw a pregnant woman struggling to give birth. "We did not know," she said, "whether to congratulate or pity her."

Katsumoto Saotome and his family, en route toward home, paused along the banks of the river, where bodies of the burned and drowned floated. He watched rescuers rope the dead, haul them onto the river-bank, and line them up like fish in a market.

"Look at it," his father said. "Don't forget it. This is what war looks like."

The family trudged through the debris, arriving to find that the rented two-story duplex in Mukojima still stood. Of all the destruction around it, their home somehow had survived; so, too, the family discovered, had the pet cat, Tomi.

Police photographer Ishikawa retraced his steps through the scorched cityscape, where he encountered an incinerated train that looked to him like the skeleton of an iron dragon. The wind whipped smoke through the streets. He passed a handful of survivors in tattered clothes, with faces blackened by soot and hair and eyebrows burned off. "For the first time, I felt alive," Ishikawa recalled. "I felt the urge to hug them." He stum-

Workers hustle to assemble B-29 bombers, which were manufactured at four plants around the country.

A member of an engineer aviation battalion operates a twelve-foot grader
during the construction of an airfield on Guam.

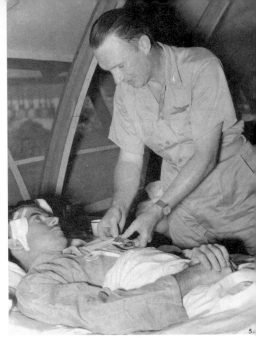

Richard M. Miller of Massachusetts, a radar operator on a B-29, unwinds with a book on the tail of a bomber.

Brig. Gen. Haywood Hansell, Jr., presents the Purple Heart to Carl W. McKinney, a bombardier wounded on a Superfortress during the first strike against Tokyo on November 24, 1944.

Gen. Hap Arnold, who learned to fly from the Wright brothers, was the father of the B-29, the single most expensive weapons system of the war.

Men with the Third Reconnaissance Squadron lay out a mosaic of Tokyo, sections of which were taken on the first photo recon mission over Japan on November 1, 1944.

Ground crews on Saipan load ammunition and two-thousand-pound bombs, adding a few personal notes to the weapons.

Incendiary bombs from two B-29s drop on a Japanese target.

Aviation engineers use bulldozers to extinguish fires after a Japanese raid on Saipan on November 27, 1944, destroyed three B-29s.

Soldiers in the Marianas, hunkered down in a four-by-eight-foot foxhole, keep a running tally of Japanese raids launched from Iwo Jima.

Maj. Gen. Curtis LeMay, pictured on the left, takes command of the 21st Bomber Command from Brig. Gen. Haywood Hansell, Jr., in January 1945. Brig. Gen. Roger Ramey is on the right.

Armorers on Saipan load M69 incendiary bombs into a B-29.

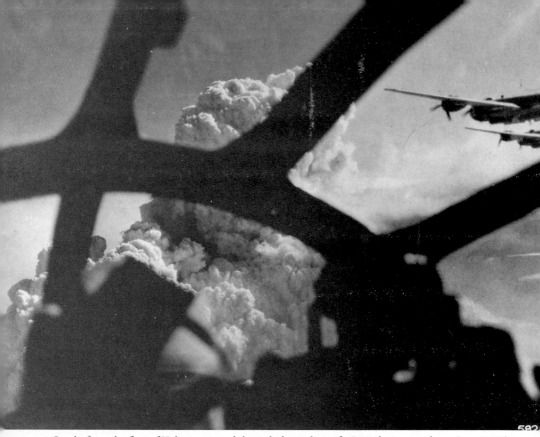

Smoke from the fires of Kobe are viewed through the cockpit of a B-29 during a strike on June 5, 1945.

Incendiary bombs rain down on Kobe on June 5, 1945, Japan's sixth-largest city. Fires already can be seen burning in the commercial dock area.

Dawn on March 10, 1945, revealed piles of charcoaled corpses.

A Japanese woman scavenges kindling amid the ruins of Tokyo.

B-29s buzz Navy Seabee Clarence Swinney of Nevada, who is operating a twenty-one-ton cat and earthmover, as he works on an unfinished section of the new airbase on Tinian.

Members of an engineer aviation battalion assemble the steel frame of a roof for a Quonset hut on Saipan.

A Japanese soldier walks through the ruins of Hiroshima after America's August 6, 1945, atomic attack on the city.

Japanese civilians were caught in the middle of America's bombing, including many children who ended the war as orphans.

bled back to the police box to find his Chevy incinerated, leaving him no choice but to continue on foot.

Ishikawa reached the police headquarters shortly before noon. The station's doctor washed out his eyes before he reported to the chief. He then had a bite of food provided by the station and went up to the rooftop for a view, where he found several spent incendiary canisters.

The photographer set out for Asakusa around two p.m. Household items littered the roads along with burned hand pumps and bodies. Ishikawa trudged along, his legs feeling tired and heavy. He paused before a pile of corpses, then removed the lens cap of his muddied Leica and raised his camera. He felt an invisible spirit reprimand him for contemplating such a tragic image, but he had no choice. It was his job.

Ishikawa pushed the shutter release.

He paused along the banks of the Sumida River before pressing on to the Susaki Police Station. Inside the building he found the chief burned to death in his office with his child in his lap and a sword still in his hands. He counted thirty-nine other bodies. Ishikawa said a prayer and returned to headquarters to find dozens of borrowed trucks. Workers loaded canned goods and hardtack to transport to aid stations. Exhausted, Ishikawa headed for his own home, where he passed out. "I fell asleep," the photographer recalled, "as if I were dead."

Shizuko Nishio left the basement of Sumida High School, stepping over the bodies that initially had blocked the door. She put her palms together and prayed. "Did I land on the moon?" she thought when she stepped into the light and surveyed the destruction. Like others, Shizuko and her mother struggled past the dead to get home, only to find the family's property in ruins. Her father arrived soon afterward, his hair burned and his face black with soot.

"Shizuko," he cried, "you are still alive."

He broke down sobbing.

Shizuko's beautiful cousin Sumiko, who had fled inside Takahashi National School, failed to return. It was obvious she had died, but Shizuko's mother could not accept the loss of her niece, so the family waited in the ruins for much of the day, before eventually leaving a note. Like so many others, the family set off for Tokyo Station to evacuate the city, a four-and-a-half-hour walk. Shizuko's parents rotated carrying her piggyback. From her perch, she saw dead dogs, horses, and of course people, reduced to charcoal. At one point, an old man carrying a dead child passed them, heading back into the wastelands. He looked lost. Near Tokyo Station the family passed several police kiosks, where desperate people fleeing the fires had crowded inside. "The bodies," Shizuko said, "were all melted together."

Haruyo Wada and her family likewise reached the ruins of her home. Amid the ashes, she found a broken shard of her favorite dish, the one with flowers printed on it. She had eaten her last meal of curry rice off it before going to bed the night before. The fires had consumed the homes of all her neighbors, including her best friend, Masao, whom she had last seen breaking ice in the family's cistern. "It was as if," she later said, "the world had ended."

For so many, it had.

CHAPTER 16

"The heart of this city is completely gutted by fire. It is the most devastating raid in the history of aerial warfare."

—MAJ. GEN. CURTIS LeMAY COMMAND DIARY
MARCH 11, 1945

The first bombers touched down on Saipan, Tinian, and Guam that Saturday morning, disgorging exhausted crew members whose uniforms stank of smoke. Ground crews marveled at the bellies of the bombers, where heat from the thermal updrafts had blistered the paint on some. Soot blackened others. A few had brought debris back with them, including a Tokyo newspaper and a page from a grocery store ledger plucked from inside engine nacelles.

LeMay stood ready to greet his airmen. The general, who only hours earlier had been pacing the floor of his headquarters, had taken an incredible gamble.

And won.

The first reconnaissance plane had lifted off in the predawn hours to photograph the damage, but even without those images, LeMay knew the mission had been a staggering success. The excited chatter of the crews only accentuated the radio reports from the night before.

General Power landed at 10:01 a.m. He had spent nearly two hours circling the dying capital, marking the outbreak of fires on a map with a red grease pencil. "There is no room for emotions in war," Power later wrote. "But the destruction I witnessed that night over Tokyo was so overwhelming that it left a tremendous and lasting impression with me."

"It was a hell of a good mission," Power hollered down to LeMay.

Debriefers swarmed the returning airmen. "Raids like that, even increasing in size and striking power, will ultimately help to bring the walls crumbling down upon the Nips and their honorable Japanese homeland," testified Staff Sgt. Robert Webb. Anxious to keep Washington updated, LeMay's headquarters fired off a message based on the reports of the first returning crews, including Power. "Largest fires covered at least a thousand blocks in center of business district and many smaller fires starting to merge into general conflagration," the cable stated. "Glow of fires could be seen clearly at a distance of 150 miles from Tokyo."

Of the 325 bombers that had climbed into the skies, 279 bombed Tokyo, unloading a total of 1,665 tons of incendiaries on the capital. Nineteen others bombed secondary targets, including the Boso Peninsula, Haha Jima, and Chichi Jima. The strike cost LeMay fourteen bombers, including four that ditched in the Pacific between Iwo Jima and Saipan, where the navy fished forty fliers out of the waters. Flak downed a couple of others, while seven bombers had simply vanished, the cause unknown, though antiaircraft fire was a likely culprit. Fighter opposition had been weak, just as LeMay had anticipated. Seventy-four Japanese pursuits made forty attacks but failed to bring down a single known bomber. The general, who had been warned that he might lose up to 70 percent of his force, in the end lost only 4.3 percent.

Reporters hungered for news, but LeMay could share only anecdotal details. "This was the most successful attack we have put on to date," he told them. "The flight reports are very good, exceptionally so." General Power filled in some gaps, telling reporters that the damage dwarfed the February 25 incendiary raid that had burned one square mile of the capital. "I saw one solid mass of flames," Power said. "It was the greatest show on earth."

Other airmen echoed the general. "It was like throwing matches on a floor covered with dry sawdust," quipped Flight Officer Frank Urso of Berwyn, Illinois.

"The town was burning like hell," added Lt. Charles Shaffer of Michigan City, Indiana, "and I mean hell."

"They won't get those fires out in a week," exclaimed Lt. James Warren of Dunn, North Carolina.

Half a world away in Washington, air force officials rushed out a three-sentence press release, stating that the mission had targeted Japanese industrial strength. "Returning aircrewmen reported smoke rising thousands of feet into the air," the communiqué stated. "Anti-aircraft fire was meager to intense, but enemy fighter opposition was slight."

Everyone now waited on the photos.

At three-thirty that morning, First Lt. Omer Cox had lifted off from Guam in his specially equipped Superfortress that sported seven cameras with six-, twenty-four-, and forty-inch focal-length lenses. "When weather conditions are good," bragged the command historian, "objects as small as human beings—even Japs—can be seen on the prints." Damage assessment photos after the February 25 incendiary raid had captured crowds on the streets below, gawking at the devastation. Two hundred and fifty miles south of the coastline, Cox pulled back on the controls and began the slow climb to 30,000 feet. Nearly six miles up in the skies over Tokyo, the cameras whirred, exposing 6,000 feet of film in less than one hour as the bomber made a 204-mile run over the target. "Results of the mission were excellent. 100 percent coverage of the area, with all cameras, was obtained," the squadron commander later reported. "Smoke, rising 15,000 feet above the target area, was observed 150 miles from the mainland."

Cox touched down at 5:34 p.m. Saturday, where airmen grabbed the film magazines and rushed them for development. The once-primitive laboratory, which had begun operating the previous fall in two tents on Saipan, would occupy, by the end of March, four Quonset huts on Guam, totaling ten thousand square feet of floor space. Sixty-eight lab technicians—divided into two twelve-hour shifts, working seven days a week—would develop 108,284 negatives plus another 103,037 prints that month. For a vital mission, like the attack on Tokyo, technicians could develop the negatives, select the images, and print photos in as little as four hours.

At midnight that Saturday, the photo interpretation officer with prints in hand jumped into a jeep and rushed to LeMay's quarters. Other senior staff officers followed, creating a parking lot in front of the general's tent. LeMay climbed out of bed and woke Norstad. Still in his pajamas, LeMay popped a cigar into his mouth and fired it up, as the photo interpretation officer spread the images across the wooden table of his bedroom. No one spoke.

LeMay leaned down, studying the contrast of the images. The torched districts appeared light gray, even white, compared to the dark unburned areas that ringed the city.

"All this is out," he said, motioning across several square miles.

"This is out," he continued, "this—this—this."

Others leaned forward.

"It's all ashes," Norstad exclaimed.

The photos, amplified by others in the days ahead, revealed that the raid had incinerated 15.8 square miles of Tokyo, including 267,171 homes, stores, and businesses. Literally one out of every four buildings in the capital had vanished. Japanese authorities, sifting through the smoldering debris, would estimate that the attack killed 83,793 men, women, and children, a figure historians would revise upward to 105,000. The strike wounded another 40,918 and left 1 million homeless. More than twice as many people died in those predawn hours in Tokyo as in Hamburg in July 1943 and roughly four times as many as in Dresden a month earlier.

This was news.

Big news.

McKelway woke newspaper correspondents at four a.m., instructing them to report to the press headquarters for a briefing, while Norstad fired off a message to Washington. "After study of the past attack pho-

TOKYO

Arakawa River

Naka River

Sumida River

Imperial
Palace
Grounds

TOKYO
BAY

N
W   E
S

0   1   2 mi

Fire damage from March
9–10, 1945, attack
········· Railroads
Streetcar lines
Target area (Zone 1)

tographs, it is very apparent that this last operation was most successful," Norstad wrote. "The results far exceed my optimistic expectations."

Before the sun rose that Sunday morning, groggy reporters hovered over the same gray and white images that showed the destruction of 440,146,000 square feet or 10,120 acres. The strike had incinerated 82 percent of the target, known as Incendiary Zone 1. That included the center of the city's residential district along with 18 percent of the capital's industrial area and 63 percent of its commercial district.

The strike had damaged or destroyed twenty-two targeted industries, including the Rising Sun Petroleum Terminal, a tank farm for aviation fuel. Gone, too, was the Ogura Oil Company, a large refinery that had produced gasoline and lubricating oil, and the Japan Machine Industry, which had hammered out airplane and engine parts. The attack went beyond war plants. The destruction of the vital Tsukiji, Kanda, and Koto markets would disrupt food distribution, while the loss of commercial equipment promised to gum up production. Burned warehouses of clothing and household necessities would increase pressure on civilians. "There is no cushion or reserve," one intelligence report noted, "with which to alleviate the immediate losses."

Along with those photos, McKelway shared a four-paragraph statement from LeMay, who congratulated his air and ground crews. "I believe that all those under my command on these island bases have by their participation in this single operation shortened this war," LeMay said. "To what extent they have shortened it no one can tell. But I believe that if there has been cut from its duration only one day or one hour, my officers and men have served a high purpose. They will pursue that purpose stubbornly. They are fighting for a quicker end to this war and will continue to fight for a quicker end to it with all the brains and strength they have."

Later that day LeMay sat for an interview with Maj. Ted Steele of the *Army Hour* radio program, firing off a message to Washington to alert Helen so she could tune in Sunday night to the show. "Almost 17 square miles—16.7 to be exact—of urban Tokyo are now twisted, gutted rubble," LeMay began, adding in the results of his earlier incendiary raid. "Hundreds of war business establishments—many important administrative buildings—and thousands of home industries were burned down in the area where the fire blazed hottest."

To illustrate the magnitude of the damage, LeMay used New York City and Washington as examples. The raid torched an area equivalent to all of downtown Manhattan, including much of the Brooklyn waterfront and nearby urban areas. Had it been Washington, it would have taken out Capitol Hill and most of Georgetown. "You can," LeMay said, "work it out for your own city or town—and can picture it lying in ruins within an area more than 160 blocks long and more than 40 blocks wide—more than 10,000 acres of destruction." He concluded with a warning. "If the Japs persist," he declared, "I now promise that they have nothing more to look forward to than the complete destruction of their cities."

In newsrooms across America, articles with Guam datelines clattered off the teletype. Editors rushed to mark up the cables, typesetters arranged the copy, and the elephantine printing presses soon rolled, spitting out headlines nationwide that trumpeted the raid.

"City's Heart Gone," announced the *New York Times*.

"Hellish Sea of Fire Engulfs Tokyo," echoed Omaha's *Evening World-Herald*.

"Havoc Wreaked by Superforts," added the *San Diego Union*.

That same day LeMay sent Arnold a copy of General Power's eyewitness report, noting in an accompanying letter that smoke still hung several miles over the enemy's capital. "Since this is the identical report handed me by one of my Wing Commanders," he wrote, "and since it relates to the heaviest strike yet made by elements of the Twentieth Air Force, the thought occurred that it might be of value to you as a personal possession."

Congratulations rattled off the teletype, none more important than the one from Arnold, who only a few weeks earlier had considered firing LeMay. "This mission, flown under most difficult operating conditions, proves again the courage and efficiency of your command," he wrote. "The high percentage of your total aircraft reaching the target and the heavy weight of bombs carried merit the highest praise upon service crews and the altitude of the attack proves your teams have the guts to tackle anything. Good luck and good bombing."

BUT LeMAY'S WORK had only begun.

The general envisioned the Tokyo strike as the first shot in a barrage to knock out Japan's major urban areas, lifting a play right out of Giulio Douhet's book. "What could happen to a single city in a single day," the airpower theorist had once written, "could also happen to ten, twenty, fifty cities." Two days after the Tokyo raid, LeMay sent his Superfortresses to firebomb Nagoya, which his crews had unsuccessfully attacked seven previous times. The target that evening, however, was not the Mitsubishi engine works or the airframe factory, but a 4.5-square-mile triangle that covered the central commercial and government districts as well as adjacent residential areas. Density, though less than in Tokyo, still hovered around 75,000 men, women, and children per square mile, more than triple the citywide average.

LeMay planned a similar low-altitude nighttime mission, but with a few modifications. To prevent bombers from wasting incendiaries on already-saturated areas, the general staggered the attacks, ordering the 313th and 314th Bombardment Wings to strike first, followed an hour later by the 73rd, allowing those crews to target areas not yet on fire. LeMay also changed the intervalometer settings from fifty feet to one hundred feet to spread out the fires. He planned to arm his tail gunners on this mission but with only two hundred rounds to blast searchlights.

Three hundred and ten Superfortresses roared into the skies that Sunday night, barely twenty-nine hours after the last Tokyo raider touched down. The aerial armada approached Nagoya from the south, to execute an upwind run. Over the course of nearly three hours, 285 bombers unloaded 1,790 tons of incendiaries at the cost of a single B-29, lost not to enemy fighters or flak but to an engine fire that forced the pilot to ditch soon after takeoff. "Lifeguard submarine," the general messaged Washington, "stationed 150 miles south of Nagoya reported that visibility was reduced to 1 mile due to smoke from wood fires."

Compared to Tokyo, however, the destruction was far less, burning a little more than two square miles. Unlike the strike on the capital, the damage to Nagoya was not concentrated but was spread across one hundred small areas. Analysts estimated that the attack damaged or destroyed eighteen industries. Only a few of those were numbered targets, the most important of which was Aichi Aircraft Works. LeMay realized that the larger intervalometer settings, combined with the time lag between the first and second waves, had given firefighters vital time to respond. "The experiment," one report noted, "proved to have been a failure." The general tempered his displeasure in his public comments. "This was not as successful as the last Tokyo mission," he told reporters. "The fires we set did not burn as furiously or spread as rapidly as they did in Tokyo. The damage done, however, was certainly not inconsiderable. We recognize, as we always have, that we are fighting a resourceful, tough, and wily enemy."

Lesson learned.

For the March 13 mission against Osaka, LeMay reverted to the strategy used over Tokyo, zeroing in on a ten-square-mile triangle over the geographical heart of the city where the population density, as in Nagoya, topped out at 75,000 people per square mile. "This zone," the target information sheet stated, "contains highly congested residential elements inextricably mingled with countless small factories and household workshops."

The strike that Tuesday night by 274 bombers, carrying 1,733 tons of incendiaries, torched more than eight square miles of Japan's second-largest city. Japanese authorities would later tally the dead at 3,987, with another 8,466 wounded and 678 missing. Fires damaged or destroyed 4,222 industrial buildings, including ten numbered targets.

Civilians shouldered the weight of the attack, which obliterated 134,744 residential buildings and left half a million homeless. The conflagration gorged on Osaka's wood-and-plaster architecture, sparking thermal updrafts that surpassed the ones crews battled over Tokyo. "Fifteen seconds after bombs away we ran into a violent thermal and for a few seconds everyone in the crew blacked-out," Capt. Louis Halton, aircraft commander of the *Patricia*, told his superiors. "The lights on the instrument panel had gone out and we were two thousand feet above bombing altitude, and still going up. I took over control from the automatic pilot which had been disturbed by the thermal, and after a procedure turn departed for our home base. I had flown many a rough mission in Europe and already completed some tough missions in the Pacific but this mission definitely gave me my greatest scare."

The back-to-back burning of Tokyo, Nagoya, and Osaka generated tremendous news coverage across America, including eight-column banners in the *New York Times* and the *Herald Tribune*. "How far away," observed the *Washington Evening Star*, "seems the day when all Nippon exulted over Pearl Harbor!" Reporters grappled with whether the missions represented a sudden abandonment of America's long-standing policy of precision strikes. "Strategy Shifts to Area Bombing," declared a headline in the New Orleans *Times-Picayune*. "The mounting fierceness and relentlessness of American Superfortress incendiary raids on Japan's industrial centers," stated an Associated Press dispatch, "strongly indicates that the B-29 command has embarked on an all-out campaign of area rather than strategic bombing."

Senior Washington officials, sensitive to charges of killing civilians in the wake of the bombing of Dresden, fired off a message to LeMay's headquarters on how best to guide the press. "Editorial comment beginning to wonder about blanket incendiary attacks upon cities therefore urge you continue hard hitting your present line that this destruction is necessary to eliminate Jap home industries and that it is strategic precision bombing," the March 14 cable warned. "Guard against anyone stating that this is area bombing."

Such concerns, however, did not faze LeMay, who day after day focused on the herculean task of returning his crews to the skies. No sooner did bombers roll onto the hardstands than ordnance and gasoline trucks pulled alongside to refuel and rearm them.

"Hey," Capt. Gus Clay of Virginia shouted down from the cockpit window. "Aren't you guys going to give us a chance to get out and stretch?"

An army of electricians, mechanics, and sheet metal workers hustled to keep bombers in service, skipping meals and even sleep. Navy Seabees joined the fight, providing floodlights so crews could work through the night. An absence of spare bomb bay doors meant that as soon as a battered plane touched down, mechanics yanked off the doors, repaired them, and rehung them, often in as little as twenty hours. To motivate service crews, LeMay ordered strike photos pinned up on bulletin boards, so everyone could share in the results. "Ground crews," one report noted, "worked 24 hour periods without rest, repairing battle damage caused by flak and enemy fighters, changing engines and making inspections, refueling and reloading by feel and by flashlight so that the returning aircraft would be ready for the next mission."

The strenuous pace likewise took a toll on the pilots, navigators, and bombardiers, who swallowed sleeping pills and Benzedrine. "A marked loss of appetite was noted due to fatigue caused by irregular eating and irritated nerves," First Lt. Charles Morgan reported to his superiors. "It was hard for us to relax and sleep as most of our rest must be acquired during the hours of daylight when the temperature and the humidity were the greatest."

On March 16, LeMay's bombers burned 2.86 square miles of Kobe, killing 2,581 people, wounding another 4,794, and leaving one-third of the city homeless. For the encore of his blitz, the general returned to Nagoya two days later. That evening his crews incinerated another three square miles, upping that city's total destruction to five square miles. LeMay's steady drumbeat of attacks accomplished precisely what he had warned the navy might happen weeks earlier, only to draw laughs. "We ran out of bombs," he said. "Literally."

In five missions flown over a span of barely ten days, LeMay's bombers had scorched a staggering thirty-two square miles of four of Japan's largest cities. House by house, block by block, district by district, American bombers reduced Tokyo, Nagoya, Osaka, and Kobe to little more than rubble and ash. The human toll was horrific. The five raids killed more than 110,000 men, women, and children, injured another 60,000, and left more than 2 million homeless, many of whom had no choice but to flee the cities. "I was not happy, but neither was I particularly concerned, about civilian casualties on incendiary raids," LeMay recalled. "I didn't let it influence any of my decisions because we knew how the Japanese had treated the Americans—both civilian and military—that they'd captured in places like the Philippines." Beyond the casualties, the attacks wrecked industry and bridges, government buildings and hospitals. Burned utility poles and toppled cables disrupted phone and telegraph services, while the Osaka streetcar system collapsed, which arrested the movement of workers and the nighttime distribution of rationed food. Kobe abandoned its subway. "The war had, indeed," concluded the U.S. Strategic Bombing Survey, "been brought home to the enemy."

The 9,365 tons of incendiaries totaled three times the tonnage dropped during the preceding three and a half months. LeMay had accomplished that with a loss of less than 1 percent of his aircrews, a better average than he had experienced flying daylight precision strikes. The missions demonstrated to LeMay that weather was no longer a challenge, nor was Japanese opposition much of a threat after dark. Not only could he increase his loads, but the majority of his bombers, even using primitive radar, could hit the target. "The end result," he told his chief of staff, "is the same as if the force had been doubled."

Newspapers and magazines continued to trumpet the attacks. "A dream come true," declared *Time*. "Properly kindled, Japanese cities will burn like autumn leaves."

"B-29s Turn Japan into Chaotic Land," added the *New York Times*.

"Heavy Blow Spreads Ruin on Homeland," stated the *Dallas Morning News*.

General Norstad, who had since returned to Washington, hosted a press conference at the Pentagon on March 23. "It is very doubtful," he crowed to reporters, "that such a high cost has ever previously been inflicted upon any people in a single eight-day period in the whole history of warfare." Norstad's remarks, in which he answered proposed sample questions, showed the air force's continued campaign to downplay accusations of area bombing. "Why in recent attacks by B-29s," Norstad asked, "has the primary purpose been to fire the targets?"

"An incendiary attack," he proceeded to answer, "was the economical method of destroying the small industries in those areas."

"What, in general terms, was the reasoning behind this switch from explosives to incendiaries?"

"It is not a switch," Norstad assured reporters. "The mission of the

Twentieth Air Force is the reduction of Japanese ability to produce war goods. That is accomplished by any and every means at the disposal of the attacking force."

"Does this large-scale emphasis on incendiary bombing reflect new considerations in the strategy of air war against Japan?"

"None whatever," the general concluded.

Back on Guam, congratulations continued to arrive for LeMay, including from his rivals in the navy. "Task Force 58 is proud to operate in the same area as a force which can do as much damage to the enemy as your force is consistently doing," one message read. "May your targets always flame." On April 3, Norstad penned his own laudatory note, in which he drew a sharp contrast to Haywood Hansell's prior operation. "Certainly your last month's operations have been the most impressive that I have seen in the field of bombardment," Norstad wrote. "Your establishment bore little resemblance to what I had seen in January."

Arnold wrote a personal letter to LeMay upon his return to Washington following his recovery from his heart attack. "I am convinced," the general wrote, "that Japan is going through a critical period, the seriousness of which will be greatly increased at the time that Germany capitulates. This fact imposes a great responsibility on the Army Air Forces, since we alone are able to make the Japanese homeland constantly aware of the price she will pay in this futile struggle." Arnold instructed LeMay to continue to pound Japan with the maximum weight of bombs, reminding him that by July his command would total a thousand B-29s, a force capable of inflicting unimaginable ruin. Arnold, who in Europe had preached the values of America's humane way of war, no longer cared. "Under reasonably favorable conditions," the general concluded, "you should then have the ability to destroy whole industrial cities should that be required."

LeMay understood.

———

AUTHORITIES IN TOKYO struggled to care for the casualties, many of whom suffered burns to the face, feet, and hands, a job made all the more difficult by the deaths of innumerable doctors and nurses. The strike had destroyed 449 out of 857 first aid stations, which served as the front line of medical defense in a raid. Hospitals fared little better, with 132 of 275 wrecked along with 97 out of 196 maternity clinics. Those losses only compounded the existing shortage of blood plasma, serums, and sulfa drugs. "Dressings," as one report noted, "had to be used over and over again—often without being properly cleaned or sterilized."

As many as 50 percent of the burn victims died within a few days of reaching an aid center and often within just a few hours. Starting that Sunday, ambulances and trucks began shuttling the seriously injured out of the destroyed districts and eventually to neighboring prefectures. City water distribution units along with army purification and antiepidemic squads rolled into the capital. "The enormous number thrown upon the first-aid stations in a few hours time, together with the drastic curtailment of first-aid facilities, the shrinkage in first-aid personnel, and the utter confusion in the midst of all," one report stated, "portray the impossible task that confronted the depleted and beaten first-aid forces."

The raid, which had lasted just 142 minutes, damaged twenty-nine of the capital's thirty-five districts. The inferno had wiped out the five wards of Fukagawa, Honjo, Asakusa, Joto, and Nihonbashi. Those areas likewise contained the majority of the fatalities. Authorities in Fukagawa tallied approximately 30,000 dead, with another 25,000 in Honjo and more than 13,000 in Joto. The strike torched half of the six other wards; eighteen additional districts suffered more moderate damage. All told, the raid incinerated 40 percent of the capital, destroying nearly 100 fire stations along with 96 fire engines, 150 hand-drawn gas pumps, and 65,000 feet of hose. Eighty-five firemen perished, while officials listed another forty as missing. "Even to her own people," recalled reporter Masuo Kato, "Tokyo's once beautiful face had become unrecognizable and misshapen."

Mortuary services, which the government had instructed to prepare for at most thirty thousand additional fatalities per year, were overwhelmed by more than three times that figure, all from a single raid. The destruction of most of the city's crematoriums complicated the task, forcing authorities to resort to mass burials, a job that fell to hastily assembled teams of police officers and firefighters, along with soldiers, city employees, and even inmates from Sugamo Prison. A fleet of trucks deployed through the streets navigated around downed utility poles and scorched vehicles to collect the dead. Workers armed with yard tools pried apart mounds of bodies, using metal roofing sheets as stretchers. "On the truck," one survivor recalled, "I saw the dead shoveled into mountains, like slaughtered cows or pigs."

Laborers resorted to grappling hooks and even copper wires salvaged from downed telephone lines to fish the dead out of rivers and canals. "We tried," one rescuer recalled, "not to hurt the faces as much as possible." In narrow canals, teams steered the bodies toward the opposite shore with bamboo poles, where workers struggled to remove the waterlogged remains, a job that at times took four men per corpse. The dead were then laid out on shore and covered from the neck down with galvanized metal. "It was impossible to attempt to identify so many corpses," recalled Kato. "The workmen labored with frantic haste to get the job done before putrefaction could become too much of a health hazard. Fortunately the weather remained cold, but even so the sickening sweet odor of dead bodies was everywhere in the area."

Hundreds of survivors crowded around to watch, all desperately searching for the remains of their families. Fukagawa resident Nisaku Kokubu, along with his eldest daughter, hunted for his wife and three children. "One by one, we examined the corpses lying in heaps by the rivers, in the parks, in the schoolyards, and on bridges," he said. "In the beginning, the bodies frightened and nauseated us; then we got used to them. For days we wandered lamely about, looking everywhere and checking lists of the dead posted in police stations and in ward offices. All our efforts proved futile. Finally we gave up."

Mortuary teams faced a similar nightmare recovering the bodies from schools, theaters, and government buildings. Investigators at times found scratch marks on the walls where victims in their final moments had tried to claw through concrete. That was the case at Chuwa National School in Honjo and at the Kameido Train Station in Joto. The intense heat inside

Kikugawa National School reduced victims to little more than ash and bones intermixed with scorched iron helmets. In the auditorium at To-sen International School, workers tried to delicately disassemble the mountain of dead, only to find that hands and feet came off. Rescuers ultimately gave up, deriving a formula to calculate the number of corpses from the artifacts left behind. One helmet and five buttons, authorities determined, equaled one victim. Twenty-four-year-old Hiroshi Maguchi, who worked as the leader of a body disposal team in Honjo and Joto, recounted the daily horror of the job. "Even if the outside of the corpse was charred surface, when we tried to hold it, the skin and flesh crumbled and the bones squeezed out," he recalled. "Warm rot spattered on the faces of the soldiers."

When possible, mortuary teams lined bodies up outside schools and in parks, giving survivors an opportunity to claim them. Family members pried open the mouths of the disfigured dead to look for telltale signs, like gold teeth. Others inspected hands for rings. Survivors learned to search the armpits of charcoaled corpses for unburned fabric that might help identify a loved one. Four days after the attack, thirteen-year-old Toshiko Kameya and her father watched workers haul corpses up from the basement of a building, which flames had reduced to steel beams. Authorities gave family members one minute to examine the dead. Toshiko moved down the line, stopping when she finally found her mother, still dressed in her baggy *monpe* trousers and *kappougi*, an apron with large sleeves designed to protect a kimono. The flames had robbed her mother of all her hair. "Close to her was my small younger brother, who had just started walking," Toshiko remembered. "His body had no head or feet below the ankles, but I recognized him from the kimono he was wearing." She likewise found only the torso of her five-year-old sister, Fumiko, whom she identified via her kimono. The *monpe* on a pair of legs helped her recognize her ten-year-old sister, Hiroko. She never found her fifteen-year-old sister, Meiko, or her twelve-year-old sister, Nobuko.

On the night of the raid, Yoshimitsu Mano managed to save his five-year-old son only to lose sight of his wife and infant son amid the blizzard of sparks on the riverbank. Fearing them dead, Yoshimitsu evacuated the city, returning fifteen days later to his old neighborhood to hold a memorial service and burn incense. "By chance, during our prayers, I spied a familiar-looking hood of the kind women wore during air raids," he recalled. "I picked it up. It was hers. I found it on the embankment where I had last seen them alive."

Yoshimitsu combed the riverbank, finally locating his wife in the muck at the water's edge. "The child was still strapped to my wife's back," he said. "They had been in the water for more than two weeks." Yoshimitsu wrested the remains from the mud and then retrieved some relatives. "We placed the bodies on an iron sheet set on two stones," he said. "It took all day to cremate the bodies with logs and whatever scraps of wood we could find."

Countless other victims, however, simply vanished.

Katsumoto Saotome sought out his classmate, Iwao Tori. He had run into his friend and his mother while fleeing, but in the chaos, the two families had separated. After the attack, Katsumoto discovered the Tori family's watch shop still standing amid the wreckage, though empty of life other than the ticking of clocks. Every day Katsumoto returned, hoping his friend would reappear. And every day he listened as the clocks slowly wound down, one by one, until the shop finally fell silent, as if time had come to an end.

Across Tokyo, families claimed just sixty-four bodies from authorities. The few surviving crematoriums handled the remains of 1,805 others; mortuary teams burned another 2,495 on makeshift pyres. Authorities identified and buried 6,002 victims in individual graves. Workers shoveled the remaining dead into mass graves capable of handling anywhere from twenty to three thousand bodies. Tokyo's few parks, where residents once strolled under the shade of cherry blossom trees, evolved into sprawling cemeteries. Laborers buried 13,000 men, women, and children at Kinshi Park, along with another 8,400 at Ueno Park and 4,900 at Sumida Park. As the city's parks filled, graves mushroomed across the grounds of schoolyards and temples, eventually totaling sixty-seven temporary cemeteries. By March 15—six days after the raid—crews had buried a staggering 77,000 bodies.

Victims had little time to grieve. The army provided blankets, and ward offices passed out charcoal and matches, toilet paper and soap. Emergency kitchens set up in those police stations that escaped damage distributed hardtack and rice balls, but the meager supplies were far too little, prompting hungry residents to carve the meat off burned animals found in the ruins. "The horse," one survivor recalled, "was stripped of all its flesh in about three days." Others salvaged sugar from a destroyed confectionery factory where syrup spilled out onto the road. A few less scrupulous people rummaged through the pockets of the dead for bank notes and coins or slipped rings from fingers. Survivors dug through ashes of homes, where all that remained were foundation stones and cracked roof tiles. The lucky ones salvaged melted tea and rice bowls. In some cases, the heat had been so intense that it fused kitchenware together with clay roof tiles and even melted coins. "To uncover a dented pot, a few knives, a broken bowl, they worked patiently from morning to night, camping out, fetching water over long distances from shattered mains, sleeping in their shelter holes," journalist Robert Guillain reported. "Theirs was almost a happy resignation: for them, the nightmare was over. They had already accepted the defeat and they did not much care what happened now as long as they were still alive."

Authorities accused America of "slaughter bombing" while downplaying the attack for domestic audiences, claiming that just 130 bombers had executed the raid and that antiaircraft fire had destroyed or damaged 65 planes. The governor of the Tokyo metro district urged citizens to remain strong, even those who had lost loved ones and homes. "We are attempting everything within our power to relieve the victims of the current air raids," Yoshizo Nishio announced. "We are calling upon the people of the capital to pledge themselves to be unafraid of the air raids, to strengthen their accord and unity with one another, and to steel themselves all the more to fulfill the great task of guarding the imperial capital and also fully to cooperate and lend support to the unfortunate sufferers with warm feelings of loving comradeship."

The government reduced or abolished taxes for victims who lost homes or businesses, while the Agricultural Central Bank made security-free loans to those who agreed to farm. Japan's leading financial institutions launched a fund drive, setting a goal of 50 million yen or more than $3 million. Emperor Hirohito donated 10 million yen for victims—the equivalent of $666,666—the same amount he had contributed twenty-one years earlier, after the Great Kanto Earthquake. But those measures made little difference, as evidenced by the government's decision to cut off free aid to victims after only five days.

On the morning of March 18, the emperor climbed into his armored burgundy-and-black limousine, a 1935 Mercedes-Benz 770 adorned with a softball-size gold chrysanthemum emblem on the door. At nine a.m. Hirohito's motorcade departed, his first time leaving the palace grounds since October. Two decades earlier the emperor had toured the damage from the Great Kanto Earthquake on horseback, a memory that came back to him this morning.

"Tokyo," he said, "has been reduced to ashes."

Despite that observation, Hirohito remained convinced that Japan needed a victory before pursuing peace. Missing from the emperor's calculus, however, was the continued suffering of his people, a fact not lost on military aide Kaizo Yoshihashi, who watched residents dig through the rubble. Empty expressions, he observed, turned reproachful as the motorcade passed. "Were they resentful of the emperor because they had lost their relatives, their houses and belongings?" he wondered. "Or were they in a state of utter exhaustion and bewilderment? I sympathized with how his majesty must have felt upon approaching these unfortunate victims."

Dressed in his military uniform with polished boots and a sword, Hirohito spent only one hour in the ruins, during which time he visited the damaged Tomioka Hachimanga Shrine in Fukagawa, a scene dutifully captured by police photographer Koyo Ishikawa. Philippine diplomat Guerrero was disappointed by the brief accounts of the visit that followed in the newspapers. "No one asked him how he felt and he did not say," he wrote in his diary. "Well, how <u>did</u> he feel, looking at the flattened ruins and the rusting debris? Was he angry, frightened, solicitous, sorry? Was he remorseful-sorry, afraid-sorry, pitying-sorry? Or was he just bored? More important perhaps, how did the people feel? Were they resentful, grateful, cynical, overwhelmed by the imperial benevolence, envious, sympathetic? Or were they too indifferent? There were no riots, no cheers, no demonstrations either way."

An army of 75,000 workers began clearing roads and salvaging roofing metal, which had to be transported by oxcart. In undamaged districts, the government ordered another 143,129 properties torn down to create additional firebreaks, displacing 644,080 people. Guerrero visited Shibuya, where chalk marked homes scheduled for demolition, a job that fell to day laborers and even schoolchildren. Out front of such properties, residents hawked household wares. Bottles, needed for soy sauce, beer, and sake rations, fetched a premium. "Tokyo was a vast flea-market," added Guillain, "in which all the articles unobtainable for months, even on the black market, suddenly reappeared: sets of porcelain, chests of drawers, European furniture, new and used sandals, charcoal, straw mats and the thousand knickknacks that adorned prosperous homes: silk paintings, luxurious cushions, vases, lacquered boxes, Japanese books, incense burners. And all of it went for a pittance."

Authorities encouraged victims to leave the city, providing free train tickets and waiving the need for ration books. Many with family in the countryside escaped. Residents scavenged scrap wood to fashion makeshift packing crates, so many that the railroads stopped accepting such parcels. Cotton curtains soon morphed into homemade luggage. Crowds swarmed Tokyo Station, waiting for hours and even days to elbow aboard a packed train. Those more fortunate souls doled out a ransom in rice to rent a black market truck or even an old bicycle blessed with a baggage rack. "The rest," recalled Danish minister Lars Tillitse, "took to the roads."

CHAPTER 17

"The forces which will soon be unleashed against Japan
are as inevitable, irrepressible and overwhelming as the force
of an earthquake or a tidal wave."

—BRIG. GEN. BONNER FELLERS
JUNE 12, 1945, LETTER

American forces closed in on the Japanese homeland. After the bloody capture of Iwo Jima on March 26, war planners aimed for Okinawa, the largest island in the Ryukyus. Seventy miles long and just seven wide, Okinawa stood like a centurion, the last line of defense guarding Japan's four principal islands; the southernmost, Kyushu, lay just three hundred miles to the north. Intelligence estimated that 80,000 Japanese troops would defend Okinawa, a task made all the more challenging by the presence of nearly half a million native islanders. The April 1 invasion, code-named Operation Iceberg, called for the largest amphibious assault of the Pacific War, including 450,000 troops and more than 1,200 ships, an armada that numbered forty flattops, eighteen battleships, and more than two hundred cruisers and destroyers.

The Japanese, starved of fuel by America's submarine blockade, had introduced kamikazes in the October 1944 invasion of Leyte Gulf in the Philippines. In the last year of the war, the suicide planes would ultimately score 474 hits on Allied vessels, sinking thirty-four ships and killing 7,000 sailors. The crashes of enemy fighters and bombers loaded with fuel and bombs proved so violent that entire planes were reduced to fragments no bigger than a few square inches. "It is one of the most spectacular things I have seen in this war," Lt. Gen. Oscar Griswold wrote in his diary after witnessing such attacks. "You've got to hand it to the Jap—he has guts!"

Okinawa promised more such horror.

In addition to airstrips scattered throughout the Ryukyus, Japan counted another fifty-five fields on Kyushu and sixty-five on Formosa. To eliminate the threat, the navy's powerful Task Force 58 targeted Kyushu from March 18 to 21, prompting a violent retaliation in which Japanese bombers landed hits on five flattops. The worst came at 7:07 a.m. on March 19, when a bomber pounded the *Franklin*, killing more than 800 sailors and wounding nearly 500 others. Fires triggered by the attack were hot enough to melt dog tags. "Instantly the planes on the deck burst into flame, their machine guns firing, their bombs going off. Ready bomb stores exploded and down below, one by one, sections of the ship blossomed into flaming death traps," reporter George Horne wrote in the *New York Times*. "High-octane gasoline spewed forth, ran in cascades over the sides, and to watchers with the rest of the fleet the great ship seemed to disintegrate."

Though LeMay's Superfortresses operated independently, General Arnold had agreed that in case of an emergency, he could be roped in to help. Admiral Nimitz felt he had no choice but to summon LeMay, who grudgingly agreed, even though he felt it diverted his bombers from more profitable urban targets. LeMay's mission: destroy the Kyushu airfields.

On March 27, LeMay's bombers roared into the skies for the first of ninety-seven missions to pound Kyushu. Seventeen airfields invited repeated attack, as photoreconnaissance planes revealed that Japanese workers hustled to repair the fields, often within a day. Strikes typically consisted of one or two squadrons, which allowed aircrews to attack four to six airfields per day. April 21 marked the peak of the operation, when 266 bombers wrecked nine airfields. "We flattened every airdrome we could find up Kyushu way," LeMay said. "We not only had the facilities

destroyed, but the runways were turned into rubble, the fields were sol-
idly cratered. It would be impossible to make those fields less effective
than they already were."

In addition to hitting airfields, LeMay's crews flew missions as part
of Operation Starvation, the navy's effort to mine the empire's waters,
beginning with Kure Harbor, Hiroshima, and the Shimonoseki Straits.
War planners designed the early missions to coincide with the invasion,
hoping to bottle up any Japanese warships that might sortie for Okinawa.
Unlike the unexpected air field strikes, Hap Arnold had previously agreed
to participate in mining missions, prompting LeMay to assign the task to
General Davies's 313th Bombardment Wing on Tinian.

Geography proved one of Japan's great handicaps. The nation's
mountainous terrain had long blocked the development of any extensive
highway or rail systems, forcing 75 percent of all transportation to go by
sea, including half of the coal that powered Tokyo, Nagoya, Kobe, and
Osaka. Japan's inland sea therefore served as a maritime superhighway, a
natural enclosed shipping route with only two viable entrances. Drawn
like sharks to chum, American submarines swarmed the Bungo Suido
entrance. That left only the Shimonoseki Straits, the narrow channel that
divided Honshu and Kyushu. Ships loaded with oil, coal, iron, and rice
transited this aquatic artery, fueling the Japanese war machine. "The Shimonoseki Straits," one report noted, "was one of the most crowded shipping lanes in the Orient."

Bombers took off on March 27, executing the first of forty-six mining
missions in what would prove to be one of the most successful campaigns
of the war. In the operation's first phase, LeMay's bombers dropped 2,030
mines, ultimately closing the Shimonoseki Straits for up to two weeks until
Japan could clear a channel, a perilous task that involved suicide boats.
Even LeMay, who begrudged any deviation from strategic bombing, could
not help but appreciate the operation's value. From that first mission until
the end of the war, the general's crews would drop a total 12,053 mines in
waters throughout Japan, China, and Korea. The undersea weapons sank
294 ships and knocked another 137 out of the war. Mines sent 239 more
into the shipyard for repairs, upping the total of lost and damaged ships to

1,251,256 tons. That averaged out to five ships sunk or damaged every day from March through the end of the war. LeMay accomplished that flying just 1,529 sorties, which represented only 5.7 percent of the 21st Bomber Command's overall effort, an incredible return on investment.

LeMay intermixed mining and airfield attacks with precision strikes, sending his bombers to the Nakajima factory near Tokyo and the Mitsubishi Aircraft Engine Works in Nagoya, the only missions he could fly until ships loaded with incendiaries arrived. He used the opportunity to experiment, further lowering bombing altitudes and ordering night strikes in which crews dropped flares in an unsuccessful attempt to illuminate the targets.

With Kyushu's airfields wrecked and smoldering, LeMay went to see Nimitz. "We've finished now," the general said. "There's not another thing we can do for you. May we go back to hitting our strategic targets? We'll do a lot more good there."

"Yes, LeMay," Nimitz replied, "you've done a very fine job. Very good. I guess it's about time you go back on your own type of operation. But let me check with Sherman."

Rear Adm. Forrest Sherman, who served as Nimitz's deputy chief of staff, balked at releasing LeMay, fearing the Japanese would simply repair the airfields. "There wasn't anything to bomb. But we were ordered to go over and keep dropping more bombs on those beat-up airdromes," LeMay complained. "All we were doing at last was plowing the fields."

LeMay appealed to Arnold to intervene, which only prompted the navy to threaten to pull out and leave troops ashore undefended. Norstad messaged LeMay several times, reminding him of the air force's duty. "The Iceberg Operation," he cabled, "continues to have first call on your resources whenever the employment of your force can be of assistance."

"Day after day," LeMay griped, "we had to go out and bomb Target Nothing."

Half a world away in Washington, members of the Joint Target Group pored over the reports of LeMay's March blitz. The mission of this new organization, which was set up inside the Joint Chiefs of Staff, was to provide target recommendations for the 20th Air Force. LeMay's decision to embrace fire raids had broadened the list of potential targets. "In just ten days," one report noted, "the entire picture changed." Unlike Germany, Japan lacked any real industrial bottlenecks beyond aircraft engines. Fire raids, the group concluded, served as the biggest threat to the enemy's industry. The group designated thirty-three urban areas as targets, noting that sprawling cities, like Tokyo, Nagoya, and Osaka, contained multiple incendiary zones. War planners divided these into three phases. The first focused on aircraft and ordnance plants; the second included electrical equipment, machine tools, and aircraft components. Analysts would consider initiating the final phase only after the first two were completed. Beyond urban areas, the group identified priority industrial targets, ranging from the Osaka Army Arsenal to Koriyama Chemical Works. This mix of targets would allow LeMay to execute both precision strikes and fire raids, depending on weather and weapons stockpiles.

A new target directive rattled off LeMay's teletype on April 3. The Nakajima plant near Tokyo, which his forces now had bombed ten times, and the Mitsubishi plant in Nagoya still ranked at the top. After those came ten urban areas in Tokyo, Kawasaki, Nagoya, and Osaka. Norstad fired off an accompanying letter to LeMay, noting that he hoped Japan might finally lose its taste for war. "I am convinced," he concluded, "that the XXI Bomber Command, more than any other service or weapon, is in a position to do something decisive."

LeMay agreed.

The fire blitz had given him a glimpse of the awesome power he possessed. Hansell had struggled for months to knock out a single factory, while LeMay in ten days had destroyed thirty-two square miles of the enemy's homeland. Like a mythical god, LeMay had the power to wield fire, to incinerate entire cities, towns, and villages, to reduce mile after mile after mile to ashes and dust. The thirty-eight-year-old general controlled the fate of an entire nation and its people. Unlike his first fire raid against Tokyo, LeMay now had Arnold's full support.

And a new list of cities to burn.

March had set a benchmark for the pace of operations. Air and ground crews had risen to the challenge, executing repeated back-to-back missions. LeMay directed his staff to determine the logistical requirements necessary to sustain a similar supercharged level of fighting in the months ahead, which he believed could knock Japan out of the war and prevent the need for a bloody invasion. That study, which assumed the arrival of the 58th Bombardment Wing in May followed by the 315th in July, predicted he could double the 2,925 sorties his crews would fly in April to 6,700 in September. But bombers represented only part of the destructive equation. LeMay needed pilots and navigators, bombardiers and gunners. Planners considered sixty hours a month the maximum crews could fly. On each mission, the Japanese shot down some, while others fell sick. After thirty-five missions, airmen could go home, creating a revolving door. The scheduled arrival of new crews was not enough. By LeMay's calculations, he would be 908 crews short by September. "It must be emphasized," he wrote in an April 13 message to Washington, "that the delivery of the additional aircraft will not permit this command to increase its sortie effort unless the aircraft are accompanied by crews."

Ten days later Washington informed LeMay that the training program could not be altered to remedy his projected shortfall of airmen. The failure to provide more crews would mean fewer sorties against the enemy's homeland. That would translate into fewer bombs, less destruction, and a prolonged war that risked more American deaths and a possible invasion. Washington's inability to provide more crews between May and September would rob LeMay of a staggering 6,789 sorties against Japan. That figure eclipsed his total projected missions for September.

Just as he had done throughout his career, LeMay dug into the problem. During the March hustle to burn Japan's cities, he discovered, crews had flown an average of eighty-six hours, far exceeding the recommended sixty. At that pace, LeMay reasoned, he could still increase his sorties and hopefully finish Japan in six months.

The question remained, however, could his crews keep up? His flight surgeon and wing commanders warned LeMay that he risked exhausting his airmen, which would only increase the likelihood of physical and emotional fatigue, mistakes, and tragedy.

But like the fire blitz, LeMay determined, it was a necessary gamble. "If Japan can be defeated without a costly ground invasion," he assured his staff, "the risk of airmen's lives is worth it." The general outlined his solution in an April 25 message to Washington. "I consider that for the first time strategic air bombardment faces a situation in which its strength is proportionate to the magnitude of its task," LeMay wrote. "I feel that destruction of Japan's ability to wage war lies with the capability of this command, provided its maximum capability is exerted unstintingly during the next six months, which is considered to be the critical period. Though naturally reluctant to drive my force at an exorbitant rate, I believe that the opportunity now at hand warrants extraordinary measures on the part of all sharing it."

The first shiploads of new incendiaries had arrived in port shortly before the middle of April. LeMay did not wait. "Anybody we could get our hands on," he said, "was hauling bombs for us." That included Seabees and Marines, often rustled out of bed in the middle of the night to greet a new arrival in port. Majors and lieutenant commanders sweated alongside seamen and privates, hauling the incendiaries straight from the ships to the bombers.

LeMay planned to mount his first fire raid since the blitz against the Tokyo Arsenal Complex, an oval-shaped area in the city's northwestern corner. The population density ranged from 30,000 to 80,000 people per square mile, with residents crowded into typical wooden homes. The area earned its name from its many gunpowder factories, chemical plants, and ordnance storehouses. "Rarely has such an opportunity for attack on industries directly contributing to the war-making power of the enemy presented itself," one intel report stated. "And rarely does the inflammable and explosive nature of the industries within the target area reach such a degree."

Three hundred and fifty-two bombers charged into the skies on April 13, hitting Tokyo with 2,042 tons of incendiaries over a span of three hours. Those bombs triggered such violent explosions that airmen saw them as far as a hundred miles away, while the ensuing fires torched 11.4 square miles. "All aircraft attacking during the later stages," the mission report observed, "had to fly through smoke clouds towering above 10,000 feet, resulting in turbulence so great that it was often necessary for both pilots to control the airplane."

LeMay ordered his crews to hit the capital again two days later as part of a joint strike on Tokyo and neighboring Kawasaki. For this mission, LeMay divided his forces. The 73rd Bombardment Wing would target Tokyo's Kamata section, along the southern shoreline of the bay, while the 313th and 314th would bomb Kawasaki, right across the Tama River.

That mission was another success, destroying six square miles of Tokyo, 3.6 of Kawasaki, and 1.5 of Yokohama. The two raids burned a total of 217,130 homes, businesses, and factories in Tokyo and Yokohama. Flames scorched 31,603 in Kawasaki. The capital's total destruction climbed to 34.2 square miles. "A quick glance at the map certainly gives the impression that something over half of Tokyo is now gone," Norstad wrote LeMay. "The three Tokyo incendiary operations have certainly been among the most effective in the entire history of bombing. Keep up the good work."

————

ON MAY 11, Nimitz finally released LeMay from his obligation to help with the Okinawa invasion. The general celebrated by ordering a massive fire raid on Nagoya three days later. His previous two efforts had burned only five square miles of Japan's third-largest city, far less than Tokyo. He hoped to remedy that with a one-two punch. His target: northern Nagoya, a nine-square-mile urban area with a population density of up to 75,000 men, women, and children per square mile. Beyond the residential congestion, the zone had critical wartime targets, including the Mitsubishi Electric Company and the Mitsubishi Aircraft Engine Works. The daylight attack by 472 bombers incinerated 3.15 square miles.

Two days later, LeMay's bombers returned, leveling 3.82 square miles along the city's southern waterfront. In five missions, aircrews had destroyed a total of 12.37 square miles, roughly one-quarter of the entire city. Blazes from the May 14 raid generated a wall of smoke that climbed more than two miles up into the sky. "We could see huge fires rising and falling in the smoke," bombardier Second Lt. Joseph O'Grady recalled. "When our element made its bombing run five formations crossed the target area abreast. It looked as if one giant bomb bay opened to let tons of bombs fall. We were too many for the Japs today."

Nagoya was finished.

Next on LeMay's list: a return visit to Tokyo.

The general once again ordered back-to-back missions, determined to finally scratch the Japanese capital as a target. The first strike he aimed at southern Tokyo, a densely populated area crowded with factories that hammered out aircraft parts and tanks along with gas and rolling stock plants. Maj. Jack Catton, the former pilot of the *Joltin' Josie*, had traded his spot in the cockpit for a job planning strikes. Antiaircraft guns prompted planners to change the axis of attack, a move LeMay seized on during the prestrike briefing.

"Who planned this mission?" the general asked.

"We planned it, sir," Catton replied.

"Why did you select this axis of attack?"

Catton explained that it provided a good initial point and radar return but also would avoid the heaviest concentrations of antiaircraft batteries.

"Let me ask just one question," LeMay said. "Is that the best axis of attack?"

"Yes, sir," Catton answered. "I think so."

"No," LeMay countered. "I don't think you do."

Catton tried to explain, but LeMay interrupted him. As he had first discovered in the skies over Germany, there was no shortcut to victory. "Let me explain something to you," LeMay said. "We will lose fewer crews and we'll destroy the target far sooner if we use the best possible axis of attack from the standpoint of getting bombs on target."

On the night of May 23, 520 bombers pummeled Tokyo, triggering an inferno that flattened another 5.3 square miles. "For two hours," one intel report noted, "bombs dropped on the target area at an average rate of 1,000 pounds per second."

But the mission revealed that Japan was still in the fight. Seventeen bombers failed to return. Fighters and flak damaged another sixty-seven. Two nights later, 464 Superfortresses roared through the skies there again, targeting the city's financial, government, and business districts in the south along with the Shinagawa Railroad Yard. One of the most important marshaling yards in Japan, Shinagawa connected the industrial complex of Tokyo, Yokohama, and Kawasaki with the rest of the nation. Destruction of the yard, planners predicted, would arrest the movement of raw materials headed to wartime factories.

Japanese fighters pounced, aided by hundreds of searchlights and antiaircraft guns. The intensity of the flak stunned veterans, including Rosie O'Donnell, who saw eight bombers go down in flames. The May 25 mission cost America a total of twenty-six Superfortresses—5.2 percent of all aircraft airborne—making it the greatest single-day loss of the war. Gunfire and flak damaged another 110 bombers. "It was one of the most violent missions that I had ever participated in," O'Donnell recalled. "Hundreds of searchlights, streams of light flak and countless bursts of heavy flak penetrated the skies while the city below took on the aspect of a flaming inferno." The brutal onslaught prompted LeMay, who rarely discussed operations with his wife, to mention it in his letter the next day. "We took quite a beating over Tokyo last night," he lamented, "but I think we did a good job, so it was worth it."

The back-to-back losses prompted O'Donnell to hold a brief service on May 30 to mark Memorial Day. At daybreak he gathered with the twelve thousand officers and enlisted men under his command on the Saipan runway. The entire service, which lasted barely five minutes, consisted of an invocation and a short address followed by a benediction and taps. "Since the beginning of operations against the Japanese homeland six months ago, over one thousand of our officers and men, having taken off from this field on combat missions, failed to return," O'Donnell began. "One thousand of our own is the terrible cost exacted thus far in the performance of our mission. That our mission has been well performed is no secret. That we have never faltered, despite our losses, in an undeniable truth. That the damage done to the enemy is all out of proportion to the cost is evident—but they are one thousand, they are our own. We miss them. We grieve for their families and loved ones, and today we humbly salute them."

Despite the losses, the sixth and final fire raid against the Japanese capital burned 16.8 square miles, bringing the total destruction to a staggering 56.3 square miles, an area more than two and half times the size of Manhattan Island. Like Nagoya, Tokyo was done.

But LeMay kept punching.

He hit Yokohama, Osaka, and Kobe again.

Then Osaka once more.

Day and night LeMay's airmen commuted north along the Hirohito Highway, hauling bellies full of bombs, while back in the Marianas ground crews hustled to swap out engines and patch bullet and flak holes. In Quonset huts on Guam, photo analysts struggled to keep up, poring over black and white images, measuring the destruction of factories and neighborhoods down to the square mile, acre, and even foot. Intelligence summaries charted Japan's wreckage with clinical precision. "A total of 6.9 square miles of the city were burned," one read.

"About 3.8 square miles," stated another.

"Approximately 3.4 square miles were destroyed by this mission."

In a few short months, LeMay had transformed the 21st Bomber Command into one of the most destructive fighting units the world had ever seen. An organization that only six months earlier had struggled to launch a hundred bombers on a mission now sent up five times that many, filling the skies over Japan with storm clouds of aluminum, rubber, and napalm. On any given night, more than 5,500 pilots, navigators, and bombardiers brought America's fury home to the enemy. To accomplish this, LeMay had revolutionized bombing tactics, revamped the maintenance system, and pushed his aircrews to the limits of human endurance. In doing so he had demonstrated the frightening potential of the B-29 Superfortress, realizing the dream Arnold had set in motion years earlier when he fought for the development of the hemispheric bomber. On June 11, LeMay's headquarters marked the destructive milestone of incinerating 102.67 square miles of Tokyo, Osaka, Nagoya, Yokohama, Kobe, and Kawasaki. The general had hit his stride. "I think I have convinced the Japs in the last two months that they are beaten," LeMay wrote in a letter to his wife, "and that I will destroy everything in Japan."

Hap Arnold welcomed such news.

On June 12, a Douglas C-54 Skymaster carrying the general touched down on Saipan at one-thirty p.m., marking Arnold's first trip to the Pacific in almost three years.

Much had changed in that time.

Only six weeks earlier in Berlin, Hitler had retreated to his study in his underground bunker, pressed the barrel of his Walther PPK to his right temple, and squeezed the trigger. Germany surrendered ten days later, ending a war that had reduced sixty-one of its cities to rubble, killed more than half a million civilians, and left another 800,000 injured. Arnold's excitement over Germany's defeat was tempered by the death of President Franklin Roosevelt, felled by a massive stroke on April 12 at his home in Warm Springs, Georgia. The president's passing had elevated Harry Truman to commander in chief. The former Missouri lawmaker, who had chaired a Senate committee designed to root out wartime waste and profiteering, had previously clashed with Arnold, which the general feared might complicate his dreams for an independent air service. "Franklin Roosevelt was not only a personal friend," Arnold lamented, "but one of the best friends the Air Force ever had."

Germany's downfall shifted America's focus from Europe to the Pacific, which had only upped the pressure on Arnold to deliver a knockout punch. On May 25, the Joint Chiefs of Staff had approved plans for the invasion of Japan—code-named Operation Downfall—which would begin on November 1 with an assault on the southernmost island of Kyushu. Five months later troops would slosh ashore on the beaches of Honshu near Tokyo. The ferocity of fighting on Saipan, Iwo Jima, and Okinawa foreshadowed a bloody battle for the enemy's homeland. Arnold remained convinced that America could bomb Japan out of the war before then, but he refused to oppose his friend George Marshall, who had advised the new president that an invasion promised the fastest path to victory. If Arnold wanted to defeat Japan via bombardment—and demonstrate the awesome power of his air force—he had to do it fast.

Time was running out.

But the general faced another challenge. Unlike the European war, which had benefited from a unified command under a single leader, the Pacific had long been divided between the army and navy. Gen. Douglas MacArthur had pushed north from Australia, while Adm. Chester Nimitz had powered west across the central Pacific. As America closed in on Japan for the war's climax, Arnold feared these titanic forces would squeeze out his air service at a critical moment. To remedy this, Arnold planned to create the U.S. Army Strategic Air Force in the Pacific under the command of Gen. Carl Spaatz, who had served as America's top airman in Europe. Arnold wanted to move the 20th Air Force from Washington to the Marianas and place it under Spaatz, along with the Eighth Air Force, led by Jimmy Doolittle, which would redeploy from England to Okinawa. The four stars that lined Spaatz's shoulders would give him—and more important, the air service—the gravitas to compete alongside Nimitz and MacArthur. All these concerns weighed upon Arnold as he climbed down from the plane to find LeMay, Rosie O'Donnell, and others waiting on the tarmac beneath the sweltering midday sun.

Arnold had long distrusted the navy, a sentiment only reinforced by his dealings with Adm. Ernest King, his irascible colleague on the Joint Chiefs of Staff. In fairness to King, few people liked the admiral, who had a reputation akin to that of a junkyard dog. He barked at subordinates, drank too much, and had wandering hands that left women reluctant to sit near him at dinner parties. Despite having earned his wings later in life, King remained a battleship sailor. "Army aviation," he once griped, "should end at the shoreline." Not only were such words blasphemy to airmen like Arnold, but they also reflected King's overall condescension toward the army air service and even toward his colleague, refusing to answer Arnold's questions during meetings of the Joint Chiefs of Staff. He directed his responses instead to General Marshall.

Arnold had earned his fifth star in December 1944, making him an equal to Nimitz, which he hoped would prove beneficial on this trip as he laid the groundwork for his new strategic air force. Soon after landing, a message from Marshall greeted him, warning him that the navy had balked at his plan to locate his new strategic bomber headquarters on Guam. Arnold fumed. Who was the navy to dictate the location of his headquarters? "They have had no strategic bomber experience," he wrote in his diary. "Time is essential and we must get things moving if we are to get maximum effectiveness of our bombing effort. Perhaps we should give up all idea of cooperating with the Navy, put the Headquarters in Manila and call it a day."

Over the next couple of days, Arnold sat through presentations by LeMay and his staff as well his counterparts in the navy. He mixed informational sessions with pep talks to the airmen, medal ceremonies, and a tour of Guam. The general marveled at the destruction. "Jungle, fruit trees, villages all gone," Arnold wrote in his diary, "wrecked by war."

Ever impatient, Arnold finally pulled LeMay aside. With the invasion date now set—and his dream for an independent air service at stake—Arnold needed a blunt and realistic appraisal of the war. No more presentations, graphs, or charts. "I'm asking this question to everyone I see out here," the general began. "When is this war going to be over?"

"We've been too busy fighting to figure out a date," LeMay confessed, "but if you'll give me thirty minutes I'll give you an estimate."

Arnold nodded.

LeMay grabbed colonels John Montgomery, James Garcia, and Stanley Emrick—his deputies for operations, intelligence, and plans—instructing them to return to headquarters and calculate when America would exhaust all industrial targets. Half an hour later one of LeMay's aides returned, handing him a slip of paper. "We'll run out of big strategic cities and targets by October 1," he said. "I can't see the war going on much beyond that date."

Arnold liked what he heard, but as his diary shows, he remained skeptical—and with good reason. Germany had seen its cities reduced to rubble and ruin yet kept on fighting. LeMay had so far burned out a hundred square miles of Japan, but his target list remained long. No one knew Japan's threshold for pain. "We did it in Germany with much more difficult targets and much more intense antiaircraft," Arnold wrote. "Why not in Japan? We will see."

The general sat down with Nimitz at 9:40 a.m. on June 14 in the admiral's headquarters on Guam to hash out details for his new air force. Arnold, who was conditioned for battle after his years of tangling with King, was stunned by the admiral's graciousness.

Could he put his new Army Strategic Air Force headquarters on Guam?

Absolutely.

With both the Twentieth and the Eighth air forces?

Of course.

And General Spaatz in charge?

Not a problem.

Arnold walked out of the meeting in disbelief. Over the course of the two-and-a-half-hour conference, the admiral had agreed to every one of the general's requests. "Nimitz is really doing what he thinks best for winning the war," Arnold confided in his diary. "He makes his decisions accordingly regardless of what the Army, Navy or Marines think."

Marshall messaged Arnold the following day, alerting him of an upcoming meeting between the president and the Joint Chiefs of Staff. The topic: could the war could be won via bombing? Arnold no doubt wanted to avoid making the eight-thousand-mile trip back to Washington, but he also knew that there was no better person to brief the Joint Chiefs than LeMay. Sending LeMay would also prevent Arnold from opposing Marshall in a public setting. "I want you to go back to Washington and give the briefing you've given me to the Joint Chiefs."

LeMay hustled to pack while Arnold flew up to survey Iwo Jima. Early that morning, more than five hundred Superfortresses had roared into the skies for a strike on Osaka. This fourth fire raid would ultimately incinerate another two and a half square miles of the city, kill or wound 1,852 people, and destroy 51,725 buildings. Within hours, bombers would render another 174,000 Japanese people homeless. In his diary, Arnold reflected on the mission with pride. The fledgling air service he had taken command of before the war had in just a few years morphed into a global strike force capable of inflicting devastating ruin. "At this writing there are 520 B-29s over Osaka, 3,000 tons of bombs," he wrote. "What a contrast with Doolittle's 18 planes and 15 tons and the first B-29 mission a year ago with its 68 planes and 181 tons."

Accompanied by fifteen officers and enlisted men, LeMay lifted off at 10:05 p.m. that evening from Guam's North Field in a B-29 bound for Washington. The bomber stopped only once, on Oahu for two hours for food and fuel, before pressing on across the ocean. LeMay, who had clearance only as far as San Francisco, failed to secure it for Washington before buzzing the Golden Gate Bridge and passing out of radio range. As a result, when he touched down at National Airport at 11:43 p.m. on that Saturday, June 16, it was much to the surprise of air control. "We don't have any record of you," airport officials said. "Where did you take off from?"

"Honolulu," LeMay replied.

"Honolulu!" came the stunned response.

The record-breaking flight, which had covered 8,420 miles in thirty eight and a half hours, landed LeMay on the front page of the *New York Times*.

At three-thirty p.m. on June 18, Truman met at the White House with War Secretary Henry Stimson, Assistant War Secretary John McCloy, Navy Secretary James Forrestal, General Marshall, Adm. William Leahy, and Admiral King. Lt. Gen. Ira Eaker attended in Arnold's place. Marshall began by arguing that the seizure of Kyushu was essential to complete the strangulation of Japan, which would allow American troops to invade Honshu. Only through invasion could the Japanese be forced to feel the "utter helplessness" that would trigger them to surrender. "Air power alone was not sufficient to put the Japanese out of the war. It was unable alone to put the Germans out," minutes show Marshall said.

"Against the Japanese, scattered through mountainous country, the problem would be much more difficult."

Truman turned to Eaker, asking the airman to share his opinion. Eaker, maintaining Arnold's refusal to openly clash with Marshall, agreed. "Those who advocated the use against Japan of air power alone," he told those gathered, "overlooked the very impressive fact that air casualties are always much heavier when the air faces the enemy alone." Absent from the printed minutes, however, was any reference to the development of the atomic bomb, which was scheduled to be tested the following month in the New Mexico desert. If successful, what role might such a new weapon play in shortening the war? "The President and the Chiefs of Staff," the minutes cryptically conclude, "then discussed certain other matters."

The president greenlit the Kyushu invasion.

LeMay met the following day at the Pentagon with the Joint Chiefs, but he was too late—and he knew it. No one cared to hear from a two-star field commander. "General Marshall slept through most of the briefing," LeMay recalled. "I can't blame him; he was probably worn down to a nub. The decision was made to invade. Here was a crazy flyboy coming in saying the war could be ended without invasion. We didn't make much of an imprint."

It now fell to LeMay to prove them wrong.

All of them.

If LeMay could not convince the Joint Chiefs, he would at least try to sell the American public. The general met that same day with the press at the Pentagon. His ink-black hair, reporters noted, had begun to gray at the temples. LeMay fingered a cigarette lighter as his staff displayed charts and photographs of fire-wrecked cities. "We have destroyed the five largest cities in Japan and any one of these would be a major disaster," he said. "We have the capacity to devastate Japan and we will do so if she does not surrender."

CHAPTER 18

"If the Japs don't give up we will completely devastate their homeland.
We will hit them so hard it will take them a century to recover."

—MAJ. GEN. CURTIS LeMAY
JUNE 21, 1945

Japan teetered on collapse.

The attacks wrecked homes and public utilities and disrupted postal and telegraphic services. Between ripped-up railways and streets clogged with evacuees, transportation ground to a halt. Worker absenteeism soared, and industrial output plummeted. To remedy this, the government passed a law, forcing laborers to remain on the job even if their homes had burned. Another required evacuated workers to return, providing them with special travel priority and free train tickets. "Large-scale strategic bombing," concluded a report by faculty at Tokyo Imperial University, "completely shattered the foundation of Japan's economy."

Residents who were able to fled the cities. After the two March strikes on Nagoya, more than 317,000 people evacuated the city, a figure equal to one-third of its prewar population. Another 170,000 departed after the raids in mid-May. Osaka experienced a similar exodus, with 425,343 leaving in March followed by 461,561 in June. Tokyo saw the largest evacuation, with more than 4,729,000 abandoning the capital, the majority of them in the last year of the war. That figure amounted to three out of every four residents. Across Japan, more than 8.5 million residents escaped cities for the countryside, roughly one-fourth of the entire urban population. "Most people," historian Thomas Havens observed, "in the timeless pattern of war refugees everywhere, wordlessly left town riding bicycles, sitting atop oxcarts, or trudging on foot."

Widespread evacuation triggered other societal problems, exposing the class divide between rural and urban residents who were suddenly thrust together. City dwellers looked down on their rural neighbors. On a train to Odawara, Guerrero overheard two Tokyo residents complaining, a scene he captured in his diary. "It seemed the country was insupportable," he wrote. "The people were such boors; conditions were so primitive. The old man climaxed it by uncovering his leg and crying: 'Look at all those fleabites! I didn't know they have so many fleas in the country!'" Rural residents likewise grew resentful of the evacuees: not only did their relative wealth spark jealousy, but most lacked skills to help farm. The government resorted to shame to prod rural residents. "Families that won't take people in are a disgrace," one slogan declared. More important, evacuees taxed already meager supplies. "Food problems were the chief cause of this," one rural schoolmaster said. "There simply wasn't enough for everyone, and the people felt that additional mouths complicated the situation, while the evacuees felt that they had as much right as anyone to eat."

Much to the frustration of the authorities, evacuees spread defeatism and contradicted the upbeat radio and newspaper propaganda. "Tokyo people," one resident complained, "had nothing new to tell us—they just brought their tales of horror and bombing."

For those who stayed in the capital, life was brutal. Japan announced plans to construct fifty thousand temporary housing units, but there were few available workers, much less building materials, even as authorities ordered lumber and nails salvaged from the wreckage. As an emergency measure, Tokyo turned standing schools and public buildings into shelters, but most refugees tired of the unsanitary and cramped communal conditions within ten days. This left residents with two options: abandon the capital or erect shanties. "Tokyo authorities," one postwar American report observed, "simply did not realize the enormity of the housing problem which was bound to follow incendiary attacks. They were unprepared for the consequences and people were therefore left for the most part to their own devices."

Refugees settled in the destroyed districts, hoping that bombers would not target those areas again. "The limitless acres of ruin," observed Masuo Kato, "seemed to spread everywhere, like a desert, in a drab and monotonous panorama of hopelessness." The only color in this otherwise empty wasteland came from the auburn rust that flourished across the abandoned remains of automobile bodies and machine lathes, printing presses and iron safes. Crafty residents salvaged charred timbers, lashing them together with wire or straw ropes. Others set up homes in old air raid trenches, laying battered tatami mats down as floors. Roofs consisted of sheet metal held in place by stones. At night survivors listened as the wind rattled the roofs. Others marveled at the view of the Ueno mountains or the cries of seabirds, sights and sounds once alien in the bustling capital. By April, a government report calculated that 227,000 people lived in such shacks in Tokyo. "It has one great advantage," a physician said of his shelter in an old bunker. "When the air-raid signal is blown, you don't have to get out of bed."

Katsumoto Saotome joined the destitute after the raids in late May destroyed his family's rented home in Mukojima, leaving only the front entryway, which framed the vast expanse of the wrecked capital in the distance. Katsumoto's father collected sheet metal, while the youth scavenged for food, including cans of sardines from a destroyed factory. "I was like a stray dog," Katsumoto said, "picking whatever looked valuable on the ground." The family's daily struggle was all too common. Playwright Kafu Nagai, who was forced out of three homes by fire raids, chronicled his ordeal in his diary. "Every day I burn scraps of wood taken from destroyed houses to cook my meals," he wrote. "Life in a defeated country—no water, no fire. One can fairly say that we have reached the extreme of misery."

News of the fire raid fatalities trickled out weeks later to the inns and temples that housed evacuated children. Forty-five days after Tokyo burned, Fukagawa native Ikuko Matsue, who turned ten that May, was summoned along with other children to the main hall of the Dairenji Temple in Niigata prefecture. The last Ikuko had heard from her family was a March 4 letter from her older sister, Toshiko, describing the February 25 attack on the capital. "I know we should never say this," her sister wrote, "but I thought the bombs were incredibly beautiful. They were like sparklers made bigger. I can hardly express how gorgeous they were."

The monks lined up in front of the main hall while the house father stepped forward. One by one, he called out each child's name and then reported on the fate of the family.

"Matsue," he finally announced, using Ikuko's surname. "Your elder brother survived. Your father, mother, and two sisters died."

Food shortages worsened as spring gave way to summer. The loss of Okinawa robbed Japan of precious rice, while aerial mining cut off vital imports from Korea and Formosa, including fertilizer. A partial crop failure stemming from that winter's brutal cold coupled with excessive rains exacerbated the crisis. The government pitched a plan to send fifty thousand urban families to the northern island of Hokkaido to raise crops, though few in the end actually moved. A revised ration system based on performance gave preference to workers, while the government encouraged residents to collect acorns and learn to eat weeds, an announcement Guerrero mocked in his diary. "If the war continues," the diplomat wrote, "they must learn to eat cinders and ashes."

Health care was another hardship. Flames had burned the left leg of Haruyo Wada's sister, a wound that had since grown infected. Haruyo used disposable chopsticks to pick out wriggling maggots. Her mother finally took Mitsuko to see a doctor.

"Do you have oil?" the physician asked.

The family, forced to live with relatives, had nothing. Her mother climbed down on her knees and prayed, which drew sympathy from a fellow burn patient, who presented her with a small bottle of oil to treat Mitsuko's leg. "You should use this."

Others were not so fortunate.

Sixth-grader and fellow Joto ward resident Kazuyo Funato had survived the March conflagration huddling in an underground shelter with her younger sister Hiroko, who suffered burns on her head and hands trying to yank off her flaming air raid hood.

"My hands hurt," the youth had cried that night. "My hands hurt."

Kazuyo dug a hole and inserted her sister's hands, using the cool soil to soothe her scorched flesh. Days later, however, Hiroko fell sick. Her father, a pharmacist whose store was destroyed, suspected tetanus, a life-threatening infection caused by bacteria in the earth. The family wheeled her to a hospital in a cart. "Hiroko's face was burned very severely and her bandages soon became soaked with blood and pus," Kazuyo recalled. "There were so few bandages available that we washed hers at home and then took them back to the hospital."

Day after day Kazuyo watched her sister decline, as her father scoured Tokyo for precious medicine. Kazuyo returned to the hospital one day with washed bandages. "Hiro-chan," she said, "why are you sleeping with your eyes open?"

Kazuyo tried to close her sister's eyelids but couldn't.

"Hiroko!" she cried. "Hiroko!"

Her father stepped back into the room. "Hiroko just died," he said, "even though I brought serum for her."

Overwhelmed with guilt, Kazuyo later watched orderlies load her sister's body onto a cart for transportation to a crematorium. "Hiroko had escaped through the fierce fires and was finally safe," Kazuyo remembered, "only to be burned again."

Over all these tragedies and challenges hung the threat of more raids, more fire, and more death, a constant fear that wore down an already-hungry and exhausted populace. "I could stand everything else," one woman lamented, "but I couldn't help worrying about the air raids." Superstitious rumors spread. Rubbing an onion on one's head promised to make a person safe; so did placing a pickled onion atop a bowl of rice and beans, or eating leeks. Others whispered that certain cities had been spared because friends of Harry Truman or Douglas MacArthur lived there. Another falsely asserted that Kyoto was off limits because MacArthur's mother was buried there. The rise in such rumors coincided with growing resentment. "The survivors," one report noted, "of those who have been killed in the bombings weep, saying that those dying on the battlefield are regarded as the heroic war dead, but that those who lose their lives in the bombings are treated as persons who have died an undesirable death."

By summer, the torrent of disastrous events at long last eroded the foundation of Japan's political resistance. Germany's surrender had left the embattled empire alone to fight, while Russia's decision not to renew its neutrality pact raised the threat that the Soviets might join the Allies in the war against Japan. On the domestic front, Prime Minister Kuniaki Koiso, blamed for Japan's failures to check American advances in the Philippines, resigned in April, replaced by seventy-seven-year-old Adm. Kantaro Suzuki. Despite America's prohibition against targeting the Imperial Palace, fires from the May 25 incendiary raid had leaped the moat and towering walls, killing more than two dozen employees and incinerating portions of the royal compound. For Hirohito, forced to live in an underground shelter, enough was enough. On June 22—the same day America secured Okinawa—the emperor told the Supreme War Leadership Council to find a diplomatic way out of the fight. "We have heard enough of this determination of yours to fight to the last soldier," he said. "Now we want action. We want you to consider methods of ending this war."

In the meantime, authorities continued to publicly downplay American attacks, censoring news of some raids. Other times the press exaggerated the number of enemy bombers shot down, while minimizing the growing size of America's aerial armadas. Indeed, the government tried to convince civilians that suffering on the home front was minor compared to what frontline troops endured. "We must overcome all the unfavorable conditions and fight to the last," welfare minister Tadahiko Okada said in a speech. Such statements, however, rang hollow to the hungry and exhausted citizenry. "There was no one," observed journalist Robert Guillain, "who did not know that the war was lost and that defeat would be total. The population had only to contemplate the black deserts where once their cities had stood."

The government blamed America for intentionally killing civilians to undermine morale in advance of an invasion. Though hostility toward the enemy was widespread, efforts to focus public outrage backfired, sparking fears of more air attacks, while highlighting the failure of the air defense corps to guard the citizenry. "We were unprotected. It was the same all over Japan," a Kokura resident told investigators after the war. "The blame is on our leaders. They did nothing to protect us after getting us into this war." That sentiment proved common as sirens howled and hungry residents bedded down in shanties. "I felt bitter toward the government," added a Yokohama resident, "and wished we had never started the war."

As Japan's fortunes faded, LeMay's star rose.

The general's decision to firebomb Japan earned accolades from fellow air commanders whose letters filled his inbox on Guam. Maj. Gen. Claire Chennault, who had once flown acrobatic shows with Hansell before he organized the Flying Tigers, lauded LeMay's magnificent work. "The two decisions, to use incendiaries *en masse* and to go in low, must have cost you a good many sleepless nights, but they have proved to be brilliantly wise," Chennault wrote. "You and your fellows are visibly shortening the war."

Even Hansell reached out from his new post in Roswell, New Mexico. It was no doubt difficult for Possum to witness the success of his replacement, but ever the southern gentleman, he demonstrated grace in his congratulations even though as his letter showed he remained convinced of the efficacy of daylight precision bombing. "I have been watching your operations with great interest and admiration," Hansell wrote. "The decision to go into Japan at such low altitude, at night, was certainly a very courageous one, but obviously it was a correct one. Personally, I believe we will have to return to daylight bombing of selected targets, before we beat the Japanese down to the level needed. However, the successful bombing and burning of the great population centers has certainly offered a tremendous contribution."

The headlines that filled newspapers nationwide made LeMay a celebrity, prompting strangers to request autographs and 21st Bomber Command insignia. Letters came from Cub Scouts and Rotarians, high school students and housewives. Postmarks revealed that LeMay's fans ranged from South Carolina and Ohio to California and Connecticut. Others arrived from as far away as Ireland, Egypt, and South Africa. A woman in Springfield, Ohio, mailed LeMay a Bible, while Paul Warwick, Jr., of Smyrna, Georgia, drew a portrait of the general. Angelo Giarratana of Cambridge, Massachusetts, walked eighteen miles just to see a B-29 at Bedford Field. "It was worth it," he wrote LeMay. "I think I would do it again."

Others praised the efforts of the general and his men.

"As long as I live," wrote Ernest Costello of Norwich, Connecticut, "I will never forget what you all have done for me and the people of our country."

"Writing you this letter is, indeed, my privilege," added Billy Zawacki of Philadelphia.

"May God make us worthy of your sacrifices," pleaded Naydene Lohr of Kansas City, Missouri.

LeMay's meteoric rise landed him that summer on the cover of *Time* magazine, a cigar clenched between his teeth as B-29s roared through the skies overhead. The scowling general with ink-black hair had become the face of destruction—the architect of Armageddon. "Can Japan," the magazine asked, "stand twice the bombing that Germany got?"

Few questioned the morality of burning Japan's cities. Years of war had exhausted most Americans, who were sick of sending their husbands and sons, brothers and fathers to fight on the beaches and in the malarial jungles of faraway islands and atolls. Why should the nation that had started the war on a peaceful Sunday morning at Pearl Harbor warrant any sympathy? A public opinion survey conducted three days after that surprise attack revealed that seven out of ten Americans favored bombing Japan's cities. Polls showed that those passions remained high even as the weeks turned to months and then years. When asked in December 1944 what America should do with the enemy after the war, 13 percent of the public supported killing all Japanese people. Another 33 percent wanted the nation destroyed as a political entity. Such sentiments could even be found among top American officials. In a speech on April 5, 1945, the chairman of the War Manpower Commission, Paul McNutt, who had previously served as governor of Indiana and high commissioner of the Philippines, told attendees that he favored "the extermination of the Japanese in toto." When a reporter asked if he meant the military or the people, McNutt said the latter. "I know," he declared, "the Japanese people."

Japan had done much to earn the world's enmity.

The nation that had prided itself on the elegance of the tea ceremony and the beauty of flower arrangement had hacked a bloody path across much of Asia, killing as many as 20 million men, women, and children over the course of eight years in just China. Along the way, soldiers had tortured, terrorized, and murdered civilians by the thousands. Troops buried priests alive and skewered infants on the steel tips of bayonets. Others raped women and mutilated victims, slicing off breasts and penises. "When the Japanese soldier goes into battle," wrote Walter Simmons of the *Chicago Daily Tribune,* "he becomes little better than an animal, raging for blood. He has no more mercy than a mad dog." After the December 1937 capture of the Chinese capital of Nanking, soldiers slaughtered as many as 350,000 men, women, and children. The carnage was so vast that bodies piled along the banks of the Yangtze turned the mighty river red. Associated Press reporter Yates McDaniel, who managed to escape, penned his last memory of Nanking in his diary: "Dead Chinese, dead Chinese, dead Chinese."

Nanking only foreshadowed the evil to come. In the wake of the April 1942 Doolittle Raid, Japanese soldiers unleashed a retaliatory campaign of rape and murder across rural China that claimed an estimated 250,000 lives. Troops set villagers on fire, drowned entire families in wells, and unleashed bacteriological warfare in the form of plague, anthrax, and cholera. "The whole countryside," recalled one missionary, "reeked of death." A similar horror played out during the February 1945 Battle of Manila, where an estimated 100,000 civilians died, many victims of horrific cruelty. In one of the most gruesome atrocities, troops cut a hole in the second floor of a home and then led blindfolded civilians upstairs one after the other, forcing them to kneel. A soldier chopped off each victim's head with a saber before kicking the body down the hole, ultimately filling the room below. War crimes investigators, by counting skulls, later determined that two hundred men died this way. "A more brutal and cold-blooded series of murders," the investigative report concluded, "can hardly be imagined."

Americans suffered alongside Asians. The Japanese shuttled prisoners around the empire crammed inside the belly of so-called hell ships, where soaring heat prompted the desperate to drink urine and even blood. "If you fell down," one survivor recalled, "you just suffocated." Guards beat captives to death, while starvation claimed others. Lt. Col. Ed Dyess, a fighter pilot who was captured in the Philippines in April 1942, survived the notorious Bataan Death March followed by a year in prison before he managed to escape. Dyess serialized his story in twenty-four installments that ran in early 1944 in the *Chicago Daily Tribune* and a hundred associated newspapers. "I saw," the airman began, "Japs bayonet malaria-stricken American soldiers who were struggling to keep marching down the dusty roads that led to hell." Dyess's account sparked outrage across America, including on Capitol Hill. "The Japs," declared Sen. Ernest McFarland of Arizona, "will pay and pay dearly through their blood and the ashes of their cities."

American leaders understood the emotional power of such accounts, weaponizing the release of them to drive public opinion. "This was propaganda of the most sophisticated sort," observed historian John Dower, "turning concrete events into icons and symbols." By 1945, the parade of savage stories had long since shaped American views of the enemy as barbaric. Editorial cartoonists, embracing racist stereotypes, caricatured the Japanese as bow-legged and buck-toothed. Others portrayed them as rattlesnakes and cockroaches. Following the execution of three captured Doolittle Raiders, *Time* ran a cartoon that depicted a cocked pistol labeled "Civilization" pointed at the head of an ape on whose chest was written "Murderers of American Fliers." The *New York Herald Tribune* in May 1945 ran a three-column photograph of a Japanese soldier with a sword raised above his head, about to decapitate a blindfolded and kneeling flier. "This," the paper trumpeted, "is the enemy the Allies still face in the Pacific."

The American press, if anything, now celebrated LeMay's nightly destruction.

"The Japs are tasting a bitter dose of retribution for their Pearl Harbor infamy," argued the *Los Angeles Times*.

"They who sowed the wind now reap the whirlwind," added the *New York Herald Tribune*.

"For the Japanese," concluded the *New York Times*, "the worst is yet to come."

Columnists at times appeared gleeful over the wreckage of Japan. "When a Jap goes to bed at night," wrote California correspondent Ed Ainsworth, "he doesn't know whether he is going to wake up in Tokyo or in ancestor land."

"The Japanese are queer people," added the *Christian Science Monitor*. "Not so long ago they were eagerly buying scrap iron from Uncle Sam. And now that the B-29s are delivering it free, they don't seem to like it at all."

There were, of course, some dissenters, even at the highest levels of the American military and government. Brig. Gen. Bonner Fellers, who served as an aide to Douglas MacArthur, was one of the first senior officers to visit Manila after the liberation of thousands of starving American soldiers and civilians from Japanese camps, a scene that horrified him. "The Japanese," Fellers wrote his wife, "are fiends." Despite that, Fellers viewed the burning of Japan as "one of the most ruthless and barbaric killings of non-combatants in all history." War Secretary Henry Stimson, who told President Harry Truman that he did not want America "outdoing Hitler in atrocities," confided in others that it was "appalling that there should be no protest in the United States over such wholesale slaughter."

Among the public, a few voices of criticism emerged, creeping onto the editorial pages of papers. A letter in the *Hartford Courant*—signed "Thoughtful"—criticized the "exultant" tone of news stories. "We must remember," the individual wrote, "that when a city like Tokyo, third largest in the world, is utterly destroyed, in the process of destruction thousands upon thousands of men, women and children, innocent of any personal guilt, are condemned to die a horrible death. Let us, therefore, in hailing each new blow against Japan as a step toward ultimate victory, temper our jubilation with the thought that it is the little citizen as usual, not the big moguls, who suffers most from these aerial blows."

THE JUNE 15 MISSION to Osaka, which Hap Arnold lauded in his diary, marked the end of LeMay's campaign against Japan's principal industrial cities. In three months, his aircrews had incinerated 56.3 square miles of Tokyo, 15.6 of Osaka, 12.4 of Nagoya, 8.9 of Yokohama, 8.8 of Kobe, and 3.6 of Kawasaki, for a total of 105.6 square miles.

But LeMay was far from finished.

He simply moved down the list to Japan's secondary cities, which ranged in size from the prefectural capital of Fukuoka with a population of 323,200 to the minuscule port town of Tsuruga, home to just 31,350 men, women, and children. The majority of LeMay's targets, however, were on the smaller scale, including forty cities with a population of less than 150,000. Half of those, in fact, were home to fewer than 75,000. Despite the air force's public claims that fire raids were aimed at industry, the number-one factor driving target selection was a city's "combustibility." War factories, transportation, and size ranked as subsequent reasons. "The preponderant purpose appears to have been to secure the heaviest possible morale and shock effect by widespread attack upon the Japanese civilian population," one postwar report observed. "Certain of the cities attacked had virtually no industrial importance."

LeMay ordered the first such strike on June 17. There was no need, with smaller targets, to send aerial armadas of five hundred planes. Just as he had done with his earlier attacks on Kyushu's airfields, LeMay divided the cities among his wings, a move that allowed him to blast multiple municipalities in a single night. For this first raid, LeMay set his sights on Omuta, Hamamatsu, Yokkaichi, and Kagoshima, all midsize cities

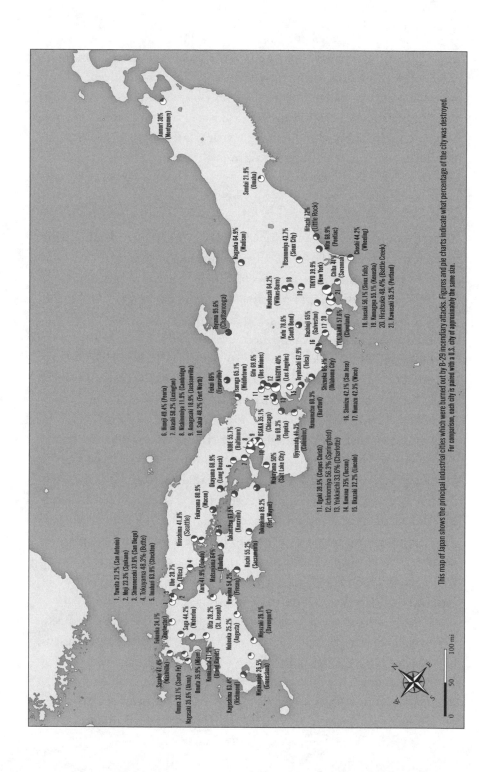

This map of Japan shows the principal industrial cities which were burned out by B-29 incendiary attacks. Figures and pie charts indicate what percentage of the city was destroyed. For comparison, each city is paired with a U.S. city of approximately the same size.

Aomori 30% (Montgomery)

Sendai 21.9% (Omaha)

Nagaoka 64.9% (Madison)

Hitachi 72% (Little Rock)

Utsunomiya 43.7% (Sioux City)

Mito 68.9% (Pontiac)

Choshi 44.2% (Wheeling)

Toyama 95.6% (Chattanooga)

Maebashi 64.2% (Wilkes-Barre)

Kofu 78.6% (South Bend)

Hachioji 65% (Galveston)

18
19

TOKYO 39.9% (New York)

Chiba 43% (Savannah)

21

16

17 20

YOKOHAMA 57.6% (Cleveland)

18. Isesaki 56.1% (Sioux Falls)
19. Kumagaya 55.1% (Kenosha)
20. Hiratsuka 48.4% (Battle Creek)
21. Kawasaki 35.2% (Portland)

Himeji 49.4% (Peoria)

Akashi 50.2% (Lexington)

Nishinomiya 11.9% (Cambridge)

Amagasaki 18.9% (Jacksonville)

Sakai 48.2% (Fort Worth)

Fukui 86% (Evansville)

Tsuruga 65.1% (Middletown)

11

14

13

Gifu 69.6% (Des Moines)

12

NAGOYA 40% (Los Angeles)

15

Toyohashi 67.9% (Utica)

Shizuoka 66.1% (Oklahoma City)

Hamamatsu 60.3% (Hartford)

16. Shimizu 42.1% (San Jose)
17. Numazu 42.3% (Waco)

Fukuyama 80.9% (Seattle)

Okayama 68.9% (Long Beach)

KOBE 55.7% (Baltimore)

Tsu 69.3% (Topeka)

Ujiyamada 41.3% (Columbus)

8

9

OSAKA 35.1% (Chicago)

Wakayama 50% (Salt Lake City)

11. Ogaki 39.5% (Corpus Christi)
12. Ichinomiya 56.3% (Springfield)
13. Yokkaichi 33.5% (Charlotte)
14. Kuwana 75% (Tucson)
15. Okazaki 32.2% (Lincoln)

Hiroshima 41.8% (Seattle)

Kure 41.9% (Toledo)

Takamatsu 67.5% (Knoxville)

Tokushima 85.2% (Fort Wayne)

Kochi 55.2% (Sacramento)

1. Yawata 21.2% (San Antonio)
2. Moji 23.3% (Spokane)
3. Shimonoseki 37.6% (San Diego)
4. Tokuyama 48.3% (Butte)
5. Imabari 63.9% (Stockton)

Fukuoka 24.1% (Rochester)

1 2

Ube 20.7% (Utica)

4

Saga 44.2% (Waterloo)

3

Uwajima 54.2% (Fresno)

Matsuyama 64% (Duluth)

Oita 28.2% (St. Joseph)

Nobeoka 25.2% (Augusta)

Miyazaki 26.1% (Davenport)

Sasebo 41.4% (Nashville)

Omura 33.1% (Santa Fe)

Nagasaki 35.6% (Akron)

Kumamoto 31.2% (Grand Rapids)

Kagoshima 63.4% (Richmond)

Miyakonojo 26.5% (Greenshoro)

0   50   100 mi

with populations between 100,000 and 200,000 and wartime factories. "All wings were instructed to compress their force over the target in a 70-minute period," the mission report stated. "This was expected to saturate the firefighting defenses and also to saturate the antiaircraft defenses."

The sun rose the next morning to reveal that airmen torched more than six square miles of the four cities. The mission cost LeMay only one out of 485 bombers, a loss rate of just 0.2 percent. The general ordered a similar strike two days later, this time against the cities of Toyohashi, Fukuoka, and Shizuoka, blasting another 5.32 square miles. On June 28, airmen burned another four square miles of Okayama, Sasebo, Moji, and Nobeoka.

The pace of operations accelerated as LeMay worked through the list of fifty-eight secondary cities he would eventually destroy. Each morning at five, planners pored over reports on the number of bombers available, while a maintenance check revealed how many ground crews could return to service in time for takeoff. Planners studied weather forecasts to determine if aircrews would execute a fire raid or precision strike. LeMay would then meet with his intelligence and operations officers to gather the information he needed to brief his aircrews. "Most of the time I didn't know when my day started and when it ended," the general wrote. "When you have things to do, you do them, and you lose track of time and days."

LeMay stole a few minutes most days to fire off a quick letter home to Helen, often just a few two- or three-sentence paragraphs in which he skimmed over the day's events, including his occasional visits to the navy's skeet range to unwind, one of his favorite pastimes. The general, who every night sent his bombers to burn cities filled with women and children, rarely expressed his own feelings about such devastation in letters to his family. If anything, his private views echoed his blunt public statements that news correspondents relished. "I am beginning to feel very optimistic about the war out here," he wrote. "I definitely have them squalling for mercy." Ever the professional, LeMay left no doubt that fighting the war was his top priority. "Sure, I miss you and Janie, but I would like to finish up the war too, especially since it is so close to the end," he wrote. "The way I figure it, a few more months at the most will see it over."

The 315th Bombardment Wing began operations from Guam in late June, swelling LeMay's command to 63,811 airmen, a figure that included 10,027 officers and 53,784 enlisted men. The air force equipped the new arrivals with a more advanced radar system, allowing crews to execute nighttime precision raids against Japan's oil industry. Superfortresses with the 313th Bombardment Wing continued to fly missions as part of Operation Starvation, parachuting mines into the vital Shimonoseki Straits as well as the harbors of Kyushu and Honshu. On days when weather permitted, LeMay's crews flew precision strikes, blasting arsenals in Kure and Osaka along with the Mitsubishi and Kawanishi aircraft plants in Himeji, Tamashima, and Kagamigahara. When the weather deteriorated, LeMay returned to fire raids. "Our strength was increasing enormously," he said, "as new units flew in to join us."

On Tinian, members of the newly arrived 509th Composite Group under the command of Col. Paul Tibbets hustled to prepare for the highly secret atomic attack against Japan planned for later that summer, pending a successful test detonation. LeMay had first learned of the secret new weapon on March 30, when Col. Elmer Kirkpatrick touched down on Guam, requesting space to establish the new group. LeMay had personally flown him around the Marianas, where Kirkpatrick selected the flat coral island on April 4. Navy Seabees had since erected an administrative building, warehouses, and hardstands to accommodate the eighteen specially equipped B-29s. Tibbets had arrived in May, followed in June by his aircrews, who would spend the next two months flying training missions against Iwo Jima, Truk, Marcus Island, and later Japan. The latter missions involved dropping "pumpkins," conventionally armed weapons designed to mimic the actual bomb. "My job," Tibbets said, "was to wage atomic war."

On his brief trip to Washington, LeMay had met with Maj. Gen. Leslie Groves, director of the Manhattan Project. Unlike the decision to firebomb Tokyo, which LeMay had made on his own, the order to use the atomic bomb would come from the president. That said, execution of the operation would fall to LeMay. Groves walked him through the bomb's specifications, including its weight and projected power as well as the proposed target lists, cities LeMay had earlier agreed not to firebomb. "I was highly impressed with him," Groves recalled of LeMay. "It was very evident that he was a man of outstanding ability." LeMay recommended that when the time came for the operation, it would be best to send a single B-29, since the Japanese were used to weather and reconnaissance missions and rarely targeted them with fighters or flak. Even with his engineering background, LeMay later admitted that he struggled with the science. "I knew this would be a big bang," he said, "but I didn't know how big."

In the meantime, LeMay's crews continued to hammer Japan's smaller cities. Few Americans could pronounce the names of his targets, much less find them on a map. Yet night after night, week after week, LeMay's bombers returned, like fire-breathing dragons. In the latter half of June, the general's forces attacked eleven secondary cities, gutting 15.24 square miles. LeMay more than tripled that figure in July, pounding thirty-seven cities for a total of 35.41 square miles destroyed. "Enemy air opposition was practically non-existent," one report noted. "The small cities proved to have meager flak and searchlight defenses."

LeMay scratched city after city from his list.

Kochi and Himeji.

Then Akashi.

And Kofu.

The general boasted of his success in a July 10 letter to his wife. "We are certainly giving the Japs a going over," LeMay wrote. "In the last two missions, we have burned down eight towns of over 100,000 population, each without losing a man. Over 1200 sorties without a loss. If they don't give up soon, they are a lot dumber than I think they are."

LeMay torched Utsunomiya, Tsuruga, and Uwajima.

Another week passed.

Bombers hit Namazu, Oita, Kuwana, and Hiratsuka, then days later blasted Fukui, Hitachi, Choshi, and Okazaki, each week delivering more fire and ruin, while the enemy absorbed the blows like an exhausted boxer pinned against the ropes. "The record will show," LeMay said, "that in the last two months of the war it was safer to fly a combat mission over Japan than it was to fly a B-29 training mission back in the U.S."

America's command of the air eased earlier fears of flak and fighters, replaced by a weariness brought on by the realization that it was no longer a fair fight. Night after night airmen looked down on the blazes that destroyed cities, while the aroma of barbecued flesh wafted through the bombers. "I imagined," recalled gunner Hoyt Clark, "that the people in the cities below us were crouched in fear as the drone of our engines approached them, and that they were wondering if we were coming to destroy them, and if this would be their last night, the night on which they and their homes would be destroyed." Radarman Michael Giroski likewise struggled. "If a guy is shooting at me, I can kill him," he said. "But these women, children and babies down there didn't have a chance." The emotional drain drove some of the airmen to take sleeping pills. Others questioned why so many people had to die and how much more Japan was willing to endure. "We were going to incinerate the whole damn island," exclaimed pilot Bob Vaucher, "if they didn't give up."

General Spaatz landed on Guam on July 20 to assume command of the new U.S. Army Strategic Air Force in the Pacific. A veteran of the European war, he, too, opposed area bombing, so much so his family later said he had been reluctant to take the job for fear it would be worse than Germany. "I have never," Spaatz said, "favored the destruction of cities as such with all inhabitants being killed." But the Pacific war was a different fight—and the decision to burn Japan had long since been made. Just that month, as world leaders gathered in Germany for the Potsdam Conference, Arnold passed out booklets with photos of the empire's wrecked cities. "The war with Japan is over as far as creative work is concerned," he said. "The die is cast." Stalin, during a toast, suggested a follow-up conference in Tokyo. "If our B-29s continue their present tempo," Arnold gloated, "there would be nothing left of Tokyo in which to have a meeting." Spaatz agreed with that statement. "Unless Japan desires to commit national suicide," he cabled to Washington, "they should quit immediately."

With Spaatz as overall commander, the press speculated LeMay would take charge of the 20th Air Force, but Hap instead tapped Lt.

Gen. Nathan Twining, who outranked LeMay by a star. Reporters questioned whether Arnold had "kicked" LeMay upstairs, his wings clipped. "The most spectacularly successful airman produced in the Army's Pacific war," *Time* magazine observed, "was no longer his own on-the-spot boss." Senior leaders tamped down such speculation, though years later LeMay would admit he had been disappointed. He had taken over America's bombing efforts against Japan at a low point, turned the force around, and exacted incredible damage on the enemy, only for Arnold on the eve of victory to muscle him aside, just as he had done to Hansell. Arnold once again demonstrated that his loyalty was not to his people but rather to his dream of an independent air force.

The fifty-eight-year-old Spaatz, whose red hair had grayed, likely sensed LeMay's frustration when he chose him as his chief of staff. One of his first moves was to message Washington, applauding LeMay's work. "Have had opportunity to check up on Baker Two Nine Operations," Spaatz cabled, "and believe this is the best organized and most technically and tactically proficient military organization that the world has seen to date." Spaatz no doubt meant what he wrote, as evidenced by the efficiency report he filed on LeMay. "An officer of great force," he observed. "Among top commanders of World War II."

The shuffling of leaders had little effect on the operation. "LeMay was the Twentieth Air Force," recalled Tibbets. "He ran the whole show." Until Spaatz and Twining acclimated, LeMay continued to run his missions. The general had long since destroyed Japan's major cities. His aircrews now picked the bones of the enemy's empire. All the work to build up America's new forces would be for nothing. "I don't think, General," LeMay leveled with Spaatz, "that they'll get fields built for these people before the war is over."

The detonation of the first atomic bomb in the New Mexico desert just days before Spaatz's arrival added a new variable to the conflict's climatic final equation. The bomb was no longer a $2 billion theory but a potential war-ending weapon, the first components of which reached Tinian aboard the cruiser *Indianapolis* on July 26. That same day at Potsdam, Truman joined British prime minister Winston Churchill and Chinese Nationalist ruler Chiang Kai-shek to urge Japan to accept unconditional surrender. "The alternative," the leaders warned, "is prompt and utter destruction." In his diary, Truman, who described the weapon as "the most terrible bomb in the history of the world," wrote that he approved its use against purely military objectives. "Soldiers and sailors are the target and not women and children," he wrote. "Even if the Japs are savages, ruthless, merciless and fanatic, we as the leader of the world for the common welfare cannot drop this terrible bomb on the old capital or the new."

Such comments, however, were woefully unrealistic, particularly since the one-page order to drop the bomb made no reference to either military or civilian objectives. The targets listed were simply four cities: Hiroshima, Kokura, Niigata, and Nagasaki. While all contained military or industrial elements, ranging from arsenals to oil refineries, all likewise were home to tens of thousands of civilians. How could any commander corral the force of such a bomb once it was released over a city? Others in the administration, however, agreed with Truman's decision, including War Secretary Henry Stimson, who disliked LeMay's firebombing campaign. Stimson's only insistence was that Kyoto, the ancient cultural heart of Japan, not be struck as a potential target. "The atomic bomb was more than a weapon of terrible destruction," Stimson wrote, "it was a psychological weapon." That was what Gen. George Marshall believed Japan needed. The army chief of staff pointed to Tokyo as an example. If the destruction of the capital and the deaths of 100,000 people in a single night failed to break Japan, then hopefully a more terrifying weapon might finally shock the nation's leaders into surrender. "We had to end the war," Marshall said, "We had to save American lives."

While technicians on Tinian worked to assemble the bomb, LeMay continued to pound Japan. In late July, he hatched a new plan. He powwowed with the navy's Psychological Warfare Office to design a new leaflet that he could drop over Japan. One side showed a picture of B-29s unloading bombs. Around the image, planners listed the names of eleven cities. The flip side carried a warning. "Attention Japanese People: Read this carefully as it may save your life or the life of a relative or friend." America, the message stated, planned to bomb at least four of the listed cities. "Heed this warning and evacuate these cities immediately."

LeMay gathered with news reporters on July 28 to announce this plan, a cigar firmly between his lips. Only the night before, bombers had dropped sixty thousand leaflets over all the targeted cities. "The Japanese have refused to come up and fight. We have been roaming their air at will, burning down their cities. Now we are telling the citizens what towns we are going to burn down," LeMay told correspondents. "We hope to convince the Japanese people that they can do nothing about it, that we can destroy any target we want to, city after city."

To hammer home his point, LeMay sent his bombers that night to strike six of the listed cities, obliterating a total of 4.26 square miles of Tsu, Aomori, Ichinomiya, Uji Yamada, Ogaki, and Uwajima. The general warned another twelve cities on the night of July 31, then proceeded to burn six square miles out of Hachiojo, Toyama, Nagaoka, and Mito a day later.

How much more could Japan tolerate?

CHAPTER 19

"Hiroshima was no longer a city, but a burnt-over prairie."

—DR. MICHIHIKO HACHIYA
AUGUST 6, 1945, DIARY ENTRY

At 2:45 a.m. on the morning of August 6, 1945, Colonel Tibbets stared through the cockpit windshield down the mile-and-a-half-long chipped-coral runway on Tinian. The newly christened *Enola Gay*—a B-29 named in honor of his red-haired mother back home in Miami—shuddered under the power of the four Wright Cyclone engines. Though the thirty-year-old was the veteran of more than two dozen bomb missions over Europe and North Africa, Tibbets couldn't shake the tension that left his palms sweaty as he gripped the controls. His payload this morning consisted of a single weapon, one that promised to devastate cities and fulfill the dream first articulated twenty-four years earlier by airpower visionary Giulio Douhet. Experts estimated that the 9,000-pound atomic bomb—nicknamed "Little Boy"—packed the punch of more than 20,000 tons of TNT, a horrific force that would take two thousand loaded B-29s to rival. "With its coat of dull gunmetal paint," Tibbets observed, "it was an ugly monster."

"Ready for takeoff on Runway Able," he radioed the tower.

"Cleared for takeoff," came the reply.

Tibbets released the brakes, and the *Enola Gay* thundered down the runway, hitting 155 miles per hour before climbing into the dark sky. The mission that Monday morning represented the last stop on America's march toward total war, a journey that had begun in earnest with LeMay's destruction of Tokyo in March. Sensitive to the awesome power of the new weapon—as well as the controversy that would no doubt surround it—General Spaatz had demanded his orders for the mission in writing. The use of the atomic bomb, however, struck many of the Pacific's veteran airmen as gratuitous, though not necessarily for moral reasons. Professional jealousy likely colored that judgment, as the officers recognized that the new bomb threatened to steal the spotlight from the hard-fought B-29 campaign. But as Arnold had said at Potsdam the previous month, the creative work in destroying Japan was done. "Atomic bomb or no atomic bomb," he said, "the Japanese were already on the verge of collapse." Few understood that as well as LeMay, who each day charted the empire's eradication via black and white photos of gutted cities. The only reason a few sizable targets still existed on which to test the new weapon was that LeMay previously had marked those cities as off limits. "I think it was anticlimactic," LeMay said, "in that the verdict was already rendered."

Tibbets reached Iwo Jima at 5:55 a.m., circling Mount Suribachi at 9,300 feet so that two trailing B-29s carrying scientific equipment could catch up. The trio then departed twelve minutes later. Tibbets had three possible targets. His priority was Hiroshima, with Kokura and Nagasaki designated as backups. Three weather planes—*Straight Flush*, *Full House*, and *Jabbitt III*—had taken off at 1:37 a.m. to scout conditions over the cities.

Tibbets puffed his Kaywoodie briar pipe as the ocean passed beneath him. He eased back on the controls, slowly climbing to the bombing altitude of 30,700 feet. The coded message with the target arrived from *Straight Flush*, which the radio operator jotted down.

"It's Hiroshima," Tibbets announced to the crew over the intercom.

At eight-thirty a.m., the bomber crossed the shoreline of the Japanese island of Shikoku. Eight minutes before the scheduled release, the city appeared ahead. "The early morning sunlight," Tibbets recalled, "glistened off the white buildings in the distance."

"Do you all agree that's Hiroshima?" he asked the crew.

The men concurred.

Fifteen and a half miles from the city, Tibbets picked up the initial point and began his three-minute run. He reminded the crew to slip on goggles to protect themselves from the bomb's glare, which would rival the intensity of ten suns. To Tibbets's relief, no enemy planes had come up to fight. Ten miles out, bombardier Maj. Thomas Ferebee spotted the Aioi Bridge, a T-shaped span in the heart of Hiroshima that served as the aiming point.

"Okay," he announced, "I've got the bridge."

Capt. Dutch Van Kirk, the mission's navigator, stood behind him, comparing the bridge ahead to an aerial photo. "No question about it," he confirmed.

The *Enola Gay* closed in on the target. Ninety seconds before the release, Tibbets let go of the controls to allow bombardier Ferebee to take command.

"It's all yours," he announced.

Hiroshima, which had begun as a fishing village in 1591, was shaped by the Ota River, whose watery tentacles divided the deltaic city into seven slender islands before emptying into the bay and the Inland Sea. A system of eighty-one bridges connected the city, which spread across twenty-six square miles. The heart of the city, however, centered on four square miles, a dense mix of one- and two-story wooden structures that housed 75 percent of the city's residents. Before the war, Hiroshima had ranked as Japan's seventh-largest city, behind Kobe, with a peak wartime population of 380,000. Five ordered evacuations had slashed those numbers to 245,000 people, yet Hiroshima's population density remained high, with 31,600 persons per square mile, an average greater than that of even New York City.

Other than a few naval air raids, Hiroshima had largely escaped the attacks that had transformed the landscape of dozens of other Japanese cities, a fact that surprised Tadataka Sasaki, a twenty-five-year-old army conscript previously based in Tokyo. "When I returned to Hiroshima, the city was beautiful, untouched, like nothing had ever happened in Japan," he recalled. "It was a strange scene for me." That facade of serenity obscured the reality. Hiroshima, home to the Second General Army headquarters and the Fifth Division, made an inviting target. The city housed not only scores of barracks, administrative buildings, and ordnance depots but nearly 25,000 troops. "Hiroshima," one intelligence report noted, "is an army city."

At 7:09 a.m. that Monday morning, Japanese authorities issued an air raid alert after lookouts spotted the weather reconnaissance plane *Straight Flush*. The bomber departed, and officials lifted the warning at 7:31 a.m. With the alarm canceled, residents left for work, including 8,400 mobilized students who were tasked to clean up broken roof tiles, nails, and lumber from homes demolished under the city's firebreak program. Others headed toward war factories, listening to the whir of summer cicadas, or cooked breakfast over charcoal stoves.

The wind that morning blew out of the south at 4.5 miles per hour. Hiroshima had not seen rain in three weeks; nor did forecasters predict any this muggy morning as the sun climbed into the sky, which was dotted by only a handful of clouds at high altitudes.

The Matsunago lookout station detected two bombers at 8:06 a.m. Three minutes later the station corrected that report to up the total spotted to three. At 8:14 a.m., the Nakano searchlight battery reported the roar of engines closing in on the city. The army conscript Tadataka Sasaki, accompanied by two other soldiers, was walking past Hiroshima Castle to return a handcart when he heard the buzz of the bombers.

"There's a B-29!" one of the soldiers announced.

The rumble of *Enola Gay's* four 2,200-horsepower engines caught the attention of others throughout the city, including twelve-year-old Nobuo Takemura, who was working with his schoolmates clearing debris that sultry morning. "It was very beautiful," the youth recalled. "Most of my classmates stopped working and looked at the shining plane."

Six miles overhead bombardier Ferebee pressed his left eye against the viewfinder of the sight, watching the streets, bridges, and canals pass below.

"We're on target," he announced.

Anticipation soared as the pneumatic bomb doors sprang open. Seventeen seconds past nine-fifteen a.m., the bomb plummeted toward the ground below.

The sudden loss of weight prompted *Enola Gay*'s nose to rise, as Tibbets immediately banked the bomber 155 degrees to the right with engines at full power, hoping to gain as much distance as possible before the blast. Ten seconds turned to twenty.

Then thirty.

Silence hung over the airmen. Tibbets struggled with the controls, while assistant weaponeer Second Lt. Morris Jeppson counted the seconds in his head. "To some in the plane," Tibbets remembered, "it seemed an eternity."

The bomb detonated after forty-three seconds, unleashing powerful radioactive forces that not only exposed X-ray films stored in the basement of a concrete hospital a mile from ground zero but made the fillings in Tibbets's teeth tingle. "If Dante had been with us in the plane," the commander later wrote, "he would have been terrified."

"My God," co-pilot Capt. Robert Lewis scribbled in his makeshift diary on the back of War Department forms, "what have we done?"

By the time the shock wave hit the bomber, a minute later and nine miles out from the target, a purple mushroom cloud boiled up into the heavens. "Fellows," Tibbets announced, "you have just dropped the first atomic bomb in history."

LITTLE BOY DETONATED approximately 2,000 feet in the air, just 700 feet southeast of the aiming point. Temperatures soared to 6,300 degrees. The blast carbonized people on the streets and vaporized birds in flight. A violent rush of air, like an atomic hurricane, toppled trees and utility poles and flattened 60,000 of the city's 90,000 homes, schools, and businesses. Survivors inside the city center never even heard the explosion. "We saw blue-white lightning," recalled fourteen-year-old Ichiso Hori. "It was like the flash of a camera." That flash left haunting reminders of life at the split-second when the bomb exploded, including the shadow of a castor bean plant's leaves on a charred utility pole, the outline of a person seated on the steps of Sumitomo Bank, and the image of a man pulling a cart across the Bantai Bridge.

Dust from the shattered city, which would rise more than eight miles, blotted out the summer sun, turning day into night. Survivors crawled out from under piles of debris, only to choke on air thick with pulverized concrete and timbers, hair and skin. "I saw a train stopped on the Aioi Bridge," recalled seventeen-year-old Hiroko Uchida. "The driver and the passengers, seated and standing both, were completely charred." The blast had left many naked, while glass from blown-out windows riddled bodies, gouged out eyes, and sliced open bellies. Flash burns blistered victims, whose skin ruptured and dangled, as one survivor later described it, like potato peelings. Victims crouched in the rubble, pleading for help. "Everywhere I looked," remembered Setsuko Iwamoto, "I saw the most horrible misery." Fifteen-year-old Michiko Yamaoka, who was walking to work at the Hiroshima Central Telephone Office, witnessed the carnage just half a mile from the hypocenter. "This wasn't the world I knew—it was a living hell."

But the hell had only begun.

The explosion had reduced block after block to a kindling pile of splintered lumber mixed with busted tables, chests of drawers, and shredded tatami mats. Radiant heat coupled with electrical shorts and toppled stoves sparked fires. In those few concrete buildings that still stood, dark cotton blackout curtains ignited; so did offices filled with papers. The blast blew out windows and doors, allowing air to rush through, while open staircases served as chimneys. Within ten minutes of the explosion, hundreds of fires erupted throughout Hiroshima. Twenty minutes later a firestorm emerged, with winds of up to forty miles per hour.

Debris blocked roads and fire hydrants, but that proved irrelevant since the blast had killed or wounded 80 percent of Hiroshima's more than four hundred on-duty firemen. Seven out of ten of the city's fire trucks and more than half the fire stations lay crushed amid the rubble.

"The public fire department," one postwar report noted, "sustained an instantaneous, paralyzing blow." Survivors struggling to recover from the shock of the explosion now battled an inferno that would incinerate 4.4 square miles of the city center. "Hiroshima," recalled seventeen-year-old Haruto Seo, "became a sea of fire."

First aid teams failed to form, and thirty hours would pass before the first outside emergency responders reached the blast area. Those survivors who were able had no choice but to abandon the burning city, climbing over debris. Others followed rail lines or limped along dry riverbeds. "Some carried dead children on their backs," recalled fourteen-year-old Yoko Shineda, "aimlessly wailing out their names." In an effort to prevent the rubbing of raw flesh, victims shuffled forward with arms raised in front of them, reminiscent, one witness recalled, of a kangaroo. "I found myself watching," recalled Rikio Yamane, "like some hellish marathon, a procession of ghastly, inhuman figures fleeing from the city."

The blast wiped out two army hospitals along with all but three of Hiroshima's forty-five civilian ones. Of the city's two hundred doctors, 90 percent suffered casualties. Nurses fared similarly. Of the 1,780 in Hiroshima, a total of 1,654 nurses were killed or wounded. "Just to find a doctor," said Akihiro Takahashi, "was a matter for rejoicing." Casualties swarmed the few surviving clinics. Inside the Hiroshima Communications Hospital, located barely fifteen hundred yards from the hypocenter, patients sprawled out on tatami mats, wallowing in excrement and vomit. "The people who were burned suffered most because as their skin peeled away, glistening raw wounds were exposed to the heat and filth," Dr. Michihiko Hachiya wrote in his diary. "This was the environment patients had to live in. It made one's hair stand on end."

With so few hospitals, the majority of the injured crowded inside schools that doubled as primitive rescue centers, often overflowing into classrooms. The broiling heat exacerbated the stench of blood and burnt skin, while swarms of flies laid eggs in rotten flesh. "I was scared," recalled eleven-year-old helper Akiyo Tagawa, "by the sounds of people wailing and screaming out in pain." Burns comprised the majority of the wounds, since those with severe fractures and internal injuries often were unable to escape the wreckage and the subsequent fires. Medics applied the topical antiseptic Mercurochrome, while orderlies passed out meager supplies of hardtack and rice gruel. Victims resorted to sliced cucumbers to cool burns. Others applied mashed potatoes or coated wounds with olive and tempura oil. "All we had," recalled Iwamoto, "was folk medicine."

Survivors arrived daily, prowling hospital hallways in search of missing loved ones. "Parents, half crazy with grief, searched for their children," Hachiya wrote in his diary. "Husbands looked for their wives, and children for their parents. One poor woman, insane with anxiety, walked aimlessly here and there through the hospital calling her child's name. It was dreadfully upsetting to patients, but no one had the heart to stop her."

The firebombing of Tokyo had occurred in late winter, when the temperatures hovered around freezing, but in the summertime bombing of Hiroshima, the heat and humidity swelled bodies, which erupted under the August sun. Workers hustled to collect the voluminous dead, including horses and dogs. Teiichi Teramura, a field officer with the 52nd Ship Construction Battalion, was assigned to recover corpses from the river. "We had to pull the charred bodies aboard with ropes and then take them ashore, where others were waiting to deal with them," he remembered. "There was no way of distinguishing the bodies by sex or age. Most had completely lost their clothes, and all were brown and swollen. Their skin had peeled off and hung dangling, like the peelings of a bruised, black loquat, and all their hair had fallen out."

Laborers dug burn pits throughout the city in schoolyards, empty lots, and along the riverbanks. Seventeen-year-old Tadaomi Furuishi was recruited for the job, searching the dead for name tags or personal items that might help with identification. "We carried the bodies on bamboo mats and wooden shutters to the trenches and ignited them with oil," he said. "The crackling of the burning bodies sounded like fish grilling." The pyres burned day and night. "Each evening," recalled Katsuyoshi Yoshimura, "we could hear the bugles blown by the soldiers and smell the indescribable odor of burning flesh." Families at times chose to cremate their own loved ones. That was the case for twenty-two-year-old Mitsuko

Tsuchikawa. "It was a horrible thing," she recalled, "to have to burn your own mother."

———

BACK ON GUAM, intelligence analysts pored over aerial photos of Hiroshima. A stunned LeMay traced the route of the blast's shock waves. "It was," he uttered to a reporter, "quite a piece of work." The general's command diary likewise reflected that amazement: "Early reports indicate that the destruction wrought on this city is incalculable." Other senior officers analyzed the photos, including Lt. Col. David Burchinal. "If you had that much power at your disposal," he said, "you just knew that things couldn't go on."

Sixteen hours after the attack, President Truman released a statement, warning that Japan faced a rain of ruin such as never before had been seen on earth. "The force from which the sun draws its power has been loosed against those who brought war to the Far East," the president declared. "Let there be no mistake; we shall completely destroy Japan's power to make war." Bombers carried that message to the Japanese people, showering leaflets over the enemy's cities. "We are in possession of the most destructive explosive ever devised by man," one warned. "We have just begun to use this weapon against your homeland. If you still have any doubt, make inquiry as to what happened to Hiroshima when just one atomic bomb fell on that city."

Hiroshima was only the beginning, but still Japan would not yield.

Russia declared war on Japan on August 8, upping the pressure on Emperor Hirohito to surrender. The following morning, the B-29 *Bockscar* thundered down Tinian's darkened runway. The target that morning originally was Kokura, but heavy clouds forced the crew to divert to Nagasaki, whose natural harbor had made the city one of Japan's great ports for foreign trade dating back to the fifteenth century. At 11:02 a.m., a second atomic bomb, dubbed Fat Man, detonated approximately seventeen hundred feet above the city. Unlike the flat delta of Hiroshima, a horseshoe of hills that ringed Nagasaki blocked some of the blast, but the explosion still wiped out two square miles and initially killed an estimated forty thousand, a figure that would roughly double as victims succumbed from illness in the weeks, months, and years ahead.

Japan was finally beaten.

At 7:21 a.m. on August 15, radio announcer Morio Tateno's voice crackled over the nation's airwaves. "His Imperial Majesty the Emperor," he began, "has issued a Rescript. It will be broadcast at noon today. Let us all respectfully listen to the voice of the Emperor."

Tateno then paused.

"Let us all," he reiterated, "respectfully listen to the voice of the Emperor."

Across Japan, utilities planned to transmit power to districts normally blacked out during the day, while authorities set up radio receivers in police stations, post offices, and government buildings, so that the public could listen. Late that morning Guerrero, who had evacuated Tokyo for a hotel in Odawara, stepped into the bird room, so named for its several cages. Other foreign guests and hotel staff joined him. "There was complete silence as the clocks ticked toward noon," Guerrero noted in his diary. "The waiting was oppressive." Dr. Michihiko Hachiya and other physicians in Hiroshima crowded into the hospital's communications bureau, where a radio had been set up. In Niigata prefecture, Ikuko Matsue, who had lost her mother, father, and two sisters in the March firebombing of Tokyo, gathered with other evacuated children in the main hall of the Dairenji Temple. Eight-year-old Haruyo Wada was playing in the yard of the family's temporary home in Nagano prefecture when her mother came for her. "There is an important announcement to be made," she said. "Come inside the house."

Hours earlier the emperor, in whose name millions had fought and died, had stepped up to the microphone in a makeshift recording booth set up on the palace grounds. It had taken two tries for engineers to capture on a gramophone record the words designed to bring an end to the war that for America had begun 1,347 days earlier at Pearl Harbor. Those intervening years had claimed the lives of more than 2.5 million Japanese and witnessed the destruction of sixty-six cities. At noon, radios nationwide buzzed to life, playing the *Kimigayo*, Japan's national anthem. Hirohito's reedy voice then followed, marking the first time many had ever heard him. The emperor's speech, which totaled 625 words when translated, lasted just four and a half minutes. Though he never mentioned the word surrender, his message was clear. "The enemy has begun to employ a new and most cruel bomb, the power of which to do damage is, indeed, incalculable, taking the toll of many innocent lives," Hirohito said. "Should we continue to fight, not only would it result in an ultimate collapse and obliteration of the Japanese nation, but also it would lead to the total extinction of human civilization."

Guerrero looked at the Japanese people around him as the emperor spoke. "All were expressionless as they stood, stiffly upright, their hands at their sides with the palms turned backward, head and shoulders bent low with reverence," he wrote in his diary. "Not a sound came from them. Perhaps it was blasphemy to weep." The emotion came when the speech ended and the radio fell silent. "They wept quietly," he wrote, "the sobs of the women were muffled in their sleeves, and the tears of the men ran undried along their pale cheeks."

At the hospital in Hiroshima, Dr. Hachiya could barely hear the radio. "The broadcast was in the Emperor's own voice," the director finally announced, "and he has just said that we've lost the war. Until further notice, I want you to go about your duties."

"I had been prepared for the broadcast to tell us to dig in and fight to the end," Hachiya wrote in his diary, "but this unexpected message left me stunned."

Others felt the same.

"Only a coward would back out now!" someone hollered.

"The one word—surrender—had produced a greater shock than the bombing of our city," Hachiya observed. "The more I thought, the more wretched and miserable I became."

Many others, however, felt relief.

"What was that about?" Haruyo asked her mother.

"The war is over," she replied, "but we lost."

The youth jumped to her feet and clapped.

"No more raids," she cried. "No more raids."

The adults in the room stared at her. "They all looked apathetic," she recalled. "They had no energy left."

At the Dairenji Temple, Ikuko didn't understand the broadcast.

"We lost," a fellow student told her. "It's over."

To her, the war's outcome made little difference. "Whether we lost it or won it, my father and mother died," she said. "They were not going to come back."

The elimination of blackout restrictions surprised twelve-year-old Katsumoto Saotome. "Peace is bright," the youth thought that first night. "We still had empty stomachs," he recalled, "but this evening we had no worries of going into the shelter."

———

AROUND TEN P.M., LeMay and several aides finished a late dinner and collapsed into chairs on the porch of his quarters on Guam. The general, as always, was tired. He had stayed up late the night before playing poker at General Spaatz's quarters, ultimately winning $250. "I still haven't caught up on my sleep," he wrote his wife, "and I would much rather have gone to bed."

Loudspeakers on Guam blared the news.

"Let's go home!" some soldiers hollered in the distance.

A few rounds of celebratory gunfire crackled in the night, then one by one the lights flickered off, and darkness settled over the base. LeMay did the same, taking just a few moments to pen a follow-up letter to Helen. "I didn't think they could last much longer," he wrote. "No one could take the beating we have been giving them the last few weeks."

The exhausted general, who for years had lamented his lack of sleep in letters to his wife, then climbed beneath the sheets. At long last, the war was over.

EPILOGUE

"Life seems to be worth so little in Japan."

—JAMES SALANGO
OCTOBER 14, 1945, LETTER

On September 1, 1945, LeMay touched down at five p.m. at Atsugi Airdrome in a C-54 transport. The general, whose B-29s had spent the last two weeks dropping crates of canned food, medicine, and clothes to American prisoners of war, had come to witness the official Japanese surrender, which was planned for the following morning on the deck of the battleship *Missouri*, moored in Tokyo Bay. The drive from the airfield through Yokohama gave LeMay a chance to experience his handiwork beyond the aerial black and white photographs he had studied after each strike. What impressed LeMay, as his car rolled along the now-cleared streets, were the skeletal remains of scorched machinery. "Darkened out, rusty drill presses and lathes," he observed, "were specters of Japan's once great home industry."

That vast sea of destruction exemplified the differences between LeMay and his predecessor. Haywood Hansell, the son of a doctor, had fought with a scalpel.

LeMay had wielded a sledgehammer.

The general's firebombing campaign had run just 159 days, from the first midnight strike against Tokyo on March 9 until Emperor Hirohito took to the airwaves on August 15 to announce Japan's surrender. In that time, LeMay's bombers burned more than 178 square miles of sixty-six cities, which were home to more than 20 million men, women, and children. "Tokyo," one Army Air Forces report wryly noted, "got the super-deluxe treatment." Hundreds of thousands were now bedded down there in shanties, growing crops amid the ash and rubble. "Vines and creepers now cover the ruins that remain, while cleared patches are bright and symmetrical with rows of potato and pumpkin plants," Guerrero observed in his diary. "Literally the grass is growing in the street of what was once the third largest city in the world, the proud capital, for a brief spell of glory, of a great new empire of East Asia."

Beyond Tokyo, LeMay had directed America's fury at the industrial cities of Nagoya, Osaka, Yokohama, and Kobe. Nearly half of all the incendiaries had targeted those five cities, whose destruction added up to 102 square miles. Japan's secondary cities likewise suffered tremendously, as many of them had been undefended. The worst hit was Toyama, a seaside town home to 128,000. Bombers flattened 99.5 percent of the city. All told, America dropped 147,000 tons of bombs in the nine-month campaign, which equated less than one-tenth of the tonnage Germany received. Of that total, LeMay had aimed 104,000 tons at Japan's urban areas. Incendiaries were the dominant weapon, comprising two-thirds of all bombs dropped. In months of maximum pressure, like March and July, that figure jumped to three-quarters. Along with home industries, America had damaged or destroyed six hundred factories, including twenty-five major aircraft plants, eighteen oil refineries and storage facilities, and six major arsenals. "The firebombs," noted military reporter Sgt. Peter Grodsky, "did their jobs thoroughly."

The human toll likewise was catastrophic. The U.S. Strategic Bombing Survey, tasked to investigate the effects of the air war, estimated that the attacks had killed 330,000 men, women, and children and injured another 473,000. Those estimates, compiled soon after the war, are likely low. Hiroshima, Nagasaki, and Tokyo accounted for the majority of those killed. The attacks left more than 8 million others homeless, including 2,861,857 just in Tokyo. The capital's colossal casualties, which far exceeded similar fire raids on other major cities, stemmed in part from a confluence of spontaneous factors, including weeks of cold, dry weather coupled with high winds, which fed the inferno. Many other factors, however, proved years in the making, from the development of the sophisticated Superfortress and the napalm-filled M69 to America's detailed analysis of Tokyo's vulnerabilities in construction and density. Complacent Japanese leaders, despite months of air attacks, had failed to evacuate the capital of nonessential workers, provide adequate shelters and fire lanes, or bolster the flagging fire department. Government censorship and propaganda likewise had left the citizenry ignorant of the peril such raids posed, while civil defense regulations mandating residents stay home and battle blazes prevented many from escaping. In the days and weeks that followed, however, as word of the capital's destruction spread, millions of residents abandoned Japan's cities, a fact that would reduce casualties in other targeted locales. "Probably more persons," concluded one bombing survey report, "lost their lives by fire at Tokyo in a six-hour period than at any time in the history of man."

Those deaths were but a fraction, however, of the civilian lives lost each month the war continued. March 1945, for example, saw 240,000 noncombatants killed across Asia, an average of 8,000 people a day. LeMay shrugged off the fatalities from his raids. "These operations," he said in a speech that November, "were not conceived as terror raids against the civilian population of Japan. But we had to be realistic." Japan's dependence on home industries to hammer out parts and equipment made crowded residential areas a legitimate target. Such factories, concluded the Strategic Bombing Survey, accounted for half of Tokyo's total industrial output. Civilian deaths were the price of victory. Even with the passage of time, LeMay's views never softened; nor did he ever publicly express remorse. "We knew we were going to kill a lot of women and kids when we burned that town," he wrote in 1965. "Had to be done." LeMay's work drew applause from other commanders, thankful that America did not have to invade and risk the deaths of thousands more. "What a miracle," Brig. Gen. Bonner Fellers wrote to his wife. "Think what it would have cost to take Japan."

The miles of flattened cityscape stunned American forces, who peered down from the windows of inbound planes at ruins that sparkled, like jewels, from the sunlight reflecting off the shards of shattered glass. On the ground, workers had collected the corrugated sheet metal, organizing it into piles, along with larger pieces of broken glass. Sergeant Grodsky was amazed to find survivors living in old bank vaults that dotted the horizon. "The more I see of these Japanese, their equipment, their hunger and destitute condition," added Chaplain James Salango in a letter, "the more I wonder how they kept going in the war as long as they did." Architect Antonin Raymond, who had helped develop the mock Japanese village at Dugway Proving Ground in the Utah desert, returned to help with the rebuilding. He, too, was shocked. "Complete devastation met our eyes," he wrote. "It is no exaggeration that I was so deeply moved that I could not help crying. It was infinitely worse than I had imagined."

The vast destruction overshadowed the role American submarines had played in jump-starting Japan on the road to ruin, a fact the bombing survey highlighted in its postwar analysis. Week after week, month after month, submarines had sent ships loaded with bauxite, iron ore, salt, and oil to the sea floor. That drumbeat of destruction had crippled Japan fatally even before the first B-29 lifted off for Tokyo on November 24, 1944. The efforts, in short, had been duplicative. "Japan's economy," the bombing survey concluded, "was in large measure being destroyed twice over, once by cutting off of imports, and secondly by air attack." In the end, the aluminum industry ground to a halt. Steel production plummeted to one-fifth of its wartime peak, while fertilizer shortages threatened to slash food production so that Japan faced the risk of famine in 1946. On the civilian front, the average caloric intake fell to 1,680 per day as the government instructed hungry residents to eat potato vines and mulberry leaves. "To speak of rice is too much like thinking of peacetime," one radio commentator broadcast shortly before the conflict's end. "We must eat anything that is available—anything that is edible."

Bombing only compounded that misery. Hunger and exhaustion are hard to visualize compared to miles of rubble and ash, rivers choked with bloated bodies, and roads clogged with millions of evacuees. So concentrated were the attacks that two out of every three people experienced air raids. "The bomber offensive," as one report observed, "brought the war home to the Japanese." Shintaro Motora, former president of Mitsubishi Heavy Industries, said LeMay's switch to firebombing was the catalyst for defeat. "Morale stood up as long as plants only were bombed," he said, "but when homes and towns were bombed and deaths occurred in the families, absenteeism increased and morale became very low." Fear enveloped daily life, as its soundtrack of air sirens sent residents scurrying into earthen bunkers. If Japan had continued to fight, Prime Minister Kantaro Suzuki said, it risked annihilation from the air: "I myself, on the basis of B-29 raids, felt that the cause was hopeless." Many others agreed, including Rear Adm. Toshitano Takata, the navy's deputy chief of military affairs. "Superfortresses," Takata said, "were the greatest single factor in forcing Japan's surrender."

Just as Marshall and Stimson had predicted, the atomic bomb served largely as a political weapon, altering Japan's domestic calculus. Equally as important, though less dramatic, was Russia's declaration of war, which ended Japan's unrealistic hopes that the Soviets might help broker a peace deal that would spare the empire from America's insistence on an unconditional surrender. The impact of this one-two punch was best summarized by navy minister and former prime minister Yonai Mitsumasa. "The atomic bombs and the Soviet entry into the war," he said, "are, in a sense, gifts from the gods." American leaders, including Hap Arnold, understood the enemy's political reality. "From the Japanese standpoint, the atomic bomb was really a way out," Arnold told reporters on August 17, 1945. "Because the bomb was incredibly destructive, it was possible for the emperor, without too much loss of face, to give up, as the only answer to this unheard of development." Arnold concluded by echoing his earlier view: "The Japanese position was hopeless even before the first atomic bomb fell."

Victory had cost America 437 bombers and 297 crews, a relatively small loss compared to the damage exacted. "As a percentage of aircraft airborne on combat missions," one Army Air Forces analysis noted, "the loss rate for aircraft averaged only 1.3% and, for crews, only .9%." The navy fished 596 airmen out of the water, from eighty-three bombers forced down in the Pacific. The capture of Iwo Jima likewise was a godsend for battle-damaged B-29s unable to limp back to the Marianas. "It ceased to be a hazard," Hansell once remarked of the island, "and became a haven." Airmen forced to bail out suffered horribly at the hands of the enemy. Guards shot arrows in some and chopped heads off others. War crimes investigators determined that sixty-two fliers burned to death during the May 25 raid after guards refused to let them out of their cells at the Tokyo Military Prison. In one of the more gruesome events, scientists at Kyushu Imperial University conducted medical experiments on eight captured airmen, including injecting them with seawater and performing vivisections on them. Flight engineer Fiske Hanley, who was shot down on a mining mission on March 27, 1945, was one of the lucky ones to survive. He emerged at the war's end weighing just ninety-six pounds. "This intense hatred built up in me," Hanley said, "until sometimes I thought I would choke."

The bombing campaign made a tremendous impact on Japanese society. On average, attacks had incinerated 43 percent of the 66 targeted cities. Along with mass evacuations and homelessness, those strikes disrupted families, killing children, parents, and grandparents. One of the more visible signs of that societal distress were the 120,000 war orphans, many of whom congregated under overpasses, like the one near Ueno Station. To survive, orphans shined shoes and hawked newspapers. Others recycled cigarette butts or resorted to theft. Relatives adopted the more fortunate children, but life in a defeated nation was hard. Not only were children bullied in new schools, but families resented the extra burden of feeding another child. That was the case for Yumiko Yoshida, whose parents were killed when she was three. Her aunt abused her, forcing her to stand barefoot in the snow. "I wish you had died with your parents," she spat at her one time, "because if you were dead, I wouldn't have to raise you." Others wrestled with depression. Toshiko Kameya, who also lived with an aunt after the raid robbed her of six family members, struggled for years with her sorrow. She eventually took pills to kill herself but fortunately survived. "I thought about death all the time," Toshiko said. "I wanted to go to my mother. I wanted to see my sisters."

Tokyo was a city of the dead with scores of temporary graveyards scattered across the grounds of schools, parks, and temples. Some of these held the remains of a few; others contained thousands. The wartime plan had called for an eventual proper disposal of the remains of an estimated 105,000 men, women, and children. In 1948, laborers began exhuming the bodies. The gruesome chore was performed over three winters, a staggered move that allowed the cold to preserve the remains. Workers likewise toiled at night, hoping to minimize attention. Morticians then cremated the dead and deposited the ashes in 450 white porcelain urns. Those large vessels joined the cremated remains of 58,000 victims from the Great Kanto Earthquake, whose ashes filled another 260 urns. All are housed at Tokyo Memorial Hall, built on the grounds of the former Army Clothing Depot, where thousands died in 1923.

The war nearly killed Hap Arnold, who suffered four heart attacks before Japan's defeat. The tempestuous general, who had staked his career on the B-29, congratulated LeMay. "The part you played in developing and commanding the 21st Bomber Command represents one of the outstanding personal achievements of this war," he cabled. "Your imagination, resourcefulness and initiative have reflected credit on the entire Army Air Forces. We are intensely proud of what you have done." Arnold's pride masked his fears that the air force would not receive the credit it deserved. How then could he justify the need for an independent air service? "I am afraid," he wrote to Carl Spaatz, "that from now on there will be certain people who will forget the part we have played." Others shared his concerns, including LeMay. "It has been a tremendous victory for Air Power," LeMay wrote to Helen. "We licked them with our B-29, but whether we will ever get credit for it is something else again."

Lost in the tug-of-war over credit for Japan's defeat was a greater appreciation of what the war meant for the advancement of airpower. The canvas-and-wire biplanes that had formerly buzzed the muddy trenches of Europe were replaced by muscular bombers able to bridge oceans and incinerate cities. "Air power can carry the battle to the enemy on any part of the globe—on land or sea," Norstad declared in a 1945 speech. "It can destroy, at its source, the enemy's ability to wage war. Those are strong

statements. They used to be considered the dreams of the visionary." He
was right. In his 1921 book *Command of the Air*, Giulio Douhet had fore-
told a future when bombers would devastate city after city, erasing the
distinction between soldiers and civilians. "Victory," he wrote, "smiles
upon those who anticipate the changes in the character of war." LeMay's
firebombing campaign was the ultimate realization of Douhet's vision.
The arrival of atomic weapons only raised the postwar stakes. "World
War II ended as World War I had," Hansell said in 1951, "with the birth of
a tremendous new power in the air."

The burning of Japan would forever haunt some of the airmen who
flew those missions. "We hated what we were doing," recalled flight engineer Jim Marich. Gunner Hoyt Clark agreed. "We spent much of our
time," he said, "killing civilians, destroying property, and making those
who survived as miserable as possible." After the war, Clark spent countless nights reflying his missions, recalling the terror of searchlights and
bursting flak in skies filled with exploding and burning bombers. "As time
went on, for many reasons I began to lose sleep thinking not of me, but of
them: the unbelievable numbers of women, children, mothers, old folks,
and the horrendous pain and suffering I helped to inflict on them," the former gunner wrote in a letter in 2017. "The almost endless fires that we set
represented the holocaust that is never talked about." Marich and Clark
were not the only airmen to wrestle with such guilt. "We didn't like it, but
we had to do it," radarman Michael Giroski said amid tears during an oral
history in 2009. "And I ask the Lord to forgive me time and time again."

In the months following the war, Arnold continued his crusade for an
independent air service, one he had begun decades earlier as a young aco-
lyte of the airpower pioneer Billy Mitchell. The cause had come to define
him. "He never ceased pushing for a separate air force," his wife, Bee,
said in 1970. "I never remember a time when he wasn't fighting for it."
Arnold sent his generals out to give speeches, including Spaatz, Norstad,
and LeMay, imploring people to call members of Congress. The future of
warfare, the airmen preached, would lie in the skies. "We are not organizing a security system against a threat of Redcoats marching through the
wilderness to attack Fort Ticonderoga or a Spanish fleet sailing against

us from Guantanamo Bay," Norstad told attendees in Philadelphia. "We know that the last war began with bombs on Pearl Harbor and, to all intents and purposes, ended with a single B-29 over Hiroshima."

Arnold's fears in the end proved unfounded. America realized Mitchell's dream of an independent air force when President Truman signed the National Security Act of 1947. By then, the irascible Arnold, who had learned to fly from the Wright brothers in an Ohio cow pasture nearly a half century earlier, had retired to a small ranch in California near Sonoma, thanks in part to the bullying of his doctor. "I'm not aware of how long you want to live," his physician warned him, "but I can tell you how long you are going to live if you keep up this racket." Arnold planned to spend his days until his death—which came in 1950 at the age of sixty-three—under the shade of an oak tree. "From there," he said of his quiet perch, "I'll look across the valley at the white-faced cattle. And if one of them even moves too fast, I'll look the other way."

LeMay's career continued its meteoric rise. He served for nearly a decade as the head of Strategic Air Command, building America's all-jet bomber force during the Cold War. To accomplish that mission, he reassembled his war-winning team from the Pacific, including Rosie O'Donnell, Thomas Power, and John Montgomery. The pinnacle of his career came in 1961, when President John Kennedy appointed him chief of staff of the U.S. Air Force, an amazing accomplishment for an impoverished son of Ohio who worked his way through college in a steel mill. He ultimately clashed during the Vietnam War with Defense Secretary Robert McNamara. "LeMay never learned," one aide said, "that he could not deal with the political problems in Washington as if he were a combat commander in the field."

In a surprise move in 1964, Japan honored LeMay with its the highest award for nonnatives, the First Order of Merit of the Grand Cordon of the Rising Sun. The decoration, which recognized LeMay for his postwar service in helping to build Japan's self-defense system, drew bitter criticism in parliament. How could Japan honor the general who had incinerated Tokyo along with dozens of other cities, a man the press once labeled a "wanton killer" and a "bloodthirsty maniac"?

Premier Eisaku Sato, however, defended the honor. "Bygones," he said, "are bygones."

The controversy in Japan paled compared to the ones that would dog LeMay following his retirement from the air service. In 1965, he published his autobiography *Mission with LeMay*, which was ghostwritten by journalist and novelist MacKinlay Kantor. In the final pages of the hefty tome, LeMay gave advice on how to end the war in Vietnam. "My solution to the problem would be tell them frankly that they've got to draw in their horns and stop their aggression, or we're going to bomb them back into the Stone Age." The statement was not far off from comments LeMay had made in July 1945, when he threatened to return Japan to the "Dark Ages." Much had changed, however, in the intervening two decades. Reviewers seized on the quotation, which cast LeMay in the minds of a war-weary public as a brute. "That statement," wrote his biographer Thomas Coffey, "did more damage to LeMay's public image than anything he ever did say."

But LeMay's problems were not finished.

Segregationist George Wallace, who in 1963 notoriously stood in the door at the University of Alabama to block entrance to black students, ran a doomed campaign for president in 1968. Wallace selected LeMay as his running mate, who after much badgering agreed to join the campaign. Former aides and friends pleaded with him to turn down the offer, including Spaatz, Montgomery, and Ralph Nutter. LeMay was a warrior, everyone recognized, not a politician. But LeMay refused to listen, hoping to use the platform to challenge America's Vietnam policy. "He was," his daughter Janie later lamented, "not prepared to be thrown into the lion's den." LeMay's impolite comments on the campaign trail once again led the press to ridicule him, even caricaturing him as a caveman in a jet bomber, cementing a reputation that would overshadow his wartime success and haunt him until his death in 1990. "History," Nutter lamented, "should judge LeMay by his deeds, not by his lack of political and diplomatic skills." LeMay recognized the damage done. "I was a hero one day," he said, "and a bum the next."

Haywood Hansell retired to Hilton Head Island, along the South

Carolina coast, where he wrote several valuable memoirs chronicling his years helping to shape American bombardment policy. His personal writings, which are on file at the U.S. Air Force Academy, show that the wound caused by his firing never fully healed. In 1975, he wrote to Ira Eaker that he was convinced America could have won the war without burning Japan's cities. That said, Hansell, always a southern gentleman, never blamed LeMay. In fact, until his death in 1988, Hansell held his successor up in awe. "General LeMay," he later said, "was an excellent combat commander." When asked in 1976 to name the war's top leaders, Hansell included LeMay alongside such esteemed commanders as Spaatz and George Marshall. The general admitted in a speech at the Air Force Academy that he personally would not have had the bravery to order his crews to attack Tokyo at such a low altitude. "To my mind," Hansell wrote to an air force historian, "that decision was one of the most important decisions of the entire war. It was a personal decision, not a consensus, and he alone should bear the credit."

On June 11, 1972, construction workers at the site of a new subway line in Fukagawa dug up a damaged sidewalk. Five feet down workers unearthed an air raid shelter that contained the skeletons of two children and four adults. One of the bodies clutched a family's mortuary tablet, which helped authorities track down the surviving family members. Katsumoto Saotome, who at age twelve had survived the firebombing of Tokyo, read news accounts of that discovery, which awakened his own memories of that March night. Armed with a notepad and pen, he knocked on doors, asking to interview other survivors. In 1971, he published *The Great Tokyo Air Raid*, which became a best seller and helped establish him as Japan's leading historian on the raid. Saotome has since dedicated his life to the story of that frightening March night, publishing or helping to publish scores of books by survivors.

Through his leadership, the Center of the Tokyo Raids and War Damage opened in 2002, a museum paid for by private donations and housed in a three-story brick building. The museum counts among its artifacts pieces of dishware fused together with clay roof tiles, a child's burned kimono, and even spent incendiary casings. Schoolchildren visit, while veterans share personal experiences, including Haruyo Wada, who at eight years old survived the conflagration in her father's embrace at the bottom of a pile of scorched strangers.

Only hours before the raid, she had played with her best friend, Masao, the young boy who lived next door and comforted her when she got in trouble. The last she had seen of him was when he was breaking up the ice in his family's cistern. After the raid, Haruyo abandoned Tokyo; when she finally returned, her family had settled elsewhere. The uncertainty over the fate of her friend haunted her as she resumed school, married, and became a librarian.

Seven decades after the raid, a television producer reached out to Haruyo. As part of his research, he had located Masao's younger brother. Through him, Haruyo learned that Masao's family had fled up the same hill that night, but the little brother had got scared and run home. His father, who had stayed back to battle the blaze, put the youth in the family's shelter and splashed water on top from the cistern through the night. Masao's efforts to break up the ice, Haruyo learned, had helped save the life of his brother. The family searched for Masao but never found him. Like so many others, he had simply vanished. His father erected a memorial to Masao in the family's cemetery. After all these years, Haruyo visited the cemetery and prayed for the soul of her lost friend. "I was able at last," she concluded, "to settle my mind."

ACKNOWLEDGMENTS

Writing a work of history is always a collaborative effort. Along those lines, I am grateful to the army of archivists, librarians, fellow researchers, and historians who have kindly assisted me. A few individuals deserve special recognition, including Nate Patch and Erik Van Slander at the National Archives and Records Administration in College Park, Maryland, who have helped me over the years on multiple books. Thank you as well to Mary Elizabeth Ruwell at the U.S. Air Force Academy Library and to my good friend Jim Zobel with the MacArthur Memorial Archives and Library in Norfolk, Virginia, who has hosted me multiple times at the archives and in his incredible home. George Cully and Katie Rasdorf, independent researchers and good friends, proved, as always, to be indispensable. Thank you as well to Michael Krehl, Nancy Samp, and the late Edwin Lawson with the 500th Bombardment Group. I was fortunate to interview B-29 pilots, flight engineers, and gunners, including Ben Nicks, Bob Minto, Bob Vaucher, Fiske Hanley, Glenn Barnhart, John Angel, and Peter Paul Hatgil. Thank you as well to the members of the 504th Bombardment Group, who graciously welcomed me to their reunion in Myrtle Beach, South Carolina.

I am grateful to Manuel "Manolo" Quezon III in Manila, who shared with me the diary of Philippine diplomat León María Guerrero, which provides a fascinating window into life in Tokyo during the last year of the war. In Japan, I would like to thank the marvelous staff at the Center

of the Tokyo Raids and War Damage, who lent me the use of their conference room so I could interview survivors of the March 9, 1945, firebombing. I am indebted to Akiko Masaki, Haruyo Nihei, Ikuko Nagata,
Shizuko Nishio, and Shizuyo Takeuchi, who generously shared their letters, photos, and personal stories of survival with me. I would like to add
a special thanks to Katsumoto Saotome, who is not only a survivor of the
raid but also Japan's foremost historian on the destruction of Tokyo. Mr.
Saotome graciously welcomed me into his home in the suburbs of Tokyo
for hours of fascinating conversation. I am beholden as well to his wonderful daughter Ai, whom I first met in Tokyo and who has since helped
me tremendously by answering my many questions from afar. Others I
want to thank include Seishi Ishibashi, who arranged many of my interviews and also gave me a personal tour of the Yasukuni Shrine and the
Yushukan War Memorial Museum. Thank you as well to Mine Takada
for the warm hospitality and to Masahiko Yamabe for a private tour of
the Wadatsumi no Koe Memorial Hall.

In Kyoto, I am indebted to Kazuyo Yamane and Ikuro Anzai at the
Kyoto Museum of World Peace. Down in Hiroshima, I want to say a special thanks to Shigeaki Mori, who survived the atomic attack on August
6, 1945. Mr. Mori generously spent two days with me in Hiroshima, inviting me into his home, sharing with me his powerful story, and escort-
ing me on a personal tour of the Hiroshima Peace Memorial Museum.
He likewise showed me the memorial he helped construct, honoring the
twelve American prisoners of war killed in the atomic attack. Despite
having once lived and worked as an educator in Japan, I still depended
on invaluable interpreters and assistants, including the excellent Kumiko
Magome, who helped translate documents and interviews. None of this
work, however, would have been possible without the tireless dedication
of my dear friend Yukako Ibuki. A retired English teacher, Yuka helped
arrange many of my interviews and served as my personal translator and
travel companion. In addition, Yuka pored over countless books and witness statements, helping to translate them for inclusion.

Closer to home, I want to thank doctors Kyle Sinisi, David Preston,
and Brian Laslie at the Citadel, where I worked on this book as part of

my master's in military history. All three are brilliant military historians whom I am fortunate to count as friends. I have benefited tremendously over the years from a cadre of fellow World War II historians and authors who have shared records, given me insightful advice, and allowed me to bounce ideas off them. Along those lines, I am especially grateful to Nigel Hamilton, Conrad Crane, John Bruning, Ray Boomhower, and the late Jim Hornfischer, whose June 2021 passing has left a professional and personal hole in the lives of so many. Richard Frank, author of the excellent book *Downfall* and one of the nation's top World War II historians, went above and beyond, poring over this manuscript in detail and offering invaluable insight. I am grateful as well to Charles Lodge, grandson of Curtis LeMay, who likewise reviewed the manuscript and has graciously granted me permission to quote from his grandfather's autobiography. I owe a special thanks to my dear friends and fellow writers George Getschow and Erik Calonius as well as the entire gang at the Archer City Writers Workshop, which doubles as a support group for narrative nonfiction writers in the tiny Texas town made famous by novelist Larry McMurtry. Thanks to Jason Ryan, Julia Flynn Siler, Ben Montgomery, Erik Nishimoto, and Kathy Floyd.

I owe a very special thanks to my wonderful editor John Glusman at Norton, whom I have had the privilege of working with now on three books. John not only immediately embraced the idea for this project but has tirelessly worked at every step to elevate the quality of the manuscript. Thank you as well to the ever-patient Helen Thomaides at Norton, who has helped to keep me to my deadlines. Copyeditor Janet Biehl, whom I have had the privilege of working with on past projects, has demonstrated yet again why she is the best in the industry. As always, much is owed to Norton's terrific art and marketing departments. Thank you to my marvelous agent Wendy Strothman, whom I have now worked with on five books, and who has always given me her best. Last but certainly not least, thank you to my amazing and patient wife, Carmen, and children, Isa and Grigs, who have put up with my travel and countless weekends of work, not to mention all the war stories. This book is just as much theirs as it is mine.

A NOTE ON SOURCES

Narrative nonfiction is like a jigsaw puzzle, requiring the meticulous assemblage of military reports, letters, diaries, oral histories, and interviews to bring a historical story into sharper focus. The task of finding those pieces led me on a search through the collections and papers of nearly three dozen archives, libraries, and museums scattered across several continents. The Marianas-based air war against Japan, which ran less than nine months, produced tens of thousands of pages of records. The National Archives and Records Administration in College Park holds the files of the 21st Bomber Command, though microfilmed duplicates are available at the Air Force Historical Research Agency in Montgomery, Alabama. Bomber Command records, which range from cables and memos to after-action reports, fill thirty-three rolls of microfilm. That adds up to more than forty-five thousand pages, a figure that does not include the records of the individual bombardment wings, groups, and squadrons.

Haywood Hansell helped pioneer America's air wars against both Germany and Japan. In addition to the three memoirs he wrote during retirement, researchers can peruse his extensive personal papers, which are divided between the Air Force Historical Research Agency and the U.S. Air Force Academy Library in Colorado Springs. These two collections include Hansell's wartime letters, lectures, and vast postwar correspondence. Curtis LeMay, who spent his life in uniform, likewise left extensive personal papers, which fill more than 250 boxes at the Library of Congress in Washington. Those records include official reports, letters, diaries, and speeches. Another valuable resource is LeMay's official military personnel file, which is available at the National Personnel Records Center in St. Louis. This more-than-four-thousand-page file includes his efficiency reports, commendations, and correspondence, allowing researchers to track the rise of one of America's top combat commanders. In addition to LeMay, the Library of Congress houses the collections of many other airpower luminaries, including Hap Arnold, Billy Mitchell, Ira Eaker, Carl Spaatz, and Jimmy Doolittle.

Japan has done a tremendous job documenting the experiences of air raid survivors. Unfortunately, very few of those records are available in English, which until now has limited the ability of American historians to tell the story of what it was like in Tokyo during the air war. A vital resource for anyone studying the air raids is the five-volume set *Tōkyō Daikūshū Sensaishi*, which was published between 1973 and 1974 and includes survivor testimonies and government records. The first volume, which totals 1,052 pages, largely comprises firsthand accounts of the March 9, 1945, raid on Tokyo. The volume, complete with maps and photographs, is organized by ward, allowing researchers to chart the conflagration, deaths and injuries, as well as property destruction neighborhood by neighborhood. Another important resource is *Tōkyō Kūshū Shashinshū*. This 2015 book includes more than fourteen hundred photographs of attack damage, ranging from Jimmy Doolittle's first raid on Tokyo on April 18, 1942, through the sixth and final incendiary strike on the capital on May 25, 1945. Many other personal accounts of the March 9 raid have also been published in Japanese. Three of the best include Kōyō Ishikawa's *Tōkyō Daikūshū no Kiroku* (1992), Shigenori Kubota's *Tōkyō Daikūshū Kyūgo Taichō no Kiroku* (1973), and Katsumoto Saotome's *Tōkyō Daikūshū* (1971).

Some of the richest sources for this work were the memories of those who fought and survived the air war against Japan. I married archival research with interviews with airmen who flew the missions out of the Marianas, including pilots, flight engineers, and gunners. I also consulted extensive oral history collections, from the University of North Texas to the National Museum of the Pacific War. In Japan, I spent valuable time at the Center of the Tokyo Air Raids and War Damage, a must-visit for anyone interested in the raid. The three-story private museum, which opened in 2002, has an extensive collection of materials on the raid and provides a forum for survivors to give lectures to schoolchildren and the public. The museum likewise showcases important artifacts, including spent incendiary casings, melted dishware, and fused coins. The museum staff were gracious in allowing me to use the conference room to conduct interviews with survivors, while others I did in homes and even karaoke booths. The Great Kanto Earthquake Memorial and Museum is another important locale for researchers, housing the cremated remains of the dead from the 1923 earthquake as well as the March 1945 firebombing. The adjacent museum likewise displays fascinating artifacts from both tragedies.

I have provided extensive notes and a bibliography of all the collections, archives, museums, and libraries consulted as well as secondary sources. All quotes and dialogue in this book come from military reports, memos, cables, letters, diaries, survivor statements, author interviews, oral histories, news stories, and memoirs of participants.

NOTES

ABBREVIATIONS

PART I

1   "There has never": William Mitchell, testimony, February 5, 1926, in U.S. Cong., House, *Department of Defense and Unification of Air Service: Hearings Before the Committee on Military Affairs,* 69th Cong., 1st sess., January 19 to March 9, 1926 (Washington, D.C.: U.S. Government Printing Office, 1926), p. 397.

CHAPTER 1

3   "It is Thanksgiving Day": Tim Leimert, broadcast transcript, November 24, 1944, Box 17, RG 38, World War II Oral Histories and Interviews, 1942–1946, NARA.

3   Brig. Gen. Haywood Hansell, Jr.: Background on Hansell's early struggles in the Marianas and with this mission are drawn from: Haywood S. Hansell, Jr., *The Strategic Air War Against Japan* (Washington, D.C.: Air Power Research Institute, 1980), pp. 33–40; Haywood S. Hansell, Jr., *The Strategic Air War Against Germany and Japan: A Memoir* (Washington, D.C.: Office of Air Force History, 1986), pp. 171–90; and Haywood S. Hansell, Jr., to James M. Boyle, January 4, 1965, Microfilm Roll # A7794, AFHRA.

3   "The delays": Chester Marshall diary, November 18, 1944, in Chester Marshall, *Sky Giants over Japan: A Diary of a B-29 Combat Crew in WWII* (Winona, Minn.: Apollo Books, 1984), p. 45.

3   Others had quipped: Narrative History of the 497th Bombardment Group, November 1–30, 1944, p. 11, Microfilm Roll # B0663, AFHRA.

4   Hansell had spent: Charles Griffith, *The Quest: Haywood Hansell and American Strategic Bombing in World War II* (Maxwell Air Force Base, Ala.: Air University Press, 1999), pp. 23–56; Sidney Shalett, "This Possum Is Jap Poison," *Saturday Evening Post,* November 25, 1944, p. 17.

4   "The idea": Hansell, *Strategic Air War Against Germany and Japan*, p. 13.

4   The mission: 73rd Bombardment Wing, Consolidated Mission Report No. 7, November 24, 1944, Microfilm Roll # C0032, AFHRA; see also Wesley Frank Craven and James Lea Cate, eds., *The Army Air Forces in World War II,* vol. 5, *The Pacific: Matterhorn to Nagasaki, June 1944 to August 1945* (Washington, D.C.: Office of Air Force History, 1983), pp. 556–60.

4   The target: USSBS, *Nakajima Aircraft Company, LTD* (Washington, D.C.: U.S. Government Printing Office, 1947), pp. 96–102.

4   "There is": Target Information Sheet, 90.17–357: Nakajima Aircraft Company, Musashino-Tama Plant, March 30, 1945, Microfilm Roll # A7092, AFHRA.

4   The United States had spent: Kenneth P. Werrell, *Blankets of Fire: U.S. Bombers over Japan During World War II* (Washington, D.C.: Smithsonian Institution Press, 1996), p. 82.

5   "It was": Bruce M. Petty, *Saipan: Oral Histories of the War* (Jefferson, N.C.: McFarland, 2002), p. 103.

5   "It's just the damnedest": James D. Hornfischer, *The Fleet at Flood Tide: America at Total War in the Pacific, 1944–1945* (New York: Bantam Books, 2016), p. 294.

5   "The artillery fire": Henry E. Williams diary, July 31, 1944, included with Monograph IV, History of the VHB Construction in the Marianas and on Iwo Jima, September 1945, Microfilm Roll # A7107, AFHRA.

5   "Day and night": 804th Engineer Aviation Battalion, "Operations of 804th Engineer Aviation Battalion on Saipan," November 22, 1944, Microfilm Roll # A0242, AFHRA.

6 "He ran over": Headquarters Army Garrison Force, Award of the Silver Star Medal to 2D Lt. Henry E. McCoy, September 13, 1944, Microfilm Roll # A0241, AFHRA.

6 "Tropical downpours": Clinton Green, "Our B-29 Base: An Epic Job," *New York Times,* December 10, 1944, p. SM8.

6 "A handful": Report of Col. C. S. Irvine, November 30, 1944, Box 21, EOP. A copy of this report can also be found in Box B16, CLP.

6 "A great cheer": Narrative History of the 497th Bombardment Group, October 1–31, 1944, p. 16, Microfilm Roll # B0663, AFHRA.

6 "Ground crews": Hansell, *Strategic Air War Against Japan,* p. 34.

7 Aircrews fortunately: 3rd Photo Reconnaissance Squadron, History of Advance Ground Echelon and Squadron, November 1–30, 1944, pp. 1–2, 15, Microfilm Roll # A0862, AFHRA.

7 "We've learned": "What B-29s Are Saying with Bombs: Now Tokyo Too Feels the Scourge," *Newsweek,* December 4, 1944, p. 13.

7 "Every crew": Hansell, *Strategic Air War Against Japan,* p. 36.

8 "I hope to launch": Haywood S. Hansell, Jr., oral history by Murray Green, January 2, 1970, Box 66, MGC.

8 "Possum, I hope": Barney Giles, oral history by Murray Green, May 12, 1970, Box 65, MGC.

9 "The effect": Hansell, *Strategic Air War Against Japan,* p. 37.

9 "Failure of the mission": Haywood S. Hansell, Jr., to Rollin C. Reineck, January 9, 1978, Microfilm Roll # 34142, AFHRA.

9 "Are you": Wilbur H. Morrison, *Point of No Return: The Story of the 20th Air Force* (New York: Times Books, 1979), p. 184.

9 "Hansell": Ibid., p. 183.

10 "Stick together": Hansell, *Strategic Air War Against Japan,* p. 38.

10 "Yep, we'll go": Chester Marshall diary, November 24, 1944, in Marshall, *Sky Giants,* p. 48.

11 rabbit hunt: "Target Tokyo," *Brief* 2, no. 2 (1944): 3.

11 "Men": John W. Cox, *Friendly Monster: A Warbird and Its Crew* (Bloomington, Ind.: Xlibris, 2007), pp. 44–45.

11 "I don't think": Chester Marshall diary, November 24, 1944, in Marshall, *Sky Giants,* p. 50.

11 Flashbulbs popped: Narrative History of the 497th Bombardment Group, November 1–30, 1944, pp. 8–13, Microfilm Roll # B0663, AFHRA.

11 "Right now": Denis Warner, "The Sea Is Waiting Below," *Boeing Magazine* 15, no. 1 (1945): 6.

12 "It is": Gene Rider, broadcast transcript, November 24, 1944, Box 24, RG 38, World War II Oral Histories and Interviews, 1942–1946, NARA.

CHAPTER 2

13 "No part": "Industry Blasted," *New York Times,* November 24, 1944, p. 1.

13 The fifty-eight-year-old: H. H. Arnold, *Global Mission* (New York: Harper & Brothers, 1949), pp. 1–29.

13 Arnold completed: A. L. Welch, "Flying Report: Summary of Lt. Hen. H. Arnold's Training," May 3–13, 1911, Microfilm Roll # 3, HHAP.

13 "More than anyone": Arnold, *Global Mission,* p. 28.

14 Arnold applied: Ibid., pp. 30–47, 100–1; Thomas M. Coffey, *Hap: The Story of the U.S. Air Force and the Man Who Built It* (New York: Viking Press, 1982), pp. 48–87; "Breaks Army Altitude Flight," *New York Times,* June 2, 1912, p. 4; "General Arnold Wins Mackay Trophy Again," *New York Times,* March 16, 1935, p. 32.

14 "At the present time": H. H. Arnold to Commanding Officer, Signal Corps Aviation School, Washington, D.C., "Report Upon Test of Aeroplane in Connection with Artillery Fires," November 6, 1912, Microfilm Roll # 3, HHAP; see also H. H. Arnold to Charles De F. Chandler, November 7, 1912, ibid.

14 "That's it": Round Table Discussion on Early Aviation with Generals Benjamin Foulois, Frank Lahm, and Thomas Milling hosted by Gen. Carl Spaatz, June 29, 1954, AFHRA.

14 "When I'm going": Coffey, *Hap,* p. 87.

14 In the waning days: Douglas Waller, *A Question of Loyalty: Gen. Billy Mitchell and the Court-Martial That Gripped the Nation* (New York: HarperCollins , 2004), pp. 4–10, 54–55, 119–22, 130–31, 141–55.

15 "Bolshevik Bug": Peter R. Faber, "Interwar US Army Aviation and the Air Corps Tactical School: Incubators of American Airpower," in Phillip S. Meilinger, ed., *The Paths of Heaven: The Evolution of Airpower Theory* (Maxwell Air Force Base, Ala.: Air University Press, 1997), p. 186.

15 "An Air Force": John J. Pershing to Maj. Gen. Charles T. Menoher, January 12, 1920, in the "Annual Report of the Director of the Air Service," *Aerial Age Weekly,* December 20, 1920, p. 396.

15 "Billy, take it easy": Arnold, *Global Mission,* p. 114.

15 "Keep cool": Waller, *Question of Loyalty,* p. 155.

15 "When senior officers": Arnold, *Global Mission,* p. 114.

15 That explosion: Waller, *Question of Loyalty,* pp. 17–23.

15 "The lives": Statement of William Mitchell Concerning the Recent Air Accidents, undated, Box 38, William Mitchell Papers, LOC.

15 "Billy was licked": Arnold, *Global Mission,* pp. 120–21.

16 "You can resign": Coffey, *Hap,* pp. 5–6.

17 "They seemed": Arnold, *Global Mission,* p. 122.

17 "Inclined to be disloyal": George O. Squier, Efficiency Report for H. H. Arnold, December 27, 1919, Henry H. Arnold OMPF, National Personnel Records Center, St. Louis, Mo.

17 "In an emergency": Mason M. Patrick, Efficiency Report for H. H. Arnold, April 8, 1926, ibid.

17 "It's so bad": Arnold, *Global Mission,* p. 46.

17 Arnold even managed: Ibid., pp. 186, 194.

17 "Oh boy": John W. Huston, ed., *American Airpower Comes of Age: General Henry H.*

"Hap" Arnold's World War II Diaries (Maxwell Air Force Base, Ala.: Air University Press, 2002), p. 1:99.

17   "His idea of a good time": Eugene Beebe, oral history by Murray Green, October 1, 1969, Box 59, MGC.

17   "Arnold was not": Haywood S. Hansell, Jr., oral history by Murray Green, January 2, 1970, Box 66, MGC.

17   "Hap": Emmett "Rosie" O'Donnell, oral history by Jack Loosbrock, March 27, 1970, Box 73, MGC.

17   "He was utterly ruthless": Emmett O'Donnell to T. D. Stamps, April 11, 1946, Box 1, EOP.

18   "He's kind of like an elephant": Barney Giles, oral history by Murray Green, May 12, 1970.

18   "Awfully rough": Hunter Harris, oral history by Murray Green, April 28, 1971, Box 66, MGC.

18   The general: Coffey, *Hap,* p. 2.

18   "People have become": Arnold, *Global Mission,* p. 158.

18   "No war": Ibid., p. 182.

18   The air war in Europe: Donald L. Miller, *Masters of the Air: America's Bomber Boys Who Fought the Air War Against Nazi Germany* (New York: Simon & Schuster, 2006), pp. 3–7.

19   "He'd have fired": James Parton, *"Air Force Spoken Here": General Ira Eaker and the Command of the Air* (Bethesda, Md.: Adler & Adler, 1986), p. 115.

19   "These first few": H. H. Arnold to H. S. Hansell, Jr., November 13, 1944, Microfilm Roll # 34142, AFHRA.

19   The tortuous path: Background on the development of the B-29 comes from Jacob Vander Meulen, *Building the B-29* (Washington, D.C.: Smithsonian Institution, 1995), pp. 11–20.

20   "It was so large": Arnold, *Global Mission,* p. 478.

20   "His life": Lauris Norstad, oral history by Murray Green, July 15, 1969, Box 72, MGC.

20   "Hap took the chances": Curtis E. LeMay and Bill Yenne, *Superfortress: The Story of the B-29 and American Air Power* (New York: McGraw-Hill, 1988), pp. 23–24.

20   Over the course: Vander Meulen, *Building the B-29,* pp. 21–29, 36–37, 69, 74–75.

21   Boeing's Wichita: Ibid., pp. 38–45; Julie Courtwright, "Want to Build a Miracle City? War Housing in Wichita," *Kansas History* 23, no. 4 (Winter 2000–1): 218–39; Peter Fearon, "Ploughshares into Airplanes: Manufacturing Industry and Workers in Kansas During World War II," *Kansas History* 22, no. 4 (Winter 1999–2000): 298–314; Ralph G. Martin, "Home Folks," *Stars and Stripes,* August 17, 1944, p. 4.

21   "Miracle City": Courtwright, "Want to Build a Miracle City?" p. 223.

21   "Grandmothers": Foster Hailey, "Superfortress Is Largest and Swiftest Bomber in the World; It Carries Heaviest Load," *New York Times,* June 16, 1944, p. 4.

22   The $73 million: Joe Kirby, *The Bell Bomber Plant* (Charleston, S.C.: Arcadia, 2008), pp. 7–8, 29.

22   On the West Coast: Bill Yenne, *Panic on the Pacific: How America Prepared for a West Coast Invasion* (Washington, D.C.: Regnery History, 2016), pp. 161–66.

22 The completed B-29: "The Mighty B-29: Facts About the Army's Plane That Is Blasting Japan," editorial, *New York Times,* August 5, 1945, p. 67.

23 "aerial battleship": LeMay and Yenne, *Superfortress,* p. 28.

23 "staggers the imagination": Jimmy Doolittle, press statement, July 23, 1945, Box 38, James H. Doolittle Papers, LOC.

23 Engineers put: LeMay and Yenne, *Superfortress,* p. 60.

23 "She flies!": Thomas Collison, *The Superfortress Is Born: The Story of the Boeing B-29* (New York: Duell, Sloan & Pearce, 1945), p. 140.

23 More tests followed: LeMay and Yenne, *Superfortress,* p. 61.

23 "Tell us": Ibid., pp. 62–63; Collison, *Superfortress Is Born,* pp. 147–48.

24 "Flames were shooting": "14 Killed in Crash of a Bomber Igniting Seattle Packing Plant," *New York Times,* February 19, 1943, p. 21.

24 "There was a blinding": Ibid.

24 "It was": LeMay and Yenne, *Superfortress,* p. 63.

24 "Look": Coffey, *Hap,* p. 303.

24 Despite more than two thousand: Gene Gurney, *Journey of the Giants: The Story of the B-29 "Superfort"—The Weapon That Won the War in the Pacific* (New York: Coward-McCann, 1961), p. 39.

24 "You could hardly": Paul Tibbets, oral history by Kenneth Leish, December 1960, USAFAL.

24 "I was just sitting": Kenneth Wolfe, oral history by Robert Piper, June 1966, AFHRA.

25 "Within the air force": Ibid.

25 Arnold faced: LeMay and Yenne, *Superfortress,* pp. 66–70.

25 "Everything seems": Craven and Cate, *Army Air Forces in World War II,* p. 5:21.

25 "The B-29 business": Herman S. Wolk, *Cataclysm: General Hap Arnold and the Defeat of Japan* (Denton: University of North Texas Press, 2010), p. 84.

25 "It is my desire": Werrell, *Blankets of Fire,* p. 80.

25 Design changes: Vander Meulen, *Building the B-29,* pp. 34–35.

25 "This is the plane": "Arnold Extra Special," *Boeing Magazine,* February 1948, p. 12; Steve Birdsall, *Saga of the Superfortress: The Dramatic History of the B-29 and the Twentieth Air Force* (Garden City, N.Y.: Doubleday, 1980), p. 36.

26 "I was appalled": Arnold, *Global Mission,* p. 479.

26 "We charted": Clarence "Bill" Irvine, oral history by Murray Green, August 5, 1974, Box 67, MGC.

26 "How are we": Ibid.

26 "It was so big": William Cooper, oral history by Ronald E. Marcello, September 7, 1944, UNT.

26 "There may be": Jack Tarver, "Japs Had Nothing to Be Thankful For," *Atlanta Constitution,* November 25, 1944, p. 4.

26 "She was a thoroughbred": Haywood S. Hansell, Jr., "Flying the B-29," undated, Box 9, Addendum 1, HSHP.

26 "The most pleasing": John Alebis, oral history by Richard Misenhimer, April 29, 2002, National Museum of the Pacific War, Fredericksburg, Tex.

27 "The B-29": Lauris Norstad, oral history by Murray Green, July 15, 1969, Box 49, MGC.

27 "The most courageous": Haywood S. Hansell, Jr., oral history by Murray Green, January 2, 1970, Box 66, MGC.

27 "Never before": Curtis E. LeMay, "The Role of VLR Aircraft in Victory over Japan," undated, Box B40, CLP.

CHAPTER 3

28 "The sight": Robert Morgan to Dorothy Morgan, November 27, 1944, Box 49, EOP.

28 Hansell had watched: 73rd Bombardment Wing, Consolidated Mission Report No. 7, November 24, 1944, Microfilm Roll # C0032, AFHRA.

29 "The Wright brothers": Clark Lee, "Correspondent Aboard B-29 Recounts Ill Luck of One Super-Fort Crew on Tokyo Raid," *Port Arthur News,* November 26, 1944, p. 16.

29 The first bombs-away: Clinton Green, "Precision Marked Take-Off of B-29's," *New York Times,* November 25, 1944, p. 3.

29 Hansell's headquarters: Narrative History of the 73rd Bombardment Wing, 1 October 1944 to 30 November 1944, p. 152, Microfilm Roll # C0031, AFHRA.

29 "A large task force": "The Texts of the Day's Communiques on the Fighting in Various War Zones," *New York Times,* November 25, 1944, p. 2.

29 The first bomber: 73rd Bombardment Wing, Consolidated Mission Report No. 7, November 24, 1944.

29 "We caught them": Lee, "Correspondent Aboard B-29," p. 16.

29 "The Japs": "O'Donnell Says B-29s Caught Foe Off Guard," *New York Herald Tribune,* November 25, 1944, p. 2.

29 "Boy": "Tokyo Raider O'Donnell Can Do Anything, His Son, 7, Is Sure," *Baltimore Sun,* November 25, 1944, p. 2.

29 News of the raid: Marc Weingarten, "He Captured Scoundrels on Paper," *Los Angeles Times,* February 14, 2010, p. E6.

30 "His communiques": Robert Gardner, "Aplomb: Some Have It, Some Don't," *Daily Pilot,* May 8, 2005, https://www.latimes.com/socal/daily-pilot/news/tn-dpt-xpm-2005-05-08-export2028-story.html.

30 McKelway applied: Narrative History of the XXI Bomber Command, 1 November 1944 to 31 December 1944, pp. 28–29, Microfilm Roll # A7780, AFHRA; St. Clair McKelway to Historical Officer, XXI Bomber Command, January 13, 1945, Historical Notes (Public Relations), ibid,; Narrative History of the 73rd Bombardment Wing, 1 October 1944 to 30 November 1944, pp. 152–54, Microfilm Roll # C0031, ibid. See also Mac R. Johnson, "Over Tokyo in a Superfortress: 6 Big Fires in Bomber's Wake," *New York Herald Tribune,* November 25, 1944, p. 1; William Hipple, "What B-29s Are Saying with Bombs: Now Tokyo Too Feels the Scourge," *Newsweek,* December 4, 1944, p. 10.

30 "Correspondents were advised": Narrative History of the XXI Bomber Command, 1 November 1944 to 31 December 1944, p. 28.

30   "Tokyo Airplant Smashed": "Tokyo Airplant Smashed, Fires Rage in City," *New York Times,* November 25, 1944, p. 1.

30   "B-29s Took": Elton C. Fay, "B-29s Took Jap Capital by Surprise," *Washington Post,* November 25, 1944, p. 1.

30   "Just the Beginning": "Just the Beginning," editorial, *Christian Science Monitor,* November 25, 1944, p. 18.

30   To complement: "Superfortress to Be Shown Here Sunday," *Washington Post,* November 24, 1944, p. 7; James V. Piersol, "B-29 of Type That Hit Tokyo Goes on Display Here Today," *Washington Post,* November 26, 1944, p. M1; Emily Towe, "100,000 See B-29 at Close Range Here," *Washington Post,* November 27, 1944, p. 1.

31   "I want the Japs": Towe, "100,000 See B-29."

31   "No wonder": Ibid.

31   In contrast: 73rd Bombardment Wing, Consolidated Mission Report No. 7, November 24, 1944; Hansell, *Strategic Air War Against Japan,* pp. 39–40; USSBS, *Nakajima Aircraft Company,* pp. 115–16; Mac R. Johnson, "Crew of B-29 Tokyo Raider Found Adrift Off Marianas: Rescue," *New York Times,* November 27, 1944, p. 1.

31   "The bombing": Hansell, *Strategic Air War Against Japan,* p. 39.

31   "This Possum": Sidney Shalett, "This Possum Is Jap Poison," *Saturday Evening Post,* November 25, 1944, p. 17.

32   "He was in no mood": Ralph H. Nutter, *With the Possum and the Eagle: The Memoir of a Navigator's War over Germany and Japan* (Novato, Calif.: Presidio, 2002), p. 200.

32   A thirty-eight-year-old: Emmett O'Donnell, Jr., official bio, undated, Box 73, MGC.

32   "I thought": Emmett O'Donnell, Jr., oral history by members of the Air Force Academy History Department, December 2, 1967, USAFAL.

32   "I would do anything": Jack J. Catton, oral history by James C. Hasdorff, July 19–20, 1977, AFHRA. See also Kenneth B. Bergquist, oral history by Arthur Marmor, October 1965, USAFAL.

32   "Your job": Huston, *American Airpower Comes of Age,* p. 2:2.

32   O'Donnell had used: Griffith, *Quest,* p. 156.

33   "Requires less fuel": Emmett O'Donnell, Jr., to H. S. Hansell, Jr., "Target Selection," June 7, 1944, Box 19, EOP.

33   "Opposition to this change": Hansell, *Strategic Air War Against Japan,* p. 32.

33   "Civilian morale": Emmett O'Donnell to H. H. Arnold, August 8, 1944, Box 11, EOP.

33   LeMay shot down: Curtis E. LeMay to H. H. Arnold, August 19, 1944, ibid.

33   "I realize": Haywood S. Hansell, Jr., to H. H. Arnold, August 19, 1944, ibid.

33   But O'Donnell continued: Emmett O'Donnell diary, entry for November 4, 1944, Box 44, EOP.

34   "I have 108": Emmett O'Donnell diary, entry for November 21, 1944, ibid.

34   "The lack of flexibility": Ibid.

34   "We lost": Ibid.

34   "I was torn": Haywood S. Hansell, Jr., to John L. Frisbee, August 2, 1983, Box 1, Addendum 2, HSHP.

34 "Rumors are": Samuel Harris diary, entry for November 18, 1944, in Samuel Russ Harris, Jr., *B-29s over Japan, 1944–1945: A Group Commander's Diary,* ed. Robert A. Mann (Jefferson, N.C.: McFarland, 2011), pp. 49–50.

34 "I look at the mission": Emmett O'Donnell diary, entry for November 24, 1944, Box 44, EOP.

35 "This first mission": Nutter, *With Possum and Eagle,* p. 200.

35 Anxious to rebound: 73rd Bombardment Wing, Consolidated Mission Report No. 8, November 27, 1944, Microfilm Roll # C0032, AFHRA.

35 So was the third: 73rd Bombardment Wing, Consolidated Mission Report No. 9, November 29, 1944, Microfilm Roll # C0032, AFHRA.

35 "The weather": Haywood S. Hansell, Jr., *The Air Plan That Defeated Hitler* (Atlanta: Arno Press, 1972), p. 121.

35 Impenetrable clouds: "The Weather Problem in Attacking Japan," *Impact* 3, no. 2 (1945): 48; "The B-29ers," *Impact* 3, no. 9 (1945): 63, both located in Box B41, CLP.

36 "The bombsight": Richard H. Kohn and Joseph P. Harahan, eds., *Strategic Air Warfare: An Interview with Generals Curtis E. LeMay, Leon W. Johnson, David A. Burchinal, and Jack J. Catton* (Washington, D.C.: U.S. Government Printing Office, 1988), p. 54.

36 "You would be there": Ibid., p. 55.

36 "Experience to date": Narrative History of the XXI Bomber Command, 1 November 1944 to 31 December 1944, p. 87.

36 Hansell was: Griffith, *Quest,* pp. 27–31.

36 "From the minute": Ibid., pp. 30–31.

36 "We did every": Claire Lee Chennault, *Way of a Fighter: The Memoirs of Claire Lee Chennault* (New York: G. P. Putnam's Sons, 1949), p. 25.

37 "It is sheer": Griffith, *Quest,* p. 36.

37 "We considered": Lee Kennett, *The First Air War, 1914–1918* (New York: Free Press, 1991), p. 225.

37 "The skies": Robert S. Dudney, "Douhet," *Air Force Magazine* 94, no. 4 (2011): 64.

37 Much like Mitchell: Phillip S. Meilinger, "Giulio Douhet and the Origins of Airpower Theory," in Meilinger, ed., *Paths of Heaven,* pp. 1–40.

37 "To have command": Giulio Douhet, *The Command of the Air,* trans., Dino Ferrari (Maxwell Air Force Base, Ala.: Air University Press, 2019), p. 20.

37 "Normal life": Ibid., p. 53.

38 "Nothing could stop": Laurence S. Kuter, oral history by Hugh N. Ahmann and Tom Sturm, September 30–October 3, 1974, AFHRA.

38 "The Douhet book": Chennault, *Way of a Fighter,* p. 20.

38 "egotistical and narrow-minded": Haywood S. Hansell, Jr., to Phillip S. Meilinger, May 13, 1974, Box 3, Addendum 1, HSHP.

38 "Chennault": Griffith, *Quest,* p. 35.

38 "There were no": Hansell to Meilinger, May 13, 1974.

38 "Tell Possum": Griffith, *Quest,* p. 47.

39   "We may find": Ronald Schaffer, *Wings of Judgment: American Bombing in World War II* (New York: Oxford University Press, 1985), p. 30.

39   Hansell further: Hansell, *Air Plan That Defeated Hitler,* pp. 59–99.

40   "A well-organized": Tami Davis Biddle, *Rhetoric and Reality in Air Warfare: The Evolution of British and American Ideas About Strategic Bombing, 1914–1945* (Princeton, N.J.: Princeton University Press, 2002), p. 142.

40   "When you put": James C. Gaston, *Planning the American Air War: Four Men and Nine Days in 1941* (Washington, D.C.: National Defense University Press), p. 22.

40   The wood-and-fabric: Kennett, *The First Air War*, pp. 220–221.

40   "The European War": William Mitchell, *Winged Defense: The Development and Possibilities of Modern Air Power—Economic and Military* (Mineola, N.Y.: Dover, 2006), p. 29.

40   "If the task was staggering": Hansell, *Air Plan That Defeated Hitler*, p. 69.

40   "We wrestled": Hansell, *Strategic Air War Against Germany and Japan*, p. 33.

41   "the most important": Haywood S. Hansell, Jr., oral history by Murray Green, January 2, 1970, Box 66, MGC.

41   "The ruthless bombing": Cordell Hull to Joseph Kennedy, September 1, 1939, in Matilda F. Axton et al., eds., *Foreign Relations of the United States Diplomatic Papers, 1939*, vol. 1, *General* (Washington, D.C.: U.S. Government Printing Office, 1956), p. 542.

41   "The scope": Hansell, *Strategic Air War Against Germany and Japan*, p. 37.

41   "slumbering dread": Ibid., p. 112.

41   "A plan": Gaston, *Planning the American Air War*, p. 103.

42   The first was: Wayne Whittaker, "The Bombsight That Thinks," *Popular Mechanics,* February 1945, pp. 7–10, 160–62; Volta Torrey, "The War's Most Closely Guarded Secret Revealed: How the Norden Bombsight Does Its Job," *Popular Mechanics,* June 1945, pp. 70–73, 220–24, 228, 232; "Norden Bomb Site Is Revealed as Almost Self Sufficient Device," *New York Times,* November 25, 1944, p. 11.

42   "We hung": Interview with Generals Charles P. Cabell and Haywood S. Hansell, Jr., September 11, 1970, Box 2, Addendum 3, HSHP.

42   "God knows": Parton, *"Air Force Spoken Here,"* p. 130.

42   "Many a B-17 crew:" Chennault, *Way of a Fighter,* p. 27.

42   "In order to see": Mark K. Wells, *Courage and Air Warfare: The Allied Aircrew Experience in the Second World War* (London: Frank Cass, 1995), p. 65.

42   "I'll give you": Ibid., p. 145.

43   "I'd go back": Robert Morgan, with Ron Powers, *The Man Who Flew the* Memphis Belle*: Memoir of a WWII Bomber Pilot* (New York: Dutton, 2001), p. 133.

43   "I dreaded them": Hansell, *Air Plan That Defeated Hitler,* p. 139.

43   "He was a proud": Nutter, *With Possum and Eagle,* p. 39.

44   "After working": Ibid., pp. 38–39.

44   "Without fighter": Ibid., p. 43.

44   "Who": Ibid.

44 "What's the use": Ibid., p. 44.

44 "I could hear": Ibid., p. 46.

44 "Compliments": Ibid.

45 "Our fears": Hansell, *Air Plan That Defeated Hitler*, p. 147.

45 Another crisis: Ibid., pp. 149–51.

45 "Young man": Ira Eaker, oral history by Murray Green, August 1, 1969, Box 64, MGC; see also Parton, *"Air Force Spoken Here,"* pp. 216–22.

45 "We couldn't envision": Curtis E. LeMay, with MacKinlay Kantor, *Mission with LeMay: My Story* (Garden City, N.Y.: Doubleday, 1965), p. 295.

46 "Combat experience": Hansell, *Strategic Air War Against Germany and Japan*, p. 113.

46 "Hansell has been": Ira Eaker to H. H. Arnold, June 12, 1943, quoted in Parton, *"Air Force Spoken Here,"* p. 272.

46 "We were operating": Arnold, *Global Mission*, p. 550.

47 "He's a very fine": Barney Giles, oral history by Murray Green, May 12, 1970.

47 "Americans": Hansell, *Air Plan That Defeated Hitler*, p. 255.

48 "It's my air plan": Nutter, *With Possum and Eagle*, p. 201.

CHAPTER 4

49 "Today the enemy": Kiyoshi Kiyosawa diary, entry for December 27, 1944, in Kiyoshi Kiyosawa, *The Wartime Diary of Kiyosawa Kiyoshi*, trans. Eugene Sovial and Tamie Kamiyama (Princeton, N.J.: Princeton University Press, 1980), p. 295.

49 The forty-three-year-old: Herbert P. Bix, *Hirohito and the Making of Modern Japan* (New York: HarperCollins, 2000), pp. 5–6, 48, 58–62, 75, 87–89.

50 A pile: Hiroyuki Agawa, *The Reluctant Admiral: Yamamoto and the Imperial Navy*, trans. John Bester (New York: Kodansha International, 1979), p. 284; "Foe Celebrates Singapore's Fall," *New York Times*, February 19, 1942, p. 4.

50 "Our men": "A Unique Kigensetsu," editorial, *Japan Times & Advertiser*, February 13, 1942, p. 6.

50 "We are the greatest": Joseph C. Grew, *Report from Tokyo: A Message to the American People* (New York: Simon & Schuster, 1942), p. 57.

50 "The contention": "Can the United States Be Invaded?" editorial, *Japan Times & Advertiser*, January 9, 1942, p. 6.

50 Japan's wartime failures: Robert Guillain, *I Saw Tokyo Burning: An Eyewitness Narrative from Pearl Harbor to Hiroshima*, trans. William Byron (Garden City, N.Y.: Doubleday, 1981), pp. 117–29; Thomas R. H. Havens, *Valley of Darkness: The Japanese People and World War II* (New York: W. W. Norton, 1978), pp. 118–47; and Hiroyo Arakawa, "The End of a Bake Shop," in Haruko Taya Cook and Theodore F. Cook, *Japan at War: An Oral History* (New York: The New Press, 1992), p. 180.

51 "Tokyo had never": Guillain, *I Saw Tokyo Burning*, p. 117.

51 "This was a politician's:": Havens, *Valley of Darkness*, p. 101.

51 The government eliminated: Ibid., pp. 90–113.

51 "A geisha": Guillain, *I Saw Tokyo Burning*, p. 109.

51 "sea leather": Havens, *Valley of Darkness,* p. 120.

51 "Traveling through": Masuo Kato, *The Lost War: A Japanese Reporter's Inside Story* (New York: Alfred A. Knopf, 1946), p. 160.

52 "One borrows": Kiyoshi Kiyosawa diary, entry for January 23, 1945, in Kiyosawa, *Wartime Diary,* p. 310.

52 "Money": Kimi Tatebayashi, "Kimonos and Potatoes," in Women's Division of Soka Gakkai, *Women Against War: Personal Accounts of Forty Japanese Women,* trans. Richard L. Gage (Tokyo: Kodansha International, 1986), p. 105.

52 "Everything was rationed": Ayako Koshino, "Dressmaker," in Cook and Cook, *Japan at War,* p. 186.

52 "The trains were packed": León María Guerrero, diary introduction, July 4, 1946, copy courtesy of Manuel Quezon III.

52 "Merely to subsist": Kato, *Lost War,* p. 9.

52 The government mobilized: Havens, *Valley of Darkness,* p. 103.

52 One of those: Katsumoto Saotome interview with author, November 21, 2019.

53 "The hunger": Ibid.

53 In another blow: Havens, *Valley of Darkness,* pp. 161–66; Cary Lee Karacas, "Tokyo from the Fire: War, Occupation, and the Remaking of a Metropolis," PhD diss. (University of California, Berkeley, 2006), p. 78; Samuel Hideo Yamashita, *Daily Life in Wartime Japan, 1940–1945* (Lawrence: University of Kansas Press, 2015), pp. 61–110.

53 "Let's all die": Yoneko Moriyama, "Neither Flowers Nor Fruit," in Women's Division of Soka Gakkai, *Women Against War,* p. 160.

53 "Every good thing": Ibid.

53 "Mother, as soon": Havens, *Valley of Darkness,* p. 165.

53 The evacuees: Yamashita, *Daily Life in Wartime Japan,* pp. 111–24.

53 "On sunny days": Mitsuko Ôoka, "No Regrets," in Women's Division of Soka Gakkai, *Women Against War,* p. 173.

54 The infant mortality: USSBS, *The Effects of Bombing on Health and Medical Services in Japan* (Washington, D.C.: U.S. Government Printing Office, 1947), pp. 88–90; Joseph Newman, *Goodbye Japan* (New York: L.B. Fischer, 1942), p. 212.

54 "We simply are": Tamura Tsunejiro diary, entry for November 20, 1944, in Samuel Hideo Yamashita, *Leaves from an Autumn of Emergencies: Selections of Wartime Diaries of Ordinary Japanese* (Honolulu: University of Hawai'i Press, 2005), p. 102.

54 Food vanished: Yamashita, *Daily Life in Wartime Japan,* pp. 162–64.

54 "Japan has become": Kiyoshi Kiyosawa diary, entry for April 19, 1944, in Kiyosawa, *Wartime Diary,* p. 180.

54 "All that was pleasing": Guillain, *I Saw Tokyo Burning,* p. 120.

54 Under the guise: Ben-Ami Shillony, *Politics and Culture in Wartime Japan* (Oxford: Clarendon Press, 1981), pp. 99–109.

54 "At that point": Wilfrid Fleisher, *Volcanic Isle* (Garden City, N.Y.: Doubleday, Doran, 1942), p. 317.

54 "By the time": Kato, *Lost War,* p. 190.

54 "We are clearly": Jun Takami diary, entry for May 11, 1945, in Donald Keene, *So Lovely a Country Will Never Die: Wartime Diaries of Japanese Writers* (New York: Columbia University Press, 2010), p. 82.

55 "We should have": Aiko Takahashi diary, entry for July 18, 1944, in Yamashita, *Leaves from an Autumn of Emergencies*, p. 174.

55 In the years: Richard H. Mitchell, *Thought Control in Prewar Japan* (Ithaca, N.Y.: Cornell University Press, 1976), pp. 39–147; Shillony, *Politics and Culture in Wartime*, pp. 11–16.

55 "During recess": Newman, *Goodbye Japan*, p. 235.

55 "We used to talk": USSBS, *The Effects of Strategic Bombing on Japanese Morale* (Washington, D.C.: U.S. Government Printing Office, 1947), p. 214.

55 "Are you a Japanese": Ibid., p. 81.

55 "It's not possible": Kiyoshi Kiyosawa diary, entry for December 30, 1944, in Kiyosawa, *Wartime Diary*, p. 296.

55 "The people": Shillony, *Politics and Culture in Wartime*, p. 68.

56 "By covering": USSBS, *Effects of Strategic Bombing on Japanese Morale*, p. 124.

56 "Nothing's quite": Tamura Tsunejiro diary, entry for December 9, 1944, in Yamashita, *Leaves from an Autumn of Emergencies*, p. 105.

56 "People in the bath": Futaro Yamada diary, entry for January 6, 1945, in Keene, *So Lovely a Country*, pp. 24–25.

56 "People in Tokyo": Guillain, *I Saw Tokyo Burning*, p. 117.

56 "The days are": Kiyoshi Kiyosawa diary, entry for January 1, 1944, in Kiyosawa, *Wartime Diary*, p. 131.

56 On December 3: 73rd Bombardment Wing, Consolidated Mission Report No. 10, December 3, 1944, Microfilm Roll # C0033; USSBS, *Nakajima Aircraft Company*, p. 116.

57 "The results": 73rd Bombardment Wing, Consolidated Mission Report No. 10, December 3, 1944.

57 In more modern: USSBS, *Mitsubishi Heavy Industries, LTD* (Washington, D.C.: U.S. Government Printing Office, 1947), pp. 127–41, 154–61.

57 "This is the largest": Target Information Sheet, Target 90.20–3611, Nagoya, April 27, 1945, Microfilm Roll # A7800, AFHRA.

57 Ten days after: 73rd Bombardment Wing, Consolidated Mission Report No. 12, December 13, 1944, Microfilm Roll # C0033, AFHRA; USSBS, *Mitsubishi Heavy Industries*, pp. 58–59, 137.

57 Hansell's bombers returned: 73rd Bombardment Wing, Consolidated Mission Report No. 13, December 18, 1944, and Consolidated Mission Report No. 14, December 22, 1944, Microfilm Roll # C0033, AFHRA.

57 In the last strike: 73rd Bombardment Wing, Consolidated Mission Report No. 16, December 27, 1944, ibid.

58 "The results of the bombing": ibid.

58 "The weather": Gen. Charles P. Cabell, interview, and Gen. Haywood S. Hansell, Jr., interview, September 11, 1970, Box 2, Addendum 3, HSHP.

58 "High Winds Hamper": Citation information is incomplete for this and the following two articles, which are included in the newspaper clipping folder in Box 49, EOP.

58 At twelve-fifteen a.m.: Samuel Harris diary, entry for November 27, 1944, in Harris, *B-29s over Japan,* p. 75.

58 "It was immediately": Nutter, *With Possum and Eagle,* p. 203.

59 "The smoke went": John Ciardi diary, entry for November 27, 1944, in John Ciardi, *Saipan: The War Diary of John Ciardi* (Fayetteville: University of Arkansas Press, 1988), p. 23.

59 "Are you hurt?": Nutter, *With Possum and Eagle,* p. 204.

59 "I watched": Ibid.

59 "Little could be done": Samuel Harris diary, entry for November 27, 1944, in Harris, *B-29s over Japan,* p. 75.

59 "The strafing came": Narrative History of the 497th Bombardment Group, November 1–30, 1944, p. 17, Microfilm Roll # B0663, AFHRA.

60 "As we came": Hansell, *Strategic Air War Against Germany and Japan*, p. 191.

60 "The noise": Chester Marshall diary, entry for November 27, 1944, in Marshall, *Sky Giants,* p. 80.

60 "There were pieces": John Ciardi diary, entry for November 27, 1944, in Ciardi, *Saipan*, p. 26.

60 "It was an extremely": Samuel Harris diary, entry for November 27, 1944.

61 "There was a tremendous": Narrative History of the 73rd Bombardment Wing, 1 October 1944 to 30 November 1944, pp. 90–91, Microfilm Roll # C0031, AFHRA.

61 "There are Jap raids": "The Japs Hit Back," *Impact* 3, no. 7 (1945): 32.

61 "It's a pitiable": John Ciardi diary, entry for November 30, 1944, in Ciardi, *Saipan*, p. 32.

61 "Well, boys": Chester Marshall diary, entry for December 4, 1944, in Marshall, *Sky Giants,* p. 89.

61 "A couple of B-29s": Hansell, *Strategic Air War Against Japan*, p. 41.

62 "It was the most": Ibid.

62 "It was a gruesome": Chester Marshall diary, entry for December 7, 1944, in Marshall, *Sky Giants,* p. 92.

62 "In the hardstand": Ibid.

62 "Flames and smoke": Cox, *Friendly Monster,* p. 65.

62 "Well": Chester Marshall diary, entry for December 7, 1944, in Marshall, *Sky Giants,* p. 93.

62 "Occasionally, they": Nutter, *With Possum and Eagle,* p. 206.

63 On December 17: Narrative History of the 497th Bombardment Group, December 1–31, 1944, pp. 9–10, Microfilm Roll # B0663, AFHRA.

63 "That was the most": George J. Savage, oral history by Jason Snow, October 21, 1996, UNT.

63 "Overhead": St. Clair McKelway, "A Reporter with the B-29s: I—Possum, Rosie, and the Thousand Kids," *New Yorker,* June 9, 1945, p. 34.

63   "Visibility zero": Hansell, *Strategic Air War Against Japan,* p. 40.

63   "The rain fell": McKelway, "Reporter with B-29s," p. 37.

64   "It's breaking": Ibid.

64   "They began landing": Ibid.

64   "I don't want": Ibid.

64   "A hundred airplanes": Ibid.

64   On the December 3: 73rd Bombardment Wing, Consolidated Mission Report No. 10, December 3, 1944.

64   Ten days later: 73rd Bombardment Wing, Consolidated Mission Report No. 12, December 13, 1944.

64   "Nose window": Ibid.

64   "Bombardier's window": Ibid.

64   "Exploding shells": Ibid.

65   "Last seen": 73rd Bombardment Wing, Consolidated Mission Report No. 10, December 3, 1944.

65   "Circumstances surrounding": 73rd Bombardment Wing, Consolidated Mission Report No. 9, November 29, 1944, Microfilm Roll # C0032, AFHRA.

65   "This airplane has more bugs": Samuel Harris diary, entry for December 18, 1944, in Harris, *B-29s over Japan,* p. 122.

65   "Sometimes we wondered": Edward M. Cifelli, *John Ciardi: A Biography* (Fayetteville: University of Arkansas Press, 1997), p. 77.

65   "I do not feel": Parton, *"Air Force Spoken Here,"* p. 276.

65   "The machine worked": Hansell, *Strategic Air War Against Japan,* p. 28.

65   "I cannot understand": H. H. Arnold to H. S. Hansell, Jr., December 19, 1944, Microfilm Roll # 34142, AFHRA.

66   "In my opinion": Ibid.

66   "We must not": H. H. Arnold to H. S. Hansell, Jr., December 30, 1944, ibid.

66   "Arnold's staff": Nutter, *With Possum and Eagle,* p. 208.

66   "He appeared lonely": Ibid.

66   "From the very first day": Emmett O'Donnell to L. G. Saunders, March 30, 1945, Box 19, EOP.

67   "We don't mind": Rollin C. Reineck to John L. Frisbee, July 23, 1983, Box 1, Addendum 2, HSHP.

67   "It was with deep regret": Emmett O'Donnell to Raymond J. McElwee, Sr., December 26, 1944, Box 16, EOP.

67   "I realize": Emmett O'Donnell to Diane H. Campbell, January 18, 1945, ibid.

67   "Please accept": Emmett O'Donnell to Alvin J. Rogers, January 18, 1945, ibid.

67   "Dick's ship": Emmett O'Donnell to Claire King, December 18, 1944, ibid.

68   "There is uncertainty everywhere": Samuel Harris diary, entry for November 29, 1944, in Harris, *B-29s over Japan,* p. 81.

68   "Someone has to start": Samuel Harris diary, entry for December 12, 1944, ibid., p. 108.

68 "I don't agree": Nutter, *With Possum and Eagle,* pp. 208–9.

68 "I was distinctly": Emmett O'Donnell diary, entry for December 29, 1944, Box 44, EOP.

68 "This was not": Nutter, *With Possum and Eagle,* p. 209.

69 "You can't be serious": Ibid., pp. 210–11.

CHAPTER 5

70 "We want to emphasize": "Industries, Not People, B-29 Aim, Harmon Says," *New York Times,* November 25, 1944, p. 3

70 From 1939: Lloyd E. Eastman, "Nationalist China During the Sino-Japanese War, 1937–1945," in John K. Fairbank and Albert Feuerwerker, eds., *The Cambridge History of China,* vol. 13, *Republican China, 1912–1949,* pt. 2 (Cambridge: Cambridge University Press, 1986), p. 567; "Chungking: Free China's Much-Bombed Capital Fights On," *Life,* March 31, 1942, p. 93.

71 The single worst: Diana Lary, *The Chinese People at War: Human Suffering and Social Transformation, 1937–1945* (New York: Cambridge University Press, 2010), p. 87.

71 "The city of Chungking": Robert B. Ekvall, "The Bombing of Chungking," *Asia,* August 1939, p. 472.

71 For the baptismal: Peter Stansky, *The First Day of the Blitz* (New Haven, Conn.: Yale University Press, 2007), p. 1; Frederick Taylor, *Coventry: November 14, 1940* (New York: Bloomsbury Press, 2015), p. 60.

71 "I'd never seen": Stansky, *First Day of the Blitz,* pp. 31–32.

71 "At first": Virginia Cowles, *Looking for Trouble* (New York: Harper & Brothers, 1941), p. 415.

72 "You could actually": Stansky, *First Day of the Blitz,* p. 32.

72 "Send all": Margaret Gaskin, *Blitz: The Story of December 29, 1940* (Orlando, Fla.: Harcourt, 2005), p. 36.

72 "The sky": Stansky, *First Day of the Blitz,* p. 38.

72 "You didn't need": Ibid., p. 89.

72 German bombers: Juliet Gardiner, *The Blitz: The British Under Attack* (London: Harper Press, 2010), pp. 14, 23.

72 "The monstrous inferno": Stansky, *First Day of the Blitz,* pp. 108–9.

72 By the end: Gardiner, *Blitz,* p. 115.

72 "The stench": Ibid., p. 107.

73 Terrified residents: Ibid., pp. 79–95.

73 German bombs damaged: Ibid., p. 116.

73 "We were saturated": Ibid., p. 113.

73 The Germans saved: Ibid., pp. 230–46.

73 "You have all seen": Ernie Pyle, *Ernie Pyle in England* (New York: Robert M. McBride, 1941), p. 31.

74 A medieval city: Taylor, *Coventry,* pp. 6–42, 265.

74 "When we reached": Ibid., p. 127.

74 "I saw a dog": Jennifer Harby, "The Coventry Blitz: 'Hysteria, Terror and Neurosis,'" BBC News, November 13, 2015, https://www.bbc.com/news/uk-england-coventry -warwickshire-34746691.

74 *coventrieren*: Taylor, *Coventry*, p. 240.

74 "Coventry had quickly": Ibid., p. 245.

74 The bombing campaign: Gardiner, *Blitz*, pp. 359, 367.

74 "They sowed the wind": Bill Yenne, *Hap Arnold: The General Who Invented the U.S. Air Force* (Washington, D.C.: Regnery History, 2013), p. 106.

75 The British had begun: Keith Lowe, *Inferno: The Fiery Destruction of Hamburg, 1943* (New York: Scribner, 2007), pp. 49–53.

75 "The primary objective": Jörg Friedrich, *The Fire: The Bombing of Germany, 1940– 1945*, trans. Allison Brown (New York: Columbia University Press, 2006), p. 70.

75 A former farmer: Max Hastings, *Bomber Command* (New York: Dial Press, 1979), pp. 148–53, 278–80.

75 "He gave": Ibid., p. 149.

75 "We can wreck": Ibid., p. 295.

75 "panacea": Ibid., p. 153.

75 "He believed": Ibid., p. 154.

75 These trial attacks: Friedrich, *Fire*, p. 71.

76 "Community life": Hastings, *Bomber Command*, p. 167.

76 Harris sent: Ibid., p. 170; Friedrich, *Fire*, p. 73.

76 "Our new methods": Winston Churchill to Franklin Roosevelt, April 1, 1942, in Winston Churchill, *The Second World War*, vol. 4, *The Hinge of Fate* (Boston: Houghton Mifflin, 1950), p. 203.

76 "We learned": Arthur Harris, *Bomber Offensive* (Novato, Calif.: Presidio Press, 1990), p. 85.

76 "The Germans invented": Ibid., p. 86.

77 "Tens of thousands": Report by the Police President and Local Air Protection Leader of Hamburg on the Large Scale Raids on Hamburg in July and August 1943, Experiences, Volume 1: Report, I.O. (T) 45, Home Office, Civil Defense Department, Intelligence Branch, January 1946, p. 16, USAHEC.

77 "The heat": USSBS, *The Effect of Bombing on Health and Medical Care in Germany* (Washington, D.C.: U.S. Government Printing Office, 1945), p. 21.

77 "They fell": Lowe, *Inferno*, p. 198.

77 "The very small children": Ibid., p. 211.

77 The hell storm: Ibid., pp. 293–94.

77 "Hamburg": Albert Speer, *Inside the Third Reich: Memoirs by Albert Speer*, trans. Richard and Clara Winston (New York: Galahad Books, 1995), p. 284.

77 Such horrific: Nutter, *With Possum and Eagle*, pp. 98–99.

78 Before the war: Louis F. Fieser, *The Scientific Method: A Personal Account of Unusual Projects in War and in Peace* (New York: Reinhold, 1964), pp. 9–27, 45–53.

78 On Independence Day: Robert M. Neer, *Napalm: An American Biography* (Cambridge, Mass.: Harvard University Press, 2013), pp. 5–6.

79   To test: Standard Oil Development Company, "Design and Construction of Typical German and Japanese Test Structures at Dugway Proving Grounds, Utah," May 27, 1943, Frances Loeb Library, Harvard University, Cambridge, Mass.

79   "The enormity": Hoyt C. Hottle, oral history by James J. Bohning, November 18 and December 2, 1985, Science History Institute (formerly the Chemical Heritage Foundation), Philadelphia.

79   "It certainly": Antonin Raymond, *An Autobiography* (Rutland, Vt.: Charles E. Tuttle, 1973), p. 188.

80   "In the bedroom": "Photographs, Written Historical and Descriptive Data, Reduced Copies of Measured Drawings," HAER No. UT-92-A, Historic American Engineering Record, Intermountain Support Office—Denver, National Park Service, LOC.

80   "The M69 bomb": National Defense Research Committee, *Summary Technical Report of Division 11*, vol. 3, *Fire Warfare: Incendiaries and Flame Throwers* (Washington, D.C.: Columbia University Press, 1946), p. 76.

80   "These towns": Michael S. Sherry, *The Rise of American Air Power: The Creation of Armageddon* (New Haven, Conn.: Yale University Press, 1987), p. 58.

81   "There won't be": Ibid., p. 109.

81   In May 1943: Narrative History of the Committee of Operations Analysts, November 16, 1942, to October 10, 1944, pp. 63–64, Microfilm Reel # A1000, AFHRA; see also R. H. Ewell to G. R. Perera, May 3, 1943, with enclosed memo from R. H. Ewell to R. P. Russell and E. P. Stevenson, April 17, 1943, ibid.

81   "The type of bomb": "Japan, Incendiary Attack Data," October 15, 1943, Microfilm Roll # A1299, AFHRA.

81   The report went: Narrative History of the Committee of Operations Analysts, November 16, 1942, to October 10, 1944, pp. 93–94.

81   "I felt that it was wrong": Guido R. Perera, *Leaves from My Book of Life,* vol. 2, *Washington and War Years* (Boston: privately printed, 1975), p. 110.

82   "The effect upon": "Report of Committee of Operations Analysts on Economic Objectives in the Far East," November 11, 1943, Microfilm Roll # A1001, AFHRA.

82   The following February: Narrative History of the Committee of Operations Analysts, November 16, 1942, to October 10, 1944, pp. 111–15.

82   On May 12: Guido R. Perera, "Status of Studies on Incendiary Attack on Japanese Urban Industrial Areas," August 29, 1944, Microfilm Roll # A1000, AFHRA; Byron E. Gates to G. R. Perera, "Re-evaluation of Target System," May 12, 1944, ibid.

82   The six major: Report to the Committee of Operations Analysts, "Economic Effects of Successful Area Attacks on Six Japanese Cities," September 4, 1944, Box 8, RG 18, Headquarters, 20th Air Force, Decimal File, 1944–1945, NARA.

83   "The best chance": Ibid.

83   "Successful incendiary": Perera, "Status of Studies on Incendiary Attack on Japanese Urban Industrial Areas."

83   "The principal product": Report to the Committee of Operations Analysts, "Economic Effects of Successful Area Attacks on Six Japanese Cities," September 4, 1944.

83 The full Committee: L. S. Kuter to Byron E. Gates, "Revision of Basic Study (Report of COA 11 Nov. 1943)," September 8, 1944, Microfilm Roll # A1001, AFHRA.

83 "These six cities": Minutes of Meeting of COA, September 13, 1944, Microfilm Roll # A1005, AFHRA.

84 "It is clear": Minutes of Meeting of COA, September 14, 1944, ibid.

84 "Would bedlam": Minutes of Meeting of COA, September 27, 1944, ibid.

84 "The Japanese": Ibid.

84 "The closer": Ibid.

84 The committee's revised: "Report of Committee of Operations Analysts," October 10, 1944, Microfilm Roll # A1001, AFHRA.

85 "In the past eighteen": Hastings, *Bomber Command,* p. 385.

85 "abhorrent to our humanity": Crane, *Bombs, Cities, Civilians,* p. 69.

85 "This is a brutal": Ibid.

86 "Urban areas": Sherry, *Rise of American Air Power,* p. 171.

86 "The purpose": COMGENAF 20 to COMGEN BOMCOM 21, Telecon Msg. S-18–2, Microfilm Roll # A7782, AFHRA.

86 "Future planning?": Hansell, *Strategic Air War Against Japan,* p. 51.

CHAPTER 6

87 "We just couldn't": Chester Marshall diary, entry for December 3, 1944, in *Sky Giants,* p. 88.

87 The thirty-seven-year-old: James V. Piersol, "When B-29s Hit Japs It's General Norstad Who Sees Job Through," *Washington Post,* November 26, 1944, p. B2.

87 "Norstad so impressed": Dwight D. Eisenhower, *Crusade in Europe* (Baltimore: Johns Hopkins University Press, 1997), p. 119.

88 "These first accomplishments": Lisle Shoemaker, "General Gives Sober Report on Bomber Results over Japan," *Honolulu Advertiser,* December 28, 1944, on Microfilm Roll # A7812, AFHRA.

88 "sober report": Ibid.

88 "utter absolute": Lauris Norstad, oral history by Murray Green, July 15, 1969, Box 72, MGC.

88 "I was more than": Ibid.

88 "The Old Man": Ibid.

89 "I thought the earth": Haywood S. Hansell, Jr., oral history by Murray Green, January 2, 1970, Box 72, MGC.

89 Hansell knew: Nutter, *With Possum and Eagle,* pp. 220–25.

90 "I had every confidence": Hansell, *Strategic Air War Against Germany and Japan,* p. 215.

90 "I am being relieved": H. S. Hansell, Jr., to H. H. Arnold, January 8, 1945, Microfilm Roll # 34142, AFHRA.

90 "All we'd heard": LeMay, *Mission with LeMay,* p. 338.

90 "We'll select": Ibid.

90   "Just as fast": Ibid., pp. 338–39.

91   "If he was going": Nutter, *With Possum and Eagle,* p. 224.

91   "When the war": Ibid., p. 225.

91   "Mac, I think": St. Clair McKelway, "A Reporter with the B-29s: II—The Doldrums, Guam, and Something Coming Up," *New Yorker,* June 16, 1945, pp. 30–32.

92   "We're personal friends": Ibid., p. 32.

PART II

95   "We'll make them": "Jap Industry Won't Survive Air Blows—Arnold," *Boston Globe,* January 14, 1945, p. 21.

CHAPTER 7

97   "I had to select": H. H. Arnold to Sammy Gordon, November 7, 1948, Box 49, MGC.

97   The thirty-eight-year-old: Curtis E. LeMay Physical Examination, October 8, 1945, Curtis E. LeMay OMPF, National Personnel Records Center, St. Louis, Mo.

97   "The Diplomat": Thomas M. Coffey, *Iron Eagle: The Turbulent Life of General Curtis LeMay* (New York: Crown, 1986), p. 1.

97   "Iron Ass": LeMay, *Mission with LeMay,* p. 217.

98   "Never shall I": Ibid., p. 20.

98   "My father": Ibid., p. 30.

98   "I didn't stay": Ibid.

98   "Oscar was gone": Ibid., p. 212.

98   Poet Carl Sandburg: Frank Marrero, "The Forgotten Father of Aerobatics," *Flight Journal,* April 1999, p. 43.

98   "the most wonderful": Ibid.

99   "At that moment": "Beachey Killed in a Taube Drop," *New York Times,* March 15, 1915, p. 1.

99   "I wondered": LeMay, *Mission with LeMay,* p. 24.

99   "There may have been": Ibid., p. 32.

100   "LeMay, you will": Ibid., p. 35.

100   "It was hard work": Ibid., p. 37.

100   "By sleeping in one": Ibid., p. 38.

100   "One after another": Ibid., p. 41.

101   "Sir": Ibid., pp. 42–43.

101   "My application": Ibid., p. 44.

101   "Urgently request": Curtis E. LeMay to Chief Personnel Division Office, September 25, 1928, Curtis E. LeMay OMPF.

101   "Your enlistment": James E. Fechet to Curtis E. LeMay, September 26, 1928, ibid.

102   "I used to wake": LeMay, *Mission with LeMay,* p. 46.

102   "God damn it!": Ibid., p. 56.

102   "Altogether it wasn't" Ibid., p. 58.

102   "Well, son": Ibid.

103 "We had our normal": Ibid., p. 66.

103 "Most of the people": Ibid., p. 78.

103 "I think I'll take": Ibid., p. 79.

103 "I was attracted": Ibid.

104 "It's up to you": Ibid., p. 80.

104 "It would be necessary": Ibid., p. 81.

104 "I had the world": Ibid., p. 83.

104 "I was thunderstruck": Ibid., p. 100.

105 "Well, Curt": Ibid.

105 LeMay had previously: F. Raymond Daniell, "Fliers Near Exhaustion," *New York Times,* July 2, 1931, p. 1.

105 "The fighter aircraft": LeMay, *Mission with LeMay,* p. 125.

105 "I can't imagine": Ibid., p. 131.

106 "The Navy": Ibid., p. 143.

106 "You were selected": Ibid., p. 146.

107 "I remember": Ibid., p. 150.

107 "The Navy raised": Arnold, *Global Mission,* p. 157.

107 "Bob, this is": Ira C. Eaker, "Old 'Iron Pants' Turns 70," undated, Box 138, Ira C. Eaker Papers, LOC.

108 "We proved": Curtis E. LeMay, interview by Dr. Bruce C. Hopper, September 7, 1943, Box 136, Carl Spaatz Papers, LOC.

108 "You have brought": E. S. Adams to Curtis E. LeMay, "Commendation," June 29, 1938, Curtis E. LeMay OMPF.

108 "This outstanding": "Citation for Distinguished Flying Cross," undated (ca. February 1942), ibid.

108 "Forceful and aggressive": John C. McDonnell, Efficiency Report for Curtis E. LeMay, June 30, 1936, ibid.

108 "A level headed": Joseph C. A. Denniston, Efficiency Report for Curtis E. LeMay, January 14, 1941, ibid.

108 "Has a brilliant": Caleb V. Haynes, Efficiency Report for Curtis E. LeMay, January 20, 1940, ibid.

108 "If a man": Curtis E. LeMay, interview by Dr. Edgar F. Puryear, Jr., November 17, 1976, AFHRA.

108 "Humor": Edward D. Gray, "The Old Man," in History of the Third Bombardment Division, June 1944, Box B39, CLP.

109 "He was much softer": Paul K. Carlton and Helen S. Carlton, oral history by Scottie S. Thompson, August 13–15, 1979, AFHRA.

109 "Very few people": Paul K. Carlton interview by Dr. Edgar F. Puryear, Jr., May 4, 1979, AFHRA.

109 LeMay, who in: Janie LeMay Lodge, oral history by Barbara W. Sommer, September 10, 1998, Nebraska State Historical Society, Lincoln.

109 "I understand": Curtis E. LeMay to Helen LeMay, September 15, 1944, in Benjamin

Paul Hegi, *From Wright Field, Ohio, to Hokkaido, Japan: General Curtis E. LeMay's Letters to His Wife Helen, 1941–1945,* ed. Alfred F. Hurley (Denton: University of North Texas Libraries, 2015), p. 247.

109   "Most had never": Curtis E. LeMay, interview by Dr. Bruce C. Hopper, September 7, 1943.

109   "He didn't look": Nutter, *With Possum and Eagle,* p. 6.

109   "When he gives": Ibid., p. 9.

110   "I can forgive a mistake": Miller, *Masters of Air,* p. 104.

110   "Enjoy it": Nutter, *With Possum and Eagle,* p. 12.

110   "Something was radically": LeMay, *Mission with LeMay,* p. 221.

110   "You've got Bell's": Ibid., p. 121.

111   "But if you": Maj. Gen. Curtis Emerson LeMay Bio, August 1, 1944, Box B39, CLP.

111   "It is a source": Robert Olds to Curtis E. LeMay, August 29, 1942, Curtis E. LeMay OMPF.

111   Miles above: Miller, *Masters of Air,* pp. 2, 90–94.

111   "Every position": Ibid., p. 7.

111   "What do you know": LeMay, *Mission with LeMay,* p. 217.

112   "The mud": Ibid., p. 247.

112   "We had practically": Curtis E. LeMay, interview by Dr. Bruce C. Hopper, September 7, 1943.

112   "If you fly straight": LeMay, *Mission with LeMay,* p. 230.

112   "complete debacle": Richard H. Kohn and Joseph P. Harahan, *Strategic Air Warfare: An Interview with Generals Curtis E. LeMay, Leon W. Johnson, David A. Burchinal, and Jack J. Catton* (Washington, D.C.: Office of Air Force History, 1988), p. 27.

112   "Top turret": LeMay, *Mission with LeMay,* p. 233.

113   "We've got to circle": Nutter, *With Possum and Eagle,* p. 24.

113   "As soon as you": LeMay, interview by Hopper, September 7, 1943.

113   "Why the hell": LeMay, *Mission with LeMay,* p. 237.

114   "You've got to": Ibid., p. 238.

114   "If we're going": Ibid., p. 242.

114   "We flew": Ibid., p. 245.

114   "I felt if ever": Nutter, *With Possum and Eagle,* p. 36.

115   "If LeMay said": Al Dopking, "B-29 Boss Lets Bombs Talk for Him," *Cleveland Plain Dealer,* July 22, 1945, p. 1.

115   "As long as LeMay": Nutter, *With Possum and Eagle,* p. 37.

115   "We'll shoot our way": Ibid., p. 25.

115   "We were more afraid": Miller, *Masters of Air,* p. 104.

115   "The only thing": Sherry, *Rise of American Air Power,* p. 179.

115   "I'm not supposed": Nutter, *With Possum and Eagle,* p. 49.

115   "He taught me": Ibid.

116   "We aren't fighting": Ibid., p. 50.

116   "Doesn't the general": Eaker, "Old 'Iron Pants' Turns 70," undated.

116 "His group": Leon Johnson, oral history by Murray Green, June 14, 1971, Box 49, MGC.

116 "German fighters": Ira C. Eaker, "LeMay," *Daedalus Flyer,* March 1965, reprinted in L. R. Carastro, comp. and ed., *Of Those Who Fly,* Air Force Reserve Officer Training Corps, Air Training Command, 1972, p. 29.

116 "The superior": H. S. Hansell, Jr., to Curtis E. LeMay, March 5, 1943, Curtis E. LeMay OMPF.

116 "This officer": J. H. Doolittle, Efficiency Report for Curtis E. LeMay, July 1, 1944, ibid.

116 "Devoted to his command": F. L. Anderson, Efficiency Report for Curtis E. LeMay, December 31, 1943, ibid.

117 "Most nights": Curtis E. LeMay to Helen LeMay, February 8, 1943, in Hegi, *From Wright Field,* p. 119.

117 "I wonder": Curtis E. LeMay to Helen LeMay, May 15, 1944, ibid., p. 208.

117 "It certainly": Curtis E. LeMay to Helen LeMay, April 20, 1944, ibid., p. 201.

117 "I'm sorry": Curtis E. LeMay to Helen LeMay, April 15, 1944, ibid., p. 197.

117 "Daddy": LeMay, *Mission with LeMay,* p. 302.

117 "Janie wanted": Ibid., p. 302.

118 "I sometimes wonder": Ibid., p. 283.

118 "You're going": Ibid., p. 321.

118 "With all due": Craven and Cate, *Army Air Forces in World War II,* p. 5:104.

118 "There would be": LeMay, *Mission with LeMay,* p. 310.

119 "B-29s had as many": Ibid., p. 321.

119 On August 29: Curtis E. LeMay Daily Diary, entry for August 29, 1944, Box B7, CLP, Curtis E. LeMay to Helen LeMay, August 30,1944, Hegi, *From Wright Field,* p. 225.

119 "As we piled": Werrell, *Blankets of Fire,* p. 96.

119 "From what I": Curtis E. LeMay to Helen LeMay, September 1, 1944, in Hegi, *From Wright Field,* p. 227.

119 In preparation: Craven and Cate, *Army Air Forces in World War II,* pp. 5:62–73.

119 "The strips": LeMay, *Mission with LeMay,* pp. 324–25.

119 Aircrews had flown: Craven and Cate, *Army Air Forces in World War II,* pp. 5:94–103.

120 "Now we'll see": LeMay, *Mission with LeMay,* p. 330.

120 "I finally got:": Curtis E. LeMay to Helen LeMay, September 10, 1944, in Hegi, *From Wright Field,* p. 236.

120 "The scheme": LeMay, *Mission with LeMay,* p. 322.

120 "It was a grueling": LeMay and Yenne, *Superfortress,* p. 72.

121 "They are finding": Curtis E. LeMay to Lauris Norstad, September 12, 1944, Box B11, CLP.

121 "Airplanes were going": LeMay, *Mission with LeMay,* p. 325.

122 "What am I": LeMay and Yenne, *Superfortress,* p. 87.

122 "You have the full": H. H. Arnold to Curtis E. LeMay, November 13, 1944, Box B11, CLP.

122 "The fine work": H. H. Arnold to Curtis E. LeMay, November 17, 1944, ibid.

122 "Keep up": H. H. Arnold to Curtis E. LeMay, December 17, 1944, ibid.

122 "I believe": Curtis E. LeMay to Lauris Norstad, October 20, 1944, ibid.

122 "One of our major": H. H. Arnold to Curtis E. LeMay, November 13, 1944, ibid.

123 "The Marianas": LeMay and Yenne, *Superfortress,* p. 91.

CHAPTER 8

124 "I don't mind": Ira C. Eaker, "LeMay," *Daedalus Flyer,* March 1965, reprinted in L. R. Carastro, comp. and ed., *Of Those Who Fly,* Air Force Reserve Officer Training Corps, Air Training Command, 1972, p. 29.

124 "The climate": Curtis E. LeMay Daily Diary, entry for January 19, 1945, Box B7, CLP.

124 The general's reserved: St. Clair McKelway, "A Reporter with the B-29s: II—The Doldrums, Guam, and Something Coming Up," *New Yorker,* June 16, 1945, p. 32.

124 "Praise be": Samuel Harris diary, entry for January 11, 1945, in Harris, *B-29s over Japan,* pp. 167–68.

125 "Possum was a weak": Edward Bowles, oral history by Murray Green, May 6–7, 1971, Box 59, MGC.

125 "He should never": Clarence "Bill" Irvine, oral history by Murray Green, August 5, 1974, Box 67, MGC.

125 "General, please": McKelway, "Reporter with B-29s: II," p. 36.

125 "My God": Ibid., p. 37.

126 "Well Ralph": Nutter, *With Possum and Eagle,* p. 228.

126 "I was learning": Ibid.

126 "I'm sure": Ibid.

126 "I feel, on reflection": H. S. Hansell, Jr., to H. H. Arnold, January 14, 1945, Microfilm Roll # 34142, AFHRA.

126 "I am cognizant": H. H. Arnold to H. S. Hansell, Jr., February 1, 1945, ibid.

126 "Every important": Hansell, *Strategic Air War Against Japan,* p. 58.

127 "Then I'll be ready": McKelway, "Reporter with B-29s: II," p. 36.

127 "Old pilots never die": Ibid., p. 34.

127 "He had one consolation": Nutter, *With Possum and Eagle,* p. 229.

128 "That just gives you": Jack J. Catton, oral history by James C. Hasdorff, July 19–20, 1977, AFHRA.

128 "The road ahead": Curtis E. LeMay to Lauris Norstad, January 31, 1945, Box B11, CLP.

128 "worthless": Ibid.

128 "My first job": Ibid.

128 "I'll tell you": Emmett "Rosie" O'Donnell, oral history by Murray Green, March 27, 1970, Box 73, MGC.

128 "Rosie's outfit": Curtis E. LeMay to Lauris Norstad, January 31, 1945.

128 "I have my legs": Curtis E. LeMay to Helen LeMay, January 26, 1945, in Hegi, *From Wright Field,* p. 312.

129 "The Navy had been": LeMay, *Mission with LeMay,* p. 340.

129 "Everyone was standing": LeMay and Yenne, *Superfortress,* p. 110.

129 "Cocktails, hors d'oeuvres": LeMay, *Mission with LeMay,* p. 342.

129 "The Navy always": LeMay and Yenne, *Superfortress,* p. 111.

129 "We took especial pains": LeMay, *Mission with LeMay,* p. 342.

130 LeMay followed: Curtis E. LeMay, oral history by Murray Green, August 5, 1974, Box 70, MGC.

130 "The extra 5,000 feet": John Ciardi diary, entry for February 16, 1945, in Ciardi, *Saipan,* p. 101.

130 "complete expendability": John Ciardi diary, entry for January 23, 1945, ibid., p. 90.

130 "I'd frankly": Ibid.

130 Three days later: 73rd Bombardment Wing, Consolidated Mission Report No. 21, January 23, 1945, Microfilm Roll # C0033, AFHRA.

130 "From landfall": Ibid.

130 "Bombing results": Ibid.

130 LeMay followed: 73rd Bombardment Wing, Consolidated Mission Report No. 22, January 27, 1945, Microfilm Roll # C0033, AFHRA.

131 "Crews reported": Ibid.

131 "The worst part": Morrison, *Point of No Return,* p. 204.

131 "You can't drop": "Battle of Japan," *Time,* August 13, 1945, p. 22.

131 "Go ahead": Morrison, *Point of No Return,* p. 205.

131 Airborne planes: Narrative History of the XXI Bomber Command, March 1–31, 1945, p. 27, Microfilm Roll # A7782, AFHRA; LeMay and Yenne, *Superfortress,* pp. 113–14.

131 LeMay analyzed: XXI Bomber Command, "Analysis of Incendiary Phase of Operations Against Japanese Urban Areas," undated, Box B37, CLP.

132 "It is imperative": Curtis E. LeMay to H. H. Arnold, "Analysis of Radar Bombing and Navigation," February 4, 1945, Microfilm Roll # A7782, AFHRA.

132 "Within one day": Cox, *Friendly Monster,* p. 87.

132 "He seems to know": Samuel Harris diary, entry for January 24, 1945, in Harris, *B-29s over Japan,* p. 182.

132 LeMay instituted: XXI BOMCOM Chief of Staff to COM GEN BOM WG 73, 313, 314, February 5, 1945, Microfilm Roll # A7782, AFHRA.

132 "All kinds": St. Clair McKelway, "A Reporter with the B-29s: III—The Cigar, the Three Wings, and the Low-Level Attacks," *New Yorker,* June 23, 1945, p. 26.

132 "If you can't lead": Jack J. Catton, oral history by James C. Hasdorff, July 19–20, 1977, AFHRA.

132 "It was the damndest": Ibid.

133 "We were ordered": Chester Marshall diary, entry for February 3, 1945, in Marshall, *Sky Giants,* p. 124.

133 "What General Arnold": Lauris Norstad to Curtis E. LeMay, January 19, 1945, Box B11, CLP.

133 "General Arnold has crawled": Morrison, *Point of No Return,* p. 207.

133 "If you don't get": LeMay, *Mission with LeMay,* p. 347.

133 Across the Marianas: Gerard S. Johnson to Historical Officer, "Special Service and

Information-Education Section Report, Months of January and February 1945," March 24, 1945, Microfilm Roll # A7782, AFHRA.

133 *The Buckaroos*: Narrative History of the 73rd Bombardment Wing, December 1944 and January 1945, p. 20, Microfilm Roll # C0032, AFHRA.

133 *Coral Times*: Narrative History of the 9th Bombardment Group, March 1–31, 1945, p. 38, Microfilm Roll # B0065, AFHRA.

133 *Poop from Group*: Narrative History of the 504th Bombardment Group, March 1–31, 1945, p. 17, Microfilm Roll # B0673, AFHRA.

133 Pious airmen: James H. Hubbell to Joseph C. Sides, March 12, 1945, Microfilm Roll # A7782, AFHRA.

134 "The club": Narrative History of the 73rd Bombardment Wing, February and March, 1945, p. 18, Microfilm Roll # C0033, AFHRA.

134 "I'm getting started": Louis Kestner, Jr., letter to family, January 19, 1945, Box 2, Louis T. Kestner, Jr., Papers, USAHEC.

134 "Nudism had its heyday": "Coral Canebrake and C-Rations," undated, Microfilm Roll # B0058, AFHRA.

134 "Galleries of pin-up": "The B-29ers," *Impact* 3, no. 9 (1945): 63, Box B41, CLP.

134 "We found you can grow": Bob Geiger, "B-29 Crews Raise Vegetables Almost as Fast as They Fly," *Washington Post*, March 11, 1945, p. B5; see also "B-29 Fliers Grow Crops on Saipan," *Christian Science Monitor*, March 19, 1945, p. 11.

134 "Everything we eat": John Barcynski to family, February 24, 1945.

134 "For every rat": "The B-29ers," *Impact*, p. 63.

134 Officers on Tinian: W. M. Rice, ed., *Pirate's Log: A Historical Record of the Sixth Bombardment Group* (Manila, 1946), p. 71, Microfilm Roll # B0058, AFHRA.

135 "Tojo's a bastard": Ibid., p. 70.

135 By the end of February: 33rd Statistical Control Unit, "XXI Bomber Command: Monthly Activity Report," March 1, 1945, Box 16, CLP.

135 Saipan's rolling landscape: Craven and Cate, *Army Air Forces in World War II*, pp. 5:517–20; "U.S. Tinian Airport World's Largest," *New York Times*, February 17, 1945, p. 2.

135 "Sometimes I awake": Louis Kestner, Jr., letter to family, January 23, 1945, Box 2, Louis T. Kestner, Jr., Papers, USAHEC.

135 One hundred miles: 314th Bombardment Wing, "North Field, Guam," December 10, 1944–March 6, 1945, Microfilm Roll # C0150, AFHRA.

135 "The roar of planes": Ernie Pyle, "Yanks Building on Almost Every Inch of Usable Land," *Boston Globe*, February 25, 1945, p. A11.

135 "Metal was our enemy": John Ciardi diary, entry for February 16, 1945, in Ciardi, *Saipan*, p. 100.

136 "Old Man Ocean": Wilfred N. Lind, "With a B-29 over Japan—A Pilot's Story," *New York Times*, March 25, 1945, p. SM3.

136 "Most of the bombers": LeMay and Yenne, *Superfortress*, p. 140.

136 Medical records showed: "Analysis of Combat Wounds Incurred by Crew-Members over Japan as of 31 May 1945," June 13, 1945, Microfilm Roll #A7812, AFHRA.

136 "As bad as were the beatings": Robert F. Goldsworthy oral history by Sharon Boswell, undated, Washington State Oral History Program, Olympia.

136 "We all often lived": Hoyt E. Clark, "Ruminations of a (Reluctant) B-29 Gunner," October 3, 2016, unpublished memoir, p. 60.

137 "It might have been": John Ciardi diary, entry ca. January 5, 1945, in Ciardi, *Saipan,* p. 82.

137 "Left wing burned": Ollie J. Dear, Missing Air Crew Report, April 7, 1945.

137 "I saw the wing": Lloyd A. Bowman, Missing Air Crew Report, February 11, 1945.

137 "How we ever got back": "B-29 Is Back 'With Prayer,'" *Baltimore Sun,* February 4, 1945, p. 4.

137 On Saipan: Martin Sheridan, "Folk Songs of Negro Garrison Bring Japs out of Saipan Caves," *Canton Repository,* March 25, 1945, p. 16; John Cashman, "Jap Hunt on Guam," *Tulsa Sunday World,* Magazine Section, March 18, 1945, p. 1.

137 "I know you like it": Gordon Cobbledick, "Sound Truck Lures Guam's Lurking Japs," *Cleveland Plain Dealer,* March 12, 1945, p. 1.

137 "Each month here": James Connally to Fay Connally, April 7, 1945, in Fiske Hanley, *Tales from the Wild Blue Yonder: 504th Bomb Group (VH) in World War II* (Fort Worth, Tex.: Tattered Cover Press, 2013), p. 198.

137 "Honey, I don't want": James Connally to Fay Connally, January 28, 1945, ibid., p. 193.

137 "Our bombs": Ciardi, "Poem for My Twenty-ninth Birthday," in Ciardi, *Saipan,* p. 111.

137 In one poem: John Ciardi, "Death of a Bomber," in John Ciardi, *Other Skies* (Boston: Little, Brown, 1947), p. 30.

137 "a rip cord": John Ciardi, "Elegy Just in Case," ibid., p. 45.

138 "Clouds had them": John Ciardi, "Elegy: For Kurt Porjescz, Missing in Action, 1 April 1945," ibid., p. 52.

138 "We waken": Ciardi, "Poem for My Twenty-ninth Birthday," in Ciardi, *Saipan,* p. 109.

138 "Our crews": XXI Bomber Command, "Analysis of Incendiary Phase of Operations Against Japanese Urban Areas," undated, Box B37, CLP.

138 "The first beer": David Braden, oral history by Alfred Hurley, February 4, 2005, UNT.

138 "In spite of": Fiske Hanley, *Accused American War Criminal: One of the Few Survivors of Japanese Kempei Tai Military Police Brutality* (Brattleboro, Vt.: Echo Point Books and Media, 2016), p. 27; see also Bob Cassedy, "Raisin Jack," in Hanley, *Tales from the Wild Blue Yonder,* p. 23.

138 "flak alley": USSBS, *Effects of Incendiary Bomb Attacks on Japan (A Report on Eight Cities)* (Washington, D.C.: U.S. Government Printing Office, 1947), p. 227.

138 "One minute": James R. Krantz, "Head First over Japan," *Brief,* January 30, 1945, p. 3; see also "Flier Sucked out of a B-29 as 'Blister' Pops; Dangles in Icy Air 5 Minutes Till Rescued," *New York Times,* January 8, 1945, p. 2.

139 "I was the first man": Ibid.

139 "With each pass": Cox, *Friendly Monster,* p. 91.

140 "Don't worry": Ibid., p. 92.

140 Medical records: D. M. Green, "The Use of Plasma on VLR Aircraft," Microfilm Roll

C0033, AFHRA; see also Emmett O'Donnell to John K. Miller, April 18, 1945, Box 16, EOP.

140   "Everything not bolted": Cox, *Friendly Monster,* p. 92.

140   "Miller just died": Ibid., p. 94.

140   "His fatigue": Ibid., p. 95.

141   "Are you going": Ibid.

141   "They're down": Ibid., p. 96.

141   "Looking at the rest": Ibid., p. 98.

141   "John": Ibid., p. 99.

CHAPTER 9

142   "It takes a little time": John Ciardi diary, entry for December 16, 1944, in Ciardi, *Saipan,* p. 58.

142   "fantastic glass": Guillain, *I Saw Tokyo Burning,* p. 178.

142   "regularly scheduled": Kato, *Lost War,* p. 207.

142   "Housewives stood": Ibid.

143   "Why should we": Ibid., p. 205.

143   "We must face": Kenteki, "Face Foe Air Raids Calmly," *Mainichi,* December 3, 1944, p. 2.

143   "Everyone in the country": Kenteki, "Prepare for Further Air-Raids," *Mainichi,* December 5, 1944, p. 2.

143   "22 of Enemy Planes": "22 of Enemy Planes Raiding Tokyo Are Downed by Anti-Air Raid Units," *Mainichi,* January 29, 1945, p. 1.

143   "More than 90 Per Cent": "13 B-29's Shot Down 50 Damaged out of 70 Raiders over Nagoya Area," *Mainichi,* January 25, 1945, p. 1.

143   The *Mainichi* newspaper: "Exterminate All Enemy Air Raiders," editorial, *Mainichi,* January 26, 1945, p. 2.

143   Another article described: "Home Front Remains Unruffled," *Mainichi,* January 6, 1945, p. 4.

143   Other times the press: "Doom of So-Called 'Super Flying Fortress,'" *Mainichi,* December 4, 1944, p. 1; see also "Wreckage of B-29 Downed by Nippon Units," *Mainichi,* January 29, 1945, p. 1.

143   "Well, we'll build": León María Guerrero diary, entry for February 12, 1945.

144   "We want to lay": "'Members of Special Attack Forces Human; Do Not Wish to Die in Vain,'" *Mainichi,* December 16, 1944, p. 2.

144   "Hell is on us": Interrogation of Fleet Admiral Osami Nagano, November 20, 1946, in USSBS, *Interrogations of Japanese Officials* (Washington, D.C.: U.S. Government Printing Office, 1946), p. 2:356.

144   "The final decisive": General Staff of GHQ, *Reports of General MacArthur: Japanese Operations in the Southwest Pacific Area,* vol. 2, pt. 2 (Washington, D.C.: U.S. Government Printing Office, 1994), p. 585.

144   At the same time: Robert J. C. Butow, *Japan's Decision to Surrender* (Stanford, Calif.: Stanford University Press, 1954), pp. 44–51.

145   "When I think": Bix, *Hirohito and Modern Japan*, p. 492.

145   "Regrettably": Ian Nish, *The Japanese in War and Peace, 1942–48: Selected Documents from a Translator's In-Tray* (Kent: Global Oriental, 2011), p. 424.

145   "Is that possible": Bix, *Hirohito and Modern Japan*, 489.

145   "If we hold out": Ibid, p. 490.

145   Interception devices: USSBS, *Final Report Covering Air-Raid Protection and Allied Subjects in Japan* (Washington, D.C.: U.S. Government Printing Office, 1947), pp. 33–40.

145   Tokyo had seventy-seven: USSBS, *Field Report Covering Air Raid Protection and Allied Subjects in Tokyo, Japan* (Washington, D.C.: U.S. Government Printing Office, 1947), pp. 16–18.

146   "Strangely enough": Guerrero diary, entry for January 7, 1945.

146   To mitigate the threat: USSBS, *Final Report Covering Air-Raid Protection and Allied Subjects in Japan*, p. 190; see also USSBS, *Field Report Covering Air Raid Protection and Allied Subjects in Tokyo, Japan*, pp. 155–56.

146   Workers leveled: USSBS, *Final Report Covering Air-Raid Protection and Allied Subjects in Japan*, p. 190.

146   The government paid: Ibid., p. 169.

146   "Grids were traced": Guillain, *I Saw Tokyo Burning*, p. 173.

146   The job of defending: USSBS, *Field Report Covering Air Raid Protection and Allied Subjects in Tokyo, Japan*, pp. 21–58.

147   "The Tokyo fire department": Ibid., p. 63.

147   To guard the ancient: USSBS, *Field Report Covering Air Raid Protection and Allied Subjects in Kyoto, Japan* (Washington, D.C.: U.S. Government Printing Office, 1947), p. 11.

147   Japan's second-largest: USSBS, *Final Report Covering Air-Raid Protection and Allied Subjects in Japan*, p. 8.

147   "Firefighting equipment": Ibid.

147   Japan, in contrast: USSBS, *Field Report Covering Air Raid Protection and Allied Subjects in Tokyo, Japan*, pp. 11–13.

147   "I can see light!": Havens, *Valley of Darkness*, pp. 156–57.

148   Kisako Motoki's mother: Tôkyô Daikûshû Sensai Shiryô Sentâ, *Ano Toki Kodomo Datta* (Tokyo: Sekibundô, 2019), p. 153.

148   To guarantee compliance: "National Air Defense Law," No. 47, April 5, 1937, in USSBS, *Final Report Covering Air-Raid Protection and Allied Subjects in Japan*, pp. 218–19.

148   "To fight ultramodern": Guillain, *I Saw Tokyo Burning*, pp. 174–75.

148   Not until July 1942: USSBS, *Final Report Covering Air-Raid Protection and Allied Subjects in Japan*, pp. 136–50.

148   Masako Sato's family: Tôkyô Daikûshû Sensai Shiryô Sentâ, *Ano Toki Kodomo Datta*, p. 228.

148   "Last year": Edward Seidensticker, *Kafû the Scribbler: The Life and Writings of Nagai Kafû, 1879–1959* (Stanford, Calif.: Stanford University Press, 1965), p. 165.

148   "The government's interest": USSBS, *Final Report Covering Air-Raid Protection and Allied Subjects in Japan,* p. 7.

149   Most hospitals: Ibid., pp. 74–81.

149   "Under these circumstances": Ibid., p. 80.

149   Tokyo experienced: USSBS, *Field Report Covering Air Raid Protection and Allied Subjects in Tokyo, Japan,* pp. 81–82.

149   The military had: USSBS, *Final Report Covering Air-Raid Protection and Allied Subjects in Japan,* p. 86.

149   "Directives sent out": Ibid.

149   "We must once": "Foe's Intention Obvious," editorial, *Mainichi,* January 17, 1945, p. 4.

149   "The war situation": "Koiso Delivers Administrative Speech as 86th Session of Imperial Diet Is Reopened," *Mainichi,* January 22, 1945, p. 1.

150   "Some people": Kikuko Ueda, "Worse than the Deprivation," in Women's Division of Soka Gakkai, *Women Against War,* p. 115.

150   "The sidewalk ditch-shelters": Guerrero diary, entry for January 4, 1945.

150   "How will the war": Hisako Yoshizawa diary, entry for January 12, 1945, in Yamashita, *Leaves from an Autumn of Emergencies,* p. 195.

150   On that frigid: 73rd Bombardment Wing, Consolidated Mission Report No. 22, January 27, 1945, Microfilm Roll # C0033, AFHRA.

151   "Until the very day": Shûichi Katô, *A Sheep's Song: A Writer's Reminiscences of Japan and the World,* trans. Chia-Ning Chang (Berkeley: University of California Press, 1999), p. 151.

151   "An infant": Kôyô Ishikawa, *Tôkyô Daikûshû no Kiroku* (Tokyo: Iwanami Shoten, 1992), p. 37.

151   "It was from": Guillain, *I Saw Tokyo Burning,* p. 179.

151   Faced with hellacious: Craven and Cate, *Army Air Forces in World War II,* pp. 5:568–69.

151   Kobe contained: USSBS, *Effects of Air Attack on Osaka-Kobe-Kyoto* (Washington, D.C.: U.S. Government Printing Office, 1947), pp. 149–56.

152   "The area selected": XXI Bomber Command, Tactical Mission Report No. 26, February 4, 1945, Microfilm Roll # A7800, AFHRA.

152   Out of the 129 planes: Craven and Cate, *Army Air Forces in World War II,* pp. 5:569–70.

152   Despite the small size: USSBS, *Effects of Air Attack on Osaka-Kobe-Kyoto,* pp. 159, 162.

152   "Of the dozen": Ibid., p. 169.

152   His crews flew: XXI Bomber Command, Tactical Mission Report No. 29, February 10, 1945, Microfilm Roll # A7800, AFHRA.

152   This 200-acre complex: USSBS, *Nakajima Aircraft Company,* p. 50.

153   Five days after: XXI Bomber Command, Tactical Mission Report No. 34, February 15, 1945, and Tactical Mission Report No. 37, February 19, 1945, Microfilm Roll # A7800, AFHRA.

153   "Kawasaki Plant": "Kawasaki Plant Gutted by B-29s," *New York Times,* January 21, 1945, p. 5.

153 "Huge Air Plant": "Huge Air Plant North of Tokyo Razed by B-29s," *Chicago Tribune,* February 7, 1945, p. 7.

153 "B-29s Again": Frank Tremaine, "B-29s Again Hit Tokyo with Record Force," *Washington Post,* February 20, 1945, p. 1.

153 McKelway rushed: St. Clair McKelway to COMGEN 20 AF, "Non-Conservative Press Matter," January 22, 1945, Microfilm Roll # A7782, AFHRA; St. Clair McKelway to COMAF 20, "News Handling," February 4, 1945, ibid.

153 "Instead the correspondents": Narrative History of the XXI Bomber Command, 1 January 1945 to 28 February 1945, p. 142, Microfilm Roll # A7781, AFHRA.

153 The stress of the war: Curtis E. LeMay to Helen LeMay, December 25, 1944, December 28, 1944, and January 3, 1945, in Hegi, *From Wright Field,* pp. 287–91.

153 "I'm still having": Curtis E. LeMay to Helen LeMay, February 1, 1945, ibid., p. 317.

154 "Tell Janie": Curtis E. LeMay to Helen LeMay, January 31, 1945, ibid., p. 316.

154 "How is Janie": Curtis E. LeMay to Helen LeMay, February 5, 1945, ibid., p. 319.

154 "Did Janie": Curtis E. LeMay to Helen LeMay, February 14, 1945, ibid., p. 324.

154 "What happened": "Minutes of Critique on Mission No. 29," February 12, 1945, Microfilm Roll # A7781, AFHRA.

154 "Our whole campaign": Morrison, *Point of No Return,* p. 212.

155 "The word": John B. Montgomery, oral history by Mark C. Cleary, April 30–May 1, 1984, AFHRA.

155 LeMay also couldn't escape: Craven and Cate, *Army Air Forces in World War II,* pp. 5:571; USSBS, *Nakajima Aircraft Company,* p. 116.

155 "Unless something": H. H. Arnold to Lauris Norstad, January 14, 1945, in Coffey, *Hap,* pp. 357–58.

155 "I know that there": H. H. Arnold to Barney M. Giles, February 16, 1945, Box 22, LNP.

156 "When he took over": Barney M. Giles to H. H. Arnold, February 21, 1945, ibid.

156 "The system": LeMay and Yenne, *Superfortress,* p. 121.

156 "I have been here": Curtis E. LeMay to Lauris Norstad, "Visit to Guam," February 15, 1945, Microfilm Roll # A7782, AFHRA.

157 "What do you think": John B. Montgomery, oral history by Mark C. Cleary, April 30–May 1, 1984, AFHRA.

157 The orders: COMAF 20 to BOMCOM 21, "Target Directive," February 19, 1945, Microfilm Roll # A7782, AFHRA.

157 229 bombers: XXI Bomber Command, Tactical Mission Report No. 38, February 25, 1945, Microfilm Roll # A7800, AFHRA.

158 "It was only": Guerrero diary, entry for February 25, 1945.

158 "The house is burning": Tôkyô Daikûshû Sensai Shiryô Sentâ, *Ano Toki Kodomo Datta,* p. 79.

158 "My heart": Ibid.

159 "The wind blew": Shizuyo Takeuchi, interview by author, November 17, 2019.

159 That Sunday raid: Craven and Cate, *Army Air Forces in World War II,* pp. 5:572–73.

159 "Whole districts": Guillain, *I Saw Tokyo Burning,* p. 180.

159   "Living each day": Hisako Yoshizawa diary, entry for February 26, 1945, in Yamashita, *Leaves from an Autumn of Emergencies,* p. 199.

159   "This raid": Narrative History of the XXI Bomber Command, 1 January 1945 to 28 February 1945, p. 27, Microfilm Roll # A7781, AFHRA.

159   "Japan would burn": Richard H. Kohn and Joseph P. Harahan, *Strategic Air Warfare: An Interview with Generals Curtis E. LeMay, Leon W. Johnson, David A. Burchinal, and Jack J. Catton* (Washington, D.C.: Office of Air Force History, 1988), p. 61.

159   "Extend my sincere": BOMCOM XXI to Wing Commanders: 73rd Wing, 313th Wing and 314th Wing, February 27, 1945, Microfilm Roll # A7782, AFHRA.

160   "Since the eighteenth": Hastings, *Bomber Command,* p. 399.

160   Air raid sirens: Frederick Taylor, *Dresden: Tuesday, February 13, 1945* (New York: HarperCollins, 2004), pp. 2–4.

160   "We were told": Allen Hall, "'People Were Boiled Alive on the Streets,'" *Sun,* February 14, 2015, https://www.thesun.co.uk/archives/news/27717/people-were-boiled -alive-on-the-streets/.

160   "Nobody dared": Larry Rue, "The Night They Bombed Dresden," *Chicago Tribune,* May 21, 1950, p. D14.

160   The first attackers: Taylor, *Dresden,* p. 257.

160   "Everywhere we turned": Ibid., p. 260.

160   A second wave: Ibid., p. 274.

161   "The streets": Ibid., p. 280.

161   "Sudden gusts": Anne Wahle, as told to Roul Tunley, *Ordeal by Fire: An American Woman's Terror-Filled Trek Through War-Torn Germany* (Cleveland: World, 1965), p. 36.

161   More than 300: Wesley Frank Craven and James Lea Cate, eds., *The Army Air Forces in World War II,* vol. 3, *Europe: Argument to V-E Day, January 1944 to May 1945* (Washington, D.C.: Office of Air Force History, 1983), p. 731.

161   The attack incinerated: Taylor, *Dresden,* p. 7; Richard Overy, *The Bombers and the Bombed: Allied Air War over Europe, 1940–1945* (New York: Viking, 2013), p. 314.

161   "Dresden was like": Miller, *Masters of the Air,* p. 436.

161   "corpse mining": Taylor, *Dresden,* p. 348.

161   The bodies were: Ibid., pp. 350–52.

162   "A great city": "Dresden, Once Reich Pride, Erased by Bombs, German Radio Asserts," *New York Times,* March 5, 1945, p. 1.

162   "The Allied air commanders": Howard Cowan, "Terror Bombing Gets Allied Approval as Step to Speedy Victory," *Evening Star,* February 18, 1945, p. 1.

162   Twenty-four Christian: "British Clergy Protest Bombing of German Cities," *Morning World Herald,* February 13, 1945, p. 5.

162   "We shall live to rue": Richard Stokes remarks before the House of Commons, March 6, 1945, https://hansard.parliament.uk/Commons/1945-03-06/debates/ d2469098-3d07-4c87-8974-0f62ccec6d9c/Supply#.

162   "Are we beasts?": Christopher C. Harmon, *"Are We Beasts?" Churchill and the Moral*

Question of World War II "Area Bombing" (Newport, R.I.: Naval War College, 1991), p. 3.

162 "It seems to me": Hastings, *Bomber Command,* p. 401.

163 "Terror Bombing": Howard Cowan, "Terror Bombing Gets Allied Approval as Step to Speedy Victory," *Evening Star,* February 18, 1945, p. 1.

163 "Ruthless Terror Bombing": "Ruthless Terror Bombing of Reich Decided to Speed German Collapse," *Boston Herald,* February 18, 1945, p. 18.

163 "Allies to Bomb": "Allies to Bomb Cities of Reich Unmercifully," *Arkansas Gazette,* February 18, 1945, p. 1.

163 "This story": Tami Davis Biddle, "Sifting Dresden's Ashes," *Wilson Quarterly* 29, no. 2 (Spring 2005): 74.

163 "Our policy": "Stimson Denies Allies Plan Terror Bombing of German People," *Evening Star,* February 23, 1945, p. A5.

CHAPTER 10

164 "No other industrial": Report to the Committee of Operations Analysts, "Economic Effects of Successful Area Attacks on Six Japanese Cities," September 4, 1944, Box 8, RG 18, Headquarters, 20th Air Force, Decimal File, 1944–1945, NARA.

164 "I could never be": LeMay, *Mission with LeMay,* pp. 346–47.

164 "God": Ibid., p. 346.

165 "Altitude fifty feet": John B. Montgomery, oral history by Mark C. Cleary, April 30–May 1, 1984, AFHRA; see also Morrison, *Point of No Return,* pp. 213–14.

166 As ordered: Charles L. Phillips, Jr., *Rain of Fire: B-29s over Japan, 1945* (Moreno Valley, Calif.: B-Nijuku, 1995), p. 34.

166 "That is a great": John B. Montgomery, oral history by Mark C. Cleary, April 30–May 1, 1984, AFHRA.

166 "We are convinced": Lauris Norstad to Carl Spaatz, March 3, 1945, Box 22, LNP.

166 "Look": LeMay, *Mission with LeMay,* pp. 345–46.

166 "We participated": Chester Marshall diary, entry for March 1, 1945, in Marshall, *Sky Giants,* p. 140.

167 "Hell": Gurney, *Journey of Giants,* p. 205.

167 "We have been": Curtis E. LeMay to Lauris Norstad, March 3, 1945, Box 22, LNP.

167 Of the 192 planes: XXI Bomber Command, Tactical Mission Report No. 39, March 4, 1945, Microfilm Roll # A7800, AFHRA; Katsumoto Saotome, ed., *Tōkyō Kūshū Shashinshū* (Tokyo: Bensei Shuppan, 2015), p. 239.

167 LeMay hunkered down: Gurney, *Journey of Giants,* pp. 210–12.

167 In 2,037 sorties: XXI Bomber Command, "Analysis of Incendiary Phase of Operations Against Japanese Urban Areas," undated, Box B37, CLP.

168 "That's just about like searching": LeMay, *Mission with LeMay,* p. 289.

168 "You've got to kill": Warren Kozak, *LeMay: The Life and Wars of General Curtis LeMay* (Washington, D.C.: Regnery, 2009), p. xi.

169 "One Square": "Report on Tawara," *Time,* December 6, 1943, p. 24.

169   "Along the beach": Robert Sherrod, "It Was Sickening to Watch . . ." *Time,* March 5, p. 27.

169   "If anything should happen": Bonner F. Fellers to Dorothy Fellers, February 14, 1945, Box 2, RG 44a, Bonner F. Fellers Papers, MMAL.

170   "If we lose": Robert S. McNamara, "We Need Rules for War," *Los Angeles Times,* August 3, 2003, p. M5.

170   "We should never": Sherry, *Rise of American Air Power,* p. 144.

171   "Norstad would never": Curtis E. LeMay, oral history by Murray Green, March 14, 1970, Box 70, MGC.

171   "You know General Arnold": LeMay, *Mission with LeMay,* p. 347.

172   "It was my decision": Curtis E. LeMay, oral history by Murray Green, March 14, 1970.

172   "You don't gamble": Ibid.

172   "Dear General": LeMay, *Mission with LeMay,* p. 348.

172   "No, Pinky": Gurney, *Journey of Giants,* pp. 211–12.

173   With a peak: USSBS, *Field Report Covering Air Raid Protection and Allied Subjects in Tokyo, Japan,* pp. 1–2.

173   The Imperial Palace: Background on the Imperial Palace is drawn from Otto D. Tolischus, "The Riddle of the Japanese," *New York Times,* September 7, 1941, p. 123; Sekijiro Takagaki, ed., *Japan Yearbook, 1941–1942* (Tokyo: Foreign Affairs Association of Japan, 1941), p. 7; USSBS, *Field Report Covering Air Raid Protection and Allied Subjects in Tokyo, Japan,* p. 3.

173   The Imperial Diet: Hugh Byas, "New $8,500,000 Diet Will Open in Tokyo," *New York Times,* November 1, 1936, p. N12.

174   On the eve: Takagaki, *Japan Yearbook,* p. 835.

174   "Kawasaki": USSBS, *Effects of Air Attack on Urban Complex Tokyo-Kawasaki-Yokohama* (Washington, D.C.: U.S. Government Printing Office, 1947), p. 4.

174   Westerners accustomed: Otto Tolischus diary, entry for February 7, 1941, in Otto D. Tolischus, *Tokyo Record* (New York: Reynal & Hitchcock, 1943), p. 5.

175   "Everything was gray": Helen Mears, *The Year of the Wild Boar: An American Woman in Japan* (Philadelphia: J. B. Lippincott, 1942), pp. 22–23.

175   "This was squalor": Ibid., p. 63.

175   "These homes": Willard Price, *Key to Japan* (London: William Heinemann, 1946), p. 94.

175   "These conveniences": Mears, *Year of the Wild Boar,* p. 43.

175   "How long it lasted": Otis Manchester Poole, *The Death of Old Yokohama in the Great Japanese Earthquake of 1923* (London: George Allen & Unwin, 1968), p. 32.

176   "It was as if": Ibid., p. 37.

176   "In the obscurity": Joseph Dahlmann, *The Great Tokyo Earthquake, September 1, 1923: Experiences and Impressions of an Eye-Witness,* trans. Victor F. Gettelman (New York: America Press, 1924), pp. 45, 47.

176   "Hell was indeed": Bureau of Social Affairs and Morihiko Fujisawa, eds., *The Great Earthquake of 1923 in Japan* (Tokyo: Sanshusha Press, 1926), p. 56.

176   "Frantic cries": Kazutomo Takahashi, *The Story of Japan's Great 1923 Earthquake: With Details of the Tremendous Conflagration Which Swept Tokyo and Yokohama in Consequence* (Tokyo: The Japan Times, 1923), p. 5.

177   "The Yokohama": J. Charles Schencking, *The Great Kantô Earthquake and the Chimera of National Reconstruction in Japan* (New York: Columbia University Press, 2013), p. 72.

177   In the years after: Ibid., pp. 288–90; USSBS, *Field Report Covering Air Raid Protection and Allied Subjects in Tokyo, Japan*, pp. 71–72.

177   "Tokyo would be": LeMay and Yenne, *Superfortress*, p. 122.

CHAPTER 11

178   "Behind every combat": Curtis E. LeMay speech, November 19, 1945, B41, CLP.

178   LeMay summoned: Curtis E. LeMay Daily Diary, March 6, 1945, Box B7, CLP.

178   Answering to the nicknames: E. Bartlett Kerr, *Flames over Tokyo: The U.S. Army Air Forces' Incendiary Campaign Against Japan, 1944–1945* (New York: Donald I. Fine, 1991), p. 125.

178   The newest arrival: Thomas S. Power, oral history by Kenneth Leish, July 1960, Box 8, Thomas S. Power Papers, Syracuse University Library, Syracuse, N.Y.

179   "He was": Paul K. Carlton and Helen S. Carlton, oral history by Scottie S. Thompson, August 13–15, 1979, AFHRA.

179   "I want to get": Coffey, *Iron Eagle*, p. 157.

179   "I'm going to send": Ibid.

179   "I'm removing": Morrison, *Point of No Return*, p. 220.

179   "Do you have": Nutter, *With Possum and Eagle*, p. 235.

179   "You've convinced": Ibid., p. 237.

179   Nutter could not: Ibid., p. 239.

179   "He never": Ibid.

180   "We got": St. Clair McKelway, "A Reporter with the B-29s: III—The Cigar, the Three Wings, and the Low-Level Attacks," *New Yorker*, June 23, 1945, p. 26.

180   "This outfit": Ibid., p. 27.

180   "If I don't": Ibid., p. 28.

180   "I could no more": Ibid., p. 29.

181   On March 7: Field Order No. 43, March 7, 1945, included with XXI Bomber Command, Tactical Mission Report No. 40, March 10, 1945, Microfilm Roll # A7800, AFHRA.

181   "Radio silence": Ibid.

181   "The most capable": Ibid.

182   "The M47": Ibid.

182   LeMay set his sights: USSBS, *Effects of Incendiary Bomb Attacks on Japan*, pp. 65–87.

183   "Employment at scores": Target Information Sheet, Tokyo Urban Industrial Area, March 9, 1945, Box 45, RG 18, Headquarters 20th Air Force, 21st Bomber Command, Mission Reports, 1944–1945, NARA.

183 A staggering: USSBS, *A Report on Physical Damage in Japan* (Washington, D.C.: U.S. Government Printing Office, 1947), p. 105.

185 "It was calculated": Ibid., p. 54.

185 "No mission": Nutter, *With Possum and Eagle,* p. 238.

185 "Weather over Japan": BOMCOM XXI to COMGEN 20 AF, March 8, 1945, Box 45, RG 18, Headquarters 20th Air Force, 21st Bomber Command, Mission Reports, 1944–1945, NARA.

185 Norstad touched down: Curtis E. LeMay Daily Diary, March 9, 1945, Box B7, CLP.

186 "Operations tonight": Lauris Norstad to Hartzell Spence, March 9, 1945, Box 45, RG 18, Headquarters 20th Air Force, 21st Bomber Command, Mission Reports, 1944–1945, NARA.

186 "We felt a major": Cox, *Friendly Monster,* p. 138.

186 "It's a big one": Gurney, *Journey of Giants,* pp. 214–15.

186 Briefers began: "Briefing Notes," March 9, 1945, Microfilm Roll # B0065, AFHRA.

187 "Tonight there is": Gurney, *Journey of Giants,* p. 216.

187 "The attack altitudes": 498th Bombardment Group diary, entry for March 9, 1945, Microfilm Roll # B0664, AFHRA.

187 "Most of us sat": Chester Marshall diary, entry for March 9, 1945, in Marshall, *Sky Giants,* p. 144.

187 "We were dumbfounded": Gordon Bennett Robertson, Jr., *Bringing the Thunder: The Missions of a WWII B-29 Pilot in the Pacific* (Oklahoma City, Okla.: Wide Awake Books, 2016), p. 1.

188 "We were appalled": Cox, *Friendly Monster,* pp. 138–39.

188 "Five thousand": Nutter, *With Possum and Eagle,* p. 240.

188 "This is stupid": Ibid.

188 "I would not lead": Ibid.

188 An army of thirteen thousand: Morrison, *Point of No Return,* p. 222.

188 "Nobody ever did": LeMay, *Mission with LeMay,* p. 368.

189 "He was risking": McKelway, "Reporter with the B-29s: III," pp. 32, 34.

189 "The war correspondents": Ibid., p. 36.

190 "I shall never": Martin Sheridan, "My 30 Seconds in Hell," *Chicago Tribune,* November 25, 1962, p. C26.

190 "I sat there": Ibid.

190 "I went out there": Myrna Oliver, "Martin Sheridan, 89; Survivor of Nightclub Fire Became War Reporter," *Los Angeles Times,* January 12, 2004, p. B11.

190 "You're Martin Sheridan": " . . . For Heroism," *Chicago Tribune,* November 25, 1962, p. C8.

190 "I was stunned": Oliver, "Sheridan Became War Reporter"; see also "Finds Rescuer in '42 Fire," *New York Times,* October 14, 1944, p. 15.

191 "We moped": Chester Marshall diary, entry for March 9, 1945, in Marshall, *Sky Giants,* pp. 145–46.

191 The aircraft commander: "Official Pilot's Check List, B-29," June 20, 1944, Box 18, EOP.

191   "Good luck, men": Earl Snyder, *General Leemy's Circus: A Navigator's Story of the 20th Air Force in World War II* (New York: Exposition Press, 1955), p. 112.

191   On board: AN 01–20EJA-1, "Pilot's Flight Operating Instructions for Airplanes Army Models B-29 and B-29A," May 20, 1945, pp. 21–23.

191   "Sonofabitch": Robert F. Dorr, *Mission to Tokyo: The American Airmen Who Took the War to the Heart of Japan* (Minneapolis: Zenith Press, 2012), p. 65.

192   "Stand by": AAF Manual 51-126-6, "B-29," Headquarters Army Air Forces, Washington, D.C., December 15, 1945, pp. 31–35.

192   "For almost a week": Nutter, *With Possum and Eagle,* p. 243.

PART III

195   "In a single": Katsumoto Saotome, "Reconciliation and Peace Through Remembering History: Preserving the Memory of the Great Tokyo Air Raid," trans. Bret Fisk, *Asia-Pacific Journal* 9, no. 4 (2011): 2.

CHAPTER 12

197   "We must not": Sherry, *Rise of American Air Power,* p. 262.

197   "Filthy houses": Guillain, *I Saw Tokyo Burning,* p. 180.

197   The headlines: "Nippon Forces Resist Enemy Attacks in Vicinity of Kita Village on Iojima," *Mainichi,* March 9, 1945, p. 1.

198   Only a few days: "Daily Pilgrimage," *Mainichi,* March 7, 1945, p. 2; "Citations Granted to 5 Army Heroes for Valiant Attacks," *Mainichi,* March 9, 1945, p. 1.

198   "All indications": "Crush Foe's Designs on Mainland at Once," editorial, *Mainichi,* March 7, 1945, p. 4.

198   Tokyo authorities: León María Guerrero diary, entry for March 2, 1945.

198   This followed: Havens, *Valley of Darkness,* p. 150.

198   The threat of defeat: Guerrero diary, entry for March 8, 1945.

198   "The impression": Guerrero diary, entry for March 9, 1945.

199   "If enemy planes": Cary Karacas, "Buckets, Bombs, and Bodies: Rights to the Japanese City & the Tokyo Air Raids," April 14, 2006, UC Berkeley, Breslauer Symposium.

199   "Not even one": Ibid.

199   "It's going to be": Ibid.

199   "Don't you ever": Haruyo Nihei, interview by author, November 18, 2019.

199   Those at home: "Radio Program," *Mainichi,* March 9, 1945, p. 2.

199   "The town": Nihei interview.

199   "Don't you dare": Ibid.

200   "Boys would be": Ibid.

200   "I will see you": Ibid.

200   "I have all the ingredients": Shizuko Nishio, interview by author, November 17, 2019.

200   "I was so happy": Ibid.

201   "I prayed": Ishikawa, *Tōkyō Daikūshū no Kiroku,* p. 13.

201   "It was a battlefield": Ibid., p. 22.

201   "I appreciate": Ibid., p. 4.

201   "I'd like you to rush": Ibid.

201   "I wish you": Ibid.

202   "We had hours": Cox, *Friendly Monster,* p. 116.

202   "At such low:" Charles W. Morgan statement, March 31, 1945, Microfilm Roll # B0665, AFHRA.

202   "We were relying": Robert C. Webb statement, undated, ibid.

203   "I can't do this": Dorr, *Mission to Tokyo,* pp. 65, 71.

203   "Don't Fence Me In": Chester Marshall diary, entry for March 10, 1945, in Marshall, *Sky Giants,* p. 146.

203   "We flew": Phillips, *Rain of Fire,* p. 40.

203   "Victory here": Warren Cox, "Marines Hew Out 500-Yard Gains in Hand-to-Hand Fighting on Iwo," *New York Times,* March 8, 1945, p. 1.

204   "This fire": 505th Bombardment Group, Consolidated Mission Report, March 10, 1945, Microfilm Roll # B0675, AFHRA.

204   "Smoke Gets in Your Eyes": Preliminary Mission Report Annex, Radio Interceptions, Box 3177, RG 18, Records of the Army Air Forces, World War II Combat Operations Reports, 1941–1946, NARA.

204   "During the night": Martin Sheridan, "He Smelled Inferno in Plane Which Was Blistered by Heat," *Boston Globe,* March 11, 1945, p. D1.

205   "I would have rather": LeMay, *Mission with LeMay,* pp. 10–11.

206   "virtually no firebreaks": XXI Bomber Command, Tactical Mission Report No. 40, March 10, 1945.

207   Aiko Matani's father: Aiko Matani, "What Condolences?" in Youth Division of Soka Gakkai, comp. Richard L. Gage, ed., *Cries for Peace: Experiences of Japanese Victims of World War II* (Tokyo: Japan Times, 1978), p. 107.

207   "A strong wind": Tsuta Kawai, "The Luckier," ibid., p. 110.

207   "It was necessary": Kato, *Lost War,* p. 208.

207   Haruyo Wada prepared: Haruyo Nihei, interview by author, November 18, 2019; see also Tôkyô Daikûshû Sensai Shiryô Sentâ, *Ano Toki Kodomo Datta,* pp. 93–106; and Hiroomi Takii, *Tôkyô Daikûshû wo Wasurenai* (Tokyo: Kodansha, 2015), pp. 49–78.

208   "The darkest hour": Havens, *Valley of Darkness,* p. 178.

208   The alarm prodded: Katsumoto Saotome, interview by author, November 21, 2019.

208   "I'll repeat": Katsumoto Saotome, *Tôkyô Daikûshû* (Tokyo: Iwanami Shinsho, 1971), p. 21.

208   Police photographer: Ishikawa, *Tôkyô Daikûshû no Kiroku,* pp. 82–85.

209   The 100-pound: 314th Bombardment Wing, Consolidated Mission Report, March 9–10, 1945, Microfilm Roll # C0150, AFHRA; Katsumoto Saotome, *Shashinban Tôkyô Daikûshû no Kiroku* (Tokyo: Shinchôsha, 1987), pp. 74–78.

209   Winds at that moment: USSBS, *Effects of Incendiary Bomb Attacks on Japan,* p. 94.

210   On the ground: Saotome, *Shashinban Tôkyô Daikûshû no Kiroku,* p. 78.

210 "Katsumoto, get up!": Saotome, *Tōkyō Daikūshū*, p. 11.

210 "In every direction": Katsumoto Saotome lecture to students at Ikebukuro Number 3 Elementary School, November 22, 2018, copy courtesy of Ai Saotome.

210 "Katsumoto, what": Saotome, *Tōkyō Daikūshū*, pp. 11–14.

211 Seven minutes: XXI Bomber Command, Tactical Mission Report No. 40, March 10, 1945.

211 "The Jap defenses": 313th Bombardment Wing, Tactical Mission Report, March 14, 1945, Microfilm Roll # C0141, AFHRA.

211 "We headed": Robert C. Webb statement, undated.

211 "I watched": Thomas S. Power with Albert A. Arnhym, *Design for Survival: A Crucial Message to the American People Concerning Our Nuclear Strength and Its Role in Preserving Peace* (New York: Coward-McCann, 1965), p. 28.

CHAPTER 13

212 "I know what": Arthur Tomes, oral history by Thomas Saylor, October 26, 2002, Minnesota Historical Society, St. Paul.

212 Up on the rooftop: Ishikawa, *Tōkyō Daikūshū no Kiroku*, pp. 86–89; Saotome, *Tōkyō Daikūshū*, pp. 54–56.

212 "Are you sure": Ishikawa, *Tōkyō Daikūshū no Kiroku*, p. 86.

212 "Be careful": Ibid.

213 "The congestion": Ibid.

213 "You should evacuate": Saotome, *Tōkyō Daikūshū*, p. 56.

213 "Everywhere I looked": Ishikawa, *Tōkyō Daikūshū no Kiroku*, p. 88.

213 "The heat": Saotome, *Tōkyō Daikūshū*, p. 107.

213 "Don't die": Ibid.

214 "The flames": Ibid.

214 "Wake up!": Shizuko Nishio, interview by author, November 17, 2019.

214 "Tokyo will be finished": Ibid.

214 "Go to that public": Ibid.

215 "You all have": Ibid.

215 "It's different tonight": Haruyo Nihei, interview by author, November 18, 2019.

216 "The sounds came": Ibid.

216 "Get out": Ibid.

216 "Stay here": Ibid.

217 "I pushed the back": Katsumoto Saotome, lecture to students at Ikebukuro Number 3 Elementary School, November 22, 2018.

217 "Once we reached": Ibid.

218 "The air might": Saotome, *Tōkyō Daikūshū*, p. 58.

218 "Everywhere is burning": Ibid., p. 59.

218 "Idiot": Ibid.

218 "Oh, you": Ibid., p. 60.

219 "Did you bring": Ibid.

219 "The fire was like": Clyde Haberman, "Tokyo Recalls a Fiery Night When 100,000 Died," *New York Times,* March 11, 1985, p. A2.

219 "I immediately ran": Katsumoto Saotome lecture to students at Ikebukuro Number 3 Elementary School, November 22, 2018.

219 "They're falling": Ibid.

219 "Katsumoto": Saotome, *Tōkyō Daikūshū,* p. 62.

220 Two bombers exploded: 9th Bombardment Group, Tactical Narrative, March 9, 1945, Microfilm Roll # B0065, AFHRA.

220 "I saw several": Bayard R. "Bob" Van Gieson, *Doc's Deadly Dose: B-29s and the Army's Aerial War Against Japan* (privately published, 2007), p. 76.

220 "Brilliant blue light": Ibid.

220 "It is difficult": Thomas Power handwritten report, March 10, 1945, copy courtesy of Dr. Conrad Crane.

220 "It was mind boggling": Bob Vaucher, interview by author, September 20, 2019.

221 "It felt like": David Braden, oral history by Alfred Hurley, February 4, 2005.

221 "As far as the eye": Dorr, *Mission to Tokyo,* p. 187.

221 "I not only saw": Martin Sheridan, "He Smelled Inferno in Plane Which Was Blistered by Heat," *Boston Globe,* March 11, 1945, p. D1.

221 "It was the smell": Phillips, *Rain of Fire,* p. 41.

221 "The whole area": Chester Marshall diary, entry for March 10, 1945, in Marshall, *Sky Giants,* p. 147.

221 "Crewmen rattled": Knox Burger, "Fire Raid," *Yank,* November 23, 1945, p. 2.

222 "It was tumultuous": Phillips, *Rain of Fire,* p. 41.

222 "How the hell": Michael Giroski, oral history by Richard Misenhimer, July 2, 2009, National Museum of the Pacific War, Fredericksburg, Tex.

222 "During this turn": Phillips, *Rain of Fire,* p. 44.

222 "This blaze will haunt me": Gurney, *Journey of Giants,* p. 220.

CHAPTER 14

223 "You could smell": Fiske Hanley, oral history by Ronald E. Marcello, October 13, 1999, UNT.

223 "I'm sweating": St. Clair McKelway, "A Reporter with the B-29s: III—The Cigar, the Three Wings, and the Low-Level Attacks," *New Yorker,* June 23, 1945, p. 36.

224 "The way all those people": Ibid., p. 37.

224 "First aircraft bombed": BOMCOM XXI to COMAF 20, Telecon Msg. FN-09–12, Box 45, RG 18, Headquarters 20th Air Force, 21st Bomber Command, Mission Reports, 1944–1945, NARA.

225 "Many fires": BOMCOM XXI to COMAF 20, Telecon Msg. FN-09–13, ibid.

225 "Observed reports": BOMCOM XXI to COMAF 20, Telecon Msg. FN-09–14, ibid.

225 "It looks pretty good": McKelway, "Reporter with the B-29s: III," p. 38.

225 "From reports": Bruce Rae, "Record Air Attack," *New York Times,* March 10, 1945, p. 1.

225 As the fires: USSBS, *Report on Physical Damage in Japan,* pp. 60, 96–101.

226 The fires grew: Tôkyô Daikûshû wo Kiroku suru Kai, *Tôkyô Daikûshû Sensaishi* (Tokyo: Tôkyô Daikûshû wo Kiroku suru Kai, 1973), pp. 1:242, 452, 551, 686.

226 Five fires in Joto: Ibid., p. 1:544.

226 The same occurred: Ibid., p. 1:684.

226 The flames from: Ibid., p. 1:282.

226 The Fukagawa: Ibid., p. 1:21.

226 Within half an hour: USSBS, *Effects of Incendiary Bomb Attacks on Japan*, p. 97.

226 "It seemed": Seiichi Tonozuka statement in Tôkyô Daikûshû wo Kiroku suru Kai, *Tôkyô Daikûshû Sensaishi*, p. 1:102.

226 "Galvanized iron plates": Suzue Kobayashi statement, ibid., p. 1:607.

227 "Walk with your hand": Kazuyo Shimada statement, ibid., p. 1:562.

227 Katsumoto Saotome passed: Tôkyô Daikûshû Sensai Shiryô Sentâ, *Ano Toki Kodomo Datta*, p. 208.

227 Throngs of dazed escapees: Kosuke Shindo statement in Tôkyô Daikûshû wo Kiroku suru Kai, *Tôkyô Daikûshû Sensaishi*, p. 1:279.

227 "The tops": Seiichi Tonozuka statement, ibid., p. 1:102.

227 "I couldn't breathe": Kakinuma Michi statement, ibid., p. 1:148.

227 "What will happen": Yoshiko Hashimoto statement, ibid., p. 1:153.

227 "The pain caused": Aoki Hiroshi statement, ibid., p. 1:216.

228 "The town was": Sumi Ogawa, "Corpses in a Pool, Park Turned into a Graveyard," in Frank Gibney, ed., *Sensô: The Japanese Remember the Pacific War: Letters to the Editor of the* Asahi Shimbun, trans. Beth Cary (Armonk, N.Y.: M. E. Sharpe, 1995), p. 204.

228 "As if suddenly": Minoru Tsukiyama statement, in Tôkyô Daikûshû wo Kiroku suru Kai, *Tôkyô Daikûshû Sensaishi*, p. 1:327.

228 "Help!": Fumiko Nakagawa statement, ibid., p. 1:573.

228 "Please forgive me": Ibid., p. 1:574.

228 "He held": Haruyo Nihei, interview by author, November 18, 2019.

228 "We must run": Takii, *Tôkyô Daikûshû wo Wasurenai*, p. 64.

228 "Take it off!": Haruyo Nihei, interview by author, November 18, 2019.

229 "Dad?": Ibid.; see also Takii, *Tôkyô Daikûshû wo Wasurenai*, pp. 66–67.

230 "Most of them": USSBS, *Effects of Bombing on Health and Medical Services in Japan*, p. 151.

230 "Die with me": Tomoji Ishikura statement, in Tôkyô Daikûshû wo Kiroku suru Kai, *Tôkyô Daikûshû Sensaishi*, p. 1:424.

230 At Meiji National School: Koiri Ino statement, ibid., p. 1:470.

230 "I suddenly saw": Itaru Yamaguchi statement, ibid., p. 1:381.

231 "Mommy": Sumiko Morikawa statement, ibid., p. 1:105.

231 "Soon the flames": Ibid.

231 "The windows": Mitsuko Terashima statement, ibid., p. 1:268.

231 "Throw away your luggage": Michi Kakinuma statement, ibid., p. 1:147.

231 "Kiichi, steady!": Sumiko Morikawa statement, ibid., p. 1:106.

232 "I want to see Dad": Ibid.

232   "Kiichi, let's try hard!": Ibid.

232   "I never thought": Sadaji Mimura statement, ibid., p. 1:290.

232   "Shizuko": Shizuko Nishio, interview by author, November 17, 2019.

232   "Open the door": Ibid.

232   "They were shouting": Ibid.

232   Fires ravaged: Tôkyô Daikûshû wo Kiroku suru Kai, *Tôkyô Daikûshû Sensaishi*, p. 1:357.

232   Scores more died: Ibid., p. 1:31.

232   "It burned": Masu Ishizaki statement, ibid., p. 1:803.

233   "Life and death": Saburo Koji statement, ibid., p. 1:857.

233   "Save me": Yonezou Ogishima statement, ibid., p. 1:741.

233   "You had to step": Seiko Noguchi statement, ibid., p. 1:760.

234   "You can leave": Toshie Takagi statement, ibid., p. 1:754.

234   "In an instant": Yonezou Ogishima statement, ibid., p. 1:743.

234   "The bridge is": Toshie Takagi statement, ibid., p. 1:754.

234   "The heat": Ibid.

234   "I wondered": Ibid.

234   "Lie down": Yoshiko Hashimoto statement, ibid., p. 1:153.

235   "I don't want": Ibid.

235   "Yoshiko": Saotome, *Tôkyô Daikûshû*, p. 115.

235   "I hugged": Ibid., p. 117.

235   "As soon as I raised": Genichi Suzuki statement, in Tôkyô Daikûshû wo Kiroku suru Kai, *Tôkyô Daikûshû Sensaishi*, p. 1:243.

235   "Direct hits": Saotome, *Tôkyô Daikûshû*, p. 119.

235   "There was no": Ibid., p. 120.

236   "Okay": Ibid., p. 121.

236   "It's not easy": Ibid.

236   "Mom": Ibid., p. 122.

236   "Before I knew it": Ibid., p. 123.

CHAPTER 15

237   "The raid": USSBS, *Field Report Covering Air Raid Protection and Allied Subjects in Tokyo, Japan*, p. 83.

237   "I had a fear": Shigenori Kubota, *Tôkyô Daikûshû Kyûgo Taichô no Kiroku* (Tokyo: Ushio Shuppansha, 1973), p. 76.

238   "In the black": Havens, *Valley of Darkness*, p. 179.

238   "What caught": Kubota, *Tôkyô Daikûshû Kyûgo Taichô no Kiroku*, p. 79.

239   "Everything that could": Ibid., p. 81.

239   "It was impossible": Ibid., p. 118.

240   Instead the sun: Shinobu Watanabe statement, in Tôkyô Daikûshû wo Kiroku suru Kai, *Tôkyô Daikûshû Sensaishi*, p. 1:393.

240   "It was": Ryoko Nakahama statement, ibid., p. 1:389.

240   "I doubted": Kazuko Nishino statement, ibid., p. 1:595.

240 "There was still": Guillain, *I Saw Tokyo Burning,* p. 187.

240 A rescuer: Saotome, *Shashinban Tôkyô Daikûshû no Kiroku,* p. 113.

241 "Come be born": Masako Kaneda statement, in Tôkyô Daikûshû wo Kiroku suru Kai, *Tôkyô Daikûshû Sensaishi,* p. 1:213.

241 A rescue team: Hiroshi Sengoku statement, ibid., p. 1:1019.

241 Haruyo Wada woke: Haruyo Nihei, interview by author, November 18, 2019.

241 "like roasted": Tsuguyo Ooga statement, in Tôkyô Daikûshû wo Kiroku suru Kai, *Tôkyô Daikûshû Sensaishi,* p. 1:530.

241 Moments before: Tomoji Ishikura statement, ibid., p. 1:424.

242 "There was a massive": Shizuko Nishio, interview by author, November 17, 2019.

242 Eight hundred: Tôkyô Daikûshû wo Kiroku suru Kai, *Tôkyô Daikûshû Sensaishi,* p. 1:686.

242 A similar tragedy: Ibid., p. 1:31.

242 "If you are": Tsugiyo Ohshika statement, ibid., p. 1:765.

242 "Forgive me!": Sumiko Morikawa statement, ibid., p. 1:107.

242 "Kiichi can drink": Ibid., p. 1:108.

242 "Mommy": Ibid.

242 Dawn found: Katsumoto Saotome, interview by author, November 21, 2019.

243 Police photographer: John Burgess, "The Night War Came Home to Tokyo," *Washington Post,* March 10, 1985, p. A1.

243 "We had to force": Masayoshi Nakagawa, "Death and Birth in the Flames," in Gage, *Cries for Peace,* p. 116.

243 "Not now": Haruyo Nihei, interview by author, November 18, 2019.

244 "I will never forget": Ibid.

244 "I can't tell": Havens, *Valley of Darkness,* pp. 179-180.

244 "Please kill me": Toshiko Oikawa statement, in Tôkyô Daikûshû wo Kiroku suru Kai, *Tôkyô Daikûshû Sensaishi,* p. 1:339.

244 "We did not know": Aiko Matani, "What Condolences?" in Gage, *Cries for Peace,* p. 109.

244 "Look at it": Saotome, *Tôkyô Daikûshû,* p. 136.

244 "For the first time": Ishikawa, *Tôkyô Daikûshû no Kiroku,* p. 89.

245 "I fell asleep": Ibid., p. 92.

245 "Did I land": Shizuko Nishio, interview by author, November 17, 2019.

245 "Shizuko": Ibid.

246 "The bodies": Ibid.

246 "It was as if": "Deadly WWII Firebombings of Japanese Cities Largely Ignored," *Tampa Bay Times,* March 9, 2015, https://www.tampabay.com/news/military/war/deadly-wwii-firebombings-of-japanese-cities-largely-ignored/2220606/.

CHAPTER 16

247 "The heart": Curtis E. LeMay Daily Diary, March 11, 1945, Box B7, CLP.

247 Ground crews marveled: Martin Sheridan, "He Smelled Inferno in Plane Which Was Blistered by Heat," *Boston Globe,* March 11, 1945, p. D1.

247   A few had brought: Van Gieson, *Doc's Deadly Dose,* p. 78; David Braden, oral history
      by Kepper Johnson, September 30, 2000, National Museum of the Pacific War, Freder-
      icksburg, Tex.

248   General Power landed: Bruce Rae, "Record Air Attack," *New York Times,* March 10,
      1945, p. 1.

248   "There is no room": Power, *Design for Survival,* p. 28.

248   "It was a hell": Morrison, *Point of No Return,* p. 223.

248   "Raids like that": Robert C. Webb statement, undated.

248   "Largest fires": BOMCOM XXI to COMAF 20, Telecon Msg. FN-10–1, Box 45, RG
      18, Headquarters 20th Air Force, 21st Bomber Command, Mission Reports, 1944–
      1945, NARA.

248   Of the 325: XXI Bomber Command, Tactical Mission Report No. 40, March 10,
      1945.

248   "This was": Bruce Rae, "Record Air Attack," *New York Times,* March 10, 1945, p. 1.

248   "I saw one": Philip. S. Heisler, "Rivers of Fire Flow in Tokyo," *Baltimore Sun,* March 10,
      1945, p. 1.

248   "It was the greatest": " 'Nothing But Twisted Rubble' in B-29s' Path Across Tokyo,"
      Washington Post, March 11, 1945, M1.

249   "It was like": Harold Smith, "First Out, First Back," *Chicago Tribune,* March 11, 1945, p. 1.

249   "The town was": Ibid.

249   "They won't get": Ibid.

249   "Returning aircrewmen": COMAF 20 to COMGENBOMCOM 21, "20th AF Com-
      munique No. 66," March 10, 1945, Box 45, NARA.

249   First Lt. Omer Cox: 3rd Photo Reconnaissance Squadron, Mission No. 76 Report,
      March 10, 1945, Microfilm Roll # A0863, AFHRA; see also 3rd Photo Reconnaissance
      Squadron, Analysis of Combat Mission No. 76, Microfilm Roll # A0866, AFHRA.

249   his specially: "Official Photographers of Japan," undated fact sheet, Microfilm Roll #
      A0862, AFHRA.

249   "When weather": Ibid.

249   "Results of the mission": P. B. McCarthy, Squadron Commander's Report, Mission
      No. 76, Microfilm Roll # A0866, AFHRA.

250   "All this is out": St. Clair McKelway, "A Reporter with the B-29s: III—The Cigar, the
      Three Wings, and the Low-Level Attacks," *New Yorker,* June 23, 1945, p. 38.

250   The photos: USSBS, *Effects of Incendiary Bomb Attacks on Japan,* pp. 94, 102.

250   McKelway woke: Warren Moscow, "City's Heart Gone," *New York Times,* March 11,
      1945, p. 1.

250   "After study": Lauris Norstad to Hartzell Spence, March 11, 1945, Box 45, RG 18,
      Headquarters 20th Air Force, 21st Bomber Command, Mission Reports, 1944–1945,
      NARA.

252   The strike had incinerated: Tactical Mission Report No. 40, March 10, 1945.

252   "There is no cushion": Special Intelligence Bulletin, A-2 Section, Headquarters, 73rd
      Bomb Wing, "Damage to Tokyo," undated, Microfilm Roll # C0034, AFHRA.

252   "I believe": Maj. Gen. Curtis E. LeMay, statement, March 11, 1945, Box 45, RG 18, Head-
      quarters 20th Air Force, 21st Bomber Command, Mission Reports, 1944–1945, NARA.

252   LeMay sat: Curtis E. LeMay to Helen LeMay, March 12, 1945, in Hegi, *From Wright
      Field,* pp. 330–31.

252   "Almost 17": Maj. Gen. Curtis E. LeMay on *Army Hour,* March 11, 1945, Box 45, RG
      18, Headquarters 20th Air Force, 21st Bomber Command, Mission Reports, 1944–
      1945, NARA.

253   "You can": Ibid.

253   "City's Heart": Moscow, "City's Heart Gone," p. 1.

253   "Hellish Sea": "Hellish Sea of Fire Engulfs Tokyo," *Evening World-Herald,* March 10,
      1945, p. 1.

253   "Havoc Wreaked": "Havoc Wreaked by Superforts," *San Diego Union*, March 11, 1945,
      p. 1.

253   "Since this": Curtis E. LeMay to H. H. Arnold, March 11, 1945, Box B11, CLP.

253   "This mission": H. H. Arnold to Curtis E. LeMay, "Commendation on March 9th
      Attack Upon Tokyo," March 10, 1945, Box 45, RG 18, Headquarters 20th Air Force,
      21st Bomber Command, Mission Reports, 1944–1945, NARA.

254   "What could happen": Douhet, *Command of the Air,* p. 53.

254   Two days after: XXI Bomber Command, Tactical Mission Report No. 41, March 12,
      1945, Microfilm Roll # A7800, AFHRA.

254   "Lifeguard submarine": COMGEN BOMCOM XXI to COMAF 20, Telecon Msg
      FN-13-23, Box 45, RG 18, Headquarters 20th Air Force, 21st Bomber Command, Mis-
      sion Reports, 1944–1945, NARA.

255   "The experiment": XXI Bomber Command, "Analysis of Incendiary Phase of Opera-
      tions Against Japanese Urban Areas," undated, Box B37, CLP.

255   "This was not": Curtis E. LeMay press statement, March 13, 1945, Box 45, RG 18,
      Headquarters 20th Air Force, 21st Bomber Command, Mission Reports, 1944–1945,
      NARA.

255   LeMay reverted: XXI Bomber Command, Tactical Mission Report No. 42, March 14,
      1945, Microfilm Roll # A7801, AFHRA.

255   "This zone": Target Information Sheet, Osaka Urban Industrial Area, March 10,
      1945, Box 45, RG 18, Headquarters 20th Air Force, 21st Bomber Command, Mission
      Reports, 1944–1945, NARA.

255   The strike that Tuesday: USSBS, *Effects of Air Attack on Osaka-Kobe-Kyoto,* pp. 26, 30.

255   "Fifteen seconds": Louis W. Halton, "Incendiary Raid on Osaka 14 March 1945,"
      Microfilm Roll # B0665, AFHRA.

256   "How far": "Fire in Tokyo," editorial, *Evening Star,* March 11, 1945, p. C2.

256   "Strategy Shifts": "Strategy Shifts to Area Bombing," *Times-Picayune,* March 15, 1945, p. 14.

256   "The mounting": Ibid.

256   "Editorial comment": Hartzell Spence to St. Clair McKelway, March 14, 1945, Box
      45, RG 18, Headquarters 20th Air Force, 21st Bomber Command, Mission Reports,
      1944–1945, NARA.

256 "Hey": "Supermen Worked on Superforts in Raids on Japan," *Stamford Advocate,* March 14, 1945, p. 2.

256 An army: "Ground Crew: Missed Food and Sleep So Superforts Could Bomb Japan Twice in 48 Hours," *Dallas Morning News,* March 13, 1945, p. 1.

257 "Ground crews": Lauris Norstad to Adjutant General, "War Department Distinguished Unit Citation," April 4, 1945, Box 27, LNP.

257 "A marked loss": Charles W. Morgan statement, March 31, 1945.

257 On March 16: XXI Bomber Command, Tactical Mission Report No. 43, March 14, 1945, Microfilm Roll # A7801, AFHRA; USSBS, *Effects of Air Attack on Osaka-Kobe-Kyoto,* pp. 159, 162.

257 For the encore: XXI Bomber Command, Tactical Mission Report No. 44, March 20, 1945, Microfilm Roll # A7801, AFHRA.

257 "We ran out": LeMay, *Mission with LeMay,* p. 354.

257 "I was not": LeMay and Yenne, *Superfortress,* p. 125.

258 "The war had": USSBS, *Effects of Air Attack on Osaka-Kobe-Kyoto,* p. 1.

258 The 9,365 tons: Craven and Cate, *Army Air Forces in World War II,* p. 5:623.

258 "The end result": Morrison, *Point of No Return,* p. 227.

258 "A dream come": "Firebirds' Flight," *Time,* March 19, 1945, p. 32.

258 "B-29's": "B-29's Turn Japan into Chaotic Land," *New York Times,* March 23, 1945, p. 10.

258 "Heavy Blow": "Heavy Blow Spreads Ruins on Homeland," *Dallas Morning News,* March 21, 1945, p. 1.

258 "It is very": "Remarks by Brig. Gen. Lauris Norstad, Chief of Staff, Twentieth Air Force, At Press Conference 23 March 1945, Pentagon Building," Box 26, LNP.

258 "Why in recent": Ibid.

259 "Task Force 58": Commander Task Force Fifty-eight to BOMCOM 21, March 13, 1945, Box 45, RG 18, Headquarters 20th Air Force, 21st Bomber Command, Mission Reports, 1944–1945, NARA.

259 "Certainly your last": Lauris Norstad to Curtis E. LeMay, April 3, 1945, Box 27, LNP.

259 "I am convinced": H. H. Arnold to Curtis E. LeMay, March 21, 1945, Box B11, CLP.

259 "Under reasonably": Ibid.

260 The strike had destroyed: USSBS, *Final Report Covering Air-Raid Protection and Allied Subjects in Japan,* p. 81.

260 "Dressings": Ibid., p. 9.

260 As many as 50 percent: Ministry of Welfare, Sanitation Bureau, Air Defense Section, "Rush Report of Air Defense Medical Treatment and Rescue," March 29, 1945, National Diet Library, Tokyo.

260 "The enormous": USSBS, *Field Report Covering Air Raid Protection and Allied Subjects in Tokyo, Japan,* p. 79.

260 The raid: Tôkyô Daikûshû wo Kiroku suru Kai, *Tôkyô Daikûshû Sensaishi,* p. 1:24.

260 Authorities in Fukagawa: Ibid., pp. 1:28, 284, 544.

260 All told: USSBS, *Final Report Covering Air-Raid Protection and Allied Subjects in Japan,* p. 70.

260 "Even to her": Kato, *Lost War,* p. 5.

261 "On the truck": Kimiko Koike statement, in Tôkyô Daikûshû wo Kiroku suru Kai, *Tôkyô Daikûshû Sensaishi,* p. 1:833.

261 "We tried": Yasuhiro Nagakura statement, ibid., p. 1:1031.

261 "It was impossible": Kato, *Lost War,* p. 215.

261 "One by one": Nisaku Kokubu, "Who Is to Blame?" in Gage, *Cries for Peace,* p. 120.

262 Rescuers ultimately: Saotome, *Shashinban Tôkyô Daikûshû no Kiroku,* p. 19.

262 "Even if the outside": Hiroshi Sengoku statement, in Tôkyô Daikûshû wo Kiroku suru Kai, *Tôkyô Daikûshû Sensaishi,* p. 1:1019.

262 "Close to her": Tôkyô Daikûshû Sensai Shiryô Sentâ, *Ano Toki Kodomo Datta,* p. 19.

263 "By chance": Yoshimitsu Mano, "The Day Off," in Gage, *Cries for Peace,* p. 114.

263 "The child": Ibid.

263 "We placed": Ibid.

263 Katsumoto Saotome sought: Saotome, *Tôkyô Daikûshû,* p.139.

263 Across Tokyo: USSBS, *Field Report Covering Air Raid Protection and Allied Subjects in Tokyo, Japan,* p. 83.

263 Laborers buried: Tôkyô Daikûshû wo Kiroku suru Kai, *Tôkyô Daikûshû Sensaishi,* p. 1:25.

264 "The horse": Yuji Hattori statement, in Tôkyô Daikûshû wo Kiroku suru Kai, *Tôkyô Daikûshû Sensaishi,* p. 1:459.

264 Others salvaged: Tôkyô Daikûshû Sensai Shiryô Sentâ, *Ano Toki Kodomo Datta,* p. 181.

264 A few less: Tsuguyo Ooga statement, in Tôkyô Daikûshû wo Kiroku suru Kai, *Tôkyô Daikûshû Sensaishi,* p. 1:534.

264 "To uncover": Guillain, *I Saw Tokyo Burning,* p. 193.

264 "slaughter bombing": John Dower, *War Without Mercy: Race and Power in the Pacific War* (New York: Pantheon, 1986), p. 41.

264 "We are attempting": Yoshizo Nishio, "Tokyo To Official Notes," March 10, 1945, in USSBS, *Final Report Covering Air-Raid Protection and Allied Subjects in Japan,* p. 231.

264 The government: Ibid., pp. 174–75.

265 "Tokyo": Noriko Kawamura, *Emperor Hirohito and the Pacific War* (Seattle: University of Washington Press, 2015), p. 149.

265 "Were they resentful": Bix, *Hirohito and Modern Japan,* p. 491.

265 "No one asked": León María Guerrero diary, entry for March 19, 1945.

266 An army of 75,000: USSBS, *Field Report Covering Air Raid Protection and Allied Subjects in Tokyo, Japan,* pp. 86–93.

266 In undamaged: Ibid., p. 156.

266 Guerrero visited: Guerrero diary, entry for March 26, 1945.

266 "Tokyo was a vast": Guillain, *I Saw Tokyo Burning,* p. 195.

266 Authorities encouraged: USSBS, *Field Report Covering Air Raid Protection and Allied Subjects in Tokyo, Japan,* pp. 151–67.

266 "The rest": Lars Tillitse, "When Bombs Rained on Us in Tokyo," *Saturday Evening Post,* January 12, 1946, p. 34.

CHAPTER 17

267   "The forces": Bonner F. Fellers to J. Woodall Greene, June 12, 1945, Box 4, Bonner F.
       Fellers Papers, Hoover Institution Archives, Palo Alto, Calif.

267   Intelligence estimated: USSBS, *The Campaigns of the Pacific War* (Washington, D.C.:
       U.S. Government Printing Office, 1946), pp. 324–30.

267   the suicide planes: Steven J. Zaloga, *Kamikaze: Japanese Special Attack Weapons 1944–
       45* (Oxford: Osprey, 2011), p. 12.

268   "It is one": Oscar Griswold diary, entry for January 8, 1945, Box 1, Oscar W. Griswold
       Papers, 1917–1945, USAHEC.

268   In addition: E. B. Potter, *Nimitz* (Annapolis, Md.: Naval Institute Press, 1976), pp.
       368–69; XXI Bomber Command, Analysis of Iceberg Operation, 26 March through
       11 May 1945, Microfilm Roll # A7089, AFHRA.

268   The worst came: Navy Department, Office of the Chief of Naval Operations, Naval
       History Division, *Dictionary of American Naval Fighting Ships* (Washington, D.C.:
       U.S. Government Printing Office, 1968), p. 3:707.

268   "Instantly the planes": George Horne, "Carrier Wrecked by Bombs Gets Home
       Despite Big Loss," *New York Times,* May 18, 1945, p. 1.

268   On March 27: William Fisher memo for Carl Spaatz, "Summary of Diversionary and
       Navy Coordinated Missions of Marianas-Based B-29s," November 13, 1945, Box 27,
       LNP; Narrative History of the XXI Bomber Command, May 1–31, 1945, p. 2, Micro-
       film Roll # A7784, AFHRA.

268   "We flattened": LeMay, *Mission with LeMay,* p. 371.

269   Geography proved: USSBS, *The War Against Japanese Transportation, 1941–1945*
       (Washington, D.C.: U.S. Government Printing Office, 1947), pp. 1, 13, 26–29; A-3
       Twentieth Air Force, "Phase Analysis of the Twentieth Air Force Strategic Mining
       Blockade of the Japanese Empire," undated, p. 3, Microfilm Roll # A7744, AFHRA.

269   "The Shimonoseki Straits": Narrative History of the XXI Bomber Command, March
       1–31, 1945, p. 19, Microfilm Roll # A7782, AFHRA.

269   Bombers took off: A-3 Twentieth Air Force, "Phase Analysis of the Twentieth Air
       Force Strategic Mining Blockade of the Japanese Empire," pp. 8, 33.

269   The undersea weapons: Ellis A. Johnson and David A. Katcher, *Mines Against Japan*
       (Silver Spring, Md.: Naval Ordnance Laboratory, 1973), pp. 27–32.

270   "We've finished": LeMay, *Mission with LeMay,* p. 371.

270   "There wasn't anything": Ibid., p. 372.

270   "The Iceberg Operation": COMAF 20 to COMGENBOMCOM 21, "Employ-
       ment of Units in Emergencies," Telecon Msg. G-16-7, April 17, 1945, Microfilm Roll #
       A7089, AFHRA.

270   "Day after day": LeMay, *Mission with LeMay,* p. 372.

270   Half a world: Craven and Cate, *Army Air Forces in World War II,* pp. 5:624–27.

271   "In just ten": "The Twentieth Air Force: A Brief Summary of B-29 Strategic Air Opera-
       tions, 5 June 1944—14 August 1945," undated, p. 27, Microfilm Reel # A7744, AFHRA.

271   "I am convinced": Lauris Norstad to Curtis E. LeMay, April 3, 1945, Box 27, LNP.

272 That study: COMGENBOMCOM 21 to COMAF 20, "XXI BOMCOM Aircraft and Crew Requirements," Telecon Msg. FN-13-12, April 13, 1945, Microfilm Roll # A7718, AFHRA.

272 "It must be emphasized": Ibid.

272 Ten days later: BOMCOM 21 to COMAF 20, "XXI BOMCOM Combat Effort," Telecon Msg. FN-25-11, April 25, 1945, Microfilm Roll # A7718, AFHRA.

273 "If Japan": Morrison, *Point of No Return*, p. 237.

273 "I consider": BOMCOM 21 to COMAF 20, "XXI BOMCOM Combat Effort," April 25, 1945.

273 "Anybody we could": LeMay, *Mission with LeMay*, p. 370.

273 "Rarely has such": "Tokyo Arsenal Area," *Air Intelligence Report*, May 4, 1945, p. 7, Microfilm Roll # A7784, AFHRA.

273 Three hundred: XXI Bomber Command, Tactical Mission Report No. 67, April 14, 1945, Microfilm Roll # A7801, AFHRA.

274 Those bombs: USSBS, *Effects of Incendiary Bomb Attacks on Japan*, p. 117.

274 "All aircraft attacking": XXI Bomber Command, Tactical Mission Report No. 67, April 14, 1945.

274 LeMay ordered: XXI Bomber Command, Tactical Mission Report Nos. 68–69, April 15, 1945, Microfilm Roll # A7802, AFHRA.

274 That mission: USSBS, *Effects of Air Attack on Urban Complex Tokyo-Kawasaki-Yokohama*, p. 7.

274 The two raids: Craven and Cate, *Army Air Forces in World War II*, p. 5:636; USSBS, *Effects of Incendiary Bomb Attacks on Japan*, p. 117.

274 "A quick glance": Lauris Norstad to Curtis E. LeMay, April 18, 1945, Box B11, CLP.

274 The general celebrated: XXI Bomber Command, Tactical Mission Report No. 174, May 14, 1945, Microfilm Roll # A7803, AFHRA.

274 Two days later: XXI Bomber Command, Tactical Mission Report No. 176, May 17, 1945, Microfilm Roll # A7803, AFHRA.

275 "We could see": Public Relations Office, XXI Bomber Command, "Report on Nagoya Strike," Release No. 147, May 15, 1945, Microfilm Roll # A7785, AFHRA.

275 "Who planned": Morrison, *Point of No Return*, p. 240.

275 520 bombers: XXI Bomber Command, Tactical Mission Report No. 181, May 24, 1945, Microfilm Roll A7803, AFHRA.

276 "For two hours": "B-29s Saturate Tokyo Defenses," *Air Intelligence Report*, June 9, 1945, p. 15, Microfilm Roll # A7811, AFHRA.

276 Two nights later: XXI Bomber Command, Tactical Mission Report No. 183, May 25, 1945, Microfilm Roll # A7803, AFHRA.

276 "It was one": Emmett O'Donnell, Jr., Memorial Day Speech, May 30, 1946, Box 32, EOP.

276 "We took": Curtis E. LeMay to Helen LeMay, May 26, 1945, in Hegi, *From Wright Field*, p. 358.

276 "Since the beginning": Emmett O'Donnell Memorial Day Speech, May 30, 1946.

277   Despite the losses: USSBS, *Effects of Incendiary Bomb Attacks on Japan,* p. 117.

277   "A total of 6.9": Summary of Mission No. 186, May 29, 1945, in Intelligence Section
       Reporting Unit, XXI Bomber Command, "Summary of XXI BOMCOM Missions,"
       Box B33, CLP.

277   "About 3.8": Summary of Mission No. 188, June 5, 1945, ibid.

277   "Approximately 3.4": Summary of Mission No. 187, June 1, 1945, ibid.

278   On June 11: Public Relations Office, XXI Bomber Command, Release No. 172, June 11,
       1945, Microfilm Roll # A7785, AFHRA.

278   "I think I have": Curtis E. LeMay to Helen LeMay, June 5, 1945, in Hegi, *From Wright
       Field,* p. 361.

278   "Franklin Roosevelt": Arnold, *Global Mission,* p. 548.

279   "Army aviation": Huston, *American Airpower Comes of Age,* p. 1:35.

280   "They have had no": H. H. Arnold diary, entry for June 13, 1945, ibid., p. 2:326.

280   "Jungle, fruit trees": Ibid.

280   "I'm asking": Morrison, *Point of No Return,* p. 247.

280   "We'll run out": Ibid., p. 248.

281   "We did it": H. H. Arnold diary, entry for June 13, 1945, in Huston, *American Air-
       power Comes of Age,* p. 2:326.

281   The general sat down: H. H. Arnold diary, entry for June 14, 1945, ibid., p. 2:327.

281   "Nimitz is really": Ibid.

281   "I want you": Morrison, *Point of No Return,* p. 248.

281   Early that morning: XXI Bomber Command, Tactical Mission Report No. 203, June
       15, 1945, Microfilm Roll # A7804, AFHRA; USSBS, *Effects of Air Attack on Osaka-
       Kobe-Kyoto,* pp. 31, 36.

282   "At this writing": H. H. Arnold diary, entry for June 15, 1945, in Huston, *American
       Airpower Comes of Age,* p. 2:330. Doolittle's legendary raid involved sixteen bombers,
       not eighteen, as Arnold writes in his diary.

282   "We don't have": Richard H. Kohn and Joseph P. Harahan, *Strategic Air Warfare: An
       Interview with Generals Curtis E. LeMay, Leon W. Johnson, David A. Burchinal, and
       Jack J. Catton* (Washington, D.C.: Office of Air Force History, 1988), p. 64.

282   The record-breaking: "LeMay in B-29 Breaks Record in Hop from Hawaii to Capital,"
       New York Times, June 18, 1945, p. 1.

282   At three-thirty p.m.: "Minutes of Meeting Held at the White House on Monday, 18
       June 1945 at 1530," in Richardson Dougal, ed., *Foreign Relations of the United States
       Diplomatic Papers,* vol. 1, *The Conference of Berlin (The Potsdam Conference), 1945*
       (Washington, D.C.: U.S. Government Printing Office, 1960), pp. 903–10.

282   "utter helplessness": Ibid., p. 906.

282   "Air power alone": Ibid.

283   "Those who": Ibid., p. 909.

283   "General Marshall slept": Kohn and Harahan, *Strategic Air Warfare,* p. 65.

283   "We have destroyed": "LeMay Promises 'Ruin' for Japan," *New York Times,* June 20,
       1945, p. 10.

CHAPTER 18

284 "If the Japs": "LeMay Here, Warns Japs to Beware," *Cleveland Plain Dealer,* June 22, 1945, p. 1.

284 "Large-scale": C. Maiide and Associates, "The Report on the Effects of the Urban Area Bombing on Japanese Wartime Economy," December 23, 1945, in USSBS, *The Effects of Air Attack on Japanese Urban Economy (Summary Report)* (Washington, D.C.: U.S. Government Printing Office, 1947), p. 49.

284 more than 317,000: USSBS, *The Effects of Air Attack on the City of Nagoya* (Washington, D.C.: U.S. Government Printing Office, 1947), p. 12.

284 Osaka experienced: USSBS, *Effects of Air Attack on Osaka-Kobe-Kyoto,* p. 36.

284 Tokyo saw: USSBS, *Field Report Covering Air Raid Protection and Allied Subjects in Tokyo, Japan,* p. 158.

285 "Most people": Havens, *Valley of Darkness,* p. 168.

285 "It seemed": León María Guerrero diary, entry for June 9, 1945.

285 "Families that won't": Havens, *Valley of Darkness,* p. 171.

285 "Food problems": USSBS, *Effects of Strategic Bombing on Japanese Morale,* p. 79.

285 "Tokyo people": Ibid., p. 87.

285 Japan announced: "Tokyo: Description of Urban Area," 56a(14)2(j), undated, National Diet Library, Tokyo.

286 "Tokyo authorities": Ibid.

286 "The limitless acres": Kato, *Lost War,* p. 6.

286 By April: USSBS, *Effects of Strategic Bombing on Japanese Morale,* p. 40.

286 "It has one": Guerrero diary, entry for May 5, 1945.

286 "I was like a stray": Katsumoto Saotome, interview by author, November 21, 2019.

286 "Every day I burn": Kafû Nagai diary, entry for May 1, 1945, in Keene, *So Lovely a Country,* p. 90.

287 "I know we should never": Toshiko Matsue to Ikuko Matsue, March 4, 1945.

287 "Matsue": Ikuko Nagata, interview by author, November 16, 2019.

287 "If the war": Guerrero diary, July 6, 1945.

287 "Do you have oil?": Haruyo Nihei, interview by author, November 18, 2019; see also Tôkyô Daikûshû Sensai Shiryô Sentâ, *Ano Toki Kodomo Datta,* p. 103.

287 "You should use": Ibid.

288 "My hands hurt": Kazuyo Funato, "'Hiroko Died Because of Me,'" in Cook and Cook, *Japan at War,* p. 347.

288 "Hiroko's face": Ibid., p. 349.

288 "Hiro-chan": Ibid.

288 "Hiroko had escaped": Saotome, *Shashinban Tôkyô Daikûshû no Kiroku,* p. 99.

288 "I could stand": USSBS, *Effects of Strategic Bombing on Japanese Morale,* p. 40.

288 Superstitious rumors: Ibid., pp. 36, 249–50.

289 "The survivors": Ibid., p. 40.

289 "We have heard": Edwin P. Hoyt, *Hirohito: The Emperor and the Man* (New York: Praeger, 1984), pp. 141–42.

289   "We must overcome": Narrative History of the XXI Bomber Command, June 1–30, 1945, p. 33, Microfilm Roll # A7785, AFHRA.

289   "There was no one": Guillain, *I Saw Tokyo Burning*, p. 212.

290   "We were unprotected": USSBS, *Effects of Strategic Bombing on Japanese Morale*, p. 39.

290   "I felt bitter": Ibid., p. 40.

290   "The two decisions": C. L. Chennault to Curtis E. LeMay, July 9, 1945, Box B11, CLP.

290   "I have been watching": H. S. Hansell to Curtis E. LeMay, March 29, 1945, ibid.

291   "It was worth": Angelo Giarratana to Curtis E. LeMay, August 10, 1945, Box B12, CLP.

291   "As long as I live": Ernest Costello to Curtis E. LeMay, August 17, 1945, ibid.

291   "Writing you": Billy Zawacki to Curtis E. LeMay, March 11, 1945, ibid.

291   "May God": Naydene Lohr to Curtis E. LeMay, July 25, 1945, ibid.

291   "Can Japan": "LeMay of the B-29s," *Time*, August 13, 1945, cover.

291   A public opinion: Hadley Cantril, ed., *Public Opinion, 1935–1946* (Princeton, N.J.: Princeton University Press, 1951), p. 1067.

291   When asked: Ibid., p. 1118.

292   "the extermination": "McNutt for Erasing Japanese," *New York Times*, April 6, 1945, p. 5; "M'Nutt Explains Speech," *New York Times*, April 14, 1945, p. 10.

292   The nation: Rana Mitter, *Forgotten Ally: China's World War II, 1937–1945* (Boston: Houghton Mifflin Harcourt, 2013), p. 363.

292   "When the Japanese": Walter Simmons, "How Barbaric Japs Bayoneted Wounded Yanks," *Chicago Tribune*, October 22, 1943, p. 1.

292   "Dead Chinese": C. Yates M'Daniel, "Nanking Horror Described in Diary of War Report," *Chicago Tribune*, December 18, 1937, p. 8.

292   "The whole countryside": "Japanese Vengeance Described by Priest," *New York Times*, May 26, 1943, p. 3.

293   "A more brutal": Report No. 59, "Investigation of the Murder and Attempted Murder of More Than Four Hundred Male Civilians in Paco District, Manila, Philippine Islands, on 10 February 1945," September 9, 1945, Box 1113, RG 331, Supreme Commander of the Allied Powers (SCAP), Legal Section, Administrative Division, War Crimes File, 1946–1950, NARA.

293   "If you fell": Oral Reminiscences of Master Sergeant Calvin R. Graef, U.S. Army, October 1, 1971, RG 49, D. Clayton James Collection, MMAL.

293   "I saw": William Edwin Dyess, "Dyess' Own Story!" *Chicago Tribune*, January 30, 1944, p. 1.

293   "The Japs": Walter Trohan, "Nippon Cruelty Stuns Nation," *Chicago Tribune*, January 29, 1944, p. 1.

293   "This was propaganda": Dower, *War Without Mercy*, p. 48.

293   Editorial cartoonists: Ibid., pp. 77–93.

293   "Civilization": "Murder in Tokyo," *Time*, May 3, 1943, p. 20.

294   "This is the enemy": "This Is the Enemy the Allies Still Face in the Pacific," *New York Herald Tribune*, May 12, 1945, p. 5.

294 "The Japs are tasting": "The Tokyo Target," editorial, *Los Angeles Times,* April 18, 1945, p. A4.

294 "They who sowed": "Japan's Factory Cities," editorial, *New York Herald Tribune,* June 19, 1945, p. 14.

294 "For the Japanese": "1,000 Planes over Tokyo," editorial, *New York Times,* July 10, 1945, p. 10.

294 "When a Jap": Ed Ainsworth, "As You Might Say," *Los Angeles Times,* May 11, 1945, p. A4.

294 "The Japanese are queer": "Hard to Please," *Los Angeles Times,* May 3, 1945, p. A4.

294 "The Japanese are fiends": Bonner F. Fellers to Dorothy Fellers, February 5, 1945, Box 2, RG 44a, Bonner F. Fellers Papers, MMAL.

294 "one of the most": Bonner F. Fellers to J. Woodall Greene, June 17, 1945, Box 4, Bonner F. Fellers Papers, Hoover Institution Archives, Palo Alto, Calif.

294 "outdoing Hitler": Henry Stimson diary, entry for June 6, 1945, in Schaffer, *Wings of Judgment,* p. 167.

294 "appalling that there": William W. Ralph, "Improvised Destruction: Arnold, LeMay, and the Firebombing of Japan," *War in History* 13, no. 4 (2006): 495.

294 "We must remember": "Bombing Tokyo: The Little Citizens Are the Ones Who Suffer Most," letter to the editor, *Hartford Courant,* May 29, 1945, p. 8.

295 He simply: Craven and Cate, *Army Air Forces in World War II,* p. 5:675.

295 The majority: John Dower, *Cultures of War: Pearl Harbor, Hiroshima, 9–11, Iraq* (New York: W. W. Norton, 2010), pp. 184–92.

295 "combustibility": USSBS, *Report on Physical Damage in Japan,* p. 39.

295 "The preponderant": USSBS, *The Effects of Strategic Bombing on Japan's War Economy* (Washington, D.C.: U.S. Government Printing Office, 1946), p. 38.

297 "All wings": XXI Bomber Command, Tactical Mission Report Nos. 206–9, June 18, 1945, Microfilm Roll # A7804, AFHRA.

297 The general ordered: XXI Bomber Command, Tactical Mission Report Nos. 210–12, June 20, 1945, ibid.

297 On June 28: XXI Bomber Command, Tactical Mission Report Nos. 234–37, June 28, 1945, ibid.

297 "Most of the time": LeMay and Yenne, *Superfortress,* p. 134.

297 "I am beginning": Curtis E. LeMay to Helen LeMay, June 9, 1945, in Hegi, *From Wright Field,* p. 363.

297 "Sure, I miss": Curtis E. LeMay to Helen LeMay, July 12, 1945, ibid., p. 371.

298 The 315th: 33rd Statistical Control Unit, "XXI Bomber Command: Monthly Activity Report," July 1, 1945, Box 16, CLP.

298 "Our strength": LeMay, *Mission with LeMay,* p. 376.

298 LeMay had first: Richard Rhodes, *The Making of the Atomic Bomb* (New York: Simon & Schuster, 1986), p. 679.

298 "My job": Paul W. Tibbets, Jr., with Clair Stebbins and Harry Franken, *The Tibbets Story* (New York: Stein & Day, 1978), p. 156.

299   "I was highly": Leslie R. Groves, *Now It Can Be Told: The Story of the Manhattan Project* (New York: Harper & Row, 1962), p. 283.

299   "I knew this would": Coffey, *Iron Eagle,* p. 176.

299   In the latter half: Craven and Cate, *Army Air Forces in World War II,* pp. 5:674–75.

299   LeMay more than tripled: Ibid.

299   "Enemy air opposition": Narrative History of the XXI Bomber Command, June 1–30, 1945, p. 11, Microfilm Roll # A7785, AFHRA.

299   "We are certainly": Curtis E. LeMay to Helen LeMay, July 10, 1945, in Hegi, *From Wright Field,* p. 370.

299   "The record will show": Curtis E. LeMay comments, undated, Box 49, MGC.

300   "I imagined": Clark, "Ruminations of a (Reluctant) B-29 Gunner," p. 52.

300   "If a guy": Michael Giroski, oral history by Richard Misenhimer, July 2, 2009.

300   "We were going": Bob Vaucher, interview by author, September 20, 2019.

300   A veteran: David R. Mets, *Master of Airpower: General Carl A. Spaatz* (Novato, Calif.: Presidio Press, 1988), pp. 302–3.

300   "I have never": Carl Spaatz statement, August 11, 1945, Box 21, Carl Spaatz Papers, LOC.

300   "The war with Japan": Crane, *Bombs, Cities, Civilians,* p. 183.

300   "If our B-29s": Wolk, *Cataclysm,* p. 178.

300   "Unless Japan desires": Carl Spaatz to Ira Eaker, August 2, 1945, in Crane, *Bombs, Cities, Civilians,* p. 183.

301   "kicked": Sidney Shalett, "Twining to Lead Superfort Group," *New York Times,* July 25, 1945, p. 5.

301   "The most spectacularly": "Battle of Japan," *Time,* August 13, 1945, p. 22.

301   "Have had opportunity": COMGEN USASTAF to COMGEN USASTAF REAR, August 7, 1945, Curtis E. LeMay OMPF.

301   "An officer": Carl Spaatz, Efficiency Report for Curtis E. LeMay, September 20, 1945, ibid.

301   "LeMay was": Paul Tibbets, oral history by Murray Green, January 7, 1970, Box 77, MGC.

301   "I don't think": LeMay, *Mission with LeMay,* p. 387.

302   "The alternative": "Ultimatum Sent to Japan," *Chicago Tribune,* July 27, 1945, p. 1.

302   "the most terrible": Harry S. Truman diary, entry for July 25, 1945, in Robert H. Ferrell, ed., *Off the Record: The Private Papers of Harry S. Truman* (Columbia: University of Missouri Press, 1980), pp. 55–56.

302   "Soldiers and sailors": Ibid.

302   "The atomic bomb": Henry L. Stimson, "The Decision to Use the Atomic Bomb," *Harper's Magazine,* February 1947, pp. 97–107.

302   "We had to end": George C. Marshall, oral history by Forrest C. Pogue, Tape 14, February 11, 1957, George C. Marshall Foundation, Lexington, Va.

302   "Attention Japanese": "LeMay Tells Japanese People Where 'Superforts' Will Hit," *New York Times,* July 28, 1945, p. 1.

303 "The Japanese have": "LeMay Warns 11 Nip Cities They're on B-29 Raid List," *Columbus Dispatch,* July, 27, 1945, p. 1.

303 "We hope": "LeMay Tells Japanese People Where 'Superforts' Will Hit," *New York Times,* July 28, 1945, p. 1.

303 To hammer: Craven and Cate, *Army Air Forces in World War II,* p. 5:675.

303 The general warned: W. H. Lawrence, "12 Japanese Cities Get B-29 Warnings," *New York Times,* August 1, 1945, p. 3.

CHAPTER 19

304 "Hiroshima was": Michihiko Hachiya diary, entry for August 6, 1945, in Michihiko Hachiya, *Hiroshima Diary: The Journal of a Japanese Physician, August 6–September 30, 1945,* trans. and ed. Warner Wells (Chapel Hill: University of North Carolina Press, 1955), p. 8.

304 At 2:45 a.m.: Tibbets, *Tibbets Story,* pp. 209–11.

304 Experts estimated: Notes of the Interim Committee Meeting, May 31, 1945, Misc. Historical Documents Collection, Harry S. Truman Presidential Library and Museum, Independence, Mo.

304 "With its coat": Tibbets, *Tibbets Story,* p. 201.

304 "Ready for takeoff": Ibid., p. 210.

305 Sensitive to the awesome: Mets, *Master of Airpower,* p. 303.

305 "Atomic bomb": Arnold, *Global Mission,* p. 598.

305 "I think": LeMay, *Mission with LeMay,* p. 388.

305 "It's Hiroshima": Tibbets, *Tibbets Story,* p. 220.

306 "The early morning": Ibid., p. 221.

306 "Do you all agree": Ibid.

306 "Okay": Ibid., p. 222.

306 Hiroshima, which: USSBS, *The Effects of the Atomic Bombs on Hiroshima and Nagasaki* (Washington, D.C.: U.S. Government Printing Office, 1946), pp. 5 6; USSBS, *The Effects of the Atomic Bomb on Hiroshima, Japan* (Washington, D.C.: U.S. Government Printing Office, 1947), pp. 1: 8–10, 68–73.

307 "When I returned": Tadataka Sasaki, "Asking Young People to Create a Peaceful Country," in Hiroshima Association for the Success of the Atomic Bomb Exhibition, *After 60 Years, A-Bomb Survivors Speak Out: An Anthology of the Experiences of Hiroshima Atomic Bomb Victims* (Hiroshima: Yoshimura, 2010), p. 13.

307 "Hiroshima": "Hiroshima," 90.30, undated, Microfilm Roll # A7809, AFHRA.

307 At 7:09 a.m.: USSBS, *Effects of the Atomic Bomb on Hiroshima, Japan,* pp. 1:84–85.

307 "There's a B-29": Tadataka Sasaki, "Asking Young People to Create a Peaceful Country," in Hiroshima Association, *After 60 Years,* p. 13.

307 "It was very": Nobuo Takemura, "Honoring the Wishes of Lost Schoolmates," ibid., p. 18.

308 "We're on target": Tibbets, *Tibbets Story,* p. 224.

308 "To some": Ibid., p. 225.

308 "If Dante": Ibid., p. 227.

308 "My God": "Hiroshima Diary," *Time,* December 6, 1971, p. 14.

308 "Fellows": Tibbets, *Tibbets Story*, p. 227.

308 Little Boy detonated: USSBS, *Effects of the Atomic Bomb on Hiroshima, Japan,* pp. 1:8–15.

308 "We saw blue-white": Ichiso Hori, "Caring for Injured People by Making Ointment," in Hiroshima Association, *After 60 Years,* p. 56.

309 That flash left: Averill A. Liebow diary, entries for October 19 and 31, 1945, in Averill A. Liebow, *Encounter with Disaster: A Medical Diary of Hiroshima, 1945* (New York: W. W. Norton, 1970), pp. 118–25, 137; USSBS, *Effects of the Atomic Bomb on Hiroshima, Japan*, pp. 2:29–31.

309 "I saw a train": Hiroko Uchida, "Overcoming the Atomic Bomb Disease," in Hiroshima Association, *After 60 Years,* p. 28.

309 Flash burns: Sakae Hosaka, "A Nurse in Hiroshima," in Gaynor Sekimori, trans., *Hibakusha: Survivors of Hiroshima and Nagasaki* (Tokyo: Kôsei, 2010), p. 43.

309 "Everywhere I looked": Setsuko Iwamoto, "That Day," in Hiroshima Peace Culture Foundation, *Eyewitness Testimonies: Appeals from the A-Bomb Survivors* (Hiroshima: Bunkasya, 2017), p. 46.

309 "This wasn't": Michiko Yamaoka, "Conveying the Spirit of Hiroshima to the Entire World," ibid., p. 142.

310 "The public fire": USSBS, *Effects of the Atomic Bomb on Hiroshima, Japan*, p. 1:14.

310 "Hiroshima became": Haruto Seo, "Flee in Flames," in Hiroshima Association, *After 60 Years,* p. 42.

310 "Some carried dead": Yoko Shineda, "Saving Our One and Only Life," in Hiroshima Association for the Success of the Atomic Bomb Exhibition, *After 65 Years, A-Bomb Survivors and War Victims Speak Out: An Anthology of the Experiences of Hiroshima Atomic Bomb Victims* (Hiroshima: Yoshimura, 2015), p. 37.

310 "I found myself": Rikio Yamane, "Everyone in My Department Is Dead," in Hiroshima Peace Culture Foundation, *Eyewitness Testimonies,* p. 134.

310 The blast wiped: USSBS, *Effects of the Atomic Bombs on Hiroshima and Nagasaki*, p. 6.

310 "Just to find": Akihiro Takahashi, "The Turning Point," in Sekimori, *Hibakusha,* p. 196.

310 "The people": Michihiko Hachiya diary, entry for August 7, 1945, in Hachiya, *Hiroshima Diary,* p. 12.

310 "I was scared": Akiyo Tagawa, "A Mother Holding Her Dead Baby," in Hiroshima Association, *After 60 Years,* p. 59.

311 "All we had": Setsuko Iwamoto, "That Day," in Hiroshima Peace Culture Foundation, *Eyewitness Testimonies,* p. 48.

311 "Parents, half": Michihiko Hachiya diary, entry for August 7, 1945, in Hachiya, *Hiroshima Diary,* p. 22.

311 "We had to pull": Teiichi Teramura, "The Unforgiveable," in Sekimori, *Hibakusha,* pp. 49–50.

311 "We carried": Tadaomi Furuishi, "Among the Flames," ibid., p. 165.

311 "Each evening": Katsuyoshi Yoshimura, "Weeds by the Roadside," ibid., p. 41.

312 "It was a horrible": Mitsuko Tsuchikawa, "My Child, Mother and Brother Stolen from Me by the A-Bomb," in Hiroshima Association, *After 65 Years,* p. 43.

312 "It was": Charles Murphy draft article, August 10, 1945, Box 21, Carl Spaatz Papers, LOC.

312 "Early reports": Curtis E. LeMay Daily Diary, entry for August 7, 1945, Box B7, CLP.

312 "If you had": David A. Burchinal, oral history by John B. Schmidt and Jack Straser, April 11, 1975, AFHRA.

312 "The force": Statement by President of the United States, August 6, 1945, Subject Files, Ayers Papers, Harry S. Truman Presidential Library and Museum, Independence, Mo.

312 "We are in possession": Translation of Leaflet Dropped on the Japanese (AB-11), August 6, 1945, Misc. Historical Documents Collection, ibid.

313 "His Imperial": Pacific War Research Society, *Japan's Longest Day* (Tokyo: Kodansha International, 1968), p. 308.

313 "There was complete": León María Guerrero diary, entry for August 15, 1945.

313 "There is an important": Haruyo Nihei, interview by author, November 18, 2019.

313 Hours earlier: Pacific War Research Society, *Japan's Longest Day,* pp. 209–12.

314 "The enemy": Ibid., p. 210.

314 "All were expressionless": Guerrero diary, entry for August 15, 1945.

314 "They wept": Ibid.

314 "The broadcast": Michihiko Hachiya diary, entry for August 15, 1945, in Hachiya, *Hiroshima Diary,* p. 81.

314 "I had been prepared": Ibid.

314 "Only a coward": Ibid., p. 82.

314 "The one word": Ibid.

314 "What was that about?" Haruyo Nihei, interview by author, November 18, 2019.

315 "We lost": Ikuko Nagata, interview by author, November 16, 2019.

315 "Whether we lost": Ibid.

315 "Peace is bright": Katsumoto Saotome, interview by author, November 21, 2019.

315 Around ten p.m.: Coffey, *Iron Eagle,* pp. 180–81.

315 He had stayed: Curtis E. LeMay to Helen LeMay, August 15, 1945, in Hegi, *From Wright Field,* p. 385.

315 "I still haven't": Ibid.

315 "Let's go home!": Joseph Hearst, "How Chicagoans on Guam Took the Good News," *Chicago Tribune,* August 16, 1945, p. 4.

315 "I didn't think": Curtis E. LeMay to Helen LeMay, August 15, 1945, in Hegi, *From Wright Field,* p. 386.

EPILOGUE

317 "Life seems": James Salango to family, October 14, 1945, Box 3, RG 64, Papers of Capt. James Salango, MMAL.

317 "Darkened out": "Radio Interview Between General of the Army Air Forces Arnold and General Spaatz," transcript, September 5, 1945, Box 21, Carl Spaatz Papers, LOC.

318 In that time: 33rd Statistical Control Unit, "The Twentieth Air Force: A Statistical Summary of Its Operations Against Japan," undated, pp. 8, 80–81, Microfilm Roll # A7737, AFHRA.

318 "Tokyo": Bob Speer, "The B-29s Most of All," *Brief*, undated, p. 7, in Box 41, CLP.

318 "Vines and creepers": Guerrero diary, entry for July 11, 1945.

318 Nearly half of all: Office of Statistical Control, "Summary of Twentieth Air Force Operations, June 5, 1944–August 14, 1945," October 1, 1945, pp. 16–17, Microfilm Roll # A1088, AFHRA.

318 The worst hit: 33rd Statistical Control Unit, "The Twentieth Air Force: A Statistical Summary of Its Operations Against Japan," p. 81.

318 All told: USSBS, *Summary Report (Pacific War)* (Washington, D.C.: U.S. Government Printing Office, 1946), pp. 16–17.

318 Incendiaries were: Office of Statistical Control, "Summary of Twentieth Air Force Operations, June 5, 1944–August 14, 1945," p. 1.

318 In months: Ibid., p. 23.

318 Along with home: USSBS, *The Strategic Air Operation of Very Heavy Bombardment in the War Against Japan (Twentieth Air Force)* (Washington, D.C.: U.S. Government Printing Office, 1946), p. 6.

318 "The firebombs": Peter Grodsky to family, September 24, 1945, Box 3, RG 60, Papers of Peter Grodsky Grant, MMAL.

318 The human toll: USSBS, *The Effects of Bombing on Health and Medical Services in Japan*, pp. 142–43.

318 The attacks left: USSBS, *Effects of Air Attack on Japanese Urban Economy*, p. 7; USSBS, *Effects of Incendiary Bomb Attacks on Japan*, p. 67.

319 "Probably more persons": USSBS, *Report on Physical Damage in Japan*, p. 95.

319 Those deaths: "World War II Casualty Estimates, Asian-Pacific," March 22, 2022, copy courtesy of Richard Frank.

319 "These operations": Curtis E. LeMay speech, November 19, 1945, B41, CLP.

319 Such factories: USSBS, *Summary Report (Pacific War)*, p. 18.

319 "We knew": LeMay, *Mission with LeMay*, p. 384.

319 "What a miracle": Bonner F. Fellers to Dorothy Fellers, September 6, 1945, Box 2, RG 44a, Bonner F. Fellers Papers, MMAL.

320 Sergeant Grodsky: Peter Grodsky to family, October 26, 1945, Box 3, RG 60, Papers of Peter Grodsky Grant, ibid.

320 "The more I see": James Salango to family, September 27, 1945, Box 3, RG 64, Papers of Capt. James Salango, ibid.

320 "Complete devastation": Raymond, *Autobiography*, p. 199.

320 "Japan's economy": USSBS, *Summary Report (Pacific War)*, p. 19.

320 In the end: USSBS, *Effects of Strategic Bombing on Japan's War Economy*, p. 41.

320 On the civilian: USSBS, *Effects of Bombing on Health and Medical Services in Japan*, p. 90.

320 "To speak of rice": Selden Menefee, "Japanese Told to Eat Refuse in Food Crisis," *Christian Science Monitor,* July 11, 1945, p. 11.

321 "The bomber offensive": USSBS, *Effects of Strategic Bombing on Japan's War Economy*, p. 58.

321 "Morale stood up": Assistant Chief of Air Staff—Intelligence, Headquarters Army Air Forces, *Mission Accomplished: Interrogations of Japanese Industrial, Military, and Civil Leaders of World War II* (Washington, D.C.: U.S. Government Printing Office, 1946), p. 27.

321 "I myself": Ibid., p. 39.

321 "Superfortresses": Ibid., p. 23.

321 "The atomic bombs": Bix, *Hirohito and Modern Japan*, pp. 509–10.

321 "From the Japanese": H. H. Arnold press statement, August 17, 1945, Box 45, EOP.

321 "The Japanese": Ibid.

321 Victory had cost: J. B. Montgomery to Curtis E. LeMay, "Brief Summary of Strategic Air Operations Against Japan," August 26, 1945, Box B15, CLP.

321 "As a percentage": Ibid.

321 The navy fished: USSBS, *Strategic Air Operation of Very Heavy Bombardment in the War Against Japan*, p. 24.

322 "It ceased to be": Haywood S. Hansell, Jr., to James M. Boyle, January 4, 1965.

322 War crimes investigators: "Sentence 5 Japs to Die for Letting 48 Yanks Burn to Death," *Chicago Tribune,* July 9, 1948, p. 11.

322 In one of the more: Burton Crane, "Cannibalism Laid to High Japanese," *New York Times,* March 12, 1948, p. 14.

322 "This intense hatred": Hanley, *Accused American War Criminal,* p. 165.

322 On average: USSBS, *Effects of Strategic Bombing on Japanese Morale*, p. 1.

322 One of the more: John Dower, *Embracing Defeat: Japan in the Wake of World War II* (New York: W. W. Norton, 1999), pp. 61–64.

322 "I wish you had": Tôkyô Daikûshû Sensai Shiryô Sentâ, *Ano Toki Kodomo Datta*, p. 191.

322 "I thought about death": Ibid., p. 21.

323 In 1948: Tokyo Memorial Association (Tokyo-to Irei Kyokai), "The Great Kanto Earthquake," January 1, 2015; Tokyo Memorial Association (Tokyo-to Irei Kyokai), "The Great Tokyo Air Raids," December 1, 2014; Cary Karacas, "Buckets, Bombs, and Bodies: Rights to the Japanese City & the Tokyo Air Raids," April 14, 2006, University of California at Berkeley, Breslauer Symposium.

323 "The part you played": COMGENAIR to CG USASTAF, August 15, 1945, Curtis E. LeMay OMPF.

323 "I am afraid": H. H. Arnold to Carl Spaatz, August 19, 1945, Box 21, Carl Spaatz Papers, LOC.

323   "It has been": Curtis E. LeMay to Helen LeMay, August 13, 1945, in Hegi, *From Wright Field,* p. 384.

323   "Air power can carry": Lauris Norstad speech, November 8, 1945, Box 26, LNP.

324   "Victory smiles": Douhet, *Command of the Air,* p. 27.

324   "World War II ended": Haywood S. Hansell, Jr., "The Development of the United States Concept of Bombardment Operations," February 16, 1951, Box 11, Addendum 1, HSHP.

324   "We hated": John Ismay, "'We Hated What We Were Doing': Memories from the Airmen," *New York Times,* September 6, 2020, p. F7.

324   "We spent much": Clark, "Ruminations of a (Reluctant) B-29 Gunner," p. 67.

324   "As time went": Hoyt Clark to Nancy Samp, March 17, 2017.

324   "We didn't like it": Michael Giroski, oral history by Richard Misenhimer, July 2, 2009.

324   "He never ceased": Eleanor Arnold, oral history by Murray Green, August 22, 1970, Box 57, MGC.

324   "We are not": Lauris Norstad speech, January 15, 1946, Box 26, LNP.

325   "I'm not aware": Ira Eaker, oral history by Murray Green, August 1, 1969, Box 64, MGC.

325   "From there": Arnold, *Global Mission,* p. 609.

325   "LeMay never learned": Nutter, *With Possum and Eagle,* p. 289.

325   "wanton killer": Philip S. Heisler, "Japs Handy with Epithets Hurled at 'Killer' LeMay," *Baltimore Sun,* March 25, 1945, p. 8.

325   "bloodthirsty maniac": Ibid.

326   "Bygones": Robert Trumbull, "Honor to LeMay by Japan Stirs Parliament Debate," *New York Times,* December 8, 1964, p. 15.

326   "My solution": LeMay, *Mission with LeMay,* p. 565.

326   "Dark Ages": Al Dopking, "B-29 Boss Lets Bombs Talk for Him," *Cleveland Plain Dealer,* July 22, 1945, p. 1.

326   "That statement": Coffey, *Iron Eagle,* p. 442.

326   "He was": Janie LeMay Lodge, oral history by Barbara W. Sommer, September 10, 1998, Nebraska State Historical Society, Lincoln.

326   "History should judge": Nutter, *With Possum and Eagle,* p. 291.

326   "I was a hero": Lodge oral history.

327   In 1975: Haywood S. Hansell, Jr., to Ira C. Eaker, April 2, 1975, Box 2, Addendum 1, HSHP.

327   "General LeMay": Haywood S. Hansell, Jr., speech, April 19, 1967, Box 1, Addendum 3, HSHP.

327   When asked: Haywood S. Hansell, Jr., to Edgar F. Puryear, Jr., January 15, 1976, Box 1, Addendum 1, HSHP.

327   The general admitted: Hansell speech, April 19, 1967.

327   "To my mind": Haywood S. Hansell, Jr., to James M. Boyle, January 4, 1965.

327   On June 11, 1972: Saotome, *Tōkyō Daikûshû,* pp. 3–7; Katsumoto Saotome, interview by author, November 21, 2019.

328   "I was able": Haruyo Nihei, interview by author, November 18, 2019.

BIBLIOGRAPHY

ARCHIVES, LIBRARIES & MUSEUMS

Air Force Historical Research Agency, Montgomery, Ala.
Australian War Memorial, Canberra, Australia
Center of the Tokyo Air Raids and War Damage, Tokyo, Japan
Charleston County Public Library, Charleston, S.C.
Daniel Library, The Citadel, Charleston, S.C.
Dwight D. Eisenhower Library, Abilene, Kans.
Frances Loeb Library, Harvard University, Cambridge, Mass.
George C. Marshall Foundation, Lexington, Va.
Great Kanto Earthquake Memorial Museum, Tokyo, Japan
Harry S. Truman Presidential Library and Museum, Independence, Mo.
Hiroshima Peace Memorial Museum, Hiroshima, Japan
Hoover Institution Library and Archives, Palo Alto, Calif.
Kyoto Museum for World Peace, Kyoto, Japan
Library of Congress, Washington, D.C.
MacArthur Memorial Archives and Library, Norfolk, Va.
Marlene and Nathan Addlestone Library, College of Charleston, Charleston, S.C.
McDermott Library, U.S. Air Force Academy, Colorado Springs, Colo.
Minnesota Historical Society, St. Paul, Minn.
National Archives and Records Administration, College Park, Md.
National Diet Library, Tokyo, Japan
National Fire Protection Association Library, Quincy, Mass.
National Museum of the Pacific War, Fredericksburg, Tex.
National Personnel Records Center, St. Louis, Mo.
Nebraska State Historical Society, Lincoln, Neb.
Science History Institute, Philadelphia, Pa.

U.S. Army Heritage and Education Center, Carlisle, Pa.
U.S. Naval Institute, Annapolis, Md.
Widener Library, Harvard University, Cambridge, Mass.
Willis Library, University of North Texas, Denton, Tex.
Wadatsumi no Koe Memorial Hall, Tokyo, Japan
Yushukan Museum, Tokyo, Japan
Syracuse University Library, Syracuse, N.Y.

SPECIFIC COLLECTIONS

AIR FORCE HISTORICAL RESEARCH AGENCY, MONTGOMERY, ALA.
  Committee of Operations Analysts
  Haywood Hansell, Jr., Papers
  Third Photo Reconnaissance Squadron
  804th Aviation Engineer Battalion
  21st Bomber Command
  73rd Bombardment Wing
  313th Bombardment Wing
  314th Bombardment Wing
  Sixth Bombardment Group
  Ninth Bombardment Group
  19th Bombardment Group
  29th Bombardment Group
  497th Bombardment Group
  498th Bombardment Group
  499th Bombardment Group
  500th Bombardment Group
  504th Bombardment Group
  505th Bombardment Group
DWIGHT D. EISENHOWER LIBRARY, ABILENE, KANS.
  Lauris Norstad Papers
HOOVER INSTITUTION ARCHIVES, PALO ALTO, CALIF.
  Bonner F. Fellers Papers
LIBRARY OF CONGRESS, WASHINGTON, D.C.
  Henry H. Arnold Papers
  James H. Doolittle Papers
  Ira Eaker Papers
  William D. Leahy Papers
  Curtis E. LeMay Papers
  William Mitchell Papers
  Carl Spaatz Papers
MACARTHUR MEMORIAL ARCHIVES, NORFOLK, VIRGINIA
  Bonner F. Fellers Papers

Peter Grodsky Papers

James Salango Papers

NATIONAL ARCHIVES AND RECORDS ADMINISTRATION,
COLLEGE PARK, MD.

Record Group 18—Records of the Army Air Forces

Record Group 38—World War II Oral Histories and Interviews

NATIONAL DIET LIBRARY, TOKYO, JAPAN

Materials on the Allied Occupation of Japan

Records of the U.S. Strategic Bombing Survey

NATIONAL PERSONNEL RECORDS CENTER, ST. LOUIS, MO.

Henry H. Arnold Official Military Personnel File (OMPF)

Curtis E. LeMay OMPF

SYRACUSE UNIVERSITY LIBRARY, SYRACUSE, N.Y.

Thomas S. Power Papers

U.S. AIR FORCE ACADEMY LIBRARY, COLORADO SPRINGS, COLO.

Murray Green Papers

Haywood Hansell, Jr., Papers

Laurence Kuter Papers

Emmett O'Donnell, Jr., Papers

U.S. ARMY HERITAGE AND EDUCATION CENTER, CARLISLE, PA.

Thomas F. Farrell Papers

Alexander H. Howard Papers

Louis T. Kestner Papers

James T. Stewart Papers

ORAL HISTORIES

AIR FORCE HISTORICAL RESEARCH AGENCY, MONTGOMERY, ALA.

Glenn O. Barcus

Earl W. Barnes

David A. Burchinal

Paul K. Carlton

Jack J. Catton

Louis E. Coira

Russell E. Dougherty

Ira C. Eaker

Edgar S. Harris, Jr.

Richard H. Ellis

Barney M. Giles

Joseph E. Grew

Francis H. Griswold

Haywood S. Hansell, Jr.

C. S. Irvine

David C. Jones

George C. Kenney

William C. Kingsbury

Laurence S. Kuter

Eugene B. LeBailly

Curtis E. LeMay

Roy H. Lynn

John L. McCoy

Thomas W. McKnew

John B. McPherson

John B. Montgomery

Paul W. Tibbets, Jr.

Nathan F. Twining

Kenneth Wolfe

Eugene M. Zuckert

MINNESOTA HISTORICAL SOCIETY, ST. PAUL, MINN.

Arthur Tomes   Robert Michelsen

NATIONAL MUSEUM OF THE PACIFIC WAR, FREDERICKSBURG, TEX.

John Alebis   Arthur E. Kelly
David Braden   Garvin Kowalke
Lewis I. Brinson   Chester W. Marshall
John E. Combs   Benjamin A. Nicks
Julius J. Erdos   James R. O'Donnel
Bill Freeman   George W. Peterson
Michael Giroski   Rod Rohling
Donald J. Gleacher   Joseph E. Sberro
Raymond F. Halloran   Irvin N. Spielberg
Fiske Hanley   James M. Vande Hey
Dave Hollis   Edgar L. Vincent
Ralph W. Johnson   Marcus Worde

NEBRASKA STATE HISTORICAL SOCIETY, LINCOLN, NEB.

Janie LeMay Lodge

SCIENCE HISTORY INSTITUTE, PHILADELPHIA, PA.

Hoyt Hottel

U.S. AIR FORCE ACADEMY LIBRARY, COLORADO SPRINGS, COLO.

Kenneth B. Berquist   Emmett O'Donnell, Jr.
Paul Emrick   Thomas Power
Barney M. Giles   Paul W. Tibbets, Jr.
C. S. Irvine

U.S. NAVAL INSTITUTE, ANNAPOLIS, MD.

Stephen Jurika, Jr.   Henri Smith-Hutton

UNIVERSITY OF NORTH TEXAS, DENTON, TEX.

J. C. Armstrong   William A. Hatcher
David Braden   George Savage
William E. Cooper   Jay Titus
Raymond F. Halloran   Francis Wiese
Fiske Hanley

AUTHOR INTERVIEWS

JAPAN

Ikuro Anzai   Shizuko Nishio
Mitsuyo Hoshino   Katsumoto Saotome
Akiko Masaki   Shizuyo Takeuchi
Shigeaki Mori   Masahiko Yamabe
Ikuko Nagata   Kazuyo Yamane
Haruyo Nihei

UNITED STATES

John Angel

Glenn Barnhart

Fiske Hanley

Peter Paul Hatgil

Bob Minto

Ben Nicks

Bob Vaucher

PERIODICALS

Aerial Age Weekly

Air Force Magazine

Air Power History

Asia-Pacific Journal

Atlanta Constitution

Atlantic Monthly

Aviation History

Baltimore Sun

Boeing Magazine

Boston Globe

Boston Herald

Brief

Chicago Tribune

Christian Science Monitor

Cleveland Plain Dealer

Collier's

Columbus Dispatch

Combustion Science and Technology

Dallas Morning News

Evening Star

Flight Journal

Foreign Affairs

Hartford Courant

Harper's Magazine

Impact

Japan Times & Advertiser

Journal of American-East Asian Relations

Journal of Military History

Kansas History

Los Angeles Times

Mainichi

New York Herald Tribune

New York Times

New Yorker

Newsweek

Nippon Times

Popular Mechanics

Proceedings

Saturday Evening Post

Time

Washington Post

Yank

GOVERNMENT AND INDUSTRY REPORTS

AAF Manual 51-126-6, "B-29." Headquarters Army Air Forces, Washington, December 15, 1945.

Assistant Chief of Air Staff—Intelligence, Headquarters Army Air Forces. *Mission Accomplished: Interrogations of Japanese Industrial, Military, and Civil Leaders of World War II*. Washington, D.C.: U.S. Government Printing Office, 1946.

Axton, Matilda F., et al., eds. *Foreign Relations of the United States Diplomatic Papers, 1939*, vol. 1, *General*. Washington, D.C.: U.S. Government Printing Office, 1956.

Bond, Horatio, ed. *Fire and the Air War*. Boston: National Fire Protection Association, 1946.

Brophy, Leo P., and George J. B. Fisher. *The Chemical Warfare Service: Organizing for War*. United States Army in World War II: The Technical Services. Washington, D.C.: Center of Military History, 1989.

Brophy, Leo P., Wyndham D. Miles, and Rexmond C. Cochrane. *The Chemical Warfare Service: From Laboratory to Field*. United States Army in World War II: The Technical Services. Washington, D.C.: Center of Military History, 1988.

Carastro, L. R., comp. and ed. *Of Those Who Fly*. Air Force Reserve Officer Training Corps, Air Training Command, 1972.

Craven, Wesley Frank, and James Lea Cate, eds. *The Army Air Forces in World War II*. 7 vols. Washington, D.C.: Office of Air Force History, 1983.

Crowl, Philip A. *Campaign in the Marianas*. United States Army in World War II: The War in the Pacific. Washington, D.C.: Center of Military History, 1993.

Dod, Karl C. *The Corps of Engineers: The War Against Japan*. United States Army in World War II: The Technical Services. Washington, D.C.: Center of Military History, 1987.

Dougal, Richardson, ed. *Foreign Relations of the United States Diplomatic Papers*, vol. 1, *The Conference of Berlin (The Potsdam Conference), 1945*. Washington, D.C.: U.S. Government Printing Office, 1960.

The Effect of the Atomic Bombs at Hiroshima and Nagasaki: Report of the British Mission to Japan. London: His Majesty's Stationery Office, 1946.

General Staff of GHQ. *Reports of General MacArthur: Japanese Operations in the Southwest Pacific Area*, vol. 2, pt. 2. Washington, D.C.: U.S. Government Printing Office, 1994.

Laiming, Boris. "Tokyo Conflagration of September 1st, 1923: Report to the National Board of Fire Underwriters, New York City, New York, of November 20, 1923, with Supplements of December 28, 1923."

"Pilot's Flight Operating Instructions for Airplanes Army Models B-29 and B-29A," May 20, 1945.

"Report by the Police President and Local Air Protection Leader of Hamburg on the Large Scale Raids on Hamburg in July and August 1943." Home Office, Civil Defense Department, Intelligence Branch, January 1946.

Robinson, S. "Official Report of Capt. S. Robinson, R.N.R., Commander of the Canadian Pacific *S.S. Empress of Australia*, on the Japanese Earthquake, the Fire, and Subsequent Relief Operations," ca. 1923.

Standard Oil Development Company. "Design and Construction of Typical German and Japanese Test Structures at Dugway Proving Grounds, Utah," May 27, 1943, Frances Loeb Library, Harvard University, Cambridge, Mass.

United States Strategic Bombing Survey. *The Campaigns of the Pacific War*. Washington, D.C.: U.S. Government Printing Office, 1946.

——. *Coals and Metals in Japan's War Economy*. Washington, D.C.: U.S. Government Printing Office, 1947.

——. *The Effect of Bombing on Health and Medical Care in Germany*. Washington, D.C.: U.S. Government Printing Office, 1945.

——. *The Effects of Air Attack on Japanese Urban Economy (Summary Report)*. Washington, D.C.: U.S. Government Printing Office, 1947.

——. *Effects of Air Attack on Osaka-Kobe-Kyoto*. Washington, D.C.: U.S. Government Printing Office, 1947.

———. *The Effects of Air Attack on the City of Nagoya*. Washington, D.C.: U.S. Government Printing Office, 1947.

———. *Effects of Air Attack on Urban Complex Tokyo-Kawasaki-Yokohama*. Washington, D.C.: U.S. Government Printing Office, 1947.

———. *The Effects of Air Attacks on the City of Nagasaki*. Washington, D.C.: U.S. Government Printing Office, 1947.

———. *The Effects of Atomic Bombs on Health and Medical Services in Hiroshima and Nagasaki*. Washington, D.C.: U.S. Government Printing Office, 1947.

———. *The Effects of Bombing on Health and Medical Services in Japan*. Washington, D.C.: U.S. Government Printing Office, 1947.

———. *Effects of Incendiary Bomb Attacks on Japan (A Report on Eight Cities)*. Washington, D.C.: U.S. Government Printing Office, 1947.

———. *The Effects of Strategic Bombing on Japan's War Economy*. Washington, D.C.: U.S. Government Printing Office, 1946.

———. *The Effects of Strategic Bombing on Japanese Morale*. Washington, D.C.: U.S. Government Printing Office, 1947.

———. *The Effects of the Atomic Bomb on Hiroshima, Japan*, 3 vols. Washington, D.C.: U.S. Government Printing Office, 1947.

———. *Effects of the Atomic Bomb on Nagasaki, Japan*, 2 vols. Washington, D.C.: U.S. Government Printing Office, 1947.

———. *The Effects of the Atomic Bombs on Hiroshima and Nagasaki*. Washington, D.C.: U.S. Government Printing Office, 1946.

———. *Effects of Two Thousand, One Thousand and Five Hundred Pound Bombs on Japanese Targets (A Report on Eight Incidents)*. Washington, D.C.: U.S. Government Printing Office, 1947.

———. *Field Report Covering Air Raid Protection and Allied Subjects in Tokyo, Japan*. Washington, D.C.: U.S. Government Printing Office, 1947.

———. *Field Report Covering Air Raid Protection and Allied Subjects in Nagasaki, Japan*. Washington, D.C.: U.S. Government Printing Office, 1947.

———. *Field Report Covering Air Raid Protection and Allied Subjects in Kyoto, Japan*. Washington, D.C.: U.S. Government Printing Office, 1947.

———. *Field Report Covering Air Raid Protection and Allied Subjects in Kobe, Japan*. Washington, D.C.: U.S. Government Printing Office, 1947.

———. *Field Report Covering Air Raid Protection and Allied Subjects in Osaka, Japan*. Washington, D.C.: U.S. Government Printing Office, 1947.

———. *Final Report Covering Air-Raid Protection and Allied Subjects in Japan*. Washington, D.C.: U.S. Government Printing Office, 1947.

———. *Interrogations of Japanese Officials*, 2 vols. Washington, D.C.: U.S. Government Printing Office, 1946.

———. *The Japanese Aircraft Industry*. Washington, D.C.: U.S. Government Printing Office, 1947.

———. *The Japanese Wartime Standard of Living and Utilization of Manpower*. Washington, D.C.: U.S. Government Printing Office, 1947.

——. *Japan's Struggle to End the War*. Washington, D.C.: U.S. Government Printing Office, 1946.

——. *Mitsubishi Heavy Industries, LTD*. Washington, D.C.: U.S. Government Printing Office, 1947.

——. *Nakajima Aircraft Company, LTD*. Washington, D.C.: U.S. Government Printing Office, 1947.

——. *The Offensive Mine Laying Campaign Against Japan*. Washington, D.C.: U.S. Government Printing Office, 1946.

——. *Oil in Japan's War*. Washington, D.C.: U.S. Government Printing Office, 1946.

——. *A Report on Physical Damage in Japan*. Washington, D.C.: U.S. Government Printing Office, 1947.

——. *The Strategic Air Operation of Very Heavy Bombardment in the War Against Japan (Twentieth Air Force)*. Washington, D.C.: U.S. Government Printing Office, 1946.

——. *Summary Report Covering Air-Raid Protection and Allied Subjects in Japan*. Washington, D.C.: U.S. Government Printing Office, 1946.

——. *Summary Report (Pacific War)*. Washington, D.C.: U.S. Government Printing Office, 1946.

——. *The War Against Japanese Transportation, 1941–1945*. Washington, D.C.: U.S. Government Printing Office, 1947.

BOOKS

Agawa, Hiroyuki. *The Reluctant Admiral: Yamamoto and the Imperial Navy*. Trans. John Bester. New York: Kodansha International, 1979.

Arnold, H. H. *Global Mission*. New York: Harper & Brothers, 1949.

Astor, Gerald. *The Mighty Eighth: The Air War in Europe as Told by the Men Who Fought It*. New York: Donald I. Fine, 1997.

Behr, Edward. *Hirohito: Behind the Myth*. New York: Villard Books, 1989.

Berger, Carl. *B-29: The Superfortress*. New York: Ballantine Books, 1970.

Bertram, James. *Beneath the Shadow: A New Zealander in the Far East, 1939–1946*. New York: John Day, 1947.

Biddle, Tami Davis. *Rhetoric and Reality in Air Warfare: The Evolution of British and American Ideas About Strategic Bombing, 1914–1945*. Princeton, N.J.: Princeton University Press, 2002.

Birdsall, Steve. *Saga of the Superfortress: The Dramatic History of the B-29 and the Twentieth Air Force*. Garden City, N.Y.: Doubleday, 1980.

Bix, Herbert P. *Hirohito and the Making of Modern Japan*. New York: HarperCollins, 2000.

Boyington, Gregory. *Baa Baa Black Sheep*. New York: G.P. Putnam's Sons, 1958.

Briggs, Charlene. *Letters to Lida: World War II Told Through the Heart and Words of a B-29 Tail-Gunner*. Rhinebeck, N.Y.: Epigraph Books, 2015.

Bureau of Social Affairs and Morihiko Fujisawa. *The Great Earthquake of 1923 in Japan*. Tokyo: Sanshusha Press, 1926.

Busch, Noel F. *Two Minutes to Noon: The Story of the Great Tokyo Earthquake and Fire*. New York: Simon & Schuster, 1962.

Butow, Robert J. C. *Japan's Decision to Surrender*. Stanford, Calif.: Stanford University Press, 1954.

Caidin, Martin. *The Night Hamburg Died*. New York: Ballantine Books, 1960.

———. *A Torch to the Enemy*. New York: Ballantine Books, 1960.

Cantril, Hadley, ed. *Public Opinion, 1935–1946*. Princeton, N.J.: Princeton University Press, 1951.

Chappell, John D. *Before the Bomb: How America Approached the End of the Pacific War*. Lexington: University Press of Kentucky, 1997.

Chennault, Claire Lee, and Robert Hotz, ed. *The Way of the Fighter: The Memoirs of Claire Lee Chennault*. New York: G.P. Putnam's Sons, 1949.

Ciardi, John. *Saipan: The War Diary of John Ciardi*. Fayetteville: University of Arkansas Press, 1988.

———. *Other Skies*. Boston: Little, Brown, 1947.

Clanton, Raymond W. *Fire, Fear and Guts: The B-29 and Her Gallant Crewmen*. Privately published, 2005.

Coffey, Thomas M. *Decision over Schweinfurt: The U.S. 8th Air Force Battle for Daylight Bombing*. New York: David McKay, 1977.

———. *Hap: The Story of the U.S. Air Force and the Man Who Built It*. New York: Viking Press, 1982.

———. *Iron Eagle: The Turbulent Life of General Curtis LeMay*. New York: Crown, 1986.

Cohen, Jerome B. *Japan's Economy in War and Reconstruction*. Minneapolis: University of Minnesota Press, 1949.

Collison, Thomas. *The Superfortress Is Born: The Story of the Boeing B-29*. New York: Duell, Sloan & Pearce, 1945.

Committee for Compiling the Writings of the University of Tokyo Students Killed in the War. *In the Faraway Mountains and Rivers: Writings of the University of Tokyo Students Killed in World War II*. Trans. Joseph L. Quinn and Midori Yamanouchi. Scranton, Pa.: University of Scranton Press, 2005.

Committee for the Compilation of Materials on Damage Caused by the Atomic Bombs in Hiroshima and Nagasaki. *Hiroshima and Nagasaki: The Physical, Medical, and Social Effects of the Atomic Bombs*. Trans. Eisei Ishikawa and David L. Swain. New York: Basic Books, 1981.

Cook, Haruko Taya, and Theodore F. Cook. *Japan at War: An Oral History*. New York: The New Press, 1992.

Cowles, Virginia. *Looking for Trouble*. New York: Harper & Brothers, 1941.

Cox, John W. *Friendly Monster: A Warbird and Its Crew*. Bloomington, Ind.: Xlibris, 2007.

Crane, Conrad. *American Airpower Strategy in Korea, 1950–1953*. Lawrence: University Press of Kansas, 2000.

———. *Bombs, Cities, Civilians, and Oil: American Airpower Strategy in World War II*. Lawrence: University Press of Kansas, 2016.

Crosby, Harry H. *A Wing and a Prayer: The "Bloody 100th" Bomb Group of the U.S. Eighth Air Force in Action over Europe in World War II*. New York: HarperCollins, 1993.

Dahlmann, Joseph. *The Great Tokyo Earthquake, September 1, 1923: Experiences and Impressions of an Eye-Witness*. Trans. Victor F. Gettelman. New York: America Press, 1924.

Dallek, Robert. *Franklin Roosevelt and American Foreign Policy, 1932–1945*. New York: Oxford University Press, 1995.

Dorr, Robert F. *Mission to Tokyo: The American Airmen Who Took the War to the Heart of Japan*. Minneapolis: Zenith Press, 2012.

Doty, Andy. *Backwards into Battle: A Tail Gunner's Journey in World War II*. Palo Alto, Calif.: Tall Tree Press, 1995.

Douhet, Giulio. *The Command of the Air*. Trans. Dino Ferrari. Maxwell Air Force Base, Ala.: Air University Press, 2019.

Dower, John. *Cultures of War: Pearl Harbor, Hiroshima, 9–11, Iraq*. New York: W. W. Norton, 2010.

———. *Embracing Defeat: Japan in the Wake of World War II*. New York: W. W. Norton, 1999.

———. *War Without Mercy: Race and Power in the Pacific War*. New York: Pantheon, 1986.

Downes, Alexander B. *Targeting Civilians in War*. Ithaca, N.Y.: Cornell University Press, 2008.

Ferrell, Robert H., ed. *Off the Record: The Private Papers of Harry S. Truman*. Columbia: University of Missouri Press, 1980.

Fieser, Louis F. *The Scientific Method: A Personal Account of Unusual Projects in War and in Peace*. New York: Reinhold, 1964.

Finney, Robert T. *History of the Air Corps Tactical School, 1920–1940*. Washington, D.C.: Air Force History and Museums Program, 1998.

Fitzgibbon, Constantine. *The Winter of the Bombs: The Story of the Blitz of London*. New York: W. W. Norton, 1957.

Fleisher, Wilfrid. *Volcanic Isle*. Garden City, N.Y.: Doubleday, Doran, 1942.

———. *Our Enemy Japan*. Garden City, N.Y.: Doubleday, Doran, 1942.

Frank, Richard B. *Downfall: The End of the Imperial Japanese Empire*. New York: Random House, 1999.

Friedrich, Jörg. *The Fire: The Bombing of Germany, 1940–1945*. Trans. Allison Brown. New York: Columbia University Press, 2006.

Gardiner, Juliet. *The Blitz: The British Under Attack*. London: Harper Press, 2010.

Gaskin, Margaret. *Blitz: The Story of December 29, 1940*. Orlando, Fla.: Harcourt, 2005.

Gaston, James C. *Planning the American Air War: Four Men and Nine Days in 1941*. Washington, D.C.: National Defense University Press, 1982.

Gibney, Frank, ed. *Sensō: The Japanese Remember the Pacific War: Letters to the Editor of the Asahi Shimbun*. Trans. Beth Cary. Armonk, N.Y.: M. E. Sharpe, 1995.

Grayling, A. C. *Among the Dead Cities: The History and Moral Legacy of the WWII Bombing of Civilians in Germany and Japan*. New York: Walker, 2006.

Greer, Ron, and Mike Wicks. *Fire from the Sky: A Diary over Japan*. Altona, Man.: Friesens, 2005.

Grew, Joseph C. *Report from Tokyo: A Message to the American People*. New York: Simon & Schuster, 1942.

Griffith, Charles. *The Quest: Haywood Hansell and American Strategic Bombing in World War II*. Maxwell Air Force Base, Ala.: Air University Press, 1999.

Grimsley, Mark, and Clifford J. Rogers, eds. *Civilians in the Path of War*. Lincoln: University of Nebraska Press, 2002.

Groves, Leslie R. *Now It Can Be Told: The Story of the Manhattan Project*. New York: Harper & Row, 1962.

Guillain, Robert. *I Saw Tokyo Burning: An Eyewitness Narrative from Pearl Harbor to Hiroshima*. Trans. William Byron. Garden City, N.Y.: Doubleday, 1981.

Gurney, Gene. *Journey of the Giants: The Story of the B-29 "Superfort"—The Weapon That Won the War in the Pacific*. New York: Coward-McCann, 1961.

Hachiya, Michihiko. *Hiroshima Diary: The Journal of a Japanese Physician, August 6–September 30, 1945*. Trans. and ed. by Warner Wells. Chapel Hill: University of North Carolina Press, 1955.

Hall, Cargill R., ed. *Case Studies in Strategic Bombardment*. Washington, D.C.: Air Force History and Museums Program, 1998.

Hammer, D. Harry. *Lion Six*. Annapolis, Md.: United States Naval Institute, 1947.

Hammer, Joshua. *Yokohama Burning: The Deadly 1923 Earthquake and Fire That Helped Forge the Path to World War II*. New York: Free Press, 2006.

Hanley, Fiske. *Accused American War Criminal: One of the Few Survivors of Japanese Kempei Tai Military Police Brutality*. Brattleboro, Vt.: Echo Point Books and Media, 2016.

———. *Tales from the Wild Blue Yonder: 504th Bomb Group (VH) in World War II*. Fort Worth, Tex.: Tattered Cover Press, 2013.

Hansell, Haywood S., Jr. *The Air Plan That Defeated Hitler*. Atlanta: Arno Press, 1972.

———. *The Strategic Air War Against Japan:* Washington, D.C.: Air Power Research Institute, 1980.

———. *The Strategic Air War Against Germany and Japan: A Memoir*. Washington, D.C.: Office of Air Force History, 1986.

Harris, Arthur. *Bomber Offensive*. Novato, Calif.: Presidio Press, 1990.

Harris, Carol. *Blitz Diary: Life Under Fire in World War II*. Stroud, Gloucestershire, U.K.: History Press, 2010.

Harris, Samuel Russ, Jr. *B-29s over Japan, 1944–1945: A Group Commander's Diary*. Edited by Robert A. Mann. Jefferson, N.C.: McFarland, 2011.

Hasegawa, Tsuyoshi. *Racing the Enemy: Stalin, Truman, and the Surrender of Japan*. Cambridge, Mass.: Harvard University Press, 2005.

Hastings, Max. *Bomber Command*. New York: Dial Press, 1979.

Havens, Thomas R. H. *Valley of Darkness: The Japanese People and World War II*. New York: W. W. Norton, 1978.

Hegi, Benjamin Paul. *From Wright Field, Ohio, to Hokkaido, Japan: General Curtis E. LeMay's Letters to His Wife Helen, 1941–1945*. Edited by Alfred F. Hurley. Denton: University of North Texas Libraries, 2015.

Hiroshima Association for the Success of the Atomic Bomb Exhibition. *After 60 Years, A-Bomb Survivors Speak Out: An Anthology of the Experiences of Hiroshima Atomic Bomb Victims*. Hiroshima, Japan: Yoshimura, 2010.

————. *After 65 Years, A-Bomb Survivors and War Victims Speak Out: An Anthology of the Experiences of Hiroshima Atomic Bomb Victims.* Hiroshima: Yoshimura, 2015.

Hiroshima Peace Culture Foundation. *Eyewitness Testimonies: Appeals from the A-Bomb Survivors.* Hiroshima: Bunkasya, 2017.

Hoito, Edoin (Edwin P. Hoyt). *The Night Tokyo Burned: The Incendiary Campaign Against Japan, March–August 1945.* New York: St. Martin's Press, 1987.

Hornfischer, James D. *The Fleet at Flood Tide: America at Total War in the Pacific, 1944–1945.* New York: Bantam Books, 2016.

Hoyt, Edwin P. *Hirohito: The Emperor and the Man.* New York: Praeger, 1984.

————. *Inferno: The Firebombing of Japan, March 9–August 15, 1945.* New York: Madison Books, 2000.

Hurley, Alfred F., and Robert C. Ehrhart. *Air Power and Warfare: The Proceedings of the 8th Military History Symposium, United States Air Force Academy, 18–20 October 1978.* Washington, D.C.: Office of Air Force History and the U.S. Air Force Academy, 1979.

Huston, John. W., ed. *American Airpower Comes of Age: General Henry H. "Hap" Arnold's World War II Diaries.* 2 vols. Maxwell Air Force Base, Ala.: Air University Press, 2002.

Ienaga, Saburô. *The Pacific War: World War II and the Japanese, 1931–1945.* Trans. Frank Baldwin. New York: Pantheon, 1978.

Ishikawa, Kôyô. *Tôkyô Daikûshû no Kiroku.* Tokyo: Iwanami Shoten, 1992.

James, David H. *The Rise and Fall of the Japanese Empire.* London: George Allen & Unwin, 1951.

Japan Memorial Society for the Students Killed in the War—Wadatsumi Society. *Listen to the Voices from the Sea: Writings of Fallen Japanese Students.* Trans. Midori Yamanouchi and Joseph L. Quinn. Scranton: University of Scranton Press, 2000.

Johnson, David. *The City Ablaze: The Second Great Fire of London, 29th December, 1940.* London: William Kimber, 1980.

Kato, Masuo. *The Lost War: A Japanese Reporter's Inside Story.* New York: Alfred A. Knopf, 1946.

Katô, Shûichi. *A Sheep's Song: A Writer's Reminiscences of Japan and the World.* Trans. Chia-Ning Chang. Berkeley: University of California Press, 1999.

Kawamura, Noriko. *Emperor Hirohito and the Pacific War.* Seattle: University of Washington Press, 2015.

Keene, Donald. *So Lovely a Country Will Never Die: Wartime Diaries of Japanese Writers.* New York: Columbia University Press, 2010.

Kennett, Lee. *The First Air War, 1914–18.* New York: Free Press, 1991.

Kerr, E. Bartlett. *Flames over Tokyo: The U.S. Army Air Forces' Incendiary Campaign Against Japan, 1944–1945.* New York: Donald I. Fine, 1991.

Kirby, Joe. *The Bell Bomber Plant.* Charleston, S.C.: Arcadia, 2008.

Kiyosawa, Kiyoshi. *The Wartime Diary of Kiyosawa Kiyoshi.* Trans. Eugene Sovial and Tamie Kamiyama. Princeton, N.J.: Princeton University Press, 1980.

Kohn, Richard H., and Joseph P. Harahan. *Strategic Air Warfare: An Interview with Generals Curtis E. LeMay, Leon W. Johnson, David A. Burchinal, and Jack J. Catton.* Washington, D.C.: Office of Air Force History, 1988.

Kozak, Warren. *LeMay: The Life and Wars of General Curtis LeMay*. Washington, D.C.: Regnery, 2009.

Kubota, Shigenori, *Tōkyō Daikūshū Kyūgo Taichō no Kiroku*. Tokyo: Ushio Shuppansha, 1973.

Landas, Marc. *The Fallen: A True Story of American POWs and Japanese Wartime Atrocities*. Hoboken, N.J.: John Wiley & Sons, 2004.

Lary, Diana. *The Chinese People at War: Human Suffering and Social Transformation, 1937–1945*. New York: Cambridge University Press, 2010.

Laslie, Brian. *Architect of Air Power: General Laurence S. Kuter and the Birth of the US Air Force*. Lexington: University Press of Kentucky, 2017.

LeMay, Curtis E., with MacKinlay Kantor. *Mission with LeMay: My Story*. Garden City, N.Y.: Doubleday, 1965.

LeMay, Curtis E., and Bill Yenne. *Superfortress: The B-29 and American Airpower*. New York: McGraw-Hill, 1988.

Liebow, Averill A. *Encounter with Disaster: A Medical Diary of Hiroshima, 1945*. New York: W. W. Norton, 1970.

Lifton, Robert Jay. *Death in Life: Survivors of Hiroshima*. New York: Random House, 1967.

Lowe, Keith. *Inferno: The Fiery Destruction of Hamburg, 1943*. New York: Scribner, 2007.

Marshall, Chester. *Sky Giants over Japan: A Diary of a B-29 Combat Crew in WWII*. Winona, Minn.: Apollo Books, 1984.

Marshall, Chester, with Ray "Hap" Halloran. *Hap's War: The Incredible Survival Story of a P.O.W. Slated for Execution*. Collierville, Tenn.: Global Press, 1998.

Marshall, Chester W., with Warren Thompson. *Final Assault on the Rising Sun: Combat Diaries of B-29 Air Crews over Japan*. North Branch, Minn.: Specialty Press, 1995.

McKay, Sinclair, *The Fire and the Darkness: The Bombing of Dresden, 1945*. New York: St. Martin's Press, 2020.

McManus, John C. *Deadly Sky: The American Combat Airman in World War II*. Novato, Calif.: Presidio, 2000.

Mears, Helen, *Mirror for Americans: Japan*. Boston: Houghton Mifflin, 1948.

———. *The Year of the Wild Boar: An American Woman in Japan*. Philadelphia: J. B. Lippincott, 1942.

Meilinger, Phillip S., ed. *The Paths of Heaven: The Evolution of Airpower Theory*. Maxwell Air Force Base, Ala.: Air University Press, 1997.

Mendelssohn, Peter de. *Japan's Political Warfare*. London: George Allen & Unwin, 1944.

Mets, David R. *Master of Airpower: General Carl A. Spaatz*. Novato, Calif.: Presidio Press, 1988.

Middlebrook, Martin. *The Battle of Hamburg: Allied Bomber Forces Against a German City in 1943*. New York: Charles Scribner's Sons, 1981.

Miller, Donald L. *Masters of the Air: America's Bomber Boys Who Fought the Air War Against Nazi Germany*. New York: Simon & Schuster, 2006.

Mitchell, Richard H. *Thought Control in Prewar Japan*. Ithaca, N.Y.: Cornell University Press, 1976.

Mitchell, William. *Winged Defense: The Development and Possibilities of Modern Air Power—Economic and Military*. Mineola, N.Y.: Dover, 2006.

Mitter, Rana. *Forgotten Ally: China's World War II, 1937–1945*. Boston: Houghton Mifflin Harcourt, 2013.

Moore, Aaron William. *Bombing the City: Civilian Accounts of the Air War in Britain and Japan, 1939–1945*. Cambridge: Cambridge University Press, 2018.

Morgan, Robert, with Ron Powers. *The Man Who Flew the* Memphis Belle: *Memoir of a WWII Bomber Pilot*. New York: Dutton, 2001.

Morrison, Wilbur H. *Hellbirds: The Story of the B-29s in Combat*. New York: Duell, Sloan & Pearce, 1960.

———. *Point of No Return: The Story of the 20th Air Force*. New York: Times Books, 1979.

Mountcastle, John Wyndham. *Flame On! U.S. Incendiary Weapons, 1918–1945*. Shippensburg, Pa.: White Main Books, 1999.

Newman, Joseph. *Goodbye Japan*. New York: L. B. Fischer, 1942.

Norquist, Ernest. *Our Paradise: A GI's War Diary*. Hancock, Wis.: Pearl-Win, 1989.

Noyes, W. A., Jr., ed. *Chemistry: A History of the Chemistry Components of the National Defense Research Committee, 1940–1946*. Boston: Little, Brown, 1948.

Nutter, Ralph H. *With the Possum and the Eagle: The Memoir of a Navigator's War over Germany and Japan*. Novato, Calif.: Presidio Press, 2002.

Ogura, Toyofumi. *Letters from the End of the World: A Firsthand Account of the Bombing of Hiroshima*. Trans. Kisaburo Murakami and Shigeru Fujii. Tokyo: Kodansha International, 1997.

Overy, Richard. *The Bombers and the Bombed: Allied Air War over Europe, 1940–1945*. New York: Viking, 2013.

Pacific War Research Society. *Japan's Longest Day*. Tokyo: Kodansha International, 1968.

Parker, Van. R. *Dear Folks*. Memphis, Tenn.: Global Press, 1989.

Parton, James. *"Air Force Spoken Here": General Ira Eaker and the Command of the Air*. Bethesda, Md.: Adler & Adler, 1986.

———, ed. *Impact: The Army Air Forces' Confidential Picture History of World War II*, 8 vols. New York: James Parton, 1980.

Perera, Guido R. *Leaves from My Book of Life*, vol. 2, *Washington and War Years*. Boston: privately printed, 1975.

Petty, Bruce M. *Saipan: Oral Histories of the Pacific War*. Jefferson, N.C.: McFarland, 2002.

Phillips, Charles L., Jr. *Rain of Fire: B-29s over Japan, 1945*. Moreno Valley, Calif.: B-Nijuku, 1995.

Pogue, Forrest C. *George C. Marshall: Organizer of Victory, 1943–1945*. New York: Viking Press, 1973.

Poole, Otis Manchester. *The Death of Old Yokohama in the Great Japanese Earthquake of 1923*. London: George Allen & Unwin, 1968.

Porter, Edgar A., and Ran Ying Porter. *Japanese Reflections on World War II and the American Occupation*. Amsterdam: Amsterdam University Press, 2017.

Potter, E. B. *Nimitz*. Annapolis, Md.: Naval Institute Press, 1976.

Power, Thomas S., with Albert A. Arnhym. *Design for Survival: A Crucial Message to the American People Concerning Our Nuclear Strength and Its Role in Preserving Peace*. New York: Coward-McCann, 1965.

Price, Willard. *Key to Japan*. London: William Heinemann, 1946.

Pyle, Ernie. *Ernie Pyle in England*. New York: Robert M. McBride, 1941.

———. *Last Chapter*. New York: Henry Holt, 1946.

Raymond, Antonin. *An Autobiography*. Rutland, Vt.: Charles E. Tuttle, 1973.

Rhodes, Richard. *The Making of the Atomic Bomb*. New York: Simon & Schuster, 1986.

Robertson, Gordon Bennett, Jr. *Bringing the Thunder: The Missions of a WWII B-29 Pilot in the Pacific*. Oklahoma City, Okla.: Wide Awake Books, 2016.

Saotome, Katsumoto. *Tôkyô Daikûshû*. Tokyo: Iwanami Shinsho, 1971.

———. *Shashinban Tôkyô Daikûshû no Kiroku*. Tokyo: Shinchôsha, 1987.

———, ed., *Tôkyô Kûshû Shashinshû*. Tokyo: Bensei Shuppan, 2015.

Schaffer, Ronald. *Wings of Judgment: American Bombing in World War II*. New York: Oxford University Press, 1985.

Schencking, J. Charles. *The Great Kantô Earthquake and the Chimera of National Reconstruction in Japan*. New York: Columbia University Press, 2013.

Schigemitsu, Mamoru. *Japan and Her Destiny: My Struggle for Peace*. Edited by F.S.G. Piggott. Trans. Oswald White. New York: E. P. Dutton, 1958.

Schwabe, Daniel T. *Burning Japan: Air Force Bombing Strategy Change in the Pacific*. Washington, D.C.: Potomac Books, 2015.

Scott, James M. *Rampage: MacArthur, Yamashita, and the Battle of Manila*. New York: W. W. Norton, 2018.

———. *Target Tokyo: Jimmy Doolittle and the Raid That Avenged Pearl Harbor*. New York: W. W. Norton, 2015.

———. *The War Below: The Story of Three Submarines That Battled Japan*. New York: Simon & Schuster, 2013.

Sckimori, Gaynor, trans. *Hibakusha: Survivors of Hiroshima and Nagasaki*. Tokyo: Kôsei, 2010.

Sherry, Michael S. *The Rise of American Air Power: The Creation of Armageddon*. New Haven, Conn.: Yale University Press, 1987.

Shigenori, Tôgô. *The Cause of Japan*. Edited and translated by Tôgô Fumihiko and Ben Bruce Blakeney. New York: Simon & Schuster, 1956.

Shillony, Ben-Ami. *Politics and Culture in Wartime Japan*. Oxford: Clarendon Press, 1981.

Snyder, Earl. *General Leemy's Circus: A Navigator's Story of the 20th Air Force in World War II*. New York: Exposition Press, 1955.

Speer, Albert. *Inside the Third Reich: Memoirs by Albert Speer*. Trans. Richard and Clara Winston. New York: Galahad Books, 1995.

Stansky, Peter. *The First Day of the Blitz*. New Haven, Conn.: Yale University Press, 2007.

Stimson, Henry L., and McGeorge Bundy. *On Active Service in War and Peace*. New York: Harper & Brothers, 1947.

Tanaka, Yuki, and Marilyn B. Young, eds. *Bombing Civilians: A Twentieth-Century History*. New York: The New Press, 2009.

Takagaki, Sekijiro, ed. *The Japan Yearbook, 1941–1942*. Tokyo: Foreign Affairs Association of Japan, 1941.

Takahashi, Kazutomo. *The Story of Japan's Great 1923 Earthquake: With Details of the Tremen-*

dous Conflagration Which Swept Tokyo and Yokohama in Consequence. Tokyo: Japan Times, 1923.

Takeyama, Michio. *The Scars of War: Tokyo During World War II: Writings of Takeyama Michio.* Trans. and edited by Richard H. Minear. New York: Rowman & Littlefield, 2007.

Takii, Hiroomi. *Tōkyō Daikūshū wo Wasurenai.* Tokyo: Kodansha, 2015.

Taylor, Frederick. *Coventry: November 14, 1940.* New York: Bloomsbury Press, 2015.

———. *Dresden: Tuesday, February 13, 1945.* New York: HarperCollins, 2004.

Tibbets, Paul W., Jr., with Clair Stebbins and Harry Franken. *The Tibbets Story.* New York: Stein & Day, 1978.

Tillman, Barrett. *Whirlwind: The Air War Against Japan, 1942–1945.* New York: Simon & Schuster, 2010.

Tōkyō Daikūshū Sensai Shiryō Sentā. *Ano Toki Kodomo Datta.* Tokyo: Sekibundō, 2019.

Tōkyō Daikūshū wo Kiroku suru Kai. *Tōkyō Daikūshū Sensaishi.* 5 vols. Tokyo: Tōkyō Daikūshū wo Kiroku suru Kai, 1973–74.

Vander Meulen, Jacob. *Building the B-29.* Washington, D.C.: Smithsonian Institution Press, 1995.

Van Gieson, Bayard R. *Doc's Deadly Dose: B-29s and the Army's Aerial War Against Japan.* Privately published, 2007.

Wahle, Anne, as told to Roul Tunley. *Ordeal by Fire: An American Woman's Terror-Filled Trek Through War-Torn Germany.* Cleveland: World, 1966.

Waller, Douglas. *A Question of Loyalty: Gen. Billy Mitchell and the Court-Martial That Gripped the Nation.* New York: HarperCollins, 2004.

Webster, Philip D., with Charlotte Webster. *Thirty-Five Missions over Japan.* Morrisville, N.C.: Lulu, 2017.

Werrell, Kenneth P. *Blankets of Fire: U.S. Bombers over Japan During World War II.* Washington, D.C.: Smithsonian Institution Press, 1996.

Wolk, Herman S. *Cataclysm: General Hap Arnold and the Defeat of Japan.* Denton: University of North Texas Press, 2010.

———. *The Struggle for Air Force Independence, 1943–1947.* Washington, D.C.: Air Force History and Museums Program, 1997.

Women's Division of Soka Gakkai. *Women Against War: Personal Accounts of Forty Japanese Women.* Trans. Richard L. Gage. Tokyo: Kodansha International, 1986.

Yamashita, Samuel Hideo. *Daily Life in Wartime Japan, 1940–1945.* Lawrence: University of Kansas Press, 2015.

———. *Leaves from an Autumn of Emergencies: Selections of Wartime Diaries of Ordinary Japanese.* Honolulu: University of Hawai'i Press, 2005.

Yenne, Bill. *Hap Arnold: The General Who Invented the U.S. Air Force.* Washington, D.C.: Regnery History, 2013.

———. *Panic on the Pacific: How America Prepared for a West Coast Invasion.* Washington, D.C.: Regnery History, 2016.

Youth Division of Soka Gakkai, comp. Richard L. Gage, ed. *Cries for Peace: Experiences of Japanese Victims of World War II.* Tokyo: Japan Times, 1978.

INDEX